POLITICO'S GUIDE TO ELECTION PRACTICE & LAW

"Experience in a good many elections since the enfranchisement of women has convinced me that they cannot be 'relied upon' to vote in any particular direction. They can be delightfully perplexing in their political decisions. Mere men can only look on and marvel".

"It must be remembered too, that the women 'intellectuals' are always a small minority. It is the working and lower middle class man's wife that must be won over if victory is to be assured, and she usually has scant sympathy with 'them suffragettes'. Happy is the agent who has on his staff a woman who holds the key to the humble homes of the division. She must be of good breeding, for the working woman still loves 'a lady', but she must be able to adapt herself to every type of woman".

"I shall be surprised if in the near future there does not arise a new type of professional woman – the woman election agent, who will take her place of equality beside her masculine colleagues and command the same remuneration".

"You may talk to women electors about 'this great Empire upon which the sun never sets' till you are blue in the face, but if your rival is telling them why the purchasing power of the £ has declined, why prices are high, and why their daily task as chancellors of the domestic exchequer is so much more difficult, you may depend upon it that you are wasting your breath and he is winning votes. That does not mean that women are not patriots. On the contrary, they are intensely patriotic, but they are not going to be fobbed off with a lot of hot air about the Empire while they are perplexed by their own domestic problems. Women are practical beings, and they demand practical politics".

"Tell the electors in plain homely language what your candidate's policy is, and see that that policy bears on the actual facts of workaday life. Never mind about the Treaty of Sevres. It is very important, no doubt, but 75 per cent. of the electors have never heard of it".

"If politicians would only have faith in the sanity of the masses and not resort in a panic to an equally reckless out-bidding of the extremists, the industrial unrest of this country would be reduced to the minimum. So long as Governments regard the people as something to be fooled, so long will they themselves be fooled to the country's infinite harm".

From: 'Modern Electioneering Practice', Henry James Houston & Lionel Valdar (Charles Knight & Co. Limited, 1922)

Politico's Guide to Election Practice & Law

By
Susan Child

First published in Great Britain 2001
by Politico's Publishing
8 Artillery Row, London, SW1P 1RZ, England

Tel. 020 7931 0090

Website: www.politicos.co.uk/publishing
e-mail: publishing@politicos.co.uk

A catalogue record for this book is available from the British Library.

ISBN: 1902301811

Printed and bound in Great Britain by St Edmundsbury Press.
Cover design by Politico's Design.

CONTENTS

RELEVANT STATUTES AND DELEGATED LEGISLATION

References to the Representation of the People Act 1983 are references to the Act as amended by the following[1]:

❖ Representation of the People Act 1985 (Chapter 50)

❖ Representation of the People Act 1989 (Chapter 28)

❖ Representation of the People Act 2000 (Chapter 2)[2]

❖ Political Parties, Elections and Referendums Act 2000 (Chapter 41)

❖ The Representation of the People (Variation of Limits of Candidates' Expenses) Order 2001 (SI 2001, No. 535)

The following regulations were made under the provisions of the Representation of the People Act 1983:

❖ The Parliamentary Elections (Returning Officer's Charges) (Northern Ireland) (Amendment) Order 2001 (SI 2001, No. 1659)

❖ The Parliamentary Elections (Returning Officers' Charges) Order 2001 (SI 2001, No. 1736)

❖ The Representation of the People (Form of Canvass) (England and Wales) Regulations 2001 (SI 2001, No. 2720)

❖ The Representation of the People (Form of Canvass) (Scotland) Regulations 2001 (SI 2001, No. 2817 (S. 15))

❖ The Representation of the People (Form of Canvass) (Northern Ireland) Regulations 2001 (SI 2001, No. 2725)

---

[1] The RPA 1983 has been amended by other legislation, but not to the same extent as the Acts listed here. Other amendments to the RPA 1983 are noted elsewhere in the text.

[2] Sections 10, 11, 14, 16 and 17, Schedule 5 and paragraph 6 of Schedule 6 of the RPA 2000 came into force immediately the Act received Royal Assent. These Sections provide for: pilot schemes in local elections (Sections 10 & 11); free electoral addresses in the first London Mayoral election (Section 14 and Schedule 5); certain financial provisions (16); certain commencement provisions (17) and provisions relating to the prohibition on the publication of exit polls before the poll closes in any parliamentary election or local government election in England or Wales (extended to Northern Ireland by means of the Local Elections (Northern Ireland) (Amendment) Order 2001). New section 66A of the RPA 1983 (as inserted by the RPA 2000) states that anyone publishing such a poll is liable on summary conviction to a fine not exceeding level 5 on the standard scale or to imprisonment for a term not exceeding six months.

The Representation of the People Act 2000 repealed the following:

- ❖ The Representation of the People Act 1990 (Chapter 32)

The following regulations were made under the provisions of the RPA 2000:

- ❖ The Representation of the People Regulations (England and Wales) Regulations 2001 (SI 2001, No. 341)

- ❖ The Representation of the People (England and Wales) (Amendment) Regulations 2001 (SI 2001, No. 1700)

- ❖ The Representation of the People Regulations (Scotland) Regulations 2001 (SI 2001, No. 497 (S. 2))

- ❖ The Representation of the People (Scotland) (Amendment) Regulations 2001 (SI 2001, No. 1749 (S. 11))

- ❖ The Representation of the People Regulations (Northern Ireland) Regulations 2001 (SI 2001, No. 400)

- ❖ The Representation of the People (Northern Ireland) (Amendment) Regulations 2001 (SI 2001, No. 1877)

The Representation of the People Act 2000 repealed the whole of the Representation of the People Act 1990.

The Representation of the People (England and Wales) Regulations 2001 (SI 2001, No. 341) referred to above and made under the Representation of the People Act 2000, revoked the following regulations:

- ❖ The Representation of the People Regulations 1986 (SI 1986, No. 1081) – the whole Regulations except 1, 4 and 97 to 100

- ❖ The Representation of the People (Amendment) Regulations 1990 (SI 1990, No. 520) – the whole Regulations, except 29 to 31

- ❖ The Representation of the People (Amendment) Regulations 1991 (SI 1991, No. 1198) – the whole Regulations

- ❖ The Representation of the People (Amendment) Regulations 1992 (SI 1992, No. 722) – the whole Regulations

- ❖ The European Parliamentary Elections (Changes to the Franchise and Qualification of Representatives) Regulations 1994 (SI 1994, No. 342) – Part I of the Schedule

- ❖ The Local Government Elections (Changes to the Franchise and Qualification of Members) Regulations 1995 (SI 1995, No. 1948) – Paragraphs 12 to 16 of Schedule 2

- ❖ The Representation of the People (Amendment) Regulations 1997 (SI 1997, No. 880) – the whole Regulations

Similar provisions to those contained in the Representation of the People (England and Wales) Regulations 2001 are applied to Scotland by the Representation of the People (Scotland) Regulations 2001 (referred to above). These new regulations revoke the following regulations:

❖ The Representation of the People (Scotland) Regulations 1986 (SI 1986, No. 1111) - the whole regulations, except regulations 1, 4 and 95 to 98, regulations 75, 76 and 78 to 94 insofar as they relate to local government elections

❖ The Representation of the People (Scotland) Amendment Regulations 1990 (SI 1990, No. 629) - the whole regulations except regulations 24 and 25 insofar as they relate to a local government election, and regulations 28 to 33

❖ The Representation of the People (Scotland) Amendment Regulations 1992 (SI 1992, No. 834) - the whole regulations

❖ The European Parliamentary Elections (Changes to the Franchise and Qualification of Representatives) Regulations 1994 (SI 1994, No. 342) - Part II of the Schedule

❖ The Local Government Elections (Changes to the Franchise and Qualifications of Members) Regulations 1995 (SI 1995, No. 1948) - paragraphs 17 to 22 of Schedule 2

❖ The Representation of the People (Scotland) Amendment Regulations 1997 (SI 1997, No. 979) - the entire regulations

Similar provisions to those contained in the Representation of the People (England and Wales) Regulations 2001 are applied to Northern Ireland by the Representation of the People (Northern Ireland) Regulations 2001 (referred to above). These new regulations revoke the following regulations:

❖ The Representation of the People (Northern Ireland) Regulations 1986 (SI 1986, No. 1091) - the whole regulations

❖ The Representation of the People (Northern Ireland) (Amendment) Regulations 1989 (SI 1989, No. 1304) – the whole regulations

❖ The Representation of the People (Northern Ireland) (Amendment) Regulations 1990 (SI 1990, No. 561) – the whole regulations

❖ The Representation of the People (Northern Ireland) (Variation of Specified Documents and Amendment) Regulations 1991 (SI 1991, No. 1674) – the whole regulations

❖ The Representation of the People (Northern Ireland) (Amendment) Regulations 1992 (SI 1992, No. 832) – the whole regulations

❖ The European Parliamentary Elections (Changes to the Franchise and Qualification of Representatives) Regulations 1994 (SI 1994, No. 342) – Part III of the Schedule

❖ The Local Government Elections (Changes to the Franchise and Qualification of Members) Regulations 1995 (SI 1995, No. 1948) – paragraphs 23 to 26 of Schedule 2

❖ The Representation of the People (Northern Ireland) (Amendment) Regulations 1997 (SI 1997, No. 967) – the whole regulations

❖ The Representation of the People (Northern Ireland) (Amendment) Regulations 1998 (SI 1998, No. 2870) – the whole regulations

Provisions relating to parliamentary constituency boundaries are contained in the following orders:

❖ The Parliamentary Constituencies Act 1986 (Chapter 56)

❖ The Boundary Commissions Act 1992 (Chapter 55)

❖ The Local Government Act 1992 (Chapter 19)

❖ The Parliamentary Constituencies (England) Order 1995 (SI 1995, No. 1626)

❖ The Parliamentary Constituencies (England) (Miscellaneous Changes) Order 1996 (SI 1996, No. 1922)

❖ The Parliamentary Constituencies (England) (Miscellaneous Changes) Order 1998 (SI 1998, No. 3152)

❖ The Parliamentary Constituencies (Wales) Order 1995 (SI 1995, No. 1036)

❖ The Parliamentary Constituencies (Scotland) Order 1995 (SI 1995, No. 1037)

❖ The Parliamentary Constituencies (Northern Ireland) Order 1995 (SI 1995, No. 2992)

Provisions relating to returning officers and acting returning officers are set out in the following:

❖ The Returning Officers (Parliamentary Constituencies) (England) Order 1995 (SI 1995, No. 2061)

❖ The Returning Officers (Parliamentary Constituencies) (England) (Amendment Order) 1996 (SI 1996, No. 898)

❖ The Returning Officers (Parliamentary Constituencies) (England) (Amendment) Order 1997 (SI 1997, No. 537)

❖ The Returning Officers (Parliamentary Constituencies) (England) (Amendment) Order 1999 (SI 1999, No. 950)

❖ The Returning Officers (Parliamentary Constituencies) (Wales) Order 1996 (SI 1996, No. 897)

The following legislation relates to the voting rights of peers:

❖ The Peerage Act 1963 (Chapter 48)

❖ The House of Lords Act 1999 (Chapter 34)

❖ The Holders of Hereditary Peerages (Extension of the Franchise) (Transitional Provisions) Order 1999 (SI 1999, No. 3322)

❖ The Holders of Hereditary Peerages (Overseas Electors) (Transitional Provisions) Order 2001 (SI 2001, No. 84)

The following legislation relates to membership of the House of Commons:

❖ The House of Commons Disqualification Act 1975 (Chapter 24)

❖ The House of Commons Disqualification Order 1997 (SI 1997, No. 861)

❖ Disqualifications Act 2000 (Chapter 42)

❖ House of Commons (Removal of Clergy Disqualification) Act 2001 (Chapter 13)

❖ Recess Elections Act 1975 (Chapter 66)

❖ Representation of the People Act 1981 (Chapter 34)

The following legislation was made under the Political Parties, Elections and Referendums Act 2000 (Chapter 41)

❖ The Political Parties, Elections and Referendums Act 2000 (Commencement No. 1 and Transitional Provisions) Order (SI 2001, No. 222 (C.11))

❖ The Registration of Political Parties (Prohibited Words and Expressions) Order 2001 (SI 2001, No. 82)

❖ The Political Parties, Elections and Referendums Act 2000 (Disapplication of Part IV for Northern Ireland Parties, etc.) Order 2001 (SI 2001, No. 446)

❖ The Registered Parties (Non-constituent and Non-affiliated Organisations) Order 2000 (SI 2000, No. 3183)

The PPERA 2000 was amended (temporarily) by the following:

❖ Elections Publications Act 2001 (Chapter 5)

The following legislation was required to delay the 2001 local government elections:

❖ The Elections Act 2001 (Chapter 7)

❖ The Elections Act 2001 (Supplemental Provisions) (No. 2) Order 2001 (SI 2001, No. 1774)

The following regulations relate to the use of the Welsh language:

❖ The European Parliamentary Elections (Welsh Forms) (Amendment) Order 1999 (SI 1999, No. 1402)

❖ The Elections (Welsh Forms) Order 1995 (SI 1995, No. 830)

❖ The Elections (Welsh Forms) Order 2001 (SI 2001, No. 1204)

❖ The Local Elections (Principal Areas) (Welsh Forms) Order 1987 (SI 1987, No. 562)

❖ The Local Elections (Communities) (Welsh Forms) Order 1987 (SI 1987, No. 561)

❖ The Local Elections (Declaration of Acceptance of Office) (Amendment) (Wales) Order 2001 (SI 2001, No. 2963)

❖ The National Assembly for Wales (Elections: Nomination Paper) (Welsh Form) Order 2001 (SI 2001, No. 2914)

The following legislation relates to the City of London:

❖ City of London (Various Powers) Act 1957

The following legislation and regulations relate to elections to the Scottish Parliament:

❖ Scotland Act 1998 (Chapter 46)

❖ The Scottish Parliament (Elections etc.) Order 1999 (SI 1999, No. 787)

❖ The Scottish Parliament (Disqualification) Order 1999 (SI 1999, No. 680)

❖ The Scottish Parliament (Elections etc.) (Amendment) Order 2001 (SI 2001, No. 1399 (S. 5))

❖ The Scottish Parliament (Elections etc.) (Amendment) (No. 2) Order 2001 (SI 2001, No. 1748 (S.10))

❖ The Scottish Parliament (Elections etc.) (Amendment) (No. 3) Order 2001 (SI 2001, No 1750 (S. 12))

The following legislation and regulations relate to elections the Northern Ireland Assembly:

❖ Northern Ireland (Elections) Act 1998 (Chapter 12)

❖ The Northern Ireland Assembly (Elections) Order 2001 (SI 2001, No. 2599)

The following legislation and regulations relate to elections to the National Assembly for Wales:

❖ Government of Wales Act 1998 (Chapter 38)

❖ The National Assembly for Wales (Representation of the People) Order 1999 (SI 1999, No. 450)

The following legislation and regulations relate to elections to the Greater London Assembly:

❖ Greater London Authority Act 1999 (Chapter 29)

❖ The Greater London Authority (Assembly Constituencies and Returning Officers) Order 1999 (SI 1999, No. 3380)

❖ The Greater London Authority Elections (Expenses) Order 2000 (SI 2000, No. 789)

❖ The Greater London Authority Elections (No. 2) Rules 2000 (SI 2000, No. 427)

❖ The Greater London Authority (Elections and Acceptance of Office) Order 2000 (SI 2000, No. 308)

❖ The Greater London Authority Elections (No. 2) (Amendment) Rules 2000 (SI 2000, No. 1040)

❖ The Greater London Authority (Disqualification) Order 2000 (SI 2000, No. 432)

❖ The Greater London Authority Election (Early Voting) Order 2000 (SI 2000, No. 826)

The following regulations relate to local government elections in England and Wales:

❖ Local Government Act 1972 (Chapter 70)

❖ The Local Elections (Principal Areas) Rules 1986 (SI 1986, No. 2214)

❖ The Local Elections (Principal Areas) (Amendment) Rules 1987 (SI 1987, No. 261)

❖ Local Government and Housing Act 1989 (Chapter 42)

❖ The Local Elections (Principal Areas) (Amendment) Rules 1990 (SI 1990, No. 158)

❖ The Local Elections (Principal Areas) (Amendment) Rules 1998 (SI 1998, No. 578)

❖ The Local Elections (Principal Areas) (Amendment) Rules 1999 (SI 1999, No. 394)

❖ The Local Elections (Principal Areas) (Amendment) Rules 2001 (SI 2001, No. 81)

❖ The Local Elections (Principal Areas) (Declaration of Acceptance of Office) Order 1990 (SI 1990, No. 932)

❖ The Local Elections (Declaration of Acceptance of Office) (Amendment) (Wales) Order 2001 (Welsh SI 2001, No. 2963 (W.245))

❖ The Local Government Elections (Changes to the Franchise and Qualifications of Members) Regulations 1995 (SI 1995, No. 1948)

The following regulations relate to parish council elections:

❖ The Local Elections (Parishes and Communities) Rules 1986 (SI 1986, No. 2215)

❖ The Local Elections (Parishes and Communities) (Amendment) Rules 1987 (SI 1987, No. 260)

❖ The Local Elections (Parishes and Communities) (Amendment) Rules 1990 (SI 1990, No. 157)

❖ The Local Elections (Parishes and Communities) (Amendment) Rules 1998 (SI 1998, No. 585)

❖ The Local Elections (Parishes and Communities) (Amendment) Rules 1999 (SI 1999, No. 395)

❖ The Local Elections (Parishes and Communities) (Amendment) Rules 2001 (SI 2001, No. 80)

The following regulations relate to local elections in Scotland:

❖ Local Government (Scotland) Act 1973 (Chapter 65)

❖ The Representation of the People (Scotland) Regulations 1986 (SI 1986, No. 1111 (S. 93)) *(partially revoked)*

❖ The Scottish Local Elections Rules 1986 (SI 1986, No. 2213 (S. 163))

❖ The Scottish Local Elections Amendment Rules 1990 (SI 1990, No. 262 (S. 25))

❖ The Local Government (Transitional and Consequential Provisions and Revocations) (Scotland) Order 1996 (SI 1996, No. 739 (S. 72))

❖ The Local Government Officers (Political Restrictions) Amendment Regulations 1998 (SI 1998, No. 3116 (S. 188))

❖ The Scottish Local Elections Amendment) (No. 2) Rules 1999 (SI 1999, No. 492 (S. 34))

The following legislation and regulations relate to local elections in Northern Ireland:

❖ Electoral Law Act (Northern Ireland) 1962 (Chapter 14)

❖ Electoral Law Act (Northern Ireland) 1968 (Chapter 20)

❖ Electoral Law Act (Northern Ireland) 1969 (Chapter 26)

❖ Electoral Law Act (Northern Ireland) 1971 (Chapter 4)

❖ Elections (Northern Ireland) Act 1985 (Chapter 2)

❖ The Local Elections (Northern Ireland) Order 1985 (SI 1985, No. 454)

❖ The Local Elections (Northern Ireland) (Amendment) Order 1987 (SI 1987, No. 168)

❖ Elected Authorities (Northern Ireland) Act 1989 (Chapter 3)

❖ The Local Elections (Northern Ireland) (Amendment) Order 1992 (SI 1992, No. 809

❖ The Local Elections (Northern Ireland) (Amendment) Order 1990 (SI 1990, No. 595)

❖ The Local Elections (Northern Ireland) (Amendment) Order 1991 (SI 1991, No. 1715)

❖ The District Electoral Areas (Northern Ireland) Order 1993 (SI 1993, No. 226)

❖ The Local Elections (Northern Ireland) (Amendment) Order 1997 (SI 1997, No. 867)

❖ The Local Elections (Northern Ireland) (Amendment) Order 1998 (SI 1998, No. 3150)

❖ Local Elections (Northern Ireland) (Amendment) Order 2001 (SI 2001, No. 417)

The following legislation relates to European Parliamentary Elections:

❖ The European Parliamentary Elections Act 1978 - *repealed extensively by the following:*

❖ The European Parliamentary Elections Act 1999

❖ The European Parliamentary Elections Regulations 1999 (SI 1999, No. 1214)

❖ The European Parliamentary Election Petition Rules 1979 (SI 1979, No. 521)

❖ The European Parliamentary Election Petition (Amendment) Rules 1988 (SI 1988, No. 557)

❖ The European Parliamentary Election Petition (Amendment) Rules 1999 (SI 1999, No. 1398 (L. 15))

❖ The European Parliamentary Elections (Franchise of Relevant Citizens of the Union) Regulations 2001 (SI 2001, No. 1184)

The following legislation relates to election petitions:

❖ The Election Petition Rules 1960 (SI 1960, No. 543)

❖ The Election Petition (Amendment) Rules 1999 (SI 1999, No. 1352 (L. 14))

The following legislation and regulations relates to the new provisions relating to the structure of local government:

❖ Local Government Act 2000 (Chapter 22)

❖ The Local Government Act 2000 (Commencement No. 4) Order 2000 (SI 2000, No. 2849 C. 83))

❖ The Local Government Act 2000 (Commencement No. 1) Order 2000 (SI 2000, No. 2187 C. 58))

❖ The Local Government (Referendums) (Petitions and Directions) (England) Regulations 2000 (SI 2000, No. 2852)

❖ The Local Authorities (Elected Mayors) (Elections, Terms of Office and Casual Vacancies) (England) Regulations 2001 (SI 2001, No. 2544)

❖ The Local Authorities (Conduct of Referendums) (England) Regulations 2001 (SI 2001, No. 1298)

Miscellaneous legislation and regulations:

❖ The Crown Office (Forms and Proclamations Rules) Order 1992 (SI 1992, No. 1730)

❖ The Broadcasting Act 1990 (Chapter 42)

❖ Parliamentary Elections Act 1695 (7 & 8 Will. 3, Chapter 26)

❖ Act of Settlement 1700 (12 & 13 Will. 3, Chapter 2)

❖ Forfeiture Act 1870 (33 & 34 Vict., Chapter 23)

❖ Parliament (Qualification of Women) Act 1918 (8 & 9 Geo. 5, Chapter 47)

❖ Banking and Financial Dealings Act 1971 (Chapter 80)

❖ Forgery and Counterfeiting Act 1981 (Chapter 45)

❖ Parliamentary Writs Order 1983 (SI 1983, No. 605)

INTRODUCTION

"There is nothing quite so pathetically amusing to the young ... as the spectacle of a grave and reverend seignior deploring the changing times. Condemning the period in which one lives is an age-long pastime, and it is a form of snobbery for veterans of sluggish mentality that persists despite its obvious futility ... Politics are supposed to have undergone a sad change for the worse. They are more sordid, more concerned with bread and butter, more dependent upon the whims of the million who must be cozened by flamboyant oratory or frightened by cheap histrionics into giving their votes ... Perhaps the most dismal critics are the old-fashioned Members of Parliament and their crusted election agents. They find the modern election a trying ordeal ... What these estimable people fail to realise is that we have definitely arrived at the Age of Democracy for good or ill. No sane man imagines that the million can ever be disenfranchised. It follows therefore that the problem of electioneering has undergone a tremendous change, the significance of which few as yet appear to have properly grasped".

From: 'Modern Electioneering Practice', Henry James Houston & Lionel Valdar (Charles Knight & Co. Limited, 1922)

As the Electoral Commission points out in its first report on the 2001 General Election: *"The administration of elections tends to be a topic of little general public interest, perhaps a reflection on the invisible efficiency of the administrative machinery."*[3] To an outsider, our election practices might seem quaint and eccentric, but by and large they are remarkably efficient; the polling booth, the blunt pencil (usually attached by a piece of string to the right of the voting booth, much to the annoyance of left-handers) and the cross on the ballot paper are well understood and there seems to be little public clamour for their replacement. The electors appear disinclined to embrace the dimpled chad or rush headlong into the arms of AV-plus. During the 2001 general election, T R Reid, The Washington Post's London Bureau Chief, expressed his surprise that the political parties published lengthy manifestos and moreover, that voters actually read them. In a branch of WHSmith, he claimed to have sighted *"people paying money to buy the Liberal Democrat Manifesto"* (The Financial Times, 5/6/01). Proof, if any were needed, that the British are still loveably eccentric.

To many, the results of the 2001 general election were yet further evidence of the electorate's growing apathy and disenchantment with the political process. Turnout was the lowest since 1945[4] and during the election itself voter apathy was a persistent theme in the press. According to an analysis of election coverage by Echo Research, the main focus of 115 articles in the national daily newspapers during the course of the election campaign was voter apathy[5].

---

[3] ('Election 2001 – The Official Results', Politico's Publishing / Electoral Commission, page 25)
[4] Turnout in general elections since 1945 was as follows: 1945 – 72.7%, 1950 – 84%, 1951 – 82.5%, 1955 – 76.7%, 1959 – 78.8%, 1964 – 77.1% - 1966 – 75.8%, 1970 – 72%, 1974 (Feb) – 78.7%, 1974 (Oct) – 72.8%, 1979 – 76%, 1983 – 72.7%, 1987 – 75.3%, 1992 – 77.7%, 1997 – 71.5%, 2001 – 59.4%
[5] 'Democracy in Action: The 2001 UK General Election' (available from Echo Research, www.echoresearch.com)

The low turnout has of course resulted in some demands for compulsory voting, although whether replacing the 'right' to vote with the 'compulsion' to vote would be a positive move is debatable. As Professor Anthony King asked in The Daily Telegraph (21/5/01) *"is low turn-out really a sign of political malaise? A good case can be made out that, on the contrary, it is a sign of political health"*. He goes on to point out that turnout in elections is falling not just in the UK, but in the United States and other European countries as well. One reason, he argues, is that societies are far less 'tribal' than ever before and the pressure to turn out and support one's 'side' is far less prevalent than it used to be. As Professor King points out, some of the highest voting levels ever recorded have been in Northern Ireland. In 1951 in Fermanagh and South Tyrone turnout was 93.4 per cent.

Just as societies have become less tribal, political parties have become less extreme. The differences between all three of the main UK political parties at the last general election (apart from on the vexed question of whether the UK should join the euro) were minimal; they were less ideologically opposed than they had ever been. To quote Professor King again: *"The fact that a far smaller proportion of people will vote on June 7 owes a great deal to the narrowing of the divisions between the Conservative and Labour parties that has taken place recently, especially since Tony Blair began to shift Labour to the right."* He concluded his article on an optimistic note: *"provide the voters with a closely fought election at which a great deal is at stake and, make no mistake, they will again turn out in their droves."*

Politico's Guide to Election Practice & Law is intended as a guide to current UK electoral law and covers parliamentary elections, elections to the European Parliament, the Scottish Parliament, the National Assembly of Wales, the Northern Ireland Assembly and the Greater London Assembly. The guide also covers local elections in England and Wales, in Scotland and Northern Ireland. It is not intended as a commentary on recent election results or an analysis of election campaigning, but will hopefully be useful to those who require an introduction to the legislation governing electoral practice in the United Kingdom.

To have included even an overview of all those aspects of campaigning not governed in some way by electoral law would have required a much lengthier book. There are already many excellent guides to political campaigning and election results and the most useful are listed at the end of the book. Some aspects of campaigning are not recognised in legislation at all. As Sam Younger, the Chairman of the Electoral Commission acknowledged in an interview in the Financial Times (14/5/01): *"There is nothing in electoral law at the moment that acknowledges the existence of the internet."* A research project undertaken by De Montfort University, Essex University and BMRB International and funded by the Government, the Electoral Commission, the Improvement and Development Agency and the Society of Local Authority Chief Executives is currently undertaking a study of voting using the telephone, television and the internet and the Hansard Society has recently produced an interesting report on the subject.[6] The way in which the political parties select their candidates is another important aspect of electoral practice not governed by legislation.

Since 1997 there have been a number of major changes to our constitution, which have necessitated the production of a considerable volume of new legislation. The creation of a Parliament in Scotland and Assemblies in Wales and Northern Ireland has resulted in

---

[6] 'Electoral Law and the Internet: Some Issues Considered', Chris Ballinger & Stephen Coleman (Hansard Society / The Stationery Office, 2001)

detailed primary and secondary legislation. Two major pieces of legislation completed their passage through Parliament in 2000: the Representation of the People Act 2000 and the Political Parties, Election and Referendums Act 2000. These are both covered in the guide, as are the consequent items of delegated legislation, which have come into effect this year. While every attempt has been made to cover the major implications of these and other statutes in this guide, it has inevitably not been possible to consider every single detail of the orders and regulations made under them. Anyone who needs a more detailed account of the legislation and delegated legislation referred to in this book should consult the relevant Acts and regulations themselves. These have been listed in the previous section.

A brief note is necessary to explain the legislative position of Northern Ireland. Anyone who enjoys confusion, complexity and obfuscation will find their metier in the electoral law of Northern Ireland. While some aspects of the electoral law pertaining to England, Wales and Scotland are also applicable to Northern Ireland, many are not. Although much of the various Representation of the People Acts apply to the UK as a whole, there is a considerable amount of legislation that relates solely to Northern Ireland. The chief example of which is the Electoral Law Act (Northern Ireland) 1962, Chapter 14 (NI). This Act relates primarily to local elections in Northern Ireland, but contains some provisions relating to parliamentary elections.[7] Every attempt has been made in this book to elucidate the position regarding Northern Ireland and where election practice differs from the rest of the UK, this has been stated. Anyone who wishes to obtain a copy of the Electoral Law Act (Northern Ireland) 1962 should be aware of the fact that it is not possible to obtain it through the usual channels. As the Act is a Northern Ireland Act which pre-dates direct rule, it is not to be found in the usual reference books, such as Halsbury's Statutes, etc., and is unlikely to be lurking on the shelves of your local reference library. It is virtually impossible to obtain a copy on the mainland as it is now out of print. However, for readers with access to the internet, a copy (minus the Schedules to the Act) can be found on the excellent website provided by the British and Irish Legal Information Institute (www.bailii.org). Alternatively, readers will find the Northern Ireland Office extremely helpful in answering questions relating to electoral law in Northern Ireland.

In its report, 'Vote Early, Vote Fairly', the Elections Review set up by the Secretary of State for Northern Ireland suggests that *"It is arguable that the remaining provisions of the Electoral Law Act (Northern Ireland) 1962 should be repealed and incorporated in more suitable legislative vehicles"*. The report goes on to point out that *"This would also produce a commonality of language across the electoral provisions for Northern Ireland. There can be little doubt that a degree of consolidation would be of benefit and it may be that fresh legislation arising from the considerations of this Review would provide appropriate homes for some of the remaining responsibilities of the 1962 Act, such as the appointment, terms and conditions and staff matters of the Chief Electoral Officer"*.

The other major difference between elections in Northern Ireland and the rest of the UK is the use of proportional representation (PR). In Great Britain proportional systems have been introduced for elections to the Scottish Parliament, Welsh Assembly, Greater London Authority and the European Parliament. However, First-Past-the-Post (FPTP) is still used for both Westminster and local elections. In Northern Ireland, although parliamentary elections are conducted using FPTP, local elections, elections to the Northern Ireland

---

[7] The Secretary of State for Northern Ireland is directly responsible for the law governing elections to the District Councils and to the Northern Ireland Assembly.

Assembly and elections to the European Parliament are conducted using the Single Transferable Vote.

NOTES

Responsibility for electoral law and local byelaws has now transferred from the Home Office to the Department of Transport, Local Government and the Regions (this includes sponsorship of the Electoral Commission). This brings all responsibility for elections and for local government policy within the DTLR.

In the text, references to 'bank holidays' are in lower case, following the form used in Statute; for example, the Banking and Financial Dealings Act 1971 and the RPA 1983.

The penalties for several of the election offences referred to in this book vary depending on whether the offence was tried summarily or on indictment. The penalties imposed differ according to whether the trial was held in the magistrates court (summary offences) or in the crown court (on indictment). References to 'fines up to a maximum of ... on level ... of the standard scale' are references to the standard scale of fines for summary offences, as set out in section 37 of the Criminal Justice Act 1982, c. 48 and section 289G of the Criminal Procedure (Scotland) Act 1975, c. 21 (the corresponding Act for Scotland) as amended by section 17 of the Criminal Justice Act 1991, which sets out the following maxima:

Level on Standard Scale	Amount of Fine
1	£200
2	£500
3	£1,000
4	£2,500
5	£5,000

Some offences are 'triable either way' and the penalties on summary conviction for offences triable either way are set out in section 32 of the Magistrates Court Act 1980. Section 32(2) states that the maximum fine is £5,000 or such sum as may be substituted by an Order under section 143(1) of the Act.

Throughout this book the following abbreviations have been used:

Full Title	Abbreviation
Representation of the People Acts	RPA (followed by the relevant year; e.g., 1983, 2000)
Parliamentary Election Rules, Schedule 1, Representation of the People Act 1983	Election Rules
Political Parties, Elections and Referendums Act 2000	PPERA 2000
Member of the European Parliament	MEP

Full Title	Abbreviation
Member of the Scottish Parliament	MSP
Member of the Northern Ireland Assembly	MLA
Welsh Assembly Member	AM

Days which are designated as bank holidays are set out in Schedule 1 of the Banking and Financial Dealings Act 1971 and are as follows:

England & Wales	Scotland	Northern Ireland
Easter Monday Last Monday in May Last Monday in August 26 December if not a Sunday 27 December in a year in which 25 or 26 December is a Sunday	New Year's Day, if not a Sunday, or where it is a Sunday, 3 January 2 January, if not a Sunday or, where it is a Sunday, 3 January Good Friday First Monday in May First Monday in August Christmas Day, if not a Sunday or where it is a Sunday, 26 December	17 March, if not a Sunday or where it is a Sunday, 18 March Easter Monday Last Monday in May Last Monday in August 26 December if not a Sunday 27 December in a year in which 25 or 26 December is a Sunday

Public holidays are not necessarily bank holidays; for example, Good Friday is a public holiday in England and Wales but a bank holiday in Scotland. For example, the days excluded from the general election timetable are weekends, Christmas Eve, Christmas Day, Maundy Thursday, Good Friday and the bank holidays as set out above.

ACKNOWLEDGEMENTS

I would like to thank the following for their help:

Andy Bagnall; Ruth Best; Fiona Callison; John Child; Iain Dale; Lea Goddard, Mayoral and Electoral Services Manager, London Borough of Croydon; Cllr Hugh Malyan, Leader of Croydon Council; Cllr Simon Milton, Leader of Westminster Council; Cllr Garry Walsh; Emma Wegoda.

I am particularly grateful to the following for their assistance:

Gill Heyworth and Maureen Newman.

Susan Child – November 2001

CHAPTER ONE – THE SELECTION OF CANDIDATES

The structure and function of political parties in the UK has, until recently, been largely ignored in law. There is currently no legislation governing the way in which candidates are selected (this may change, given the inclusion in the Queen's Speech of a commitment to legislation on gender equality on shortlists in the 2001/02 Session). The fact that most candidates represent political parties, as opposed to standing for election as independents, is not recognised in law and indeed Members of Parliament are considered to be individual representatives of the people who elected them rather than party delegates, mandated to vote simply along party lines in the House of Commons. Hence, the ability of MPs to 'cross the floor of the House'; to leave one party and join another, without having to resign.

Under the terms of our unwritten constitution, MPs are elected as individuals rather than party representatives. Some would argue that an MP leaving one party to join another has a moral obligation to resign and fight a by-election, even if they have no legal obligation to do so. The tension between a party's elected representatives in the House of Commons and its paid-up membership in the country has often been in evidence, most notably in the Labour Party. In Labour's recent past, the policies supported by the party faithful, often expressed vociferously at the party's annual conference, have frequently been antithetical to those being followed by the party in Parliament, particularly when the party has been in Government. This problem has gradually been assuaged under the leadership of first Neil Kinnock, then John Smith and finally Tony Blair, with the annual conference declining in importance and the National Policy Forum taking on the role of policy making. However, in any political party there resides the potential for conflict between elected representatives (elected by members of all parties and none) and those who selected them as candidates (the party membership in one form or another).

Two aspects of party organisation are now governed by legislation: party funding and registration. These aspects of party organisation are dealt with in Chapter Nine. Although this book is primarily a guide to electoral law, the way in which the political parties select their candidates is too important to ignore. Candidates, if successful, are the people who represent us in local councils up and down the country, in the devolved assemblies, in the UK Parliament and in the European Parliament. The way in which they are selected is of legitimate concern – not just to the political parties who selected them, but also to all those voters whom they claim to represent. This begs the question of whether there should be basic regulations, set out in legislation and applicable to all registered political parties, governing candidate selection.

What follows is merely a brief summary of candidate selection in those parties that are actually represented in the major institutions covered in this book (Westminster, the European Parliament, the Scottish Parliament, the Welsh Assembly, the GLA and the Northern Ireland Assembly).

PARTIES WITH REPRESENTATION AT WESTMINSTER

THE LABOUR PARTY

The Party Leader

Until 1981, the Leader of the Labour Party was elected by means of a ballot of all Labour MPs. However, in 1981 at a special conference at Wembley, after a heated debate (in part responsible for the decision by David Owen, Shirley Williams and Bill Rodgers to leave Labour, and along with Roy Jenkins, establish the Social Democratic Party) a new system for electing the Leader was devised. Both the Leader and Deputy Leader were to be chosen by an electoral college comprising MPs (30 per cent), Constituency Labour Parties (CLPs) (30 per cent) and Trade Unions (40 per cent).

The first contest under the new procedure was the 1981 contest for the Deputy Leadership, the results of which are set out below.[1]

	Votes (percentages) – first ballot		
	Denis Healey	Tony Benn	John Silkin
Trade Unions	24.696	6.410	8.894
CLPs	5.367	23.483	1.150
MPs	15.306	6.734	7.959
TOTAL	45.369	36.627	18.004[2]

John Silkin was therefore eliminated from the contest and the results of the second ballot were as follows.

	Votes (percentages) – second ballot	
	Denis Healey	Tony Benn
Trade Unions	24.994	15.006
CLPs	5.673	24.327
MPs	19.759	10. 241
TOTAL	50.426	49.574

The first leadership contest under the new rules took place in 1983, when the contenders were Neil Kinnock, Roy Hattersley, Eric Heffer and Peter Shore. The results were as follows.

---

[1] Source: Twentieth-Century British Political Facts 1900-2000, David Butler and Gareth Butler – 8th Edition, Macmillan Press Ltd

[2] Appears as '4' in Twentieth-British Political Facts 1900-2000, but figures actually add up to 18.003

Votes (percentages)			
	Neil Kinnock	Roy Hattersley	Eric Heffer	Peter Shore
Trade Unions	29.042	10.878	0.046	0.033
CLPs	27.452	0.577	1.971	-
MPs	14.778	7.833	4.286	3.103
TOTAL	71.272	19.288	6.303	3.137[3]

In that year's contest for the Deputy Leadership the results were as follows.

Votes (percentages)			
	Roy Hattersley	Michael Meacher	Denzil Davies	Gwyneth Dunwoody
Trade Unions	35.237	4.730	-	0.033
CLPs	15.313	14.350	0.241	0.096
MPs	16.716	8.806	3.284	1.194
TOTAL	67.266	27.886	3.525	1.323

In 1988, Neil Kinnock was challenged for the leadership by Tony Benn, while Roy Hattersley was challenged for the Deputy Leadership by John Prescott and Eric Heffer. The results are set out below.

Votes (percentages)		
	Neil Kinnock	Tony Benn
Trade Unions	39.660	0.340
CLPs	24.128	5.872
MPs	24.842	5.158
TOTAL	88.630	11.370

Votes (percentages)		
	Roy Hattersley	John Prescott	Eric Heffer
Trade Unions	31.339	8.654	0.007
CLPs	18.109	7.845	4.046
MPs	17.376	7.195	5.430
TOTAL	66.823[4]	23.694	9.483

---

[3] Appears as 3.137 in Twentieth Century British Political Facts 1900-2000, but figures actually add up to 3.136
[4] Appears as 66.823 in Twentieth Century British Political Facts 1900-2000, but figures actually add up to 66.824

After the 1992 General Election, Neil Kinnock and Roy Hattersley resigned and a contest ensued between John Smith and Brian Gould for Leader and between Margaret Beckett, John Prescott and Bryan Gould for Deputy Leader. The results were as follows.

	Votes (percentages)	
	John Smith	Bryan Gould
Trade Unions	38.518	1.482
CLPs	29.311	0.689
MPs	23.187	6.813
TOTAL	91.016	8.984

	Votes (percentages)		
	Margaret Beckett	John Prescott	Bryan Gould
Trade Unions	25.394	11.627	2.979
CLPs	19.038	7.096	3.866
MPs	12.871	9.406	7.723
TOTAL	57.303	28.129	14.568

The current rules for electing the Leader and Deputy Leader are set out in the Draft Labour Party Rule Book 2002 and vary according to whether or not the party is in government or opposition. When in opposition, where there is a vacancy for Leader or Deputy Leader, candidates for either position must be nominated by 12.5 per cent of the House of Commons' members of the Parliamentary Labour Party (PLP), and must themselves be members of the House of Commons. The Deputy Leader becomes Leader in the interim between vacancy and election and the National Executive Committee (NEC) decides on whether to hold an immediate ballot or elect a new Leader at the next annual conference.

Where there is no vacancy, an election theoretically takes place each year at the party conference, but a challenger would need to be nominated by 20 per cent of House of Commons' PLP members. In opposition, if the positions for both Leader and Deputy were to fall vacant, the Shadow Cabinet would need to appoint one of their number as interim leader and the NEC would have to order a postal ballot. When the party is in government, there is only a leadership election if a majority of conference members requests one on a card vote.

When in government, if a vacancy arises, a temporary leader (this could be the Deputy Leader in which case the Cabinet and NEC would have to appoint an interim Deputy Leader to serve until the next conference) is appointed by the Cabinet in consultation with the NEC, until a ballot can be held. The post could be left vacant until the next party conference.

In 1993 the rules were altered to give the three sections of the electoral college equal weighting in any leadership or deputy leadership contest.

Any subsequent election was also to be on a 'one member, one vote' basis, with each trade union dividing its total vote in proportion to its members' preferences, as opposed to casting the entire vote for one candidate (the so-called 'block vote'). In 1994, this was put to the test after the sudden death of John Smith. The results of the election were as follows.

	Votes (percentages) *(These figures, except for the totals, are percentages of each section of the electoral college rather than percentages of the total electoral college)*		
	Tony Blair	John Prescott	Margaret Beckett
Trade Unions	52.3	28.4	19.3
CLPs	58.2	24.4	17.4
MPs & MEPs	60.5	19.6	19.9
TOTAL	57.0	24.1	18.9

If no candidate had gained over 50 per cent of the votes cast, further ballot(s) would have been required to eliminate the lowest placed candidate. Any such ballots would have been held using the alternative vote, where preferences could be expressed.
In the battle for the Deputy Leadership, the result was as follows.

	Votes (percentages) *(These figures, except for the totals, are percentages of each section of the electoral college rather than percentages of the total electoral college)*	
	John Prescott	Margaret Beckett
Trade Unions	55.6	44.4
CLPs	59.4	40.6
MPs & MEPs	53.7	46.3
TOTAL	56.5	43.5

When in opposition, the Parliamentary Labour Party (PLP) (which consists of all Labour MPs when in opposition and all backbenchers when in government) elects a Shadow Cabinet. It also elects a Chairman and two Vice-Chairmen. In July 2001, Jean Corston became the first woman to be elected as Chair of the PLP, gaining 183 votes to Tony Lloyd's 167. 351 of Labour's 412 backbenchers took part in the poll.

The Party organisation in the country, as opposed to Parliament, is headed by the National Executive Committee, which, for the purpose of electing its members is divided into five divisions. Rule 4C.2 of the Draft Labour Party Rule Book 2002 sets out the regulations governing their election.

Elections to the party's policy-making body, the National Policy Forum takes place in eight divisions and appointments are for two-year terms.

NATIONAL EXECUTIVE COMMITTEE

Division	Members and Electorate
1	12 members, at least six of whom must be women, nominated by trade unions from their delegates and elected by their delegations at the Party Conference. Members of the TUC General Council cannot stand for election.
2	One member nominated by the socialist, co-operative and other affiliated organisations from among their appointed delegates and elected by their delegations at the Party Conference.
3	Six members, at least three of whom must be women, to be nominated by their own and at least two other CLPs and elected by a ballot of all eligible individual members of the party by a national one member, one vote, postal ballot.
4	Two members of the Association of Labour Councillors, at least one of whom must be a woman, nominated by Labour groups and elected by a ballot of all individual ALC members by a national one member, one vote, postal ballot.
5	Three House of Commons' members of the PLP or EPLP, at least one whom must be a woman, nominated from among backbench Labour MPs and MEPs (except the leader of the EPLP) and elected by all Labour MPs and MEPs by a ballot. House of Commons' members of the PLP and members of the EPLP cannot stand for election to Divisions 1,2,3 and 4 of the NEC.

NATIONAL POLICY FORUM

Division	Membership	Electorate
Division 1	55 members (there must be 5 from Scotland, 5 from Wales and 5 from each of the English regions[5], of which one place is reserved for a Young Labour representative[6] and two for women)	Nominated and elected by CLPs
Division 2	30 members, 15 of whom must be women	Nominated and elected by affiliated trade unions
Division 3	22 representatives, comprising one man and one woman from each of the following areas: Scotland, Wales and each English region	Elected by the Scottish, Welsh and English regional conferences or regional policy forums
Division 4	Nine Labour local government representatives (two men and two women from the Local Government Association Labour Group and the same from the Association of Labour Councillors and one representative from the Convention of Scottish Local Authorities Labour Group)	Elected by the Local Government Association Labour Group, Association of Labour Councillors and the Convention of Scottish Local Authorities Labour Group
Division 5	Three members (at least one of whom must be a woman) from the affiliated socialist societies	Elected by the affiliated socialist societies
Division 6	Four representatives of the Labour Party Black Socialist Society (two of whom must be women)	Elected by the Labour Party Black Socialist Society
Division 7	Nine representatives of the House of Commons' members of the PLP (at least four of whom must be women)	The PLP
Division 8	Six members of the European Labour Party (at least three of whom must be women)	The EPLP
Appointees	Eight frontbench representatives appointed by the Cabinet (or Shadow Cabinet when in opposition) at least three of whom must be women	
	Two Co-operative Party representatives, at least one of whom must be a woman	
Ex-officio	NEC members	

---

[5] Eastern, Greater London, Midlands, North, North West, South East and South West.
[6] The Young Labour representative must be a woman at least every other election.

Parliamentary Candidates

The Labour Party currently has 413 MPs in the House of Commons.

The selection of candidates for any public office is based on certain fundamental principles as set out in Rule 5A of the Draft Labour Party Rule Book 2002.

❖ All individual members of six months standing, who live in the electoral area concerned are entitled to participate in selection meetings.

❖ Anyone wishing to stand as a Labour candidate must have been a party member for at least 12 months.

❖ All nominees must undertake in writing to abide by Labour Party rules and standing orders.

❖ Selection procedures must enable the inclusion and involvement of all members on an equal basis and all selections should be carried out on the basis of one member, one vote, wherever reasonably practical, including elections where an electoral college is used.

The bedrock of the Labour Party is the Constituency Labour Party (CLP). Individual members of the Party are members of a CLP, even if they joined the Party nationally. Individuals have three ways of joining the Labour Party: through a CLP, a trade union or an affiliated society. The trade unions pay an affiliation fee for each member, which must come from a political fund, from which members can contract out. Those members paying the political levy pay a reduced subscription fee for individual membership of the Labour Party, as do members of affiliated societies.

The NEC maintains a national parliamentary panel of candidates. Candidates recommended by nationally affiliated organisations through their own processes are automatically included on the parliamentary panel, subject to agreement between the NEC and the organisation concerned. Nominees do not have to be members of the national parliamentary panel to seek selection.

Where a sitting MP is up for re-selection, a so-called 'trigger ballot' takes place. If the MP concerned wins the trigger ballot, he or she is selected as the CLP's Prospective Parliamentary Candidate (PPC). If the sitting MP does not win the ballot, he or she is then eligible for nomination and is included in the shortlist. If a sitting MP is not then selected, he or she can appeal to the NEC, but only on the grounds that the correct procedures were not followed. When the Speaker of the House of Commons is standing for re-election there is no selection procedure (traditionally, the Speaker seeking re-election in a general election is unopposed, although some political parties do contest the Speaker's seat, on the grounds that the Speaker's constituents happen, rather than choose, to live in his or her constituency and therefore have as much right to vote for the party of their choice as electors in other constituencies).

Under Rule 5C.8 (a) of the Draft Labour Party Rule Book 2002, *"The Selection of a parliamentary candidate shall not be regarded as completed until the name of the member selected has been placed before a meeting of the NEC and her or his selection has been endorsed."*

The NEC also has the power to rescind an endorsement of a candidate. Under Rule 5C.10 the NEC can, in an emergency, modify the normal selection procedures.

One of the most contentious issues facing the Labour Party in the run-up to the 1997 General Election was that of all-women shortlists. The 1993 Annual Conference had agreed to introduce quotas for women and women-only shortlists were introduced in 50% of all marginal constituencies that could be won on a 6% swing and in 50% of vacant Labour-held seats. These constituencies were to be identified by meetings between local and national officials, with intervention from the NEC where no agreement could be reached. Problems surfaced immediately as some local parties resented what they saw as the imposition of women-only shortlists from the party nationally.

The matter came to a head when two candidates, Peter Jepson and Roger Dyas Elliott, who had put themselves forward for selection as candidates in women-only seats, took the matter to an industrial tribunal on the basis that quotas were in breach of the Sex Discrimination Act 1975 as well as the 1976 EU Directive on Equal Treatment. They won the case and all-women shortlists were declared illegal. The Labour Leadership decided not to contest the decision. By this time, 38 women had been selected from women-only shortlists and 34 were in winnable seats. In 15 other seats, CLPs went on to select women even though the court ruling had meant the suspension of women-only selections. The Government has now said it will introduce legislation to permit positive discrimination in the selection of candidates. Labour's 2001 General Election Manifesto stated that *"We are committed, through legislation, to allow each party to make positive moves to increase the representation of women"*. The 2001 Queen's Speech (20/6/01) simply stated that *"My Government will prepare legislation to allow political parties to make positive moves to increase the representation of women in public life"*.

Local Government

Rule 5B of the Draft Labour Party Rule Book 2002 sets out the procedures to be used in selecting local government candidates. The NEC issues guidelines to Local Government Committees (the committees corresponding to the relevant local government areas), which are responsible for implementing them. All party members of six months' standing, who are resident in the area in which the election is taking place, are entitled to take place in the process of shortlisting and selecting local government candidates. Both the shortlisting and selection of candidates is undertaken by an eliminating ballot of all eligible individual members of the electoral ward / division on the basis of one member, one vote. All potential candidates must have been party members for at least 12 months and must agree to abide by the standing orders of the relevant Labour group and to become a member of the national Association of Labour Councillors. Anyone disqualified as a parliamentary candidate by the party may not be nominated as a local government candidate.

European Elections

The Labour Party currently has 29 MEPs.

The process of selecting candidates for the first elections to the European Parliament under the new system in 1999 was initiated by an OMOV 'trigger' ballot of all European Constituency Labour Party members who were asked whether they wished to reselect their local sitting MEP. MEPs passing this hurdle were guaranteed a place on the relevant regional list. Others interested in becoming candidates had to complete an application form stating the regions in which they wished to stand. An information pack was produced for candidates as well one for European Constituency Labour Parties (ECPLs) and CLPs. Guidelines for Regional Directors and NEC designated representatives were also produced.

The application forms of those interested in standing in a particular region were then sent to all branches, CLPs, affiliated Trade Unions, Fabian Societies and Co-operative Societies within that region. Each of the aforementioned groups/societies could nominate one candidate. The candidates who were thus nominated were interviewed by the General Committee of the relevant CLP.

Each CLP had to select one female and one male candidate. There followed a one member, one vote (OMOV) ballot of members in the former European parliamentary constituencies areas to select one male and one female candidate. There were separate alternative vote ballots for the male and female candidates. Those at the top of the ballots were thereby deemed to the selected candidates (59 men and 55 women). In addition to this, 50 sitting MEPs stood again and were therefore guaranteed a place on the final list. This left 34 places for other candidates. Candidates (included the sitting MEPs) were sent another application form, indicating three electoral regions in which they were interested in standing. They were also required to sign an agreement to abide by the decisions of the Selection Board, a memorandum of agreement for regional MEPs, the EPLP's standing orders and the NEC guidelines. The application forms were assessed by a National Selection Board and counted for 30 per cent of a candidate's final score.

Finally, the candidates appeared before a panel of five NEC members, three representatives of the relevant regional board, one ethnic minority member and one member of the National Trade Union Liaison Committee and the General Secretary of the Labour Party. The panels then selected (along with all the sitting MEPs who wanted to stand again) the candidates they wanted to go forward (usually 50 per cent more than the number of list places for that region). These final candidates were again interviewed by the panel and finally ranked in five groups from 'A' to 'E'. After this the regional boards met to make the final selections.

There were some concerns about the way in which candidates were selected for the new European regional lists, used for the first time in 1999 and particularly the way in which candidates were ranked. In London, for example, Carole Tongue, a popular and successful sitting MEP, was ranked five on a list of 10, leading many to suspect that there were serious flaws in the system. In the West Midlands, Christine Oddy, the sitting Labour MEP was placed seventh out of eight on the shortlist, below Michael Cashman and Neena Gill (both elected as MEPs). When she complained she was dropped from the shortlist altogether. In February 2001, she took the Labour Party to an employment tribunal on the grounds of racial and sexual discrimination. However, as David Butler and Martin Westlake point out in their excellent account of the 1999 European Parliamentary elections ('British Politics and European Elections 1999', Macmillan Press Ltd, 2000) the Labour Party was faced with an impossible task given the transition to a proportional system in which they were bound to return fewer MEPs than under the old first-past-the-post system, which in 1992 had returned 62 Labour MEPs. Some sitting MEPs were inevitably disappointed.

The rules on selecting candidates for European parliamentary elections have recently been altered to provide for selections by one member, one vote postal ballots of all those living in the relevant region. Section 5D.5 of the Draft Labour Party Rule Book 2002 states that the party's regional boards / national executives should appoint a selections board 'representative of local CLPs and affiliated organisations as determined by the NEC'. These boards then administer the procedures for re-selecting MEPs (essentially a ballot of affiliated organisations and CLPs). MEPs receiving the support of at least 50 per cent of the affiliated organisations / CLPs who have voted, are automatically included on the shortlist for the relevant region. Those who fail this hurdle, have the same rights to nomination as other members. All eligible members in the region will then determine the successful candidates by a postal ballot in which the candidates are ranked (by simple preference voting). The NEC must endorse the selection and can dispense with the normal selection procedures in an emergency.

The Scottish Parliament

The Labour Party currently has 55 MSPs.

The Labour Party was criticised by the media for the way in which it selected its candidates for the first elections to the Scottish Parliament. The failure of party stalwarts such as Dennis Canavan to gain a place on the shortlist of candidates led many to feel that only the most 'on-message' Blairites stood any chance of success. The 1997 Annual Labour Party Conference agreed to some basic procedures to be followed in the selection of candidates for Scotland, after which details were drawn up by the Scottish and Welsh Conferences. Labour Party members of a year's standing could 'self-nominate'; i.e., apply to be a candidate. A selection board consisting of representatives from the Scottish Executive and the NEC, along with some Independent members, then selected a panel of candidates. Constituencies were then 'twinned' so that each CLP could then shortlist two men and two women from the panel with the final decision being taken by an OMOV ballot of CLP members.

As far as the list section was concerned, lists of candidates taken from the shortlisted candidates were drawn up by a committee of four members of the Scottish Executive, two members of the National Executive and the Secretary of the Scottish Party and were then put to regional electoral conferences attended by three representatives from each of the CLPs within the relevant list region. They could reject the list and refer it back to the selection committee.

The Draft Labour Party Rule Book 2002 says little on the selection of candidates for the Scottish Parliament, beyond stating that the NEC will draw up a procedural document for consultation with the Scottish Executive Committee.

The Welsh Assembly

The Labour Party currently has 28 members of the Welsh Assembly.

The contest for the position of Labour's leader in Wales proved to be yet another spectacular own goal for the Party. As in the selection process for the party's candidate for London Mayor, an electoral college was chosen to select Labour's leader in Wales. As in London, the organisations comprising the trade union section were not compelled to ballot their members. Each of the three sections of the electoral college constituted one third of the votes. The first part of the electoral college comprised 40 CLPs, five ECLPs, 22 County Labour Parties and 17 Women's Councils. The voting methods differed widely, with some CLPs restricting voting to GMs while others balloted all members. Where organisations actually balloted, Rhodri Morgan appeared to have an advantage over his rival Ron Davies. As Kevin Morgan and Geoff Mungham point out in their account of the Assembly elections ('Redesigning Democracy: The Making of the Welsh Assembly', seren), it would have been possible for someone to have been a member of a CLP/ECLP, a County Labour Party and a Women's Council and to have had three votes in this section alone. They could then have voted again if they had been members of the bodies voting in sections two and three of the electoral college. The second section consisted of trade unions (none of whom balloted their members) and the affiliated societies. The third section consisted of 34 Welsh Labour MPs, five Welsh Labour MEPs and all the approved Welsh Assembly candidates.

The votes were eventually cast as follows.

	Votes (percentages of those sections)	
	Rhodri Morgan	Ron Davies
CLPs, etc	47.83	52.7
Trade Unions, etc	91.72	8.28
MPs, MEPs and Assembly candidates	60.77	39.23

Ron Davies, duly selected as Labour's leader in Wales, proved to be as embarrassing to the Labour Party as Jeffrey Archer was to the Conservatives in London. On 27 October 1998 he was forced to resign as Secretary of State for Wales and then later as Labour's prospective Assembly leader. A new contest was required. A Task Force met to discuss procedures. They decided to re-open the selections for the panel of Assembly candidates, removing an obstacle to the Labour Leadership's preferred candidate, Alun Michael, the new Welsh Secretary. The Task Force then proposed a slightly different variant of the electoral college used in the first contest. In the first section, all members were to have a vote; in the second, affiliated bodies were to consult their members and in the third, MPs and MEPs were to be included, but only selected candidates as opposed to all approved candidates.

The TGWU said it could not afford to ballot all party members, yet found the resources to mail them a letter recommending Alun Michael. The Electoral College voted as follows.

	Votes (percentages of those sections)	
	Rhodri Morgan	Alun Michael
CLPs, etc	64.35	35.65
Trade Unions, etc	36.04	63.96
MPs, MEPs and Assembly candidates	41.57	58.43

Alun Michael therefore won with 52.68 per cent of the total votes as against Rhodri Morgan's 47.32 per cent.

The party's constituency candidates were chosen by a process which involved 'self nomination', selection by a panel and finally by a procedure designed to achieve gender balance – 'twinning' ('zipping' to the Liberal Democrats) whereby one CLP was twinned with another so that one selected a woman and the other a man. The selection panels comprised a member of the Welsh Labour Party Executive, an NEC nominee, a member of the Welsh Labour Party and a professional adviser to the panel. Unsuccessful candidates could appeal to a three-member appeals panel and then if rejected again could appeal in writing, but to the same panel. The appeals panel then presented its list of candidates whom it considered should have been selected to the Welsh Labour Party panel. They refused to accept them. They were then presented to the Welsh Executive, who did.[7] This resulted in a further eight candidates joining the existing 163 who had already been approved. Branches then nominated candidates who could then go forward to be selected by CLPs, a process made more complicated than usual by the adoption of twinning. Members voted on candidates at hustings meetings, ranking them in order. Members could also vote by post.

The list candidates were chosen in each region by representatives from each of the constituencies within that region, overseen by a panel comprising three members from the Welsh Labour Party Executive, two NEC members and two other party officials. However, the panel alone decided the shortlist and placings – the delegates were only allowed to either approve or reject the list. Alun Michael entered the contest too late to have a reasonable chance of being selected as a constituency candidate and was therefore forced to find a place on a list. It came as no surprise to many in the Welsh Labour Party to find that he eventually came top of the list in the Mid and West Wales region. Four list members were selected for each region.

The Draft Labour Party Rule Book 2002 says little on the selection of candidates for the Welsh Assembly, beyond stating that the NEC will draw up a procedural document for consultation with the Welsh Executive Committee.

The Greater London Assembly and Mayor

The Labour Party currently has nine members of the GLA.

The procedure adopted by the Labour Party in its selection of a mayoral candidate was not a public relations triumph. The process was dominated from the start by 'the Ken Livingstone problem'. A Greater London regional conference held in June 1998 had decided that mayoral candidates would need to be nominated by one eighth of all London CLPs if they were to proceed to an OMOV ballot of all London Labour Party members. However, the Regional Board thought otherwise and in November a new system was put to the NEC. 'Self nomination' was proposed, with candidates putting themselves forward to a panel of regional party and NEC members.

A committee in Millbank came up with a shortlist of three names which were then submitted to an 'electoral college' where the following had one third of the votes each: members in London, Trade Unions and affiliated co-operative societies and finally, London Labour MPs, MEPs and GLA candidates who had, by that stage, been selected. The Trade Unions and affiliated societies were to choose how to cast their block votes and whether or not to conduct internal ballots of their members. Some Trade Unions who had not paid their subscriptions in time, and who therefore missed the cut-off date, were excluded altogether.

As Mark D'Arcy and Rory MacLean recount in their excellent and enormously entertaining account of the mayor race ('Nightmare! The Race to Become London's Mayor', Politico's

---

[7] For an entertaining account of the selection procedures in Wales, see 'Dragons Led By Poodles: The Inside Story of a New Labour Stitch-Up' (Paul Flynn MP, Politico's Publishing)

Publishing), this included the Manufacturing, Science, Finance union (MSF), the National Union of Rail, Maritime and Transport Workers (RMT) and the Associated Society of Locomotive Engineers and Firemen (ASLEF). The Selection Panel eventually (after a tortuous process) included Ken Livingstone on the shortlist. The next stage was the vote by the electoral college. In the first round, Frank Dobson gained 51.526 per cent of the vote and Ken Livingstone, 48.473 per cent. Glenda Jackson gained 4.421 per cent and her votes were then redistributed to give Frank Dobson 51.526 per cent and Ken Livingstone, 48.473 per cent. In the CLP members section of the College, Ken Livingstone had gained 54.9 per cent in the first ballot, Frank Dobson 35.3 per cent and Glenda Jackson, 9.8 per cent. Once her second preferences had been redistributed, Ken Livingstone had 50.8 per cent of the votes and Frank Dobson, 49.2 per cent. In the Trade Union section, Ken Livingstone gained 24.003 per cent of the vote and Frank Dobson, 9.330 per cent (once Glenda Jackson's votes had been redistributed). In the MPs, MEPs and GLA candidates' section, on the first ballot Ken Livingstone won only nine votes and Frank Dobson 64 (Glenda Jackson's single vote was redistributed to Ken Livingstone on the second ballot).

Frank Dobson's victory turned out to be a Pyrrhic one and Labour's attempt to keep Ken Livingstone out of the Mayor's office backfired in spectacular fashion. Although he had signed up to the Electoral College process that Labour had devised, Ken Livingstone then declared that he would stand as an independent candidate, against Frank Dobson. It was not really a surprise when Ken Livingstone won the mayoral election, beating his nearest rival – not Frank Dobson but Steve Norris – on the second ballot, gaining 776,427 votes to Steve Norris' 564,137. Ken Livingstone was defeated by Frank Dobson, prompting the former to stand against the latter in the ensuing mayoral contest.

The Draft Labour Party Rule Book 2002 says little on the selection of candidates for the devolved institutions, beyond stating that the NEC will draw up a procedural document for consultation with the Scottish and Welsh Executive Committees. A similar process is to be adopted with respect to selections for the Greater London Authority or any other regional body in England. The NEC is also to draw up detailed procedural guidance with respect to selections for directly elected leaders or regional administration and local authorities.

More information about the Labour Party can be found at: www.labour.org.uk or by calling: 020 7802 1000

More information about the Scottish Labour Party can be found at: www.scottishlabour.org.uk or by calling: 0141 572 6900

More information on the Welsh Labour Party is available at: www.waleslabourparty.org.uk or by calling: 029 2087 7700

THE CONSERVATIVE PARTY

It is only recently that the Conservative Party has become a national party, in the sense of having a national, centrally held membership list. Until the leadership of William Hague, the party had no single national organisation and was really an amalgamation of three different organisations: the Parliamentary Party (MPs), the voluntary Party (the National Union, comprised of local associations) and the professional Party (Conservative Central Office). Local parties are called 'Associations' and were, until the recent reforms, merely part of a national umbrella organisation – the National Union of Conservative and Unionist Associations.

The Constitution of the Conservative Party (October 1999 edition) sets out the membership and functions of the new Governing Board, headed by the Chairman of the Conservative Party. The Board consists of the following:

❖ Two Deputy Chairmen (the Chairman of the National Conservative Convention and a Deputy Chairman appointed by the Leader)

❖ Four members elected by the National Conservative Convention (in addition to the Chairman)

❖ The elected Chairman of the 1922 Committee

❖ The Conservative Leader in the House of Lords

❖ The elected Deputy Chairman of the Scottish Conservatives

❖ The elected Chairman of the Welsh Conservatives

❖ The elected Chairman of the Conservative Councillors Association

❖ The Party Treasurer

❖ A senior member of staff nominated by the Board

❖ A member nominated by the Leader, subject to endorsement of the Board

❖ A member nominated by the Board and subject to the approval of the Leader

The Board, which meets six times a year, has three sub-committees:

❖ The Committee on Membership

❖ The Committee on Candidates

❖ The Committee on Conferences

The Area Councils consist of the Chairmen of the Conservative Associations within the relevant Area, two representatives elected by the Executive Council of each Constituency Association within the relevant area and the elected members of the Area Management Executive.

Each Area Council meets once a year and elects an Area Management Executive, which consists of a Chairman, two Deputies, one of whom has responsibility for policy and campaigning and one of whom is responsible for fund-raising and membership and up to two other officers who can be co-opted by the Area Management Executive. In Areas with more than 12 constituencies, Area Council elect to the Area Management Executive, one additional officer for every additional six constituencies (or part thereof).

In addition, Regional Co-ordinators are appointed to deal with such matters as boundary reviews, which need to be considered on a regional basis.

The National Conservative Convention meets twice a year and includes the following:

❖ Chairmen of all Constituency Associations

❖ The elected representatives of the Board

❖ The elected members of the Scottish Executive of the Scottish Conservatives

❖ The elected members of the Board of the Welsh Conservatives

❖ All members of the Area Management Executives

❖ All Regional Chairmen and Deputy Chairmen

❖ The three past Presidents of the National Conservative Convention

❖ The two immediate past Chairmen of the National Conservative Convention

❖ The immediate past Area Management Executive Chairmen for one year only

❖ The immediate past Regional Chairmen for one year only

❖ Further representation from each Recognised Organisation, Specialist Group or other body as the Board determines (elected by those organisations)

The Conservative Political Centre (CPC) has been re-launched as the Conservative Policy Forum (CPF) and is linked to local policy forums, the aim being to involve ordinary association members in policy-making to a greater extent than before. The Area Deputy Chairmen responsible for policy development elect three representatives to the CPF Council, which is chaired by a Cabinet or Shadow Cabinet member, appointed by the Leader, a senior Director of the Party, appointed by the Chairman of the Board, a representative appointed by the Scottish Conservatives and up to five people with expertise in specific policy areas who are co-opted by the Director of the Conservative Policy Forum in consultation with the CPF Council. The CPF Council meets twice a year.

An Ethics and Integrity Committee, chaired by a QC and comprised of the Chairman of the National Conservative Convention and the Chairman of the 1922 Committee considers complaints against Party Members considered to be 'bringing the Party into disrepute'. Instances of misconduct are referred to the Committee, either by the Party Leader, or by the Board. The Board appoints a Compliance Officer, whose responsibility it is to ensure that Party Members adhere to the provisions of the Constitution. The Compliance Officer is responsible for informing the Board of any breaches of the Constitution. Disagreement with Party policy is not considered evidence of having brought the Party into disrepute. The Ethics and Integrity Committee can recommend that an individual is suspended or expelled from the party.

The following are entitled to attend the Annual Party Conference:

❖ The members of the National Convention

❖ The two Deputy Chairmen each Constituency Association

❖ Three additional representatives of each Constituency Association (one of whom must be a member of a Recognised Organisation)

❖ Members and former members of the Board and its committees

❖ The Agent or Secretary of each Constituency Association

❖ MPs, MEPs, MSPs, AMs and Conservative Peers

❖ PPCs for Westminster, Scottish Parliament, the Welsh Assembly and the European Parliament

❖ Parliamentary Candidates on the Approved Lists

❖ The Chairman and members of Recognised Organisations as determined by the Board

❖ Members of the Scottish Executive of the Scottish Conservative Party

❖ Members of the Board of the Welsh Conservatives

❖ One representative of each university-based branch

❖ Honorary Vice-Presidents of the former National Union

❖ The Leaders of Conservative Groups on all local authorities in the UK

Each Conservative Association has an Executive Council, chaired by the Chairman of the Association and comprising the following:

❖ The President of the Association

❖ Another Honorary member of the Association (if the General Meeting wishes to appoint one)

❖ The Officers of the Association

❖ One or more elected representative from each Ward or Polling District Branch

❖ One or more representatives of each Committee (e.g., the Local Government Committee, the Women's Committee, etc.)

❖ One representative of each Conservative Club in the constituency

❖ The MP / PPC for the constituency

❖ The MEP / or Prospective European Parliamentary Candidate (non-voting)

❖ The Party Agent (non-voting)

❖ The Chairman of the relevant Area Management Executive (or another member nominated by the Chairman)

❖ An advisor appointed by the Board of the Party (non-voting)

❖ Up to three people co-opted by the Executive Council

Measures to reform the Party, similar to those in England, were also put in place in Scotland, effectively merging the old voluntary and professional wings of the Scottish Conservative and Unionist Party.

The Party Leader

Until 1965 there was no formal process for electing the Leader of the Conservative Party; the leader 'emerged' after an informal process of consultation.

Only one name was put forward to a meeting of Conservative MPs, peers, PPCs and the Executive Committee of the National Union.

After the party's defeat in the 1964 General Election, Sir Alec Douglas-Home recommended a new system under which the leader would be selected by a ballot of all Conservative MPs. To be successful, a candidate had to secure both a majority of votes in the first ballot, and have a lead of 15 per cent over the nearest rival candidate (15 per cent of those voting). If no such lead was secured a second ballot took place. At this stage, new candidates, who had not taken part in the first ballot, could throw their hats into the ring. In the second ballot the winning candidate needed only to secure an absolute majority. If no candidate secured such a majority, a third ballot was necessary. The third round consisted of only the three leading candidates from the second round and voters had to indicate first and second preferences. The candidate with the smallest number of first preferences was eliminated and his second preferences distributed between the other two. The first time this system was used was in the election for Leader after the resignation of Sir Alec Douglas-Home in 1965. The results of the first ballot were as follows:

Edward Heath – 150 (lead was less than requisite 15 per cent)
Reginald Maudling – 133
Enoch Powell – 15

As both Maudling and Powell withdrew, Heath was elected unopposed. In 1974 after the party's second general election defeat in a year, Sir Alec Douglas-Home was asked to propose changes to the rules to allow an incumbent leader to be challenged. As a result, it was decided that there should be an annual election for Leader and to be successful on the first ballot, a candidate required not just an overall majority, but also a lead of 15 per cent (*of those eligible to vote*) over his or her nearest rival. Under the previous system the 15 per cent related to those actually voting. This allowed a so-called 'stalking horse' candidate to challenge a leader in the first ballot, before withdrawing before the second in order to allow the real contenders to put their names forward. In the 1975 election for leader, Edward Heath was beaten into second place on the first ballot by Margaret Thatcher. The results were as follows:

Margaret Thatcher – 130
Edward Heath – 119
Hugh Fraser – 16
Abstentions – 11

Edward Heath then resigned, Hugh Fraser withdrew from the race and four new candidates entered. The result of the second ballot was as follows:

Margaret Thatcher – 146
William Whitelaw – 79
James Prior – 19
Sir Geoffrey Howe – 19
John Peyton – 11

In 1989, Mrs Thatcher was challenged by a 'stalking horse' candidate in the shape of Sir Anthony Meyer. Mrs Thatcher won 314 votes to his 33 (there were 27 abstentions). In 1990, she was challenged by Michael Heseltine and the results of the first ballot were as follows:

Margaret Thatcher – 204 (four votes short of the 15 per cent hurdle)
Michael Heseltine – 152
Abstentions – 16

Margaret Thatcher was eventually persuaded by leading figures in the party to withdraw from the second ballot. John Major and Douglas Hurd then entered the contest and the results of the second ballot were as follows:

John Major – 185 (two votes short of an overall majority)
Michael Heseltine – 131
Douglas Hurd – 56

Although, John Major needed two votes for an overall majority, a third ballot was rendered unnecessary as both Michael Heseltine and Douglas Hurd withdrew. As a result of a contest in which a Prime Minister, undefeated at the ballot box, who had won three election victories for the Conservative Party, was forced to concede defeat, further amendments were made to the election process. It was decided that in future, 10 per cent of Conservative MPs would be required to nominate anyone wishing to challenge the incumbent leader. The next contest took place in 1995, when John Major, then Prime Minister, resigned in order to provoke the right wing of the party into a contest. John Redwood challenged John Major but lost on the first ballot.

John Major – 218
John Redwood – 89
Abstentions and spoilt ballot papers – 22

After the 1997 General Election, John Major resigned and in the first ballot five candidates stood for election. The results were as follows:

Kenneth Clarke – 49
William Hague – 41
John Redwood – 27
Michael Howard – 24
Peter Lilley – 23

In the second ballot, the results were as follows:

Kenneth Clarke – 64
William Hague – 62
John Redwood – 38

After the second ballot, John Redwood withdrew, entering into what was surely one of the strangest pacts ever between left and right in Conservative Party history, by agreeing to back Kenneth Clarke. In the third ballot, William Hague emerged as the victor.

William Hague – 92
Kenneth Clarke – 70

After his election as Leader, William Hague presided over a complete overhaul of the structure of the Conservative Party and also instituted new rules for electing the leader. The influential 1922 Committee which meets weekly while Parliament sits and which consists, when the party is in opposition of all Conservative MPs and when in government, of all backbenchers, still has a key role to play in his or her election.

Under the new system, the Chairman of the 1922 Committee orders a vote of confidence in the party leader, only if he or she is petitioned to do so by 15 per cent of the parliamentary party. The Chairman then decides the date of the vote of confidence. If the incumbent leader secures a simple majority he remains leader and a further confidence vote cannot be held during the next 12 months. However, if the leader fails to obtain a majority he must resign and cannot stand in the ensuing election. If the leader is ousted, any Conservative MP can stand in the election, provided they have a proposer and seconder. All Conservative MPs then vote in a secret ballot. If there are three or more contenders, the one with the least votes in the ballot then drops out. Two days later a second ballot is held for the remaining candidates and the process is repeated until only three candidates remain, after which the candidate with the fewest votes drops out. The two surviving candidates then go forward to a postal ballot of all Conservative Party members. Only those who have been members for at least three months before the confidence vote are eligible to vote. The candidates can spend up to £100,000 on their campaign (the money must come from donations).

In the first round of the 2001 leadership contest on 10 July, Michael Ancram and David Davis tied for final place, necessitating a re-run on 12 July.

Michael Portillo – 49
Iain Duncan Smith – 39
Kenneth Clarke – 36
Michael Ancram – 21
David Davis – 21

In the second ballot, two days later, Michael Ancram was eliminated from the contest.

Michael Portillo - 50
Iain Duncan Smith – 42
Kenneth Clarke – 39
David Davis – 18
Michael Ancram – 17

David Davis then withdrew from the contest and the results of the third ballot were as follows.

Kenneth Clarke – 59
Iain Duncan Smith – 54
Michael Portillo – 53

Michael Portillo was therefore eliminated and Iain Duncan Smith and Kenneth Clarke were left to battle it out amongst the party members.

There were a number of complaints from Conservative Party members about the way in which the ballot of party members was conducted. The cut-off point for those eligible to vote for the Leader was set at 28 March 2001, meaning that those who had joined the Party in the run-up to the 2001 general election could not vote. There was no central register of those eligible to vote (only the names of 33,000 activists who have joined since 1998 are held centrally). As a result, Conservative Associations submitted lists of members to Conservative Central Office, which many claimed were inaccurate. Only those paying the minimum membership subscription of £15 qualified to vote. Several of those paying smaller amounts to local associations claimed they had not realised that this would not qualify them to vote in the leadership ballot (when the central register was set up in 1997, so-called 'Foundation Members' were allowed to pay less than the minimum subscription).

Party members returning ballot papers had to sign a declaration that they had not voted twice (some Party Members belong to more than one Conservative Constituency Association). A report in The Sunday Times (29/7/01) suggested that in some areas, members who had recently moved house and members who had recently defected to other parties might be eligible to vote. Ballot papers were not valid unless returned with a signed declaration. Ballot papers had to be placed inside a ballot paper envelope, and then returned, along with the declaration in a reply paid envelope. Ballot papers had to be received by the Independent Scrutineer at Electoral Reform Ballot Services Limited, no later than noon on Tuesday, 11 September 2001. The result was to have been declared on Wednesday 12 September, but as a result of the terrorist attacks in the USA, on the World Trade Center in New York and the Pentagon in Washington on 11 September, this was delayed until Thursday, 13 September. Iain Duncan Smith was the winner with 155,933 votes, while Kenneth Clarke gained 100,864 votes. The turnout was 79 per cent.

Parliamentary Candidates

The Conservative Party currently has 166 MPs.

Under the new constitution of the Conservative Party, the governing body of a local association is the Executive Council, elected by members at the association's Annual

General Meeting. One Deputy Chairman has specific responsibility for policy development (this provision is mirrored both at the Area and at the Regional level). The Executive Council is responsible for establishing a Candidate Selection Committee, which is itself responsible for selecting three candidates from the Party's 'Approved List'.

Anyone wishing to be a candidate, must be on the United Kingdom Parliamentary List (the 'Approved List'). There is a separate list for European Parliamentary elections – the 'European Parliament List'. Would-be candidates are interviewed by an adviser on candidates before attending a weekend parliamentary selection board. If this hurdle is passed, his or her name is added to the approved list. The only task remaining is to find a constituency looking for a candidate.

The local Association's Candidate Selection Committee, (appointed by the Executive Council of the local Association and consisting of the Chairman of the Association, the local party agent, other members appointed by the Executive Council and a person appointed by the Conservative Party Board, who can attend all meetings of the Selection Committee in an advisory capacity) shortlists candidates and may well have over 100 names from which to choose. They can decide to shortlist candidates not on the approved list, but if they do, those names must be submitted to Conservative Central Office (CCO), to the National Board's sub-committee on endorsement. If they refuse to endorse the candidate, but the local Association goes on to select them, they are not considered an official party candidate at the forthcoming election.

Usually only about eight candidates make it through to the next stage (at least three candidates must be interviewed), to be interviewed by the Executive Council. They recommend at least two candidates to a general meeting of the Association at which the final selection is made by secret ballot. If any candidate gains over 50 per cent of the votes on the first round they are elected, but if not the candidate with the least votes is eliminated and another round of voting takes place. Conservative Associations can and do deselect sitting MPs, as David Ashby in Leicestershire North West, Sir George Gardiner in Reigate and Sir Nicholas Scott in Kensington and Chelsea, discovered before the 1997 General Election. Where a sitting MP wishes to stand again, he or she must send a written application to the Executive Council. The Council votes by secret ballot on whether or not to re-adopt the MP concerned. If they vote against re-adoption, the Member concerned can ask for a postal ballot of all the Association's members or ask for his or her name to be added to the final list to be considered by the General Meeting.

Local Government

The Conservative Party's local government candidates are selected at branch level in each constituency. The Constituency Association's Executive Council can either maintain an approved list of potential local government candidates and submit names to local branches for selection, allocate candidates to fight particular wards or divisions or allow branches to select candidates of their own choosing (which must then be approved by the Executive Council and subsequently adopted at a branch meeting). Sitting councillors wishing to be re-adopted must apply in writing to the Executive Council or Branch Committee, which must then ensure that the Executive Council adds his or her name to the list submitted to the Branch.

European Elections

The Conservatives currently have 35 MEPs.

An approved list of candidates was drawn up by a panel under the chairmanship of Lord Freeman. The final list contained 200 names and was published on 5 April 1998. The selection of candidates was undertaken by Regional Selection Colleges comprising the Chairs of the former European constituencies and the parliamentary constituencies within that area. These Regional Selection Colleges then selected a sub-committee of about 20 of their members who came up with a shortlist of those they wished to be interviewed by the whole College. The shortlist was drawn from those on the approved list. The College then voted on who should go through to the final stage, a meeting where any member of the relevant Conservative associations could vote, on how the candidates should be ranked (potentially, these meetings could have been huge, given the number of party members in what are quite large geographical areas). Candidates were entitled to address the meetings for 20 minutes, followed by 10 minutes of questioning. As a result, in some cases, meetings lasted for around seven to eight hours. In the South East, around 2,500 people attended just such a meeting.

The Scottish Parliament

The Conservatives currently have 19 MSPs.

In Scotland, only candidates who had been chosen to contest the 73 constituency seats could be selected for the regional list. The list candidates were selected by a central committee assisted by the chairmen of the local Associations for the relevant regions.

The Welsh Assembly

The Conservatives currently have nine members of the Welsh Assembly (Rod Richards was elected as Conservative, but the party whip was later withdrawn).

The candidates for the Welsh Assembly were selected in a similar way to candidates for the Scottish Parliament. All list candidates had to stand for a constituency seat as well, except for those on the last four places in each regional list, as there were only 40 constituency MPs to be elected and 20 additional list members.

The Greater London Assembly and Mayor

The Conservatives currently have nine members of the GLA.

Conservatives who saw themselves as potential candidates for the GLA were required to send in an application to the London Candidates Committee, which was empowered to ask candidates to attend interviews, where necessary. The Committee comprised Conservative Party Regional and Area Officers, a London MP and a local government representative. In each GLA constituency, a selection committee was responsible for shortlisting candidates. In most cases between around eight and 14 candidates were interviewed before the list was reduced to three or four names for the next stage of the selection process in which candidates addressed a General Meeting open to all members of the relevant Constituency Association; for example, all members in Croydon and Sutton. The constituency candidate was then selected by a secret ballot. This process could be by-passed by a candidate applying directly to the constituency in which he or she lived (however, they still required the approval of the London Candidates Committee). Those who made it to the final round of the constituency selection process were eligible for selection as London members (members of the GLA, elected from a party list, who do not represent a constituency). A sifting committee consisting of the three regional officers (as far as the Conservative Party organisation in London is concerned, there are three regions: East, West and South) the Area Management officers (Chairman, two deputies and two other officers) and the Constituency Chairmen ranked the candidates who appeared on the party's final list of London members.

The Conservative Party's search for a suitable mayoral candidate in 1999 proved to be as difficult as Labour's. Their answer to Ken Livingstone came in the form of Jeffrey Archer, the flamboyant peer, whose litigious past caught up with him, causing him to withdraw from the mayoral race and resulting in an embarrassing and at times, chaotic, re-run of the Conservative's selection procedure.

A specially constituted Mayoral Selection Executive selected candidates who then went forward to an electoral college (consisting of one representative from each Constituency Association in the London area, along with 25 party officers, including regional officers from the London area) followed by a hustings meeting of all party members in London. The shortlist consisted of Lord Archer, Steve Norris, Andrew Boff, Robert Blackman, Bernard Gentry, Patrick Ground, Mark Kotecha and John Wilkinson MP. The electoral college chose four to go forward to the hustings meeting. They were chosen on a 'one member, one vote' basis. Lord Archer, Steve Norris, Andrew Boff and Robert Blackman got through this stage. The hustings meeting was charged with selecting the two candidates who would go forward to a ballot of all party members in London. Lord Archer gained 868 votes, to Steve Norris' 595 (Andrew Boff gained 156 and Robert Blackman 135). In the ensuing ballot, Lord Archer gained 15,716 votes and Steve Norris 6,350. 22,301 votes were cast and the turnout was 58.6 per cent.

After Lord Archer was forced to withdraw from the mayoral contest, the Mayoral Selection Executive decided to institute a new selection process. They selected nine candidates to go forward: Andrew Boff, Bernard Gentry, Patrick Ground QC, Baroness Hanham, Mark Kotecha, Councillor Paul Lynch, Baroness Miller and John Wilkinson MP. They were interviewed by a vetting panel with five members. The Mayoral Selection Executive then met again to decide who should go forward to the Electoral College. They were presented with a letter from the President, Chairman and two former Chairmen of the Epping Forest Conservative Association, which suggested that Steve Norris had decided not to re-contest the seat that he represented until 1997 because if he had not, he would have been deselected.

The Mayoral Selection Executive voted on all the candidates and decided not to put Steve Norris forward for the next stage. The majority of members of the Electoral College, however, wanted to see Steve Norris on the shortlist. The matter was eventually referred back to the Executive, who did not want to enlarge the shortlist. Deadlock loomed, so the matter was then referred to the Board of the Conservative Party. Two names were added, Steve Norris and Paul Lynch. The Electoral College then met again to choose the two candidates who would go forward to a ballot of all party members in London (an eliminating ballot was used). Steve Norris gained 354 votes, Andrew Boff, 210 and Baroness Miller of Hendon, 162. Steve Norris and Andrew Boff therefore went through to a final ballot, which Steve Norris won by 12,903 votes to 4,712. Steve Norris therefore became the Conservative's candidate for London Mayor.

More information about the Conservative Party can be found at: www.conservatives.com or by calling: 020 7222 9000

More information about the Scottish Conservative Party can be found at: www.scottishtories.org.uk or by calling: 0131 247 6890

More information about the Welsh Conservatives can be obtained by calling: 029 2061 6031

THE LIBERAL DEMOCRATS

The Party Leader

The Liberal Democrats are a federal party, with separate organisations in England, Scotland and Wales. The Federal Party has its headquarters in London and has three main Federal Committees: the Federal Executive, the Federal Policy Committee and the Federal Conference Committee. Local Parties elect Conference Representatives by means of an STV secret ballot of all members and the Federal Conference meets twice a year (the autumn meeting coincides with the Annual General Meeting of the Party, which all members can attend, although only elected representatives can vote). The number of conference representatives to which Local Parties are entitled is set out in the Constitution of the Federal Party and is based on the number of members; for example, a Local Party with between 30 and 50 members is entitled to two representatives and one with between 401 and 450 members is entitled to 11 (with a sliding scale in between). The Conference is the final arbiter of policy, but there are extensive discussions beforehand, overseen by the Federal Policy Committee. The policy-making process has been streamlined recently and final policy papers are preceded by brief consultation papers.

The Party in England has 12 Regional Parties, which appoint representatives to the Council, which in turn elects the English Council Executive. The Liberal Democrat equivalent to the CLP is the Local Party, which must have at least 30 members and must contain at least one parliamentary constituency. Adjacent Local Parties may combine to form a single Local Party. However, where that combined Local Party has more than 30 members in a single parliamentary constituency, those members select the parliamentary candidate. Where there are fewer than 30 members in a that constituency, the Local Party Constitution can state whether all members of the Local Party should choose the candidate or whether only those members in that particular constituency should vote.

The Liberal Democrats elect their Leader by a postal ballot of all party members (using the Alternative Vote where appropriate). In 1988, Paddy Ashdown won the leadership contest, gaining 41,401 votes, compared to Alan Beith's 16,202. The Leader can be challenged, if the Parliamentary Party passes a no-confidence motion, or if 75 Local Parties submit no-confidence motions to the Party's President. In opposition, there is a leadership election every year (this can be postponed for a year by the Federal Executive) if anyone wishes to challenge the incumbent leader. Candidates must be MPs and have to be proposed and seconded by an MP and supported by 200 members in not less than 20 Local Parties.

In 1999, Paddy Ashdown resigned and five MPs stood for the leadership: David Rendel, Jackie Ballard, Malcolm Bruce, Simon Hughes and Charles Kennedy. In the ensuing postal ballot, the first three candidates were eliminated after three rounds of counting. Charles Kennedy beat Simon Hughes in the final round by 28,425 votes to 21,833.

Parliamentary Candidates

The Liberal Democrats currently have 52 MPs.

The Liberal Democrats are a federal party and the parties in England, Wales and Scotland have a fair degree of autonomy. In many ways the Party has a model constitution, with the merits of being both democratic and relatively easy to understand. The Liberal Democrats have been using 'one member, one vote' ballots for much longer than the other Parties and their Prospective Parliamentary Candidates are elected by a one member, one vote ballot of all Party members in the relevant Local Party.

All candidate selection is overseen by a Joint States Candidates Committee, chaired by the Chief Whip, and consisting of a representative from each of the State Candidates Committees for England, Wales and Scotland. The State Candidates Committees are responsible for maintaining lists of approved candidates (Article 11 of the Liberal Democrats' Constitution). Article 11 specifies that shortlisting be carried out by the Local Party Executive or a sub-committee and that a shortlist include at least one man and one woman (two in the case of shortlists of five or more). The shortlist must consist of at least three and no more than seven names.

Names of shortlisted candidates are sent to all members of the Local Party in advance of a hustings meeting, and those attending the meeting are given ballot papers (those who cannot attend can apply for a postal vote). In some cases ballot papers are simply sent out to all members. A sitting MP can be re-selected by a majority of those voting in a secret ballot of all Local Party members in attendance at such a meeting. If he or she is not reselected, a ballot of all Local Party Members is called to make the final decision.

Local Government

Local Parties are given some discretion over the selection of local government candidates, as opposed to parliamentary candidates, where they must follow the rules set out in the relevant State and Federation Constitutions. For example, the Constitution of the Liberal Democrats in England contains a 'Model Constitution for Local Parties', which they are recommended to adopt. Local government candidates can either be selected at a meeting, at which all members in the relevant area can vote, or by a postal vote.

European Elections

The Liberal Democrats currently have 11 MEPs.

Unsurprisingly, the Liberal Democrats employed the most democratic system of all for electing their European parliamentary candidates. Candidates' statements were circulated to all party members in the region in which they wished to stand (they could stand in more than one) before the relevant regional committee drew up a shortlist. The final order of candidates was determined by a postal vote using the Single Transferable Vote. Through a procedure known as 'zipping' ('twinning' in the Labour Party) if one region had a male candidate at the top of the list, the next had a woman.

The Scottish Parliament

The Liberal Democrats currently have 16 MSPs.

In Scotland the Liberal Democrats selected their candidates for the 56 additional list seats using OMOV ballots in individual constituencies within the list regions. Constituency candidates were selected using the same procedures as used for the selection of parliamentary candidates.

The Welsh Assembly

The Liberal Democrats currently have six members of the Welsh Assembly.

In Wales, the Liberal Democrats used an approved list from which parties could shortlist constituency and regional candidates for the Welsh Assembly. Assembly Electoral Regional Committees were set up in each of the Assembly Regions. Final selections were made using OMOV ballots. Party rules state that any candidate for the position of Leader in the Welsh Assembly must be supported by 30 members of the party, five of whom must be from each Assembly Electoral Region. The election is by a postal ballot of all Welsh Party members using STV and takes place within one year of elections to the Assembly. The Leader's term of office runs until a similar time after the next set of Assembly elections, unless there is a vote of no confidence in the Leader passed by a majority of the Liberal Democrat group on the Assembly or if 10 Local parties request such a vote.

The Greater London Assembly and Mayor

The Liberal Democrats have four members of the GLA.

Candidates for the GLA were elected by all paid-up members of the relevant local parties. Advertisements were placed in Liberal Democrat News for candidates for constituency seats, the top-up list and for Mayor. Applications were then sent to either the Returning Officer for the constituency seats or the Returning Officer for the list seats and Mayoral election. The shortlisting committee for the constituencies consisted of two people (one man and one woman) from each constituency within the area, along with a regionally appointed Returning Officer or Deputy Returning Officer to act as non-voting chairman. As far as the list candidates were concerned, the selection committee was appointed by the Regional Candidates Committee. The Mayoral selection committee was appointed by the Regional Executive. The party's usual rules on gender balance on shortlists applied (one man and one woman on shortlists of between two and four and at least two for shortlists of five or more) and as far as the list members were concerned, at least one third of the shortlist had to be of each gender. Applicants were interviewed by the selection committees before it shortlisted candidates. Party members could vote for shortlisted constituency candidates either at hustings meetings or by postal vote. The election was by STV. The election of the list members and Mayor was by a postal vote of all eligible party members in the London area (again using STV).

The Liberal Democrats mayoral candidate, Susan Kramer, was selected after what was arguably, the most straightforward and democratic process of all those employed by the three main parties. Candidates were required to complete an application form before being interviewed by a panel. Liberal Democrats, being the sort of people they are, also indulged in some creative role-playing, giving their candidates an 'aide' incapable of giving advice and finally subjecting them to a fake ambush by journalists asking daft questions, arguably the best possible training for the real campaign (for a fuller and more amusing account of the Liberal Democrats mayoral campaign, see 'Nightmare! The Race to Become London's Mayor', by Mark D'Arcy and Rory MacLean). Susan Kramer was elected in a ballot of all the party's members in London, beating Keith Kerr, Mike Tuffrey and Donnachadh McCarthy.

More information about the Liberal Democrats can be found by consulting their excellent website which includes almost everything you could ever want to know about the party - www.libdems.org.uk, or by calling: 020 7222 7999.

More information about the Liberal Democrats in Scotland at: www.scotlibdems.org.uk or by calling: 0131 337 2314

More information about the Welsh Liberal Democrats can be found at: www.libdemwales.org.uk or by calling: 029 2031 3400

THE SCOTTISH NATIONAL PARTY

The SNP currently has five MPs, 35 MSPs and two MEPs.

The SNP is comprised of Constituency Associations and they are responsible for the selection of candidates both for Westminster and for the new Scottish Parliament. Candidates must be approved by the SNP's National Executive Committee and anyone who has been an SNP member for 10 months or more is eligible to apply to be a parliamentary candidate. An NEC sub-committee, the Election Committee, organises an assessment process. The Committee makes recommendations to the NEC, which then takes the final decision as to which candidates should join the list of Approved Possible Parliamentary Candidates. Candidates so approved can then approach any Constituency Organisation. At a constituency level, the Constituency Organisation puts together a shortlist of possible candidates, who are then called to appear before a Constituency Selection Meeting. The candidates are selected by means of a ballot of those present at the meeting.

As far as local government elections are concerned, nominations are invited from branch members whose area covers the ward in which the election is to take place. Candidates must first have passed the vetting procedure organised by the relevant Local Government Liaison Committee. All branch members can vote at the selection meeting, about which they are notified 14 days in advance. Members at the meeting vote on an OMOV basis using a secret ballot. If no candidate gains more than 50 per cent of the vote on the first ballot, the candidate with the fewest votes then drops out and another ballot is carried out with the remaining candidates, until one candidate gains more than 50 per cent of the votes.

As far as the European elections were concerned, candidates were drawn from the party's approved list. Candidates had to be nominated by at least two constituency associations. Those nominated went forward to regional primary selection meetings where one candidate was nominated. The Party's eight 'list' candidates were then selected and ranked at the 1998 Annual Conference. Each delegate listed his or her selection in order of preference.

Candidates for the Scottish Parliament were selected from an approved list by individual constituency meetings and by regional conferences, which decided how the regional lists should be ordered.

The party's Annual Conference is where the National Executive Committee and the National Convenor (Leader) of the Party are elected. In the last leadership election at the 2000 Conference, John Swinney beat Alex Neil by 547 votes to 268. In 2000, Roseanna Cunningham defeated Kenny MacAskill for the position of Senior Vice Convenor by 457 votes to 323 and Jim Mather beat Ian Blackford for the position of Treasurer by 632 votes to 143.

More information can be obtained at: www.snp.org.uk or by calling:
0131 525 8900

PLAID CYMRU

Plaid Cymru currently has four MPs, two MEPs and 17 members of the Welsh Assembly (AMs).

At Westminster, the Plaid Cymru MPs form a single parliamentary grouping with their Scottish National Party colleagues. Plaid Cymru members join the party either nationally or through one of its 220 local branches. As well as local branches there are rhanbarthau - committees made up of branch delegates with boundaries corresponding to Westminster constituencies or local government boundaries. At national level the party structure includes: the Annual Conference - which decides policies and changes in the party's Constitution; the National Council - which frames policies between conferences, approves election manifestos, and amends Standing Orders and which comprises rhanbarth and branch delegates and the National Executive Committee, which controls party management and finance, guides policy formation and strategy and which has around 25 members. The President of Plaid Cymru is elected by all branch members, for a two-year term of office and voting takes place over a 10-day period, enabling all 30 branches to hold election meetings. In the last leadership election in August 2000, Ieuan Wyn Jones won 77 per cent of the vote, defeating the two other candidates, Helen Jones and Jill Evans on the first ballot.

Anyone wishing to be a candidate must be on the party's National Register. They must complete an application form before being interviewed. Regional interviews are conducted by panels, whose composition is determined by the National Executive. The Selection Conference includes all members of the Constituency Committee plus one additional representative for each member each branch has on the Constituency Committee. If necessary, a shortlisting meeting is held by the Constituency Committee. Members of the Selection Conference and candidates are informed of the time of its meeting 12 days in advance. Candidates are elected using the 'second vote' system. One ballot is held and if no candidate gains more than 50 per cent of the vote on the first ballot the votes of the candidate who gained the lowest number of votes are distributed according to their second choice. Where more than one woman and one man apply, there is an election for two lists and a ballot is then held between those at the top of both lists. Plaid's rules state that no one can be accepted to be a candidate if they serve on another elected body, apart from a Town or Community Council.

Plaid Cymru selected its candidates for the Welsh Assembly by using a national approved list, from which constituency parties could select candidates. Party members were invited to apply to be on the National Register. Rhanbarth and Constituency Committees could advertise for potential candidates and then apply for those names to be included on the National Register. A National Panel decided which applications should be included on the Register. PPCs could only be chosen from the Register. Applicants had to attend a half-day pre-selection seminar and also complete a detailed form. All applicants were interviewed. A series of regional interviews (the composition of the interviewing panel is determined by the National Executive) then took place. Those successful at gaining a place on the approved list were then eligible to be nominated and could apply to any of the Constituencies. After the close of nominations, candidates were invited to a selection conference attended by members of the Constituency Committee (where necessary, the Committee could meet prior to this to draw up a shortlist).

Members of the Constituency Committee had to be notified of the Selection Conference at least 14 days before the date and candidates, 16 days before. The members of the Selection Conference selected the candidates using the Alternative Vote (if more than two candidates were involved). The National Executive had the power to decide the composition of the regional lists. Regional Committees then invited applications from all individuals on the National Register. A Selection Conference was then held, comprising all members of the various Selection Conferences of each constituency within the Regional Constituency (the branch representatives on the Constituency Committee). Votes were cast separately for male and female candidates using STV and were then placed on the list in the gender order instructed by the National Executive Committee.

A selection conference was then held in each electoral region to select the list candidates. This was done by using the Single Transferable Vote (STV) system, with members voting for male and female candidates separately. Plaid Cymru's rules state that no one can be an Assembly candidate if serving on another elected government body, except for a Town or Community Council and anyone elected to both National Assembly and a County or County Borough Council had to stand down from one or the other after one term. MPs could serve as Assembly Members for the first term only.

The Party's National Panel interviewed possible candidates for European elections who, if successful, were added to the European Parliamentary Register. The selection was made by the party's National Council. Two lists of candidates were elected, one for men and one for women, using STV. The applicant elected to first place on the list was the one receiving the greatest number of votes on either of the gender lists. The applicant given second place on the list was the one with the highest number of votes on the other gender list and the third on the list was the candidate with the second highest number of votes on the list of the first applicant selected.

Plaid Cymru's election rules stated that no one could be a candidate for both the European Parliament and the National Assembly in 1999 and that no one could be a member of both the European and Westminster Parliament for more than one term.

Plaid Cymru's local government candidates are selected by the branch in whose area the ward falls (where a ward crosses branch boundaries, the branch committees nominate one of the branch secretaries to operate the selection process). The branch secretary invites nominations from all current members living within the ward boundaries, regardless of which branch they belong to. At a meeting of all current members living within the ward boundaries, a ballot is held to decide the final candidates using 'the party's normal system of transferable voting'.

The party's constitution and standing orders are to be considered at a Special Conference on 24 November 2001 as a result of which candidate selection procedures may well be revised.

More information about Plaid Cymru can be obtained at: www.plaidcymru.org.uk or by calling: 029 2064 6000

ULSTER UNIONIST PARTY

The UUP, the largest of the unionist parties in Northern Ireland, currently has six MPs, one MEP and 28 members of the Northern Ireland Assembly.

The Ulster Unionists select their candidates for Westminster constituencies at general meetings of the party's Constituency Associations. The Associations are autonomous bodies and the composition of the general meeting therefore varies between associations. Given the autonomy of the associations, there is no national 'approved list' of candidates. As far as Northern Ireland Assembly members are concerned, each association can select a maximum of six members to contest the election; however the Association concerned may take the decision to field only three.

As far as the European Elections are concerned, the selecting body is the Ulster Unionist Council; however, as the sitting Ulster Unionist member, Jim Nicholson, was reselected to contest the 1999 elections, there was no actual contest. The Ulster Unionist Party is governed by the Ulster Unionist Council, comprising 900 party members, representing the 18 constituency associations and certain affiliated bodies; e.g., the Ulster Women's Unionist Council and the Ulster Young Unionist Council. The Council's Annual General Meeting is where the Leader of the Party is elected by means of a secret ballot.

More information on the UUP can be found at: www.uup.org or by calling:
028 9032 4601

DEMOCRATIC UNIONIST PARTY

The DUP, is staunchly unionist and has five MPs, one MEP and 21 members of the Northern Ireland Assembly. At a local level the party is based on local government and parliamentary constituencies. All local branches within a parliamentary constituency are affiliated to the Westminster Constituency Association (except for University Associations and the Ulster Young Democratic Unionist Council, which have the status of local branches). As well as local branches, Local Government Associations consist of all full members living in the relevant Local Government District. They are responsible for the organisation and selection of candidates for local elections.

The Party's Central Executive Committee (comprising five members elected by the Westminster Constituency Associations, two members from each University Association and four members from the Young Democrats and in addition the Leader and Deputy Leader) appoints a convenor for each Local Government Association who must ensure that a meeting of the Association takes place a year before local elections.

The Central Executive Committee is responsible for selecting candidates for elections to the European Parliament, the Westminster Constituency Association is responsible for elections to the Westminster Parliament and Northern Ireland Assembly and the Local Government Association is responsible for local elections. In order to vote at a selection meeting, members must have been full members of the party for the six months prior to the selection meeting. Voting at selection meetings is by a secret ballot. Successful candidates have to be endorsed by the Central Executive Committee.

The Leader and Deputy are elected each year by the party members of the Northern Ireland Assembly and ratified by the Central Executive Committee (if there is no Assembly sitting at the time, they are elected by the Committee).

More information on the DUP can be found at www.dup.org.uk or by calling: 028 9047 1155

SDLP

The SDLP (which is predominantly Catholic) is a nationalist party which believes in a united Ireland by consent. The SDLP has three MPs, 24 members of the Northern Ireland Assembly and one MEP. John Hume recently resigned as Leader and was succeeded by Mark Durkan (he became leader-designate after none of his party colleagues challenged him for the leadership).

The SDLP's candidates (for all elections based on parliamentary constituencies) are selected at a Selection Convention, organised by the Election Committee and consisting of members of the party aged over 16 years and registered by the party's headquarters as paid-up members, living within the constituency on certain registration dates, which are 31 March, 30 June, 30 September or 31 December. All candidates must be party members of one year's standing (the Election Committee can waive this requirement under exceptional circumstances). Candidates have to be proposed and seconded in writing by members of the party who live in the relevant constituency. The list of potential candidates is then sent to all paid-up members registered in the constituency on the aforementioned dates. Candidate(s) are then elected by an STV ballot.

Candidates for District Council elections in each District Electoral Area are selected at General Meetings of party members aged over 16 years, resident in the relevant District Electoral Area and registered on the dates set out above. Candidates must be party members of one year's standing (this can be waived by the Election Committee in exceptional circumstances).

Candidates for European Parliamentary elections are selected by an STV ballot at the Annual Party Conference in the year preceding the elections themselves. Candidates must be party members of at least one year's standing (this can be waived in exceptional circumstances) and must have held membership as of 31 December the preceding year. All candidates have to be proposed and seconded in writing by party members and their names sent to the Party's Management Committee no less than seven weeks before the date of the Conference. In the event of a by-election, a special conference is convened by the Election Committee in order to select a candidate. The Election Committee has the power to decide the number of candidates to be selected and also to ratify candidates once selected. An appeal lies to the party's General Council.

More information can be found at: www.sdlp.ie or by calling: 028 9023 6699

SINN FEIN

Although Sinn Fein (the political wing of the IRA) has four elected MPs, they have not taken the oath and as a result, may not sit in the House of Commons or use its facilities. The party has 18 members of the Northern Ireland Assembly (MLAs). The current structure of the party dates from 1970 when Provisional Sinn Fein split off from Official Sinn Fein (which then became The Workers' Party). This happened at the same time as the IRA divided into the Official and Provisional wings. Information on candidate selection was not forthcoming.

More information can be found at: www.sinnfein.ie or by calling:
02890 223000

PARTIES WITHOUT WESTMINSTER REPRESENTATION

The Green Party

The Green Party has three members of the GLA, two MEPs, one MSP and one member of the GLA.

The Green Party is comprised of Local Parties, Area Parties, Autonomous Area Parties, a Regional Council and the Green Party Executive. The Area Parties; for example, the South East, Greater London, Wales, elect two members to attend the Regional Council.

The Green Party selects its parliamentary candidates by informing members that nominations are open. Nominees address a selection meeting and if any member is dissatisfied with the shortlist the process can be re-opened and further nominations sought. The final selection takes place by all members within the relevant area voting (if necessary by post) using the Single Transferable Vote (STV). It is up to local parties to decide on an appropriate procedure to use for the selection of local government candidates, but the final choice of candidates is usually made by party members in an STV ballot. Candidates for elections (the list candidates) to the GLA were selected by party members in an STV ballot and gender balance was ensured by specifying that one man and one woman had to appear amongst the top three names on the list. Candidates for the constituency sections were decided in the same way as they would have been for parliamentary elections. The mayoral candidate (Darren Johnson) was selected by all members using an STV ballot (he was also first on the list of London members).

The Green Party selected its candidates for the European Parliament by a postal ballot of its members (this determined both the candidates and the final ranking). Selections took place on a regional basis, using STV or the Alternative Vote (AV). Candidates had to be nominated by at least 10 members of the Green Party from within that region and needed to have been party members for at least two years (this provision could be waived in some circumstances). It was possible to alter the ranking of candidates at a later date if for some reason a candidate wanted to be further down the list. The selection of candidates for elections to the Welsh Assembly was carried out in a similar way, with members deciding both the final list and the ranking, using an STV ballot. Party members in the relevant constituencies selected candidates as they would for a General Election.

The Green Party in Scotland is a separate party (information on candidate selection was not forthcoming).

More information can be found at: www.greenparty.org.uk or by calling:
020 7272 4474

The United Kingdom Independence Party

The UKIP has two MEPs. Another was originally elected as UKIP but now sits as an independent.

For the 2001 General Election, the UKIP formed an Election and Campaigns Committee under the chairmanship of a senior party member – Lawrie Boxall took on the role of Chairman at the beginning of 2001. It was the Election and Campaigns Committee's responsibility to recruit candidates. In 2000, the Committee had asked the party's regional workers and representatives to canvass amongst the membership for suitable candidates. Members were also invited to apply through the party's National Newsletter. Candidate Selection Panels were then formed across the country and they had the responsibility for vetting each applicant for suitability. All candidates were asked to confirm that they had never been members of any racist political party or organisation. They were also asked to supply a police certificate to indicate that they had no criminal record. Applicants who passed the Selection Panel were then entered onto a Nationally Approved List from which they could be selected by Constituency Branches as PPCs to be adopted formally as candidates once the election had been called.

For the European Parliamentary elections, the selection procedures were similar to those used in the General Election. In 1999 applicants were vetted by Selection Committees set up in the relevant regions. The final list was ranked by allowing the members of each region to vote in order of preference by postal ballot. Hustings were organised around the regions to allow members to meet and hear the applicants speak. The voting procedure was organised by a UKIP Returning Officer in each region who was responsible for the fairness and security of the voting and for the count. Procedures are now being reviewed for the 2004 elections.

A similar procedure as the one used for selecting candidates for the European Parliamentary elections was used in the Greater London Authority elections. As far as local elections are concerned, candidates were selected by Constituency Branch Committees. The UKIP Party Leader is elected by a vote of all party members, using a postal ballot, conducted using the single transferable vote. Candidates must be nominated by 20 people from at least four different Constituency Branches. The National Executive Committee was also elected using STV, but in future the party may move towards using first-past-the-post. FPTP could be used for future leadership elections.

For more information contact: www.independence.org.uk or call:
020 7434 4559

Scottish Socialist Party

The SSP has one MSP. The party selects its candidates by initially mailing all members to determine whether or not there is sufficient interest in standing in a particular area. If members want selections to proceed, nominations are then sought. The local branch meeting selects candidates from among those nominated (nominees require a proposer and seconder) and a vote is taken at the meeting itself. If there are no nominations, a request would be made to other branches in the region.

More information can be found at: www.scottishsocialistparty.org or by calling:
0141 221 7714

The Alliance Party

The Alliance Party, which has six MLAs, is non-sectarian and operates only in Northern Ireland (although it is linked to the Liberal Democrats in Great Britain). The party's governing body is the Council, which consists of the party Officers, the Executive Committee, any Alliance Party members of the European Parliament, the UK Parliament, the Northern Ireland Assembly and the District Councils, the Party Vice Presidents, 10 delegates from each Association of the Party and 10 delegates from Young Alliance. The Party Leader is the leader of the Assembly Party and is elected by the Council from the Assembly's Alliance members. He or she holds office until he or she ceases to be a member of the Assembly or (except in the case of general elections to the Assembly) or is removed by a vote of the Council.

Where another Alliance MLA wishes to challenge the incumbent Leader they can do this each year at the Annual General Meeting but must be proposed and seconded by a Council Member and supported by 10 other Council Members. The election is by secret ballot. If the Assembly is prorogued, dissolved or ceases to sit for any reason, the Council would take the place of the Assembly in the rules outlined above. The Party holds an Annual Conference which all Party members can attend. The Party has Associations throughout Northern Ireland. Each Association has an Executive Committee which appoints an Election Organiser for the relevant Parliamentary Constituency. The Organiser is the Convenor and Chair of the Constituency Election Committee, the members of which are appointed by the Election Organiser after consulting with the Association Executive Committee.

The Executive Committee of the Party consults with the Executive Committee of the association in order to appoint a Local Government Election Organiser for each Local Government District, except in Belfast City where a Local Government Election Organiser is appointed for each District Electoral Area. The Local Government Election Organiser appoints a Liaison Committee to assist with the election. The Party maintains a central list of Approved Candidates and members wishing to appear on the list are interviewed by a Candidates Sub-Committee of the Executive Committee. They must sign the Alliance Representatives' Code of Conduct. If a candidate is supported by an Association, their application is considered within 14 days. A member whose name is on the list of approved candidates can apply to be considered for a particular election, provided their request is received 72 hours before the selection meeting.

The Party's Council selects candidates for European elections, whereas Parliamentary or Assembly election candidates are selected by a selection meeting of Alliance members with the relevant Association's area. As far as local government elections are concerned, candidates are selected at meetings of members within the relevant area. A member is taken to mean a person who has been a paid up member of the party for six weeks prior to the day of the meeting. Candidates are elected by a secret ballot and candidates need over 50 per cent of the votes to win.

More information can be found at: www.allianceparty.org or by calling:
028 9032 4274

Northern Ireland Unionist Party

The NIUP has three MLAs, who were originally elected as UK Unionists, but who resigned to form the NIUP in January 1999. Roger Hutchinson was later expelled from the party and joined the DUP. The party describes itself as an 'Anti-Agreement, Pro-Union party', opposed to Sinn Fein having a place in government within Northern Ireland. As far as candidate selections are concerned, all paid-up party members are sent a letter inviting them to forward their names in writing by a certain date to the Party Secretary if they wish to be considered as candidates. Candidates are selected at a selection meeting, to which all party members are invited and at which they are all entitled to vote.

More information can be found at: www.niup.org or by calling:
028 9032 4274

United Unionist Assembly Party

The UUAP has three MLAs, originally elected as independents, but who later formed the UUAP in September 1998. However, the UUAP is a 'movement' rather than a political party as such and therefore members of the UUAP are also members of other Unionist Parties.

More information can be obtained by calling: 028 9052 1464

The Northern Ireland Women's Coalition

The NIWC was formed in 1996 and is a non-sectarian organisation, representing women of all backgrounds and religions. It aims to raise the profile of women in politics in Northern Ireland and is fully committed to the peace process. The coalition has two MLAs. Candidate selections are made centrally by a Selection Committee, which invites applicants to put themselves forward for elections. They must complete an application form and must have a proposer and seconder. The Executive of the Coalition highlights those areas in which it would particularly like to see candidates coming forward. The Coalition is organised on a constituency basis with 'constituency teams' in some areas and more informal groupings in others.

The NIWC has a very interesting and informative website (which contains a copy of their constitution) - www.niwc.org. It can also be contacted on the following numbers:
028 9023 3100 or at Stormont on 028 9052 1463

Progressive Unionist Party

The PUP has two MLAs. The PUP was formed in 1977, primarily to 'fill the obvious void that existed in relation to the Loyalist working class' at that time under-represented in Ulster politics. The party states that it is pro-union, but committed to power-sharing and accepts that 'constitutional' nationalists should have a place in government. Information on candidate selection was not forthcoming.

More information can be obtained at: www.pup-ni.org.uk or by calling: 028 9032 6233

UK Unionist Party

The UK Unionists have one MLA. The party states on its website that the party 'remains absolutely opposed to the immoral provisions of the Belfast Agreement' and goes on to say that 'there can be no role whatsoever in any democratic institution for those who remain inextricably linked to terrorist organisations'. The party is against policies that would result in the UK's 'further integration within a federal European Super-state'. Information on candidate selection was not forthcoming.

More information can be obtained at: www.ukup.org

CHAPTER TWO - PARLIAMENTARY ELECTIONS

THE TIMING OF A GENERAL ELECTION

It is a common misconception that a general election must be held every five years. In fact, it is Parliament itself that may not sit for longer than five years. As a result, a general election must be called within that period. Under the Septennial Act 1715, as amended by Section 7 of the Parliament Act 1911, a Parliament automatically terminates exactly five years after the date of its first meeting. Parliament has to be dissolved and a date set for a general election before this date. Neither House actually has to be sitting for dissolution to take place. If the Prime Minister had not called a general election when he did in 2001, the 1997 Parliament would have run until midnight on Monday 6 May 2002. If Parliament had expired at this time, there is no statutory requirement to issue a new proclamation immediately, but the most likely date for issuing a proclamation would have been Tuesday 7 May (6 May was a bank holiday). Polling day would therefore have been Thursday 30 May 2002. Some constitutional experts argue that a proclamation *must* be issued before Parliament is dissolved and the Act takes effect. A Parliament could also be brought to a conclusion if the Government were to lose a vote of confidence in the House of Commons. As it would no longer be able to command the support of a majority in the House it would be forced to call a general election.[1]

There is no statutory period of time that must be served between the calling of a general election and the dissolution of Parliament; however, there is usually a period of at least a few days, to allow for any pending parliamentary and legislative business to be completed.

In the case of the 1997 general election, the period between the prorogation of Parliament and its dissolution was slightly longer than usual (see the timetable below). In both 1992 and 1997, Parliament was prorogued before being dissolved. Prorogation is a prerogative act of the Crown, which suspends most parliamentary proceedings until Parliament sits again for a new Session. Prorogation can be effected either by a Commission in the House of Lords, or by proclamation when either House is adjourned. Parliament does not have to be prorogued before dissolution can occur, it can be dissolved following an adjournment of both Houses (an adjournment merely suspends the business of either the House of Commons or Lords for a specified period of time within a Session of Parliament). Once Parliament has been prorogued, it can be recalled for a date earlier than the date set out in the prorogation proclamation[2] and if an adjournment has taken place, the Speaker can recall the House of Commons.

When Parliament was prorogued in on 27 March 1997, the Lord Chancellor, in the House of Lords, read out the Queen's speech proroguing Parliament. The following appeared in Hansard (HL Col: 1182):

---

[1] On 28 March 1979 the Labour Government lost a vote of confidence in the House of Commons by 311 votes to 310 and Parliament was dissolved on 7 April. In 1924 (21 January) the Government lost the vote on the Debate on the Address (the Queen's Speech) and as its entire legislative programme had been rejected, a general election was called. If the Government were to be defeated on the Budget (the Finance Bill) it would probably have to call a general election.
[2] Meeting of Parliaments Act 1797, Meeting of Parliaments Act 1870 and Parliament (Elections and Meetings) Act 1943

Her Majesty's Most gracious Speech was then delivered to both Houses of Parliament by the Lord Chancellor (in pursuance of Her Majesty's Command) as follows:

(The speech was read out)

After which the Lord Chancellor said:

"My Lords and Members of the House of Commons, by virtue of Her Majesty's Commission which has been now read We do, in Her Majesty's name, and in obedience to Her Majesty's Commands, prorogue this Parliament to Tuesday, the 15th day of this instant April, to be then here holden, and this Parliament is accordingly prorogued to the 15th day of this instant April. Parliament was prorogued at twenty-one minutes before midday."

When Parliament was adjourned on Friday 11 May 2001, all that appeared in Hansard (HL Col: 1147) was the following:

Lord Carter: *My Lords, I beg to move that the House do now adjourn.*
Moved accordingly, and, on Question, Motion agreed to.
House adjourned at nine minutes before noon.

In the House of Commons (HC Col: 406) the following appeared:

Mr. Speaker: *I have to notify the House, in accordance with the Royal Assent Act 1967, that the Queen has signified her Royal Assent to the following Acts:*

(List of Acts followed)

Question put and agreed to.
Adjourned accordingly at five minutes past Twelve noon.

End of the Fourth Session (opened on 23 October 2000) of the Fifty-Second Parliament of the United Kingdom of Great Britain and Northern Ireland, in the Fiftieth Year of the Reign of Her Majesty Queen Elizabeth the Second.

The interval between the dissolution of Parliament and polling day is set out in statute – in Schedule 1, Part 1 of the Representation of the People Act 1983 and amounts to 17 working days (Saturdays, Sundays, Christmas Eve, Christmas Day, Maundy Thursday, Good Friday and all bank holidays are excluded from any calculations).

A general election is announced by the issuing of a press notice from No. 10 Downing Street. This notice also sets out the dates of the dissolution of Parliament, the date of the general election itself (by convention this is held on a Thursday), the date of the first meeting of the new Parliament and the State Opening. Formally, it is the Queen who dissolves Parliament. This prerogative power is not derived from statute, it is a common law right which has never been codified. In practice, the Prime Minister decides when to 'go to the country'.

There is no exact date on which a new Parliament must meet following a general election, except that it must meet within three years, as set out in the Meeting of Parliament Act 1694. The date for the meeting of a new Parliament is decided by the Prime Minister and is set out in the Royal Proclamation that calls the general election.

The Royal Proclamation follows a form set out in regulations[3] and a draft is submitted for approval and signature to the Queen in Council and at the same time an Order directs the Lord Chancellor to cause the 'Great Seal of the Realm' to be affixed to the proclamation. There is no constitutional requirement for the Prime Minister to obtain the approval of either the Cabinet or Parliament before calling an Election, although as Alan Watkins points out in 'The Road to Number 10' (Duckworth, 1998) the question may be considered by the Cabinet, *"but the form in which it is presented varies"*.

In the House of Commons, under SO 13 of the Standing Orders of the House of Commons, the Leader of the House simply makes a statement rearranging the parliamentary timetable before the dissolution. The meeting of Parliament after the general election, may be deferred by a further proclamation proroguing Parliament to a later day (not less than 14 days after the date the proclamation was made) under the Proclamation Act 1867.

The Royal Proclamation (the signed copy of which is sent to the Crown Office in the House of Lords) which dissolves Parliament requires writs to be sent out by the Office of the Clerk of the Crown in Chancery (the Permanent Secretary in the Lord Chancellor's Department) and the Secretary of State for Northern Ireland, to returning officers in all 659 Parliamentary Constituencies. The form of the writ is specified in an Appendix to Schedule 1 of the Representation of the People Act 1983 and is set out below:

"Whereas by the advice of Our Council We have ordered a Parliament to be holden at Westminster on the ... day of ... next We Command you that due notice being first given you do cause election to be made according to law of a Member to serve in Parliament for the said ... Constituency And that you do cause the name of such Member when so elected, whether he be present or absent, to be certified to Us in Our Chancery without delay".

Rule 3 of Schedule 1, Part II of the 1983 Act specifies that writs should be sealed and issued in accordance with the existing practice of the office of the Clerk of the Crown. Paragraph 10 of the Parliamentary Writs Order 1983 (SI 1983, No. 605) stipulates that writs must be sent by registered post and paragraph 11 adds that the Returning Officer must send a receipt to the Clerk of the Crown (also by registered post). The Royal Mail is the relevant universal postal service provider used by the Clerk of the Crown for the delivery of writs under the Postal Services Act 2000. The Royal Mail must maintain a 'parliamentary writs list', which includes the name of the officer in each constituency to whom the writ is to be sent as well as the name of the Royal Mail official who has the responsibility of ensuring its delivery. Acting returning officers are charged with informing the Royal Mail of any change in the address to which writs should be sent.

Returning Officers

The returning officer (usually the Chief Executive of the local authority) is really a figurehead and in most cases it is the acting returning officer who discharges all the electoral duties expected of the returning officer.

---

[3] The Crown Office (Forms and Proclamations Rules) Order 1992 (SI 1992, No. 1730) (as amended by The Crown Office (Forms and Proclamations Rules) (Amendment) Order 1996 (SI 1996, No. 1730)) states that Royal Proclamations must be published in the London, Edinburgh and Belfast Gazettes and that the Lord President of the Council may also send copies of the proclamations to High Sheriffs, Sheriffs, Lord Mayors in England and Wales and Sheriffs Principal in Scotland.

Section 24 of the RPA 1983 states that in England and Wales the following are to be returning officers for parliamentary elections:

❖ The sheriff of the county in a county constituency in England, which is coterminous with or wholly contained in a county.

❖ The sheriff of the county, in the case of a county constituency in Wales which is coterminous with or wholly contained in a preserved county as defined by section 64 of the Local Government (Wales) Act 1994.

❖ The chairman of the district council, in a borough constituency in England, which is coterminous with or wholly contained in a district.

❖ The Chairman of the county or county borough council in a borough constituency in Wales, which is coterminous with or wholly contained in a county or county borough.

❖ A sheriff or chairman of a district council as designation in an SI made by the Secretary of State in the case of any other constituency in England wholly outside Greater London.

❖ A sheriff or chairman of a county or county borough council as designation in an order made by the Secretary of State in the case of any other constituency in Wales.

❖ The mayor of the borough in the case of a constituency, which is coterminous with or wholly contained in a London Borough.

❖ The mayor of a London Borough or chairman of a district council as designated in an SI made by the Secretary of State in the case of a constituency wholly or partly in Greater London which is situated partly in one London borough and partly in a district or any other London borough (the City, Inner Temple and Middle Temple are treated as if together they formed a London borough).

In some cases (as outlined above) the returning officer for a particular constituency must be designated in an Order made by the Secretary of State; for example, The Returning Officers (Parliamentary Constituencies) (England) Order 1995 (SI 1995, No. 2061) which states, for example, that the returning officer for the Poplar and Canning Town constituency is to be the Mayor of the London Borough of Tower Hamlets.

In Scotland the returning officer for a parliamentary election is defined in sections 25 and 41 of the RPA 1983 as amended by the Local Government etc. (Scotland) Act 1994 as being the person appointed to be that officer by the local authority in which the constituency is situated. Where the constituency covers more than one local authority area, the returning officer may be designated in regulations.

In Northern Ireland the Chief Electoral Officer is the returning officer for each constituency.

Many of the Returning Officer's duties are carried out by the Acting Returning Officer (usually the Registration Officer). In Croydon, for example, the Returning Officer is the Chief Executive of the authority, but day-to-day running of elections is delegated to the Deputy Returning Officer who is also the Head of Electoral Services.

Even receipt of the writ may be undertaken by the acting returning officer (such a request must be made in writing to the Clerk of the Crown at least one month before the issue of the writ). However, the returning officer may reserve to himself certain duties in connection with the declaration of the result. This has to be set out in writing. Some local authorities; for example, the London Borough of Croydon, reserve the right of the Mayor to read out the declaration of results on election night.

The acting returning officer is usually the local authorities' registration officer. Section 28 of the RPA 1983 states that in England and Wales, the duties of the returning officer for a parliamentary election are to be discharged by the acting returning officer. Section 28(1)(a), (aa) and (b) state that this should be the registration officer (in some cases this has to be specifically set out in regulations; for example, The Returning Officers (Parliamentary Constituencies) (England) (Amendment) Order 1999 (SI 1999, No. 950).

According to the aforementioned section of the RPA 1983, in England, in a constituency for which the Chairman of the District Council or the Mayor (in the case of a London Borough) is the returning officer, the registration officer is to act as that council's acting returning officer. In Wales, in the case of a County Council or County Borough Council where the Chairman is the returning officer, the registration officer appointed by the council is designated as acting returning officer. In other local authorities in England and Wales, the acting returning officer is the electoral registration officer (as set out in an order made by the Secretary of State; for example, The Returning Officers (Parliamentary Constituencies) (England) Order 1995 (SI 1995, No. 2061)).

The two offices of acting returning officer and electoral registration officer are quite distinct (see section 27(1) of the RPA 1983). Acting returning officers may also appoint deputy returning officers to assist them, particularly if they are responsible for more than one parliamentary constituency. An acting or deputy acting returning officer is liable on summary conviction to a fine not exceeding £5,000 under section 63 of the RPA 1983 if he or she is guilty of any act or omission which breaches any of his or her official duties. Any Returning Officer or deputy is liable to a fine not exceeding level 5 on the standard scale if he or she is found guilty of any act or omission in breach of official duty (sections 37 and 75 Criminal Justice Act 1982 as amended). An action for damages cannot be brought against a Returning Officer.

In Scotland the returning officer for a parliamentary election is defined in sections 25 and 41 of the RPA 1983 as amended by the Local Government etc. (Scotland) Act 1994 as being the person appointed to be that officer by the local authority in which the constituency is situated. Where a constituency covers more than one constituency, the returning officer may be designated in regulations. In Northern Ireland, the returning officer is the Chief Electoral Officer. The Returning Officer for a European Parliamentary election is the Returning Officer for parliamentary elections in any one of the parliamentary constituencies wholly or partly contained in the European Parliamentary constituency (as set out in an order made by the Secretary of State; for example, The European Parliamentary Elections (Returning Officers) Order 1999 (SI 1999, No. 948). This order sets out the returning officers for the European electoral regions in England; for example, the returning officer for the South East region is the returning officer for the Winchester constituency. Every County Council must appoint someone to act as Returning Officer for county council elections and every District Council must appoint someone to act as Returning Officer for district and parish council elections. London Boroughs must also appoint Returning Officers for their elections.

The Election Timetable

An electoral timetable is shown below. By convention, general Elections are held on a Thursday and under the electoral timetable set out in Rule 1 of the Election Rules, polling stations must be open from 7.00am to 10.00pm (8.00am to 9.00pm in the case of local elections). There is no statutory requirement for a General Election to be held on a Thursday, but since 1935, every General Election has been held on this day. General Elections are usually held either in the spring or autumn. The last time a General Election was held in December was in 1918 and in January 1910.

DISSOLUTION DATES – GENERAL ELECTIONS, 1918 - 2001

Year	Date of Election Announcement	Date of Prorogation (where applicable)	Date of Dissolution	Polling Day	Date Parliament Reassembled to Elect Speaker and swear in new Members[4]
1918	14 November	21 November	25 November	14 December	4 February 1919
1922	23 October	-	26 October	15 November	20 November
1923	13 November	16 November	16 November	6 December	8 January 1924
1924	9 October	9 October	9 October	29 October	2 December
1929	24 April	10 May	10 May	30 May	24 June
1931	6 October	7 October	7 October	27 October	3 November
1935	23 October	25 October	25 October	14 November	26 November
1945	23 May	15 June	15 June	5 July (12 July in 12 constituencies and 19 July in one as a result of local holidays)	1 August
1950	11 January	21 January	3 February	23 February	1 March
1951	19 September	4 October	5 October	25 October	31 October
1955	15 April	6 May	6 May	26 May	7 June
1959	8 September	18 September	18 September	8 October	20 October
1964	15 September	-	25 September	15 October	27 October
1966	28 February	10 March	10 March	31 March	18 April
1970	18 May	29 May	29 May	18 June	29 June
1974 (Feb)	7 February	-	8 February	28 February	6 March
1974 (Sep)	18 September	-	20 September	10 October	22 October
1979	29 March	-	7 April	3 May	9 May
1983	9 May	-	13 May	9 June	15 June
1987	11 May	-	18 May	11 June	17 June
1992	11 March	16 March	16 March	9 April	27 April
1997	17 March	21 March	8 April	1 May	7 May
2001	8 May	-	14 May	7 June	13 June

---

[4] The date on which Parliament reassembles is not the same as the State Opening, which usually takes place a few days later; for example, in 1992, the House of Commons reassembled on Monday 27 April and the State Opening took place on Wednesday 6 May. In 1997, the House of Commons reassembled on Wednesday 7 May and the State Opening took place on Wednesday 14 May and in 2001, the House reassembled on Wednesday 13 June with the State Opening on Wednesday 20 June.

GENERAL ELECTION TIMETABLE
(as set out in the Parliamentary Election Rules, Schedule 1 Representation of the People Act 1983)

Day	Date at 2001 General Election	Procedure	Timing
0	Monday 14 May	Issue of writs by Clerk of the Crown in Chancery (Lord Chancellor's Office)	Usually on the same day as, but if not, as soon as possible after, the issue of the Royal Proclamation dissolving Parliament
1	Tuesday 15 May	Receipt of writs by returning officers	The day after the writs are issued
3	Thursday 17 May	Notice of the Election	No later than 4pm on second day after writs are received
6	Tuesday 22 May	Delivery of candidates' nomination papers (including appointment of Election Agent)	Between 10am and 4pm on any day after date of publication of notice of election, but no later than 6th day after day of Proclamation summoning new Parliament
6	Tuesday 22 May	Making of objections to nomination papers	Objections can be made on the last day for delivery of nominations papers, plus one hour following (i.e., up until 5pm), except that on the afternoon of the last day objections can only be made to nominations papers delivered within 24 hours of the last time for delivery (4pm). (This means that objections to nomination papers handed in up to 4pm on the day before the last day for delivery, must be made between 10am and noon on the last day of delivery, but objections to papers handed in on the last day can be objected to until 5pm on that day.)
6	Tuesday 22 May	Publication of statement of persons nominated and notice of poll (stating day and hours of polling, situation of polling stations and those electors entitled to vote at them) a copy of which must be given to each election agent	At close of time for making objections to nomination papers
7	Wednesday 23 May	Under Rule 15(2) where a Returning Officer thinks a candidate may be disqualified for nomination under the Representation of the People Act 1981 (under the provisions of this Act, anyone sentenced to more than one year's imprisonment is disqualified from membership of the House of Commons during the period of imprisonment) he or she must publish a draft statement of persons nominated stating the time when objections can be made to that person's nomination	Objections can be made between 10am and 4pm on the day after the last day for delivery of nomination papers
11	Wednesday 30 May	Last day for receipt of absent voting applications	By 5pm
13	Friday 1 June	First day for applications for replacement postal ballot papers	
15	Tuesday 5 June	Last day for appointment of polling and counting agents	
16	Wednesday 6 June	Last day for applications for replacement postal ballot papers	Before 5pm
17	Thursday 7 June	Polling Day	Between 7am and 10pm on the 11th day after last day for delivery of nomination papers[5] (postal votes can be returned up until 10pm on polling day)

---

[5] For local elections, polling stations are open between 8.00am and 9.00pm.

43

Days Excluded from the Timetable

Under Rule 2 of the Election Rules, the following days are excluded when calculating any period of time in the above timetable:

- ❖ Saturdays and Sundays
- ❖ Christmas Eve, Christmas Day
- ❖ Maundy Thursday, Good Friday
- ❖ Bank holidays (as set out in the Banking and Financial Dealings Act 1971)[6]
- ❖ Any day appointed as a day of public thanksgiving or mourning

In the case of a general election a bank holiday is taken to mean a day that is a bank holiday in any part of the UK. In the case of a by-election, a bank holiday is taken to mean any day, which is a bank holiday, in that part of the UK in which the by-election is being held. The RPA 1985 states that the electoral timetable can be suspended for 14 days on the 'demise of the Crown' (death of the monarch) if this occurs between the time when the Proclamation summoning a new Parliament is made and polling day. This would effectively delay the Proclamation for 14 days. If the delay would result in an element of the election process taking place on a day disregarded under the 1983 Act, then that part of the process would take place on the following day. It is not clear how the provisions of the 1983 Act relating to 'days of mourning' interact with the provisions of the 1985 Act relating to the death of a sovereign. The electoral timetable could be lengthened by both the 14-day period and any other days of mourning.

After the 2001 General Election, ballot papers were returned to the Clerk to the Crown in Chancery by Returning Officers on Friday 8 June 2001. The deadline for the return of writs, giving the name of the elected Members was Sunday 10 June 2001 and the deadline for the submission of candidates' election expenses to the Returning Officer was Thursday 12 July 2001. The deadline for the submission of national campaign expenditure returns to the Electoral Commission, where total expenditure was £250,000 or less, was Friday 7 September and the deadline where the total was over that amount is 7 December 2001.

The timetable for local elections is set out in the Local Elections (Principal Areas) Rules 1986 (SI 1986, No. 2214), the Scottish Local Election Rules 1986 (SI 1986, No. 2213 (S 163), the Local Elections (Parishes and Communities) Rules 1986 (SI 1986, No. 2215) and the Local Elections (Northern Ireland) Order 1985 (SI 1985, No. 454).

A Parliament can be extended beyond five years and this has happened twice in the last century. The 1911 Parliament was extended by the passage of the Parliament and Registration Act 1916 and the 1935 Parliament by the Prolongation of Parliament Acts 1940, 1941, 1942, 1943 and 1944.

---

[6] The following, as set out in Schedule 1 of the Act are bank holidays in England and Wales: Easter Monday, the last Monday in May, the last Monday in August, 26 December (if not a Sunday), 27 December in a year in which 25 or 26 December is a Sunday. The following are bank holidays in Scotland: New Year's Day (if not a Sunday, or if it is a Sunday, 3 January), 2 January (if not a Sunday, or if a Sunday, 3 January), Good Friday, the first Monday in May, the first Monday in August, Christmas Day (if not a Sunday, or if a Sunday, 26 December). The following are bank holidays in Northern Ireland: 17 March (if not a Sunday, or, if a Sunday, 18 March), Easter Monday, the last Monday in May, the last Monday in August, 26 December (if not a Sunday) 27 December in a year in which 25 or 26 December is a Sunday.

Notice of Election

In each local authority, it is the responsibility of the returning officer to ensure that before 4pm on the second day after the day on which the Election writ is received, a notice of the election, including the invitations for nominations of Parliamentary Candidates, is published in the Constituency. Rule 5 of the Election Rules, as set out in Schedule 1 of the 1983 Act, stipulates that the notice of election must state the *"place and times at which nomination papers are to be delivered"* and also *"the date of the poll in the event of a contest"*.

The notice of election must also state the date by which applications for postal and proxy votes must reach the registration officer. Under Section 200(1) of the RPA 1983 as amended, notice of the election must be given by the returning officer placing notices in *"some conspicuous public place or places in the constituency"*. Similar provisions apply under the same Section of the Act to local government elections.

WHO CAN VOTE?

UK ELECTORATES

Election	Electorate
UK Parliament	Anyone over 18 years of age, who is *resident* in a Constituency and whose name is on an *electoral register*, i.e., living in the Constituency, who is a *British, Commonwealth or Irish Citizen*, including *overseas voters* who have lived abroad for up to 20 (soon to be reduced to 15 years) but *excluding life peers* (hereditary peers may now vote in parliamentary elections).
Local Government	Those eligible to vote in a UK parliamentary election, *including life and hereditary peers and EU nationals fulfilling the residency criteria, but excluding overseas voters.*
European Parliament	Anyone entitled to vote in a parliamentary election, *including British nationals overseas, life and hereditary peers and other EU nationals who fulfil the residency criteria.*
Scottish Parliament	Those eligible to vote in local government elections, fulfilling the residency criteria.
Welsh Assembly	Those eligible to vote in local government elections, fulfilling the residency criteria.
Northern Ireland Assembly	Those eligible to vote in local government elections, fulfilling the residency criteria.

The main provisions relating to eligibility to vote in parliamentary elections are set out in Sections 1 and 4 of the RPA 1983 as amended by the RPA 2000. The following provisions relate only to the parliamentary franchise. For details of those entitled to vote in local government elections, elections to the European Parliament, the Scottish Parliament, the Welsh Assembly and the Northern Ireland Assembly and the Greater London Assembly, please see the relevant chapters later in the book.

Anyone who is **over 18** on the date of the poll , who is **resident** in a Constituency and whose name is on an **electoral register** and who is a **British, Commonwealth** or **Irish Citizen** may vote. Expatriates, who have lived abroad for up to 20 years (soon to be reduced to 15 years) can also vote (RPA 1985, 1989, 2000 and PPERA 2000). In Northern Ireland, to satisfy the residence criteria a voter must have lived in the constituency for the previous three months. *Further information on the new provisions governing the register of electors and the new system of 'rolling registration' is set out in the next section in this chapter.*

In law the term 'Commonwealth citizens' includes all British citizens and British subjects (as defined under section 37 of the British Nationality Act 1981) as well as citizens of all Commonwealth countries, as listed below.

The Commonwealth countries are: Antigua and Barbuda, Bangladesh, Belize, Brunei Darussalam, Canada, Dominica, Ghana, Guyana, Jamaica, Kiribati, Malawi, Maldives, Mauritius, Namibia, New Zealand, Pakistan, Samoa, Sierra Leone, Solomon Islands, Sri Lanka, St Lucia, Swaziland, The Gambia, Trinidad and Tobago, Uganda, United Republic of Tanzania, Zambia, Australia, Barbados, Botswana, Cameroon, Cyprus, Fiji Islands, Grenada, India, Kenya, Lesotho, Malaysia, Malta, Mozambique, Nauru, Nigeria, Papua New Guinea, Seychelles, Singapore, South Africa, St Kitts and Nevis, St Vincent and the Grenadines, The Bahamas, Tonga, Tuvalu, United Kingdom, Vanuata and Zimbabwe.

British citizens and subjects includes the following:

❖ All those who before 1983 were **citizens of the UK and its Colonies** and who are defined as **patrials** under the Immigration Act 1971 (a patrial is someone who is a Citizen of the UK and its Colonies by reason of birth, adoption, naturalisation or registration in the UK, Isle of Man or Channel islands, Citizens of the UK and its Colonies who were settled and resident in the UK, Isle of Man or Channel Islands for five or more years at the time the Act was passed, citizens of other Commonwealth countries who were born to, or adopted by, parents who at the time of the birth or adoption were UK citizens by virtue or their birth in the UK, Isle of Man or Channel Islands and women who were Commonwealth citizens and married to patrials).

❖ **British Dependent Territories' citizens** (citizens of the Channel Islands, the Isle of Man, Anguilla, Bermuda, British Antarctic Territory, British Indian Ocean Territory, British Virgin Islands, Cayman Islands, Falkland Islands, Gibraltar, Montserrat, Pitcairn, St Helena, South Georgia, South Sandwich Islands and the Turks and Caicos Islands).

❖ **British Nationals (Overseas)** (essentially British Dependent Territories citizens whose local connection was with Hong Kong could apply to become British Nationals (Overseas) under the Hong Kong Act 1985 and the Hong Kong (British Nationality Order 1986 (SI 1986, No. 948)) - Home Office Circular 416 set out the position relating to Hong Kong Chinese and Indians resident in the UK after 17 July 1997.

❖ **British subjects** (people who were born in an independent Commonwealth country before 1949 who had neither citizenship of that country nor who were Citizens of the UK and Colonies).

Under the provisions of Section 4(5) of the RPA 1983 (as amended by Section 1(4)(5) of the RPA 2000), anyone who will become 18 before the end of the period of 12 months beginning with the next 1st December following the 'relevant date' may be entered in the register along with the date on which he or she is to become 18. He or she cannot vote until that date. The 'relevant' date is the date on which an application for registration is made or in the case of someone making a declaration of local connection or a service connection, the date on which the declaration was made.

Under section 1 of the RPA 1983 as amended by the RPA 2000, no one may vote more than once in the same constituency, except where they are voting both as an elector and as a proxy and no one may vote in more than one constituency (at a general election). An elector may be on the electoral register in more than one constituency and may vote in a by-election wherever he or she is registered, but may not vote in more than one constituency at a General Election.

The provisions of section 3 of the RPA 2000, which substitutes a new section 5 in the RPA 1983 will allow homeless people to vote by stating that they may be considered as resident if *"at a particular time"* they are *"staying at any place otherwise than on a permanent basis"* and have *"no home elsewhere"*. Under section 3(3) of the RPA 2000 (new section 5 of the RPA 1983) residence is not deemed to be interrupted by employment elsewhere if the intention is to resume residence within six months. This will also apply to those absent by virtue of attendance on an education course.

Residence, for the purposes of voting, is determined by permanency rather than legality. In the case of Hepperson and Others v Newbury Electoral Registration Officer and Another ((1985) 3 WLR 61, CA) women anti-nuclear supporters had camped out on some common land. They were included on the electoral register. The matter went to the County Court where it was decided that the unlawful nature of their occupation of the land did not prevent them from being electors. The case went to the Court of Appeal, but the appeal was dismissed. Merchant seamen may vote by virtue of the fact that they are considered as resident at the place at which they would have been resident were it not for the nature of their occupation.

Under Sections 14 and 15 of the RPA 1983, members of the armed forces and their wives or husbands, may vote by virtue of a 'service qualification'. They must complete a 'service declaration'. Under Section 59(1) of the RPA 1983 members of the reserve and auxiliary forces are excluded except during an emergency. Section 16 of the RPA 1983 as amended by the RPA 2000 stipulates that the declaration must state the address at which the person concerned would have been registered had they been residing in the UK. It can be made at any point in the 12 months preceding the qualifying date. A service declaration must state the address at which the person making the declaration would have been residing if he or she had been in the UK.

Section 7 of the RPA 2000 repeals the provisions of sections 12(3) and (4) of the RPA 1983 which state that those with a service qualification can *only* register by means of a service declaration. This means that while they can still register by this means they will also be able to register in the same way as other voters, provided they meet the residence criteria contained in Section 3, or as overseas electors. Under Schedule 1 (7) and (8) of the RPA 2000, Section 15 of the RPA 1983 is amended to make service declarations valid for one year, as opposed to indefinitely, as at present. There will no longer be any difference between declarations made by members of the armed forces and their spouses and those made by others with a service qualification.

Schedule 2 of the RPA 2000 amends the provisions of the RPA 1985 relating to overseas voters. British citizens living overseas can qualify to vote in UK Parliamentary elections by fulfilling one of the two sets of criteria set out below (section 141 of the PPERA 2000 reduces the residence qualification period from 20 to 15 years but has yet to come into force and did not affect registration for the 2001 general election).

❖ *He or she was resident in the UK at some point within the previous 15 years* and was included in a register of parliamentary electors in the constituency concerned and on the date on which the register was prepared he or she was resident, or treated for the purpose of registration as resident at an address in the constituency and that the date in question fell within 15 years ending immediately before the relevant date and that, if included in any register of parliamentary electors prepared with reference to a date after the date referred to above, he or she was not at that later date, resident at a UK address.

❖ *He or she was resident in the UK at some point within the previous 15 years but was under 18 years of age* and was last resident in the UK within the period of 15 years ending immediately before the relevant date and was under 18 years of age and therefore not able to be included on a register of electors in force on the last day on which he or she was resident in the UK and that the address at which he or she was resident on that date was in the constituency concerned and that a parent or guardian was included on the register of parliamentary or local government electors in force on that day (at that address).[7]

Under the provisions of the new section 2 of the RPA 1985 (as substituted by the RPA 2000), overseas electors must make an 'overseas elector's declaration', which according to new Section 2 remains in force until *"the end of the period of 12 months beginning with the date when the entry in the register first takes effect"* or is cancelled, or the voter concerned becomes registered as an elector in another capacity. The declaration must include the date it was made, must state that the person making it is a British citizen, is not resident in the UK and that when he or she ceased to be resident, or in the case of a person relying on registration in pursuance of a service declaration, when he ceased to have a service qualification. Where an applicant is relying on registration under the second set of circumstances set out above, he or she must state his or her date of birth and the name of the parent or guardian in question. Overseas electors can now vote by post as well as proxy; the provisions of the RPA 1983 were amended by the RPA 2000, enabling ballot papers to be sent to addresses outside the UK.

The details required in an overseas elector's declaration are set out in Regulation 18 of the Representation of the People (England and Wales) Regulations 2001 (2001, No. 341).[8] Regulation 20 states that an overseas elector's declaration must be attested by a British citizen, who is not a UK resident, is 18 years of age or over and who knows the person making the declaration but who is not their husband, wife, parent, grandparent, brother, sister, child or grandchild. Under Regulation 25, the registration officer must send a reminder of the need to make a new declaration during the period beginning nine months after the day when the existing entry in the register was made. This also applies to electors who have made service declarations and declarations of local connection.

---

[7] The reference to local government electors includes a reference to a register of electors prepared for the purposes of local elections within the meaning of the Electoral Law Act (Northern Ireland) 1962.
[8] The same provisions are applied to Scotland by the Representation of the People (Scotland) Regulations 2001 (SI 2001, No. 497 (S. 2)) and to Northern Ireland by the Representation of the People (Northern Ireland) Regulations 2001 (SI 2001, No. 400).

THE REGISTER OF ELECTORS

An electoral register is compiled from returns sent to all households. Until the passage of the RPA 2000, the qualifying date for appearing on the register was 10 October. The register came into effect on 16 February of the following year and was operative for the next 12 months. One of the problems with the electoral register was that, inevitably, it was out of date and, for example, included the names of those who had either moved or died between its compilation and coming into force. This was one of the questions addressed by the House of Commons Select Committee on Home Affairs in its Fourth Report of the 1997/98 Session – 'Electoral Law and Administration' (HC 768 - 1 October 1998). The Home Office Working Party on Electoral Procedures, set up by the Government in January 1998, chaired by Home Office Minister, George Howarth MP, recommended a 'rolling register'.

The RPA 2000 introduced such a rolling register, the provisions for which were in place for the 2001 general election. Under the previous system, an elector's place of residence on 10 October each year was the key to being included on the register. The draft register was open for inspection until 16 December and mistakes could be rectified. The register came into effect on the following 16 February (this could be altered if there was to be a general election before this date). Under this system anyone changing address after 10 October could not be registered at a new address until the register was next updated.

The RPA 2000 provides for 'rolling registration' enabling anyone moving home to have a new address added to the register at the beginning of the month. The register cannot be altered once the final date for nominations for an election has passed.

The format and contents of the registration form are set out in The Representation of the People (Form of Canvass) (England and Wales) Regulations (SI 2001, No. 2720), The Representation of the People (Form of Canvass) (Scotland) Regulations 2001 (SI 2001, No. 2817 (S. 15)) and The Representation of the People (Form of Canvass) (Northern Ireland) Regulations 2001 (SI 2001, No. 2725).

Section 1 of the Representation of the People Act 2000 substitutes new sections for Sections 1 and 2 of the Representation of the People Act 1983. Section 1 of the RPA 1983 now states that:

1   (1)   A person is entitled to vote as an elector at a parliamentary election in any constituency if on the date of the poll he –
        (a)   is registered in the register of parliamentary electors for that constituency;
        (b)   is not subject to any legal incapacity to vote (age apart);
        (c)   is either a Commonwealth citizen or a citizen of the Republic of Ireland; and
        (d)   is of voting age (that is, 18 years or over)

        (2)   A person is not entitled to vote as an elector –
        (a)   more than once in the same constituency at any parliamentary election; or
        (b)   in more than one constituency at a general election

The new Section 2 of the RPA 1983 will provide for similar arrangements for local government electors.

2   (1)   A person is entitled to vote as an elector at a local government election in any electoral area if on the date of the poll he –

    (a)   is registered in the register of local government electors for that area;
    (b)   is not subject to any legal incapacity to vote (age apart);
    (c)   is a Commonwealth citizen, a citizen of the Republic of Ireland or a relevant citizen of the Union; and
    (d)   is of voting age (that is, 18 years or over).

    (2)   A person is not entitled to vote as an elector -
    (a)   more than once in the same electoral area at any local government election; or
    (b)   in more than one electoral area at an ordinary election for a local government area which is not a single electoral area

There have been recent changes to the way in which the register of electors is compiled. For the 2001 General Election, 44,403,238 people were registered and eligible to vote. Anyone who had applied to be on the electoral register by 5 April 2001 was eligible to vote, as this was the final day for inclusion on the register published on 1 May 2001. This was the last published register before the closing date for candidates' nominations on 17 May. It was not therefore possible to register to vote after the General Election was called on 7 May 2001.

Section 9 of the Representation of the People Act 2000, which substitutes new paragraphs 10 and 11 for the existing ones in Schedule 2 to the RPA 1983, provides for registration officers to produce two versions of the electoral register: a 'full register' open to public inspection and used for elections (copies of which are only to be supplied to certain categories of people prescribed in regulations) and an 'edited register' excluding the names of those who have requested not to be included in the register, but which can be sold to anyone on payment of a fee. The regulations to bring this into effect were not laid before the 2001 General Election.

New paragraph 10B of Schedule 2 to the RPA 1983 requires that regulations be made requiring registration officers to supply copies of the full register to prescribed people, either free of charge or on payment of a fee. Regulations will specify the uses to which copies of the full register can be put by those in receipt of them. Under new paragraph 11 of Schedule 2 of the RPA 1983, regulations will set out the extent to which anyone inspecting the full register can make a copy of it and to what extent those in receipt of copies of the full register can make use of the information. It will be an offence (punishable on summary conviction by a fine not exceeding level 5 on the standard scale) to contravene regulations made under new paragraph 11.

In a recent action brought against the City of Wakefield and the Home Secretary (responsibility for this issue now resides with the Department of Transport, Local Government and the Regions), Brian Robertson argued that the sale of personal details contained on the electoral register[9] was a violation of privacy and breached the European Convention on Human Rights. Mr Robertson refused to register before the General Election on the grounds that his name had been used by another to fraudulently purchase a car on credit. Wakefield Council decided not to prosecute him, but he then applied for judicial review on the grounds that his vote appeared to be conditional rather than absolute (Guardian, 6/9/01).

---

[9] Local authorities may sell the electoral register to commercial companies.

On 16 November, Justice Maurice Kay, ruled that allowing information on the electoral register to be sold for commercial use breached the European Convention on Human Rights (The Times, 17/11/01). He also stated that the council's refusal to remove Mr Robertson's name from the register was in breach of article 8 of the Human Rights Act and also resulted in a *"disproportionate and unjustified restriction on his right to vote"*. At the time of writing, the court had yet to decide on the form of order to make in the case and whether or not to allow Mr Robertson's claim for £1,000 damages.

Schedule 1 (3) of the RPA 2000 substitutes a new Section 9 in the RPA 1983 and sets out the conditions governing the maintenance of the register of electors. Each local authority registration officer must maintain a register of parliamentary electors for each constituency or part of a constituency for which he is responsible and a register of local government electors. Both registers must contain the names of those entitled to vote, their qualifying addresses and electoral numbers. These registers are usually combined, with the names of those registered as parliamentary or local government electors only, being marked to indicate the fact.

Schedule 1 (4) of the RPA 2000 substitutes a new Section 10 to the RPA 1983 and reflects the new system of rolling registration. Under the provisions of new Section 10 (2), there will still be an annual 'canvass' to determine eligibility to vote, conducted by reference to residence on 15 October of the year in question. However, this canvass will not include those resident in penal institutions, mental hospitals or other places where those eligible to make a declaration of local connection might be detained. Paragraph 6 substitutes a new Section 13 in the RPA 1983 which will mean that a revised version of both registers must be published by 1 December or by a later date if so prescribed in regulations. A revised version may also be published at any time in the year and takes effect from the time of publication. A new Section 13A will provide for rolling registration. The registration officer will be able to add new or amended entries to the register, issuing a notice of the changes on the first day of the next month, or if there are only 14 days until that date, on the first day of the following month. The change to the register will be effective from the day on which the notice is published. However, the registration officer will not have to publish such a notice on the first day of the month if a revised register is to be published then anyway; i.e., in December, nor will he have to publish such a notice at the beginning of the preceding two months; i.e., October and November.

New Section 13B provides that when an election is pending, an alteration to the electoral register which is due to take effect after the closing date for nominations will not normally have effect at that election. The exception is where an alteration takes effect on or before the fifth day before polling day and is made to correct an error or to give effect to a court ruling under Section 56 of the Representation of the People Act 1983 (decisions of the county court relating to registration or objections to registration or decisions to disallow applications to vote by proxy or post). These new provisions apply to parliamentary elections, local government elections in England and Wales, Scotland and Northern Ireland and elections to the Scottish Parliament, the European Parliament, the National Assembly for Wales and the Northern Ireland Assembly.

Regulations Relating to Registration

Part III of the Representation of the People (England and Wales) Regulations 2001[10], sets out the powers available to registration officers in gathering information needed to compile the electoral register. Anyone failing to comply with such requests for information is liable on summary conviction to a fine not exceeding level 3 on the standard scale. Objections can be made to names included on the register; these must be in writing and must be received no later than five days after receipt of the application to be on the register to which the objection relates. The registration officer can decide whether or not to allow an objection and the person making the objection then has three days from the date of the registration officer's notice to state that he wishes the objection to be heard.

The hearing of an objection cannot be earlier than the third day or later than the seventh day after the date of the notice sent to the objectors notifying them of the hearing. Under Regulation 32 of the Regulations, where the registration officer has decided not to include someone on the register, that person may appeal against the decision provided they give notice within 14 days. The matter is then decided by the county court.

Under the provisions of the Representation of the People (England and Wales) Regulations 2001 (SI 2001, No. 341), The Representation of the People (Northern Ireland) Regulations 2001 (SI 2001, No. 400) and the Representation of the People (Scotland) Regulations 2001 (SI 2001, No. 497 (S.2)), the electoral register must be set out in separate parts for every parliamentary polling district and where a district covers more than one electoral area, there has to be a separate part of the register for each part of the polling district contained in each electoral area.

Each parliamentary polling district has to have a separate letter or letters in the register (the letter forms part of the elector's number of the electoral register). Names are arranged in street order, unless this is impractical. Names are numbered consecutively with separate series of numbers for each polling district. Service voters, those who have made declarations of local connection and overseas electors are grouped alphabetically at the end of the relevant part of the register that relates to the addresses given in their declarations. There is a separate list of overseas voters, which the registration officer must publish along with the main register.

Under the provisions of Regulation 42, where an elector is registered in both the parliamentary and local government registers, no letter appears against his or her name. Electors are denoted by the letters set out in the following table.

---

[10] The same provisions are applied to Scotland by the Representation of the People (Scotland) Regulations 2001 (SI 2001, No. 497 (S. 2)) and to Northern Ireland by the Representation of the People (Northern Ireland) Regulations 2001 (SI 2001, No. 400).

Type of Elector	Letter
An elector registered in both the parliamentary and local government registers	no letter
EU citizen registered only in the register of local government electors	G
An EU citizen registered in both the register of local government electors and the register of European parliamentary electors	K
Another elector registered only in the register of local government electors	L
An overseas elector registered only in the register of parliamentary electors	F
A European Parliamentary overseas elector registered only in the register of such electors	E
Elector or proxy entitled to vote by post	A

The registration officer is obliged to supply a copy of the register and list of overseas electors, free of charge to the relevant Member of Parliament and to the relevant MEPs. He or she is also obliged to supply one copy of that part of the register which relates to the relevant electoral area to each councillor for that area and each candidate (or his or her election agent) at a local government election for that area. Each registered political party is entitled to one free copy of the register as is any prospective parliamentary candidate or his election agent. Regulation 47 of the 2001 Regulations states that on payment of a fee, the register must be supplied in data form at a rate of £20 plus £1.50 for each 1,000 entries in it and in printed form, at a rate of £10 plus £5 for each 1,000 entries.

In the case of the register of overseas electors, the rate, in data form is £20 with an additional fee of £1.50 for each 100 entries and in printed form, £10 with an additional £5 for each 100 entries.

As the Electoral Commission states in its first report on the 2001 General Election, proposals have been put forward by the Commission in partnership with the Local Government Association and the Improvement and Development Agency (I&DeA) to link registers electronically, in order to provide a standardised, centralised electronic version of the register[11]. The Commission suggests in its report that consideration should be given to adopting the practice used in Australian federal elections, where there are seven days between the announcement of the election and the deadline for inclusion on the electoral register. Under current UK legislation, electoral registration officers can amend the register up until five working days before the election.

The Functions of the Electoral Registration Officer

Every Unitary Authority, London Borough Council, Metropolitan Borough Council and Shire District or Borough Council in a two-tier area (not the County Council) has to have an Electoral Registration Officer, whose task it is to compile the electoral register. The Common Council of the City of London has to appoint an officer as Registration Officer for that part of the constituency containing the City and the Inner Temple and Middle Temple. A form is sent to each home in the area and completion of the form is compulsory. The

---

[11] 'Election 2001 – The Official Results', Politico's Publishing / Electoral Commission, page 25

following is a typical example of the functions of an electoral services division, in this case the Electoral Services Office of Croydon Council.

Welcome to Croydon's Electoral Services
The principal role of Electoral Services is to compile and maintain the Register of Electors and organise and manage all elections and referendum.
Key aims of the service include the implementation of strategies for increasing awareness of electoral matters and participation in elections. We also aim to provide a service that is available to all sections of the Community.
How to get in touch with us
The Electoral Services Office is at The Town Hall, Katharine Street, Croydon, CR9 1DE
Office hours are 8.45am to 5.15pm.
Telephone 020 8760 5730
Fax 020 8407 1308
e-mail electoral_services@croydon.gov.uk
Notice of Alteration
The Croydon results of the 2001 general election can be found here

Am I on the Electoral Register?
Because you pay Council Tax does not mean that you are on the Electoral Register. The Council Tax list is independent of the electoral register. To register to vote you must complete a voter registration application. You can check if your name is on the Electoral Register by contacting Electoral Services or look at the Register at any Council Public Information Centre. Local Libraries hold the Electoral Register for the area they cover. You cannot search the Electoral Register on line but you can use this form to find if you are on the Electoral Register.
Applying to be included on the Electoral Register
If you find your name is not included in the register you need to notify us by completing a voter registration application form. The form can be obtained from the Electoral Services Office or you can *download a copy by clicking here. This is not an on-line form, you will need to print it out complete it and send it back to Electoral Services at the address shown at the foot of the form. Each applicant must complete a separate form.
Please note that you will not be able to vote as soon as you have completed the Registration Form. Your registration details will be updated between 2-6 weeks from receipt of the application. You will be notified as soon as your name has been added to the register
Voting by post
You can apply to *vote by post by clicking here. You will need to print the form out and return it to the electoral service's office - the address is on the top of the form. Each applicant requires a separate form. Please note that you have the choice of voting by post for as long as you like or for one election only. The choice is yours
Proxy voting
If you cannot get to the Polling Station on Election Day and do not want to vote by post you can appoint someone else to cast your vote at the polling station. Please contact the Electoral Services Office on 020 8760 5591 for further details.
Suggestions
We are looking for continuous improvement and achievement for Electoral Services. If you have any ideas on how the service may be improved please contact Lea Goddard, Mayoral and Electoral Services Manager lea_goddard@croydon.gov.uk or you can use this form
Back to the Council Home page

The following, also taken from Croydon Council's website give advice on alterations to the register.

Notice of Alteration

Each month applications are submitted for addition, deletion and amendment of entries in the Register of Electors. The Electoral Registration Officer must publish a "Notice of Alteration to the Register" on the first day of the month following approval of the applications. All applications are available for inspection until they are allowed or disallowed. There is also a procedure to allow a person to object to the entry of an elector's name on the Notice of Alteration.

For further information on the monthly procedure please contact Electoral Services at
The Town Hall, Katharine Street, Croydon, CR9 1DE -
Office hours are 8.45am to 5.15pm.

Telephone 020 8760 5730 - Fax 020 8407 1308
e-mail electoral_services@croydon.gov.uk

2001			
LATEST Published 3rd September	North*	Central*	South*
Published 3rd August	North*	Central*	South*
Published 2nd July	North*	Central*	South*

Northern Ireland

Great Britain has no equivalent officer to the Chief Electoral Officer in Northern Ireland. He or she is appointed by the Secretary of State for Northern Ireland under Section 14 of the Electoral Law Act (Northern Ireland) 1962 and is responsible for the conduct of all elections in Northern Ireland. In Great Britain the conduct of elections is the responsibility of local authorities. In Northern Ireland, the Chief Electoral Officer is both the Registration and Returning Officer for each Parliamentary constituency and is also the Returning Officer for European Parliamentary elections, elections to the Northern Ireland Assembly and to District Councils. The Chief Electoral Officer is assisted by Deputy Electoral Officers and Assistant Electoral Officers, who can act as Deputy Returning Officers, except in the case of District Council elections, where the Clerk of the Council acts as the ex-officio Returning Officer (under the supervision of the Chief Electoral Officer). The Chief Electoral Officer's Office has seven regional offices (three of these deal only with the registration process and not with election duties).

ABSENT VOTERS

Until the passage of the Representation of the People Act 2000, provisions relating to absent voting were contained largely in the Representation of the People Act 1985 and the Representation of the People Regulations 1986, under which there were six categories of voters who could apply for a postal or proxy vote (where an elector appoints another person to vote on their behalf) for an indefinite period for parliamentary and local government elections (similar rules applied to European Parliamentary elections under the European Parliamentary Elections Regulations 1986).

Section 12 of the RPA 2000 repeals Sections 5 to 9 of the Representation of the People Act 1985 in so far as it relates to England, Wales and Scotland. The provisions of the RPA 2000 relating to absent voting do not apply to Northern Ireland and the aforementioned sections of the 1985 Act still apply to Northern Ireland parliamentary elections (as amended by the Representation of the People (Northern Ireland) Regulations 2001 (SI 2001, No. 400)).

As far as Great Britain is concerned, in the place of Sections 5 to 9 of the 1985 Act is substituted Schedule 4 of the RPA 2000 which contains similar rules to the original ones, but includes changes, such as the stipulation that those detained in mental hospitals, who are not offenders and remand prisoners, may only vote by post or proxy.

New regulations, the Representation of the People (England and Wales) Regulations 2000, came into effect on 16 February 2001 and replace all but regulations 1 to 4 and 97 to 100 of the aforementioned 1986 Regulations. Similar provisions are applied to Scotland by the Representation of the People (Scotland) Regulations 2001 (covering elections in Scotland to the Westminster Parliament and European Parliament and local elections, although the provisions of Part V of the regulations concerning the Issue and receipt of postal ballot papers do not apply to local government elections) and similar provisions apply to Northern Ireland by virtue of the Representation of the People (Northern Ireland) Regulations 2001.

Under Schedule 4(2)(5) a police officer or another person involved in running an election can vote at any polling station in the constituency if they are unable to vote at their allotted polling station.

Under the provisions of Schedule 4(2)(6) detained mental patients (not offenders) and remand prisoners may only vote by post or proxy.

Schedule 4(3)(1) of the RPA 2000 simply states that to apply for a postal vote an elector must be registered in the register of parliamentary elections, local government electors or both. As a result, most of the restrictions on postal voting were dispensed with in time for the 2001 general election.

Deadlines for Absent Voting

Conditions relating to the time within which applications for postal votes must be returned are set out in the Representation of the People (England and Wales) Regulations 2001 (SI 2001, 341).[12]

---

[12] The same provisions are applied to Scotland by the Representation of the People (Scotland) Regulations 2001 (SI 2001, No. 497 (S. 2)).

5pm on 11th day before polling day

The following must reach the registration officer before 5pm on the 11th day before polling day:

❖ An application by a postal voter to change to voting by proxy (and vice versa) for a definite or indefinite period.

❖ An application by a postal voter to vote by proxy at a particular election.

❖ An application by a postal voter to have a ballot paper sent to a different address for a particular election.

❖ An application by a person registered to vote by post as a proxy for either an indefinite or definite period to have a ballot paper sent to a different address for a particular election.

❖ An application by an elector registered as voting by post or by proxy to be removed from that list.

❖ An application by an elector registered to vote by post as proxy for either a definite or indefinite period or for a particular election, to be removed from that list. *

❖ A notice cancelling a proxy's appointment. *

5pm on the 6th day before polling day

The following must reach the registration officer before 5pm on the sixth day before polling day:

❖ An application for a postal or proxy vote for a definite or indefinite period.

❖ An application to appoint a proxy for a definite or indefinite period.

❖ An application to vote by post as proxy for a definite or indefinite period.

❖ An application to vote by post as proxy at a particular election.

❖ An application to vote by post at a particular election.

❖ An application to vote by proxy at a particular election.

❖ An application to appoint a proxy for a particular election.

These deadlines were applied by the provisions of the Representation of the People (England and Wales) (Amendment) Regulations 2001 (SI 2001, No. 1700) which amended the Representation of the People (England and Wales) Regulations 2001 (SI 2001, No. 341)

Saturdays, Sundays, Christmas Eve, Christmas Day, Maundy Thursday, Good Friday and bank holidays are disregarded when calculating these times.

Eligibility to Vote by Proxy

Schedule 4(3)(3) of the RPA 2000 sets out those eligible to vote by proxy for either a definite or indefinite period:

❖ Those registered as service voters (usually members of the armed forces who are serving away from home).

❖ Anyone who is blind or who has another 'physical incapacity', which prevents them travelling to a polling station.[13]

❖ Anyone whose occupation or attendance at an educational institution (or that of his or her spouse) means that they cannot reach a polling station.[14]

❖ Anyone who could only reach a polling station by means of an air or sea journey.

❖ Expatriates living abroad, last resident in the UK within the previous 20 (soon to be reduced to 15) years.

Under Schedule 4(4) of the RPA 2000 an elector can apply to vote by proxy at a particular election if he *"cannot reasonably be expected to vote in person at the polling station allotted or likely to be allotted to him"*.

Addresses for Absent Voters

Schedule 4(3)(4)(b) of the RPA 2000 states that the address supplied by a postal voter in his or her application must be the address to which the ballot paper should be sent. However, the ability of applicants to have postal ballots sent to secondary addresses is open to abuse. It is possible for an unscrupulous canvasser to apply for a postal vote in someone else's name and arrange for it to be sent to another address, from which it can

---

[13] Under Regulation 53 of the Representation of the People (England and Wales) Regulations 2001 (SI 2001, No. 341) and the Representation of the People (Scotland) Regulations 2001 (SI 2001, No. 497 (S.2)), such an application must be attested by one of the following: a registered medical practitioner, a registered nurse (within the meaning of section 7(7) of the Nurses, Midwives and Health Visitors Act 1997), a Christian Science practitioner (in the three cases above they must be treating the elector concerned) a person registered under the Registered Homes Act 1984 as running such a care home, the matron or other person in charge of residential accommodation provided by the local authority (under section 21(1) of the National Assistance Act 1948), the resident warden of a home for elderly people or home for those with disabilities. A witness is not needed to attest in this way when the application is based on the applicant's blindness and he or she is registered as blind by the local authority (as specified in the application under section 29(4)(g) of the National Assistance Act 1948) or where the application states that the applicant is in receipt of the higher rate of the mobility component of the Disability Living Allowance (payable under section 73 of the Social Security Contributions and Benefits Act 1992). Being registered as blind or disabled in this way is sufficient evidence of an elector's eligibility to vote by proxy.

[14] Under Regulation 54 of the Representation of the People (England and Wales) Regulations 2001 and the Representation of the People (Scotland) Regulations 2001 (SI 2001, No. 497 (S.2)) such applications must be attested and signed, in the case of a self-employed person, by someone who is 18 years of age or over, knows the person concerned and is not related to him or her; in the case of an employed person, by his or her employer (or other employee to whom that function has been designated by the employer); in the case of someone at an educational institution, by the director or tutor of the relevant course or the principal or head of the institution or an employee to whom this function has been designated.

be picked up and completed. However, there are many people who legitimately need postal ballots sent to work addresses if they are unable to get back to their primary address. The stipulation that the address must be one in the UK has been dropped. Under Schedule 4(3)(6) & (7) a postal voter can apply to vote by proxy instead and vice versa, provided they meet the relevant requirements as set out above.

Absent Voters List

Under Schedule 4(5) the registration officer must keep two 'absent voters lists'. The first is a list of the names of those granted a postal vote, along with the address to which postal ballot papers are to be sent and the other a list of those shown as voting by proxy along with the names and addresses of those appointed as their proxies.

The registration officer must supply free of charge a copy of the list of postal and proxy voters to each candidate or his or her election agent and these lists are published as soon as possible after the sixth day before the poll.

The Appointment of Proxies

Schedule 4(6) deals with the appointment of proxies. No one can appoint more than one proxy to vote for him or her at any one election. No one appointed as a proxy can vote at the same parliamentary or same local government election on behalf of more than two electors where he or she is not the husband, wife, parent, grandparent, brother, sister, child or grandchild of the electors concerned. No one can be appointed as a proxy in a parliamentary election if subject to any legal incapacity to vote and if he or she is neither a Commonwealth citizen nor a citizen of the Republic of Ireland.

No one can act as a proxy at a local government election if he is subject to any legal incapacity to vote or if he or she is not a Commonwealth citizen or a citizen of the Republic or Ireland or a citizen of the European Union.

Proxies must be at least 18 on the date of the poll and must be registered in the register of parliamentary electors or government electors or both, depending on whether the election in which they have been appointed as proxy is a parliamentary or local government election.

Proxy voters can, if necessary, vote by post as proxies. The registrar must keep a list of such voters showing whether they had applied to vote by post as proxy for an indefinite or a particular period. A proxy can be removed from the list if he or she applies to have his or her name removed, if the elector for which he or she is proxy ceases to be registered, if the appointment as proxy was for a particular time which has elapsed or if the application to vote by post as proxy was for a particular period which has expired.

Voters with Disabilities

Section 13 of the RPA 2000 is designed to make it easier for those with disabilities to vote and after Rule 29 in the RPA 1983, the Act adds a new Section 3A stipulating that the returning officer should provide each polling station with at least one large version of the ballot paper displayed inside the polling station for the assistance of partially-sighted voters and a 'device' (known as 'The Selector') to hold a ballot paper in place (set out in Regulation 12 of the Representation of the People (England and Wales) Regulations 2001

(SI 2001, No. 341) to enable voters who are blind or partially-sighted to vote without any need for assistance from the presiding officer or any companion.[15]   These provisions were extended to local elections in Northern Ireland by means of the Local Elections (Northern Ireland) (Amendment) Order 2001 (SI 2001, No. 417) which amends the Electoral Law Act (Northern Ireland) 1962.

If a registration officer refuses to grant an application to vote by post or proxy, the applicant can appeal, but he or she must do so within 14 days of receiving such notification from the registration officer. The registration officer then forwards notice of the appeal to the county court. Where a proxy vote has been granted on the grounds of employment or attendance at an educational institution, the registration officer must check within three years after the application has been granted to ascertain whether or not the application is still entitled to a proxy vote.

A copy of the lists of postal voters, proxy voters and postal proxy voters must be supplied free of charge to each candidate or election agent.   The lists are published as soon as possible after the sixth day before polling day.

Timetable for Despatching Postal Ballot Papers

The procedures to be followed in issuing and receiving postal ballot papers are set out in Regulations 65 to 91 of the Representation of the People (England and Wales) Regulations 2001 (SI 2001, No. 341) and the Representation of the People (Scotland) Regulations 2001 (SI 2001, No.497 (S. 2)). The new provisions of the RPA 2000 relating to absent voting do not apply to Northern Ireland and the relevant sections of the 1985 Act still apply to Northern Ireland parliamentary elections (as amended by the Representation of the People (Northern Ireland) Regulations 2001 (SI 2001, No. 400)).

Only the acting returning officer and his or her staff can be present at the issue of postal ballot papers (formerly, candidates and their agents could attend, but this has been discontinued in the 2001 regulations). Under Regulation 71(1) of the English regulations, postal ballot papers for electors and proxies who have registered to vote by post for a definite or indefinite period are sent out after 5pm on the 11th day before the date of the poll. In the case of those issued for a particular election, they must be sent out 'as soon as practicable after the registration officer has granted the application to vote by post'. Apart from the provisions set out above, there is no set time at which postal ballot papers must be sent out and no last date on which they should be issued. Local authorities usually send out postal ballot papers in batches; for example, in Croydon, there were two issues of postal ballots. The official mark on postal ballot papers must carry the official mark and the number of the elector as stated in the electoral register must be marked on the counterfoil of the ballot paper.

---

[15] The same provisions are applied to Scotland by the Representation of the People (Scotland) Regulations 2001 (SI 2001, No. 497 (S. 2)) and to Northern Ireland by the Representation of the People (Northern Ireland) Regulations 2001 (SI 2001, No. 400).

Declarations of Identity

When the Returning Officer sends out ballot papers he must also send out a declaration of identity for the elector to complete, a return envelope labelled 'B', (first class pre-paid[16]), known as the 'covering envelope' and a smaller 'ballot paper envelope', which must have the letter 'A' marked on it and the words 'Ballot Paper Envelope' as well as the number of the ballot paper. The declaration form contains voter instructions and the forms differ depending on whether the election is a parliamentary election alone or whether combined with another election.

The number of the postal ballot paper must then be marked on the declaration of identity sent with that paper. Under Regulation 76(1) of the English regulations, postal ballot papers can be despatched by the Post Office or another universal postal service provider (as defined in section 4(3) and 4(4) of the Postal Services Act 2000[17]), a commercial delivery form or the acting returning officers own clerks. The acting returning officer is reimbursed by the Royal Mail for the return of postal ballot papers.

After the postal ballot papers have been sent out, the marked copies of the absent voters list and the list of postal proxies are sealed in one packet and the counterfoils of the ballot papers must be sealed in another separate packet. If an elector inadvertently spoils a postal ballot paper, he or she can return it by post, or hand, to the Returning Officer along with the declaration of identity, the ballot paper envelope and covering envelope and unless they are returned after 5pm on the day before polling day, the Returning Officer must issue another postal ballot paper. Where a postal voter has not received a postal ballot paper by the fourth day before polling day he or she may apply to the returning officer for another. The application for a new ballot paper must be received before 5pm on the day before polling day. The acting returning officer must keep a list showing the name and electoral number of those to whom replacement ballot papers have been issued. The list should also indicate the number of any replacement ballot paper issued and where the postal voter is a proxy, his name and address. This list does not have to be available for inspection before the close of the poll. Spoilt ballot papers and accompanying material are made up into a separate packet and sealed. The total number of spoilt ballot papers returned and replacements reissued are entered in Form K (set out in the 2001 regulations – see Appendix B).

Postal ballots can either be returned by hand to a polling station or by post or hand to the returning officer. They can now be returned at any time up until the polls close, which has meant that although the majority of postal votes are counted before the main count on election night, some postal votes are now counted at the count itself. They are placed in the unopened postal voters' ballot box. Under the provisions of Regulations 68 and 83(1) of the 2001 Regulations, the candidates' agents can be present when postal ballot papers are returned. They must be given at least 48 hours' notice of the times and place for opening postal ballot papers (the bulk of which are opened before the count). There must be two separate ballot boxes:

---

[16] First class pre-paid envelopes are only sent to voters in the UK. Voters in the Channel Islands, the Isle of Man, the rest of the European Union, including the Republic of Ireland and the rest of the world must pay return postage.

[17] In 2001, the only such provider was the Post Office.

❖ The postal voters' ballot box (in which covering envelopes are placed when postal votes are returned)

❖ The postal ballot box (into which postal ballot papers are placed after the covering envelopes have been opened)

The returning officer must provide 'receptacles' for the following:

❖ Rejected votes
❖ Declarations of identity
❖ Ballot paper envelopes
❖ Rejected ballot paper envelopes

Provided the returning officer ensures that there is at least one, sealed postal voters' ballot box for the reception of covering envelopes up to the time of the close of the poll, the other postal voters' ballot boxes may be opened beforehand. This last postal voters ballot box along with the ballot box containing the previously opened ballot papers are then opened at the count in accordance with Rule 45 of the Election Rules.

When postal votes are returned, they are placed in the postal voters' ballot box, which is then opened by the returning officer in the presence of the candidates' agents. Regulation 84 sets out the procedure for the opening of covering envelopes. If a covering envelope does not contain both a declaration of identity and a ballot paper it has to be rejected. If a ballot paper covering envelope does not contain a declaration of identity but does contain a ballot paper envelope, the latter is opened to see whether the declaration of identity is inside. The declaration of identity must be checked to see if it has been signed by the voter and also by a witness (whose name and address must also be present) - If not, it is rejected. Agents can object to the rejection of a postal ballot paper and in this case the words 'rejection objected to' must be written on the paper. Ballot papers and declarations are then put in separate piles. A ballot paper envelope (or where this is missing, the ballot paper) and declaration of identity must have the same number. The returning officer must keep a list of postal ballot papers returned with no declaration of identity and another list of ballot paper numbers where a declaration of identity has been received without a corresponding ballot paper. The returning officer can compare the two lists at any time before polls close to see whether a declaration and corresponding ballot paper have been received but have gone astray (Regulation 88). After the close of the poll, any postal votes returned to polling stations are opened and the final version of the two lists compared to see whether the numbers of any ballot papers tallies with any returned declarations of identity. The words 'provisionally rejected', which would have been written on the declaration of identity, are then struck through and the declaration placed in the receptacle for declarations of identity and the ballot paper placed in the postal ballot box. Finally, the postal ballot boxes are taken to the count. After the count separate packets are made up, consisting of the following:

❖ Rejected votes
❖ Lists of spoilt and lost postal ballot papers
❖ Declarations of identity
❖ Rejected ballot paper envelopes

At some point, the acting returning officer must also place into a packet the unopened covering envelopes to postal ballot papers received after the polls had closed, those returned as undelivered or those spoilt ballot papers returned too late for a replacement to be issued.

After a parliamentary election, the returning officer sends the sealed packets of ballot papers and rejected papers to the Clerk of the Crown in Chancery and in the case of a local government election, to an officer of the relevant local authority. In the case of a parliamentary election a statement of the number of postal ballot papers issued is also sent to the Secretary of State.

Absent Voting Provisions in Northern Ireland

The provisions governing absent voting in Northern Ireland are governed by the provisions of the RPA 1985 and the Representation of the People (Northern Ireland) Regulations 2001 (SI 2001, No. 400). Under section 6(b)(ii) of the RPA 1985 and Regulation 53 of the above regulations, if a person applies to vote by post or proxy for an indefinite period on the grounds of "blindness or other physical incapacity", that application must be signed by one of the following persons, who must be treating the person concerned:

- ❖ A registered medical practitioner

- ❖ A registered nurse within the meaning of section 7(7) or the Nurses, Midwives and Health Visitors Act 1997

- ❖ A Christian Science practitioner

Or, alternatively:

- ❖ A person in charge of a residential care home or nursing home registered under the Registered Homes (Northern Ireland) Order 1992

- ❖ A person in charge of residential accommodation under article 15 of the Health and Social Services (Northern Ireland) Order 1972

- ❖ The warden of a 'premises' for elderly or disabled people

Where a person is registered as blind with a Health and Social Services Board that is deemed sufficient evidence that he or she is eligible for an absent vote and the provisions set out above do not apply.

Where an elector applies for an absent vote (proxy or postal) for an indefinite period on the grounds of self-employment, the application must be attested by a person aged 18 years and over, who knows the self-employed person concerned and is not related to him or her. Where the applicant is an employee, his or her employer must attest. Where the person concerned is studying at an educational institution, the director or tutor of the course, or the principal or head of the institution must attest.

An application for an absent vote for a particular election under section 7(1) of the RPA 1985, must be signed and attested by someone who is over 18 years of age, resident in the UK, knows the applicant, but is not related to him and has not attested any other application for that particular election. Where the application is on the grounds of illness, that application must be attested and signed by:

❖ A registered medical practitioner

❖ A registered nurse within the meaning of section 7(7) or the Nurses, Midwives and Health Visitors Act 1997

❖ A Christian Science practitioner

The person attesting the application must have seen the applicant in connection with the circumstances of the illness. The application must be received before 5pm on the sixth day before the day of the election. The standard closing date for absent voting applications is 5pm on the 14th day before polling day, but application on the grounds of illness are accepted after this day if the applicant could not have reasonably foreseen the circumstances concerned. Applications from those who will be employed in connection with the election must be received by 5pm on the sixth day before polling day.

An application by a person registered as voting either by post or proxy to change their method of voting; an application for a ballot paper to be sent to a different address and an application to vote by post as proxy must be received by 5pm on the 14th day before polling day.

Applications by electors to be removed from the register of postal or proxy voters and applications by proxy voters to be so removed, must be received by the registration officer by 5pm on the 14th day before polling day.

Saturdays, Sundays, Christmas Eve, Christmas Day, Maundy Thursday, Good Friday or bank holidays[18] are disregarded in computing the deadlines set out above.

Under Regulation 67, only the returning officer, the candidates, their election agents (or others appointed by the candidates to attend in place of their election agents) and any agents appointed by the candidates may be present when postal ballot papers are both issued and received. Each candidate can appoint one or more agents to attend the issuing and receipt of ballot papers (up to a number set by the returning officer).

Each postal ballot paper is stamped with the official mark and the elector's registration number is marked on the counterfoil attached to the ballot paper. The envelope issued for the return of the postal ballot paper and the declaration of identity, the 'covering envelope', is marked with the letter 'B'. The smaller envelope, 'the ballot paper envelope', is marked with the letter 'A' and the number of the ballot paper. Spoilt ballot papers must be returned before 5pm on the day before polling in order to receive a new ballot paper. The returning officer must keep a list of spoilt ballot papers. The regulations to be followed on the receipt and opening of postal ballot papers are set out in Regulations 79 to 86 of the Representation of the People (Northern Ireland) Regulations 2001 (SI 2001, No. 400) and are similar to the provisions which apply in England, Wales and Scotland. Provisions governing absent voting at local elections are covered by separate legislation, which is dealt with in the following chapter on local elections.

---

[18] A bank holiday is one which is designated as such under the Banking and Financial Dealings Act 1971 in any part of the UK, but in a by-election, a bank holiday is one designated as such under the Act, only in Northern Ireland. Where proceedings are commenced afresh as a result of a candidate's death, at a parliamentary general election, a bank holiday is deemed to be one designated as such under the Act, only in Northern Ireland.

Concerns About Postal Voting

The estimate of the numbers of postal votes cast in the 2001 General Election is thought to be in the region of 1.4 million, compared to 937,205 in the 1997 General Election. During the campaign there were a number of allegations of fraud, based on the fact that it was possible for one individual to make several applications for postal votes.

In an article in The Times on 21 April 2001, Andrew Pierce reported that he had telephoned the Home Office postal votes hotline and requested 13 forms to be sent to his home address. He then completed these using false names. Not wishing to break the law he did not then hand them in at Hackney Town Hall. The argument of his article is that these applications would have been counted in the election, if he had decided to hand them in. However, as the Electoral Commission points out in its report on the 2001 general election, applications were checked against the electoral register and no ballot form would have been issued if a voter had not been registered. The problem really lies with the compilation of the electoral register and the fact that someone can register at an address without any residence checks being made. However, checking every application to be included on the electoral register would entail huge expense for local authorities.

One positive move would be the establishment of a central database of all electoral registers so that it would be possible to ascertain whether an elector was included on more than one register and whether he or she had applied for more than one postal vote. In Torbay, the BBC attempted to obtain ballot papers in the name of seven registered voters who had recently died. Under the regulations introduced under the RPA 2000, electoral administrators are allowed access to the records of the Registrar of Births and Deaths. The new provisions relating to rolling registration have made it less likely that any deceased elector will remain on the register for longer than a month; for example, where a voter died in March, they would be removed from the register that appeared on 1 April. Where an elector dies after an election has been called, poll cards can be suppressed. The Electoral Commission argues in its first report[19] that the practice adopted in some areas, of the local Registrar automatically informing the local electoral registration department of deaths in that area, should be more widely adopted. However, this has always been a risk factor in elections and was not a result of new regulations governing postal voting.

Applications for postal votes are checked against the electoral register and no further identity checks are made. However, the Commission admits in its report that the extension of postal voting provides greater opportunities for fraud and will itself be producing a further report on the issues raised. There were some allegations during the 2001 General Election that local parties had collected postal ballots and completed them themselves and had collected ballot papers and destroyed those with votes for other parties. There were other administrative problems related to postal voting. The closing date for applications for postal votes meant large numbers of applications had to be dealt with in a short space of time. Postal ballot papers were still being sent out in the last week of the campaign and some voters did not receive them until after polling day. Therefore, there were some voters who attempted to vote in person at a polling station who were unable to vote as they had already registered for a postal vote and could not be issued with another ballot paper.

---

[19] 'Election 2001 – The Official Results' – Politico's Publishing / Electoral Commission, July 2001, pp35

Another problem highlighted by the Commission's report is the absence of a 'marked register' for postal votes. Registers are marked at polling stations once electors have voted, but there is no equivalent for postal votes, meaning that party officials have no way of identifying those who have not yet voted. There have been concerns about the way in which the new system of postal voting was administered. The Mail on Sunday (10/6/01) reported the concerns of the Conservative and Liberal Democrats in Stevenage that 25,000 (over half of those voting) had registered to vote by post. The local authority decided to send all electors a postal vote application form. This was also the case in Croydon, where the local authority took the decision to send all electors such a form. Postal votes in the three constituencies in Croydon usually total around 3,000, but in the last general election, this total rose to over 14,000. However, the overall turnout was only slightly lower than in 1997, in contrast to many other areas of the country, indicating that the ability to vote by post without having to give a reason may have encouraged some electors to turn out and vote who would not otherwise have done so (a copy of the form sent to electors in Croydon is attached as Appendix 1). Conservative concerns appeared to centre on the fact that some electors completed these forms 'unwittingly', failing to realise they were applying for a postal vote. However, it seems a little unfair to blame the local authority either for making it easier for the electorate to exercise their rights, or for the failure of some voters to read election literature. As George Smith, Chairman of the Association of Electoral Administrators put it: *"the malpractices are a very small proportion of the total"* (The Daily Telegraph, 5/6/01).

Some of the criticisms levelled at postal voting are completely unrelated to the new system and are nothing more than re-cycled complaints about measures that have long been normal practice. According to a report in The Daily Telegraph (5/6/01), some electors in Wigan were concerned that the Declarations of Identity they were required to send in along with their ballot papers denied them the right to vote in secret. However, the requirement for a Declaration of Identity to be signed and returned is not a new legislative requirement, nor does a vote cast in the normal way at a polling station carry an absolute guarantee of secrecy (an elector's number (from the electoral register) is written on the ballot paper counterfoil (which also carries the ballot paper number), making it theoretically possible to trace how a particular person voted. If 18-year-olds in Stevenage voted by post because they did not realise there was any other way, it indicates, not a failure on the part of Stevenage Council, but the almost total absence of voter education in schools. There is one problem, however, which does need to be addressed and that is the difficulty of ensuring that the free election addresses which the political parties are entitled to send to all electors, reach them before they return their postal ballot papers.

However, there are serious issues raised by the extension of postal voting, namely the extent to which voters can be openly influenced by others. A postal vote is a 'witnessable' vote, whereas one cast in a polling booth is not. Activists can also encourage people to apply for postal votes, which they can then complete. It is not just the postal voting system that is open to fraud; proxy votes can also be manipulated. In a recent case in Hackney, Isaac Liebowitz, a Conservative and Zev Lieberman, a Liberal Democrat, were jailed after it was proved that their activities had resulted in a 2,000 per cent rise in proxy voters in the borough in the 1998 local elections. In the Northwold Ward, proxies rose from 12 in 1994 to 241 in 1998. Both men were convicted of forgery and conspiracy to defraud the deputy returning officer. The problem lies with the way in which the electoral register is compiled, as applications to go on the register are not subject to any routine checks. However, it is difficult to see how any local authority could possibly check every registration form to ensure its authenticity.

In Northern Ireland, under the provisions of the Elections (Northern Ireland) Act 1985, voters must present identity documents at the polling station before being given a ballot paper. There have been some concerns that among the documents specified (a driving licence, passport, social security payment book, social security card, British seaman's card, medical card or, under certain conditions, a marriage certificate) only a passport and Northern Ireland driving licence contained photographs. Once a voter has identified himself, the presiding officer issues a ballot paper. If a candidate or his election or polling agent believes that the voter is not who he or she claims to be, he or she may require the presiding officer to ask if the voter in question is who they claim to be and if they have already voted in the election other than as a proxy voter. If the presiding officer is satisfied with the answer, the ballot paper is held to be acceptable unless the candidate or his election or polling agent accuses the voter of personation.

The provisions of the Electoral Fraud (Northern Ireland) Bill, introduced in the House of Commons on 28 June 2001, require a canvas form and an application for voter registration to be signed by, and include the date of birth of, each of the persons to whom the form or application relates. It provides for an electoral identity card to be issued to anyone entitled to vote, who does not have other satisfactory proof of identity. Presiding officers at polling stations will have the power to ask an elector's date of birth applying for a ballot paper.

Under the provisions of the bill, the presiding officer will be able to ask a voter (who is not a proxy) his or her date of birth. Under Clause 1 of the Bill electors will have to state their date of birth on the form for the annual canvass as well as stating name and address. The signature and date of birth will not appear on the electoral register but the information will be used in the electoral office and at polling stations in order to make checks against the name of an elector when they apply for a postal or proxy vote or when they arrive at the polling station to vote. A voter will have to sign an application to vote by post or proxy and the signature will have to correspond with the signature provided on registration. The bill also amends section 10 and 10A of the Representation of the People Act 1983 and the parliamentary election rules in Schedule 1 to the Act. The eventual aim is to allow only photographic ID, including the new electoral-ID card proposed by the bill, a passport or Northern Ireland driving licence as evidence of identity.

In its first report on the 2001 General Election, the Electoral Commission states that it will consider the value of the declaration of identity and whether there is any need to continue to offer proxy votes. More information on the Electoral Commission, postal votes and registration can be found at the Commission's website (www.electoralcommission.gov.uk) or by going directly to www.rolling.registration.co.uk or www.postalvotes.co.uk.

WHO CANNOT VOTE?

Section 49 of the RPA 1983 as amended by the RPA 2000 makes clear that a person who appears on the electoral register, but who is *not* legally entitled to vote *must not* be prevented from voting, although by so doing they are committing an offence. They could still be prosecuted and their vote could be rejected if the result of the election became the subject of an election petition.

The following list sets out the categories of persons who may not vote.

❖ Until the passage of the House of Lords Act 1999, **peers,** except for Irish peers (Peerage Act 1963) could not vote. Hereditary peers may no longer sit in the House of Lords and as a result may now vote in parliamentary elections. 90 hereditary peers were elected to remain in the House of Lords along with the Earl Marshal and Lord Great Chamberlain and they may not vote in parliamentary elections. Life peers may not vote. There is some controversy about the position regarding the voting rights of the Lords Spiritual (the Bishops and two Archbishops). It is only by *tradition* that they do not vote.[20] All peers may vote in local elections, European elections, elections to the Northern Ireland Assembly and in elections to the Scottish Parliament and Welsh Assembly.

❖ **Infants** (anyone under the age of 18) may not vote. This means anyone who has not attained that age on the day of an election, may not vote. The birthday of a person born on 29 February in a leap year is taken to be 1 March in a year that is not a leap year.

❖ **Aliens** may not vote (1698 Will 3, c 7). Anyone who is not a Commonwealth citizen, a citizen of the Republic of Ireland may not vote.

❖ Anyone who has been convicted and is serving a **prison** sentence may not vote (Representation of the People Act 1983, section 3, as amended by the Representation of the People Act 1985, Schedule 54) (a prison may not be considered a 'residence' and residence is essential in order to qualify as an elector). However, someone on remand who has not been convicted may register to vote and will be entitled to an absent vote. A prisoner who will have been released by the time of a General Election may register to vote at that election.

❖ Anyone who has committed a **corrupt electoral practice** is disqualified from voting for five years and anyone found guilty of an **illegal practice** cannot vote for three years.

❖ Under common law, 'idiots' cannot vote and 'lunatics' only in their lucid moments. The Representation of the People Act 1983 stated that a **psychiatric** hospital could not be treated as a place of residence, so if a person was a long-term, compulsorily-detained patient, they were effectively prevented from voting. Under section 7 of the Representation of the People Act 1983 a 'voluntary mental patient' could vote if they signed a declaration under section 7(4)(d)(iv) specifying an address where they would be resident if they were not a voluntary mental patient. This has now been amended by Section 2 of the Representation of the People Act 2000, which inserts a new section, 3A, after Section 3 of the Representation of the People Act 1983. This section disenfranchises 'offenders' detained in mental hospitals as opposed to those who simply have mental health problems. The new Section lists those Acts under which people may be detained and therefore may not vote in parliamentary and local government elections. They fall into two groups: enactments under which orders may be made for the detention in hospital of those suffering from a mental illness who have been convicted of a criminal offence or those who have been found to have committed the act with which they were charged; and, enactments under which people serving prison sentences and who have a mental illness may be

---

[20] Erskine May, 'Parliamentary Practice' – 22nd Edition (Butterworths) page 27

transferred to hospital.[21] Section 4 of the Representation of the People Act 2000 substitutes a new Section 7 in the RPA 1983 to permit those resident in mental hospitals who are not detained offenders to vote. It will also allow remand prisoners to vote. Those detained in mental hospitals and voluntary patients will no longer have to make a patient's declaration. Such patients will be able to register the hospital as their place of residence if they are likely to be there long enough to have the hospital regarded as a permanent place of residence. Such registrations will last for 12 months. Such patients may also register at the address at which they would normally be resident by means of a 'declaration of local connection'. However, one drawback of the new provisions is that registration officers must still undertake an annual canvass, but this need not include mental hospitals, which could result in some residents being unaware of their right to vote. Similar provisions regarding remand prisoners are set out in Section 5 of the Representation of the People Act 2000, which substitutes a new Section 7A in the RPA 1983. Remand prisoners currently have the right to vote, but if they are detained in prison at the time of the annual registration qualification date they cannot register. Under the new Section, remand prisoners will be able to register and their registration will last for 12 months. However, remand prisoners will also be able to register at their home address by means of a declaration of local connection.

DECLARATIONS OF LOCAL CONNECTION

Under the provisions of Section 6 of the Representation of the People Act, which inserts a new Section 7B and 7C in the RPA 1983, remand prisoners, patients in mental hospitals (other than offenders) and the homeless may make what is known as a 'declaration of local connection'. Such a declaration must give the person's name, an address for correspondence, the date of declaration and in the case of patients detained as a result of mental illness and those on remand, the declaration must give the name of the institution where the person is living and the address where he or she would be living were he or she not a patient or remand prisoner. Alternatively he or she can provide an address in the UK where he or she has lived at any time. In the case of a homeless person, the address must be 'the address of, or which is nearest to, a place in the United Kingdom where he commonly spends a substantial part of his time (whether during the day or at night).

For those making such declarations in Northern Ireland the declaration must also state that the person concerned has been in Northern Ireland for the whole of the three-month period ending on the date of the declaration.

Where a homeless person makes a declaration of local connection for the purpose of registering in an area where a by-election is due for either Westminster, the Scottish Parliament or Welsh Assembly, and the declaration is delivered to the registration officer during the period beginning with the date when a vacancy occurs and ending on the final nomination day then the declaration must state that during the three month period ending on the date of the declaration, the person making the declaration has spent a substantial part of his time at or near the required address.

---

[21] The Acts in question are the Mental Health Act 1983, the Criminal Procedure (Insanity) Act 1964, the Criminal Appeal Act 1968, the Criminal Procedure (Scotland) Act 1995, the Mental Health (Northern Ireland) Order 1986, the Criminal Appeal (Northern Ireland) Act 1980, the Army Act 1955, the Air Force Act 1955 and the Naval Discipline Act 1957

New Section 7B(7) states that declarations of local connection made for parliamentary elections will also apply for local government elections. Those entitled to vote only in local government elections (peers and other non-UK EU nationals) can make a declaration for the purposes of local government elections only. A declaration of local connection is valid for 12 months.

WHO CAN BE A CANDIDATE?

There is no one Statute that defines eligibility to stand as a Parliamentary Candidate. In most cases, the holding of particular offices prevents certain individuals from membership of the House of Commons - theoretically, it does not prevent them from standing for election. Returning officers are not obliged to check whether or not a candidate holds an office that would debar him from being a member of the House of Commons; their function is only to ensure that those concerned comply with the correct procedures for nominating candidates.

If a disqualified candidate is elected, an Election Court can rule that if the electors were unaware of the candidate's ineligibility, a by-election should be called. If on the other hand, it is clear that the electorate were aware of the reasons for disqualification, then the runner-up is declared the duly elected Member. For example; in 1960, Tony Benn MP, succeeded to his father's title of Viscount Stansgate and his Bristol seat was duly declared vacant (he could not sit in both the House of Lords and House of Commons at the same time). A by-election in Bristol South-East was called, at which he stood. He won the election, but the Election Court declared the Conservative runner-up to be the elected Member[22] on the grounds that the electorate was aware that Tony Benn was ineligible to stand. In this case, the runner-up resigned, precipitating another by-election, which took place after the law had been reformed. This reform was the passing of the Peerage Act 1963 which allowed anyone who had succeeded to a hereditary title to relinquish it, rendering them eligible for membership of the House of Commons.

It is a curious feature of our electoral system that nothing actually prevents a candidate from standing in as many constituencies as possible. In 1880 Charles Stuart Parnell was elected in three Irish constituencies at the same time.

The question of what to do when a Member is elected to two constituencies simultaneously is not resolved in Statute, but is covered by the so-called 'Sessional Orders' which are passed by the House of Commons at the beginning of each Session of Parliament. Where a Member is elected for more than one constituency and no one petitions against his election, he or she must decide within one week,[23] 'after it shall appear that there is no question upon the Return for that place' which constituency to represent, but where someone does petition against him or her, he or she must await the decision of the Election Court.

Since 1888, election petitions of this nature, as well as those relating to corrupt, irregular or illegal electoral practices, have been heard, in England, by the Election Court - basically a Divisional Court of the Queen's Bench Division of the High Court (consisting of two judges), by the High Court of Justice in Northern Ireland and the Court of Session in Scotland.

---

[22] Re Parliamentary Election for Bristol South East (1964) 2QB 257
[23] Election Petitions must be submitted to the Election Court within one month after the disputed election – so this effectively means one week after that date

The Election Court has the power to order a recount, disqualify a candidate from membership of the House of Commons and declare the runner-up the winner, declare the election void or declare that there have been 'corrupt or illegal practices'. For example, the result in Winchester at the 1997 General Election was challenged after the Liberal Democrat candidate, Mark Oaten won the contest by two votes after two recounts. The Conservative Candidate and sitting MP, Gerry Malone, petitioned the Election Court after some ballot papers were discounted as not having the official mark on them (the perforation which should be made in the ballot paper at the polling station). Without the mark, ballot papers are invalid.

The Liberal Democrats argued that had Richard Huggett not stood as the 'Liberal Democrat Top Choice for Parliament' candidate, receiving 640 votes, the Liberal Democrats would have had a clear victory. They had been forced to call themselves 'Liberal Democrat – Leader Paddy Ashdown', in an attempt to distinguish themselves from Mr Huggett, who had already caused problems for them in the European Elections. After an informal agreement was reached a by-election was called, at which Mr Oaten emerged the victor increasing his majority from 2 to 21,556.

Any decision of the Election Court is conveyed to the Speaker of the House of Commons and entered in the Journal of the House of Commons. Under Section 144(7) of the Representation of the People Act 1983, the House of Commons must then decide whether to confirm the result, or issue a writ for a new election. Where the Election Court has determined that the runner-up should have been elected, the Clerk of the Crown must substitute the new name on the return[24]. Under section 82(6) of the Representation of the People Act 1983 if a candidate or election agent knowingly makes a false declaration of election expenses, this is considered a corrupt practice. Where corrupt practices are alleged, the Director of Public Prosecutions can, under section 171 of the Representation of the People Act 1983, rule that the prosecution be heard in a Crown Court. A person charged with a corrupt practice can choose to be tried by jury rather than summarily before an Election Court.

A candidate found guilty of election fraud can face up to two years imprisonment or a fine (section 168, Representation of the People Act 1983 as amended by schedule 3, paragraph 8 of the Representation of the People Act 1985).

An MP found guilty of corrupt practices must immediately vacate his or her seat. A recent example is provided by the case of Fiona Jones MP, the former MP for Newark who was found guilty of making a false declaration of expenses in the 1997 General Election. The Conservative Opposition moved the writ for a by-election in Newark in the House of Commons on 29 March 1999, but this was defeated by the Government who were keen to avoid a by-election before the case was heard by the Court of Appeal on 13 April 1999. The Representation of the People Act 1983 (prior to its amendment by the PPERA 2000) was ambiguous about the exact status of an MP found guilty by an Election Court but cleared by the Court of Appeal. It depended on the Court's interpretation of Section 160(4) of the Representation of the People Act 1983, which stated that an MP found

---

[24] A 'return' is basically an entry in the 'Return Book' listing the names of those Members 'returned' to serve in Parliament after the General Election – hence the title 'Returning Officer' – the local council official whose task it is to ensure that candidates nominations are valid and whose moment of fame comes on election night when he or she is called to read out the relevant constituency's election results.

'guilty of a corrupt[25] practice should for five years from the date of the report be incapable – (a) of being registered as an elector or voting at any parliamentary election in the UK or at any election in Great Britain to any public office, (b) of being elected to and sitting in the House of Commons, and (c) of holding any public or judicial office and, if already elected to the House of Commons or holding such office, should from that date vacate the seat or office. This could be interpreted in two ways: firstly, an MP was disqualified from sitting in the House of Commons from the moment of the decision of the Election Court, but if cleared by the Court of Appeal, was therefore eligible to fight a subsequent by-election; secondly, he or she was reinstated as an MP if he or she won a case in the Court of Appeal, thereby dispensing with the need for a by-election.

In the case of Fiona Jones, the Court of Appeal overturned the original decision of the Crown Court and the matter was then handed back to the Speaker. The Court of Appeal made it clear that they did not have the power to reinstate Ms Jones or declare that there was no longer a vacancy in Newark. Unfortunately, nor did the Speaker, as was apparent from her statement to the House of Commons on 19 April 1999 (HC Col: 571). She informed the House that, *"It is for the courts, not for the House, to interpret the law"*. The High Court was therefore, *"invited to make a declaration that ... Fiona Jones is entitled to resume her seat"* and this they duly did, allowing her to retake her seat in the House.

Section 136 of the PPERA 2000 substitutes a new Section 173 in the RPA 1983 which has the effect of bringing the consequences of conviction for illegal practices into line with the those for corrupt practices. Under the existing Section, a person convicted of a corrupt practice may not sit in the House of Commons or hold any public or judicial office, but a person convicted of an illegal practice is not subject to the same penalties. The new Section 173 states that a person convicted of a corrupt or illegal practice (as set out in Sections 60 and 61 of the RPA 1983) will, for the period of time set out below, be incapable of being registered as an elector or voting at any parliamentary election in the UK or any local government election in Great Britain or being elected to the House of Commons or holding any elective office. The period of time referred to above is five years in the case of a corrupt practice and three years in the case of an illegal practice. Where an MP has to vacate his or her seat in the House of Commons, the seat must be vacated at the 'appropriate time' which is the end of the period which is prescribed by law within which notice of appeal may be given or an application for leave to appeal may be made or, if that period is extended, the end of that period as so extended or the end of the period of three months beginning with the date of the conviction, whichever is the earlier.

Under part III of the Representation of the People Act 1983, election petitions must be presented within 21 days of the relevant Election. Such petitions may only be presented by an elector registered in that constituency or a candidate for that Election (further information is provided later in the chapter).

WHO CANNOT BE A CANDIDATE?

The following categories of people are not eligible to be candidates in elections to the UK Parliament. Eligibility for candidature in elections to the European Parliament, the Scottish Parliament, the Welsh Assembly, the Northern Ireland Assembly, the Greater London Assembly and in local elections is set out in the relevant chapters later in the

---

[25] Section 164(5) of the Representation of the People Act 1983 states that where a person is found guilty of an 'illegal' as opposed to a 'corrupt' practice, they may not vote in the Constituency where the offence was committed, for the next five years.

book. It is worth noting that technically, apart from convicted criminals, those in the following categories are legally only disqualified from membership of the House of Commons; they are not disbarred in law from standing for election. However, it would be a foolish political party that decided to adopt a mentally-ill, under-aged bankrupt as a prospective parliamentary candidate. No good could possibly come of it. A candidate can in fact be nominated for more than one constituency, but if elected in more than one, would have to decide for which one he or she would serve in the House of Commons (under rules set out in Erskine May's Parliamentary Practice[26]).

Aliens

Aliens may not stand as parliamentary candidates. This is taken to mean anyone who is not a British citizen, or a citizen of the Irish Republic or Commonwealth (*British Nationality Act 1981, Ireland Act 1949*) *(please see section on 'Who Can Vote' for a definition of British nationality).*

Those Under 21

No one under 21 years of age may be a Member of Parliament *(Parliamentary Elections Act 1695, Union with Scotland Act 1706, Parliamentary Elections (Ireland) Act 1823).*

Peers

Under the Peerage Act 1963, peers of the United Kingdom, Great Britain, England or Scotland were disqualified from sitting in the House of Commons. However, since the passage of the House of Lords Act 1999, which ended the right of hereditary peers to sit in the House of Lords, hereditary peers may vote in parliamentary elections and sit as Members of the House of Commons.[27] This excludes those hereditary peers who were elected to remain in the House of Lords (along with the Earl Marshal and Lord Great Chamberlain). Under the provisions of the Holders of Hereditary Peerages (Extension of the Franchise) (Transitional Provisions) Order 1999 (SI 1999, No. 3322), which came into force on 16 January 2000, a hereditary peer registered as a local government elector was deemed to be registered as a parliamentary elector in the register of parliamentary electors to be published on 16 February 2000. Article 3 of the order enabled hereditary peers not resident in the UK to rely on former registration as a local government elector as evidence of eligibility to be included in the register of parliamentary electors, thereby enabling them to vote as overseas electors in UK parliamentary elections.

---

[26] 'Erskine May: Parliamentary Practice' is the bible of parliamentary procedure and is published by Butterworths. The last edition was the 22nd Edition and was published in 1997.

[27] Section 3 of the House of Lords Act 1999 states that holders of hereditary peerages 'shall not be disqualified by virtue of that peerage for (a) voting at elections to the House of Commons, or (b) being, or being elected as, a member of that House. However, this does not include those hereditary peers who still sit in the House of Lords by virtue of Section 2 of the Act. Under Section 2, 90 hereditary peers were elected by their fellow peers to remain in the House of Lords along with the holders of the following offices: Earl Marshal, Lord Great Chamberlain. Therefore, hereditary peers remaining in the House of Lords cannot vote at parliamentary elections or stand as candidates in elections to the House of Commons.

Clergy

Until the passage of recent legislation (House of Commons (Removal of Clergy Disqualification) Act 2001) under the provisions of the House of Commons (Clergy Disqualification) Act 1801, anyone ordained as a priest or deacon of the Church of England or anyone ordained as a minister of the Church of Scotland could not sit as members of the House of Commons. Anyone ordained after becoming a Member of the House of Commons could not remain as an MP and their election was deemed to be void. The penalty for continuing to sit and vote after being ordained was £500 per day. Under the provisions of the Roman Catholic Relief Act 1829, no Roman Catholic priest could sit as a Member of the House of Commons. The same penalties as those set out in the House of Commons (Clergy Disqualification) Act 1801 applied.

There was nothing to prevent non-conformists or clergy of the Church of Wales from becoming Members of the House of Commons (Welsh Church Act 1914) or indeed ministers of other non-Christian faiths (because they were not ordained by a bishop). Although not referred to directly in the 1801 Act, priests of the Church of Ireland were deemed to be prohibited according to Re MacManaway (Re House of Commons (Clergy Disqualification) Act 1801 [1951] A.C. 161 at 178, P.C.) The Reverend J G MacManaway, a Church or Ireland clergyman was elected in Belfast West in 1950 and was later disqualified. In this case the Privy Council ruled that the 1801 Act disqualified not just those ordained in the Church of England but anyone ordained by a Bishop. The Clergy Disqualification Act 1870 provided a means by which Church of England clergy could relinquish their clerical positions and after six months be eligible to sit in the House of Commons. However, there was no similar statutory provision for other clergy. In their Fourth Report of the 1997/98 Session of Parliament, the Home Affairs Select Committee recommended that all Ministers, of whatever religion, except for serving Bishops of the Church of England, be allowed to stand as parliamentary candidates. The restriction on bishops clearly had to remain, as some of their number sit in the House of Lords. Under Section 5 of the Bishoprics Act 1878, the number of Bishops who may sit in the House of Lords is limited to 26. The Archbishops of Canterbury and York and the Bishops of London, Durham and Winchester are always summoned to sit in the House of Lords, but the other 21 seats are taken by diocesan bishops summoned on the basis of seniority of date of consecration. These 'Lords Spiritual' are designated 'Lords of Parliament' as opposed to peers, under House of Lords Standing Order No. 6 and are therefore disqualified from membership of the House of Commons on the grounds of their ordination as clergy rather than their membership of the House of Lords.

Now that the House of Commons (Removal of Clergy Disqualification) Act 2001, has reached the statute book members of the clergy may stand for election. The Act states that *"A person is not disqualified from being or being elected as a member of the House of Commons merely because he has been ordained or is a minister of any religious denomination"*. However, this does not extend to the Lords Spiritual (the Bishops who sit in the House of Lords). The Act makes clear, however, that such Lords Spiritual will be able to sit in the Scottish Parliament, the Welsh Assembly and the Northern Ireland Assembly. The Act applies to the whole of the UK and had effect on Royal Assent. The Act was prompted by the case of a former Roman Catholic Priest, David Cairns, who was selected as a Labour Candidate for the Greenock and Inverclyde constituency (now the MP for that seat) prior to the 2001 General Election.

Mental Illness

Under the common law, 'lunacy' or 'idiocy' disqualifies a person from membership of the House of Commons. Under the Mental Health Act 1983, if an MP is compulsorily detained in a psychiatric hospital, his or her seat is vacated after six months and a by-election held. A by-election cannot take place during a recess in those cases where a Member has resigned or been detained under the Mental Health Act 1959 as amended by the Mental Health (Amendment) Act 1982. In the latter case, where an MP has been detained on the grounds of mental illness, a by-election can only take place if two psychiatrists declare, after visiting the MP on two occasions, six months apart, that the said MP is indeed suffering from some form of mental illness.

Deaf and Dumb

Extraordinary as it may seem, according to the case of Whitelocke (1766), any person who is deaf and dumb is ineligible for membership of the House of Commons.

Bankrupts

Those declared bankrupt by a court are disqualified from election to, and from sitting and voting in the House of Commons, until their bankruptcy is discharged (Insolvency Act 1986). The disqualification begins to be applied six months after the adjudication, so where the Member's bankruptcy continues for six months (i.e., it is not annulled or a grant of discharge awarded) the seat is vacated and a by-election called.

Corrupt and Illegal Practices

Those reported by the Election Court to have committed corrupt electoral practices as set out in the Representation of the People Act 1983 - this includes such practices as undue influence, impersonation of another voter, or bribery, may not sit in the House of Commons. Where a candidate is found to have committed such practices, the election is declared void and the candidate disqualified from standing again or voting in any constituency for five years in the case of a corrupt practice or three in the case of an illegal practice (sections 159 and 160, Representation of the People Act 1983 as amended by the PPERA 2000).

Prisoners

Under the Representation of the People Act 1981, anyone sentenced to more than one year's imprisonment is disqualified from membership of the House of Commons during the period of imprisonment. If nominated as a candidate their nomination would be declared void and if elected the election would be declared void. If an MP was sentenced to a year's imprisonment, their seat would be vacated and a by-election called. Convicted criminals are barred in law from being candidates as well as from membership of the House of Commons.

Treason

Under the Forfeiture Act 1870 (as amended by the Criminal Law Act 1967) those found guilty of treason are disqualified from membership of the House of Commons, for as long as the sentence is in force or until a pardon has been granted.

Office Holders

The House of Commons Disqualification Act 1975 lists certain office holders who are barred from sitting in the House of Commons. There are six classes of office holders who are disqualified:

❖ Certain judicial office holders including High Court Judges and Judges of the Court of Appeal

❖ Civil servants

❖ Members of the armed forces

❖ Police officers

❖ Members of legislatures outside the Commonwealth, other than Ireland (under the provisions of the Disqualifications Act 2000, which amends the House of Commons Disqualification Act 1975, members of the Irish legislature will no longer be disqualified from membership of the House of Commons. The Northern Ireland Act 1998 permitted members of the upper house (Seanad Eireann) to sit in the Northern Ireland Assembly, but by amending the Northern Ireland Assembly Act 1975, the Disqualifications Act 2000 will permit members of the lower house, the Dail, to sit in the Assembly and the House of Commons as well.

❖ Holders of other offices listed in Schedule 1 of the House of Commons Disqualification Act 1975 are also disqualified. Additions can be made to the list of disqualifying offices by means of their inclusion in an Order in Council supported by a resolution of the House of Commons[28]. Schedule I of the Act is divided into four parts. Part I lists those judicial offices which debar holders from membership of the House of Commons; Part II lists those organisations, all of whose members are disqualified from membership; Part III lists those bodies, some of whose members may not be MPs and Part IV lists offices which disqualify holders from being MPs for particular constituencies. There are some curious inclusions in the list; for example, it is difficult to see why membership of the Sea Fish Industry Authority or the Crofters Commission should render anyone ineligible for membership of the House of Commons (although it is hard to imagine why it would render them eligible either). An example of an officer included in Part IV of the Schedule is a Lord Lieutenant or High Sheriff of any county in England and Wales, who may not sit as an MP for any constituency within that county. He or she could stand for election in a constituency in

---

[28] Additions to and deletions from the 1975 Act are given effect by means of a draft Order in Council. A Treasury Minister (usually the Paymaster General) places a motion on the Order Paper of the House of Commons, to the effect that 'Schedule 1 to the House of Commons (Disqualification) Act 1975 be amended as follows ...'. Amendments may be tabled to this motion. If passed by the House, the 'resolution' as it is called, is embodied in an Order in Council which amends Schedule 1 of the 1975 Act. The former Member for Newham South, Nigel Spearing (Lab) tabled one such amendment when a Government Motion to amend Schedule 1 was debated on 13 February 1997. His amendment would have disqualified Recorders and Assistant Recorders from being Members of the House on the grounds that it was anomalous that temporary judges in Scotland and lay members of Industrial Tribunals should be barred from sitting as MPs, when part-time judges (Recorders) were not (at the time, three MPs were Recorders).

another county. Whilst the Chairman of the Red Deer Commission apparently has duties too onerous to permit him or her to undertake the work of a Member of Parliament, a councillor and/or a Member of the European Parliament may sit in the House of Commons. It is possible to be a councillor, MP and MEP simultaneously, but woe betide the member of the Covent Garden Market Authority or the Oil and Pipelines Agency who fails to resign his office on becoming an MP. Holding one of the offices of Bailiff or Steward of the 'Chiltern Hundreds of Stoke, Desborough and Burnham', or the 'Manor of Northstead', disqualifies an MP from retaining his seat in the House. These are two fictional offices for which MPs technically apply if they wish to resign; there is no other way in which an MP can resign his seat (section 4, House of Commons (Disqualification) Act 1975).

If anyone disqualified from being an MP under the Act, is elected, the election is considered void and if any MP becomes disqualified under the Act, then his or her seat is vacated.

There is no precise time at which the above disqualifying factors apply. For example; there is no clear statement set out in Statute to determine exactly when a candidate has to be 21 - is it, for example, at receipt of nominations or on polling day itself? Similarly, there is nothing in any Act of Parliament to indicate the legal position of a person who holds a disqualifying office when their nomination is submitted but who ceases to hold that office on the day of the Election. Under section 6(1) of the 1975 Act, if a person is elected to the House of Commons whilst disqualified under the aforementioned Act, the election is void[29]. This can only be determined on an election petition. Under section 6(2) of the Act, if it appears to the House of Commons that the grounds for disqualification no longer exist, it can order that those grounds be disregarded (for example, if the MP had resigned the offending office). This cannot, however, affect the proceedings on an election petition. If, once elected as an MP, a former candidate continues to hold a disqualifying office, he or she is deemed to have vacated his or her seat and a by-election is called.

The rules relating to disqualification grew out of the disputes between the House of Commons and the Crown and the concern of the Commons to control its own membership. As a result, anyone taking 'an office of profit under the Crown' could not at the same time be a Member of the House of Commons. The Commons was concerned that the Crown would attempt to seek influence over it by the use of patronage and by offering lucrative offices to its Members. The Succession to the Crown Act 1707 specified that no Member of the House of Commons could also hold 'an office or place of profit under the Crown'; however, Ministers were allowed to retain their seats, subject to the proviso that they seek re-election after appointment. Two of these offices, the Office of Bailiff or Steward of Her Majesty's Three Chiltern Hundreds of Stoke, Desborough and Burnham or that of the Steward of the Manor of Northstead are retained today for use by those MPs wishing to resign - hence the term, 'taking the Chiltern Hundreds'. The practice is to appoint to the two offices alternately, so that two Members may, if necessary, resign at once. If the last Member to resign took the Chiltern Hundreds, the next would take the Manor of Northstead.

---

[29] Under schedule 1, Part II, paragraph 8 of the Representation of the People Act 1983 (known as Rule 8) a candidate must sign a 'consent to nomination', stating that, 'to the best of his knowledge and belief he is not disqualified for membership of the House of Commons'.

The House of Commons (Disqualification) Act 1975 consolidated the legislation in this area and also imposed an upper limit on the number of Ministers who could sit in the House of Commons – 95 in fact (this includes Ministers of State and Parliamentary Secretaries of State). This is why some Government Ministers are peers, who sit in the House of Lords. Parliamentary Private Secretaries (PPSs) are not included in the above calculation, but can be counted upon to support the Government in the House, thus increasing the 'payroll vote'. It is only convention that dictates that all Government Ministers must sit in either of the two Houses of Parliament - legally, the Prime Minister could appoint non-Parliamentarians as Government Ministers.[30]

Until the Re-election of Ministers Act 1926, any MP had to resign on appointment as a Minister and fight a by-election. This was taken as an endorsement of their appointment as a Minister. To avoid a series of by-elections after a General Election, Ministers would be appointed before an Election. The Election itself was taken to be an endorsement of both their candidacy and their appointment as a Minister. The electorate does not elect the Prime Minister, or indeed, any other Minister; the Prime Minister only holds that office by virtue of having been elected Leader of his or her Party and Ministers hold office merely by appointment.

Schedule 1 of the Ministerial and Other Salaries Act 1975 limits the number of ministerial salaries payable at any one time. As a result, there may only be 21 Secretaries of State and 50 Ministers of State. There can be a total of 83 Secretaries of State, Ministers and Parliamentary Secretaries, excluding the Parliamentary Secretary to the Treasury, also known as the Chief Whip. There may only be four Law Officers, five Junior Lords of the Treasury (Government Whips), seven Assistant Whips and five Lords in Waiting (Government Whips in the House of Lords). There may only be one Captain of the Honourable Corps of Gentlemen-at-Arms (Government Chief Whip in the House of Lords), one Captain of the Queen's Bodyguard of the Yeoman of the Guard (Deputy Chief Whip in the House of Lords), one Treasurer of Her Majesty's Household (Deputy Chief Whip in the House of Commons), one Comptroller of Her Majesty's Household (No. 3 Whip in the House of Commons) and Vice-Chamberlain of Her Majesty's Household (No. 4 Whip in the House of Commons). This makes a grand total of 110 paid officers. There are, in addition, numerous PPSs, who whilst considered part of the 'payroll vote' are not paid members of the Government. These restrictions were the reason why, on his appointment to Parliamentary Under-Secretary of State at the DTI, in December 1998, Michael Wills MP had to accept the position on an unsalaried basis.

The Judicial Committee of the Privy Council also has jurisdiction in the case of disqualifications under the 1975 Act. Anyone can apply to the Committee for a declaration of disqualification, but the Committee cannot oblige if the matter is awaiting the decision of the Election Court.

---

[30] The last non-parliamentarian to be a member of the Government was Jan Smuts, the South African Leader, who was a member of Lloyd George's wartime Cabinet.

THE CANDIDATE'S NOMINATION

ELECTION OF A MEMBER to serve in Parliament for the Constituency

We, the undersigned, being electors for the said Constituency, do hereby nominate the under-mentioned person as a candidate at the said election.

Candidate's surname	Other names in full	Description	Home address in full
BROWN	John Edward	Merchant	52 George Street Bristol

Signatures	Electoral Number (See Note 3)	
	Distinctive Letter	Number
Proposer	....	....
Seconder	....	....
We, the undersigned, being electors for the said Constituency, do hereby assent to the foregoing nomination.		
1	....	....
2	....	....
3	....	....
4	....	....
5	....	....
6	....	....
7	....	....
8	....	....

The definition of a candidate contained in Section 118 of the RPA 1983 has been amended by Section 135 of the PPERA 2000 which inserts a new Section 118A into the RPA 1983. The new Section states that a person becomes a candidate at a parliamentary election on the date of the dissolution of Parliament (or in the case of a by-election on the date when the vacancy occurs) provided that he or she has been declared by himself or herself, or by others, to be a candidate on or before that date and in other circumstances a person becomes a candidate on the day on which he or she is declared by himself or herself or by others to be a candidate, or the day on which he or she is nominated as a candidate at the election, whichever is the earlier . The old Section had defined a candidate as being either someone who had already been elected to serve in Parliament, or someone nominated as a candidate. The new definition puts MPs on an equal footing with other candidates. A local government candidate is defined as someone who is nominated as such on the last day for publication of the notice of the election (25 days before the date of the poll).

Under Rule 8 of the Election Rules, a candidate must consent to nomination before an election otherwise his or her nomination is not valid. Consent must be given in writing on or within one month before the last day for delivery of nomination papers. The nomination requires one witness and the consent has to be handed in at the time for delivery of nomination papers. If a candidate is out of the country he or she can communicate his or her consent other than in writing and without a witness. The consent must state that the candidate is aware of the provisions of the House of Commons Disqualification Act 1975 and that 'to the best of his knowledge and belief' he or she is not disqualified from membership of the House of Commons.

In European Parliamentary elections the same provisions apply but the candidate must state that he or she knows of no reason why he or she would be disqualified from being an MEP under the provisions of the European Parliamentary Elections Act 1978. A candidate who is a member of another Member State and not a British, Commonwealth or Irish citizen, has to complete a declaration and certificate which must be delivered within the same time limit as the nomination. The declaration must state the candidate's name, nationality, home address, where appropriate, the address at which he or she was on an electoral register in his or her own Member State and must contain a declaration stating that he or she is not standing as a candidate in the same election in any other Member State. The candidate must also produce a certificate from the relevant authorities in his or her own Member State, stating that he or she is not disqualified from being an MEP in that Member State.

In local government elections, candidates must give their consent in writing in a form set out in the Local Elections (Principal Areas) Rules 1986 and the Local Elections (Parishes and Communities) Rules 1986 (SI 1986, No. 2215). This has to be attested by a witness and delivered on or within one month before the last day for receipt of nomination papers. The consent must also include a statement that the candidate is not disqualified from standing. Under Rule 6 of the Election Rules contained in the Representation of the People Act 1983, a candidate's nomination must state his or her full names[31] (with the surname written first) and home address[32], along with a description, no longer than six words, if desired. Under Rule 6(A) of the Election Rules, a description may not be one *"which is likely to lead voters to associate the candidate with a registered political party"* unless the party is a qualifying party in relation to the constituency. A registered party is a qualifying party in relation to a constituency if the constituency is in England, Scotland or Wales. Rule 6 has now been amended by Section 38 of the Political Parties, Elections and Referendums Act 2000 so that the description can either be one of six words in length or can simply be the word 'independent' or 'Speaker seeking re-election'.[33] Similar provisions apply to local elections. It is usually the candidate who completes the nomination form, but he or she can request that the Returning Officer complete the form and he or she can then simply sign the form.

Under Rule 7 of the Election Rules, a nomination has to be signed by a proposer and seconder and by eight other electors, whose names must appear on the nomination paper along with their electoral numbers and the letter or letters of the polling district in which they are registered. In the case of European Parliamentary elections, a proposer and seconder and 28 other electors are required. For a local government election a proposer and seconder and eight others are required (Local Elections (Principal Areas) Rules 1986). No one may put his or her name to more nomination papers than there are vacancies to be filled in any one electoral area and no one person may nominate a candidate for an

---

[31] Suffixes to a candidate's name (e.g., 'CBE', 'OBE', etc.) are not part of the candidate's name and must be excluded from the ballot paper.

[32] Knowingly making a false statement about a candidate's name or address in a nomination paper is a corrupt practice under section 65A of the RPA 1983 (as inserted by the RPA 2000).

[33] More information on the party names and descriptions and the registration of political parties can be found in Chapter Nine.

election in another electoral area in the same local government area at the same election. Under the Local Elections (Parishes and Communities) Rules 1986 (SI 1986, No. 2215), a candidate for a parish or community council requires only a proposer and seconder from the relevant electoral area. The proposer and seconder may not nominate more candidates than there are vacancies to be filled and may not nominate candidates in other wards at the same election. In the context of local elections, an elector is someone registered as a local government elector for the electoral area in the electoral register. Welsh language versions of nomination papers can be used as set out in the Representation of the People (Welsh Forms) Order 1989 (SI 1989, No. 429).

However, nominations in languages other than English are not acceptable. Although, in the case of Evans v Thomas (1962) 2 QB 350, it was held that a returning officer was wrong to reject the nomination paper of a candidate at a local government election on the grounds that it had been completed in Welsh (on the basis that there was nothing in either statute or common law which required nominations to be in English) the judgment relied on the fact that at local elections 'forms to the like effect' may be used. This is not the case at parliamentary elections. Nomination forms must also be intelligible to the returning officer and the other candidates in the election. The other candidates would not be able to object to a nomination in a language that they could not read. A candidate can be nominated by more than one nomination paper and this is sometimes done in order to avoid the problem of a candidate failing to be nominated because of a technical problem with one or his or her nomination papers. However, an elector can only sign one nomination paper.

Under Rule 6, nomination forms must be delivered by either the candidate, his or her proposer or seconder or election agent. If the agent delivers the nomination forms, then he or she must give, if this has not been done previously, his or her name and address to the Returning Officer. The Returning Officer has to be present when nomination papers are delivered. Under Rule 11 of the Election Rules, when a nomination paper is delivered only certain people may be present: the candidate, his or her election agent, proposer and seconder (where the candidate is also the agent, another person named by the candidate can attend). They may inspect and/or object to any candidate's nomination paper. The candidate's husband or wife can attend, but cannot inspect or object to nomination papers.

Nomination day is perhaps not quite the occasion it used to be. Messrs Houston and Valdar regarded the day as "a good opportunity for a demonstration of strength". They offer sound advice, as pertinent today as it was in 1922, on the necessity of ensuring that names on nomination forms appear as they do in the electoral register: "a man or woman should sign his or her name and address as per the electors' register, even if such entry is wrong in some particular."

In the case of a local government election, a nomination paper must be delivered no later than noon on the 19th day before polling day. There is no deposit.

Under Rule 15(2) of the Election Rules (RPA 1983) where a Returning Officer thinks a candidate may be disqualified for nomination under the Representation of the People Act 1981 (under the provisions of this Act, anyone sentenced to more than one year's imprisonment is disqualified from membership of the House of Commons during the period of imprisonment) objections can be made between 10am and 4pm on the day after the last day for delivery of nomination papers. Other objections, to nomination papers handed in up to 4pm on the day before the last day for delivery, must be made between

10am and noon on the last day of delivery, but objections to papers handed in on the last day can be objected to until 5pm on that day. An objection can be made by anyone entitled to attend the nomination (candidates, proposer and seconders, election agents or those attending in place of the election agent). Where a candidate is disqualified under the Representation of the People Act 1981, the acting returning officer can either reject the nomination paper on his or her own initiative or on the objection by one of those allowed be present. Where the acting returning officer rejects a nomination paper for this reason, he or she then publishes a 'draft statement of persons nominated', stating that anyone who wishes to object to any candidate on the ground that he or she is disqualified under the 1981 Act can do so between 10.00am and 4.00pm on the next working day after the last day for the delivery of nomination papers. If the acting returning officer is confident that none of the candidates is so disqualified or that one or more of them is so disqualified and that the remainder are not, he or she does not need to publish a notice along the lines outlined above. For example, a candidate in attendance at the time for objections to nomination papers would clearly not be disqualified under the 1981 (unless, of course, they had just participated in a daring prison escape).

Nomination papers could also be ruled invalid on the following grounds:

❖ That the particulars of the candidate or his or her subscribers were not as required by law.

❖ That the nomination paper was not subscribed in the way required.

❖ That the description of the candidate did not meet the requirements of Rule 6A of the Election Rules.

The acting returning officer can only declare a nomination paper to be invalid; he or she cannot declare a candidate unqualified, except on the grounds of the 1981 Act. For example, the acting returning officer is not expected to make a judgement about the candidate's real name or address, only whether or not it satisfies the requirements set out in the legislation. Under the provisions of section 65A of the RPA 1983 (as amended by the RPA 2000) it is a corrupt practice at a parliamentary or local government election in England and Wales to include any false information in a nomination paper. The acting returning officer's decision as to the validity of a nomination paper is final and cannot be challenged in any legal proceedings. This is not to say that a candidate's nomination cannot be challenged subsequently on the grounds that he or she is disqualified from being a Member of the House of Commons.

Under Rule 13 of the Election Rules, a candidate can withdraw from standing in an election by signing a notice of withdrawal, attested by one witness and delivered to the Returning Officer within the time limit for delivery of nominations. In the case of local government elections, the time limit is by noon on the 16th day before polling day.

Under Rule 14 of the Election Rules, the Returning Officer has to publish a list of those nominated, showing names, addresses and, in some cases, descriptions and the names of proposers, seconders, etc. The statement must also, where appropriate, give the names of those whose nominations have been rejected (stating the reason). If the election is uncontested, the statement declares that person elected. Under paragraph 6 (9) of Schedule 21 to the PPERA 2000, an acting returning officer must send a copy of the statement of those nominated and where appropriate, copies of the certificates (of party registration) required in accordance with Rule 6A, to the Electoral Commission.

Where the election is contested, the statement of persons nominated also includes a notice of poll, stating the day and times of polling.

Once an election has been called, and before a candidate submits his or her nomination papers, the party that he or she represents will usually call an adoption meeting, to formally 'adopt' the candidate. Such meetings have no legal status but are a good way of galvanising the party faithful into action and publicising the candidate locally.

THE DEPOSIT

When a candidate in an election registers his or her nomination with the returning officer, he or she must also submit a deposit of £500 (this is also the amount for both individual constituency candidates standing for election to both the Scottish Parliament and Welsh Assembly and for each party list). Elections to the Northern Ireland Assembly require a deposit of £150 per candidate. For European Parliamentary candidates the amount is £5,000 for each list or individual candidate. Rule 53 of the Election Rules (RPA 1983) stipulates that a deposit is only returned if the candidate receives one-twentieth (5 per cent) of the total votes cast in that constituency (2.5 per cent in the case of elections to the European Parliament). Tendered ballots and rejected ballot papers are not counted when calculating this total. Lost deposits are paid to the Treasury. Deposits are paid by bankers draft or 'legal tender', or with the consent of the acting returning officer, by cheque. 'Legal tender' does not mean cash. Only banknotes issued by the Bank of England, Bank of Scotland, the Clydesdale Bank and the Royal Bank of Scotland are acceptable. A candidate may not pay his or her deposit in 10p and 5p pieces.

THE SPEAKER

The Speaker's constituency (Michael Martin is the MP for Glasgow Springburn) is the one constituency that is not usually contested by the main parties at a General Election. This is a convention rather than an electoral rule and some argue it is an undemocratic one, effectively denying the voters of Glasgow Springburn the opportunity to vote Conservative or Liberal Democrat. This was certainly the view of the former SDP/Liberal Alliance, which always contested Croydon North East, the constituency of the then Speaker, Rt Hon Bernard Weatherill (now Lord Weatherill). The somewhat unconvincing argument in favour of the current practice is that the Speaker's role in the House of Commons is a non-political one. An alternative would be for the Speaker, on his or her appointment as such, to be dubbed the 'Member for the Palace of Westminster' and resign his or her seat, thereby allowing a by-election to be fought.

In the general election in 1997, the main parties contested all other seats, except for Tatton, where both the Labour and Liberal Democrat candidates stood down in favour of Martin Bell, who became the House of Commons' only Independent MP. Martin Bell stood in the Brentwood and Ongar constituency in the 2001 general election, but failed to be elected. However, Richard Taylor was elected as an independent candidate in the constituency of Wyre Forest and is therefore the only independent MP in the present House of Commons.

FORMER MEMBERS DURING ELECTIONS

Whilst Government continues during the period of a General Election, Parliament does not. No Parliament, no Members. Former Members contesting their seats, may not use any parliamentary facilities, although an exception is made in the case of Party Leaders, who may use their offices throughout the campaign period. MPs who stand down or who are not re-elected are entitled to a resettlement grant (a percentage of annual salary) based on age and length of service. Government Ministers also receive severance payments if they lose office under the age of 65 provided they do not hold office again within three weeks. The payment is equal to one quarter of the annual amount of the person's ministerial salary, reduced by one quarter of the difference between the ministerial salary and an ordinary MP's salary. MPs also receive a pension as set out in the Parliamentary and Other Pensions Act 1987 and subsequent regulations and the Ministerial and Other Pensions and Salaries Act 1991. Members contribute at a rate of 6% of salary and the pension is based on final salary, accruing at a rate of one fiftieth for each year of service, pro rata for a part year. According to rules issued by the Cabinet Secretary, Sir Richard Wilson, at the start of the 2001 general election campaign, ministers' special advisers, heading for the campaign trail, were required to relinquish contact with their departments for the duration of the campaign. Those remaining to advise ministers could not take any public part in the campaign.

POLLING DISTRICTS

Under Section 18(1) of the Representation of the People Act all parliamentary constituencies must be divided into polling districts and each district must have at least one polling place. There is no legislative requirement on local authorities to provide a minimum or maximum number of polling stations for each constituency within its boundaries. For example, in the London Borough of Croydon, at the last general election, there were 223 polling places (to cover three parliamentary constituencies). The authority attempts to ensure that electors are no further than 800 metres from a polling place and that the convenience of voters is uppermost, in terms of location and accessibility. Each parish or community is considered a separate polling district or districts. In Northern Ireland, polling districts are established under Section 130 of the Electoral Law Act (Northern Ireland) 1962. Where 30 or more electors in a constituency feel that the requirements of the electors have not been met they can appeal to the Secretary of State, who can direct the council to alter the boundaries of polling districts. If the council does not abide by his/her direction within one month, he can make the necessary amendments himself/herself.

A polling district is a sub-division of a ward, division or constituency and for each such district there has to be a polling place (this is not the same as a polling station). There is no definition of polling place in the RPA 1983, but Schofield's[34] suggests that a polling place is simply the location in which a polling station is located. As far as possible, councils must choose as polling stations, locations that are accessible to people with disabilities. Thirty or more electors can make representations to the Secretary of State if they feel that the designation of polling places is unreasonable.

---

[34] 'Schofield's Election Law', 2nd Edition (Shaw & Sons) 1996

DURING THE CAMPAIGN

"Nothing appeals more to the public than domestic felicity, and it is no use ignoring this aspect of mass psychology. On public platforms, and whenever possible elsewhere, the candidate should be accompanied by his wife. If she can speak in public, no meeting should be complete without a little heart-to-heart talk from her to the women electors. It is difficult to over-estimate the vote-winning influence of an attractive woman when she is the wife of the candidate. In the Dover election of 1921 ... the wonderful pluck and emotional eloquence of Lady Polson was regarded by many competent judges as the decisive factor in the contest. Not every candidate can have a wife with the gifts of this lady, but there is always something she can do. She is generally an excellent canvasser, and even if she can be trusted to do no more than ride about in a car and smile happily by his side, she is still doing useful work".

From: 'Modern Electioneering Practice', Henry James Houston & Lionel Valdar (Charles Knight & Co. Limited, 1922)

Meeting Rooms

Meeting rooms should not be confused with 'committee rooms', which the political parties establish once an election has been called. The parties usually establish campaign headquarters (committee rooms) in as prominent a location in the constituency as they can afford. Where a vacant high street shop or similar premises cannot be found, a hapless party member can sometimes be prevailed upon to donate the use of a front room, or two. This is not a recommended course of action for those with a history of mental instability, as it is likely to be exacerbated by uninterrupted exposure to other party workers for the duration of the campaign.

Under Section 95 of the 1983 Act, during an election campaign, a parliamentary candidate and also a European Parliamentary candidate is entitled to the free use (payment must be made for heat and light, etc.) of a suitable meeting room in a school or other public building in order to hold a public meeting. The period during which the room can be used is between the day on which the writ is received (in the case of a European Parliamentary election, the last date on which notice of an election may be published in accordance with election rules) and the day preceding polling day. The candidate, or whoever convenes the meeting, must pay heating, lighting and cleaning expenses (these provisions do not apply to Northern Ireland). Similar provisions apply in the case of local government elections (Section 96).

Postage

Under Section 91 of the RPA 1983 a candidate at a parliamentary election or European Parliamentary election is entitled to send out free of charge a communication not exceeding 60g in weight to each elector and each proxy (provided they appear on the electoral register). This also includes those voters who will reach voting age on the day of the poll. The election address can either be sent out in an addressed envelope (which necessitates party workers printing off labels from the electoral register) or in an un-addressed envelope (which makes the lives of small parties and independent candidates much easier, but which is less personal).

What sort of information should be contained in an election address? Again, Henry James Houston and Lionel Valdar have some salutary advice: *"If it contains one unfortunate phrase, your opponent will see that you are not allowed to forget it,"* they suggest. Little, it seems, has changed since 1922. Their motto was *"Cut it short"*. *"Cut out the ponderous high-brow stuff. It bores people to tears. And cut out personal attacks on your opponent. They lose more elections than anything else"*, they proclaimed. According to Houston and Valdar, this was particularly true where women voters were concerned: *"The agent of the future who imagines that he can snatch a victory by exposing some domestic or other scandal concerning the opposing candidate may receive a rude shock. Instead of exciting woman's horror, he may excite her interest and sympathy. Women often have a perverse sympathy with the 'wicked' man, and a 'spice of the devil' is not always a bar to their favour. Possibly they think that a man 'with a past', may also be a man with a future ... Women realise that many of the most virile and attractive men, the men who really accomplish things in life, have in their youth been guilty of escapades that men with less generous and less impulsive natures contrive to avoid. In their judgments of such men, women are apt to be not unkind."*

Hughes and Valdar even included an entire section in their weighty publication on the 'psychology of woman'. A few, they concluded, were motivated solely by feminist issues, but the majority *"respond to appeals based on food prices, education, religion, taxation, and wages. They do not bother much about the Supreme Council, but they do know something about the purchasing power of the £"*. So, there you have it.

What should an election address look like? Once again, our aforementioned experts are not short of advice, suggesting that *"the pica wins the sympathy of the eye more readily than minion"*. In a rash moment, they even advocate *"imitation typewriting type and purple ink"*.

Candidates' Expenses

There are two types of expenses:

❖ those incurred in connection with the conduct of the election campaign;
❖ the candidate's own personal expenses.

The limit on expenses incurred in conducting the election campaign is governed by Section 76 of the Representation of the People Act 1983 as amended by the Political Parties, Elections and Referendums Act 2000 Section 132. The new provisions give the Secretary of State power to vary such sums by order as a result of the effects of inflation and also in order to *"give effect to a recommendation of the Electoral Commission"*. Under the Representation of the People (Variation of Limits of Candidates' Election Expenses) Orders, the latest being the 2001 Order (SI 2001, No 535) which came into force on 5 March, the following limits apply to parliamentary elections:

❖ for candidates in UK parliamentary general elections in county constituencies, £5,483, with an additional 6.2p for each entry in the electoral register being used at that election;

❖ for candidates in UK parliamentary general elections in borough constituencies, £5,483, with an additional 4.6p for every entry in the electoral register to be used at that election.

The PPERA 2000 amends Section 76A of the RPA 1983 under which the above order is made, with a new Section (as set out in Section 133 of the PPERA 2000) which gives the Secretary of State power to vary such sums by order as a result of the effects of inflation and also in order to *"give effect to a recommendation of the Electoral Commission"*.

Section 132 of the PPERA 2000 amended the existing limits on by-election expenses as set out in Section 76 of the RPA 1983 (these were: for candidates in UK parliamentary by-elections in county constituencies, £19,863, with an additional 22.2p for each entry in the electoral register to be used at that election; and for candidates in UK parliamentary by-elections in borough constituencies, £19,863, with an additional 16.9p for each entry in the electoral register to be used at that election) and replaced them with one common limit, of £100,000 per candidate, regardless of whether the by-election is to be in a borough or county constituency.

At a local government election (excluding elections to the Greater London Authority and local elections in Scotland and Northern Ireland) the maximum is £242 with an additional 4.7 pence for each entry in the register of electors to be used at that election (Representation of the People (Variation of Limits of Candidates' Expenses) Order 2001 (SI 2001, No 535).[35] In Northern Ireland, the respective limits are £242 and 4.8 pence (Local Elections (Northern Ireland) (Amendment) Order 2001 (SI 2001, No. 417) (which amended the Electoral Law Act (Northern Ireland) 1962).

In the case of case of Bowman v United Kingdom (February, 1998) the European Court of Human Rights ruled that Section 75 of the Representation of the People Act 1983, was a violation of the right to freedom of expression under Article 10 of the European Convention of Human Rights. As a result, Section 131 of the Political Parties, Elections and Referendums Act 2000 amended Section 75 of the RPA 2000 so that certain expenditure was exempt from the general prohibition on expenses being incurred by anyone other than the candidate or his or her election agent. The previous level of such exempted expenditure was £5, but Section 131 raised this level to £500 in respect of a candidate at a parliamentary election and £50 in respect of a candidate at a local government election, together with an additional 0.5p for each entry in the register of local government electors for the electoral area in question. Section 131(5) of the Political Parties, Elections and Referendums Act 2000 repealed the amendments to the RPA 1983 made by Schedule 3, paragraph 20 of the Greater London Authority Act 1999.

The candidate's own personal expenses are defined in Section 118 of the Representation of the People Act 1983 and include travelling expenses and accommodation costs. Where incurred by the agent, these expenses, are unlimited; where incurred by the candidate, they are limited by Section 74(1) of the 1983 Act, as amended by the Representation of the People Act 1985 to £600. The candidate has to send a written account of his or her expenses to his or her agent within 14 days after the day the election result is declared. When the agent makes his return of expenses, the candidate's personal expenses should be stated separately, as they are not used in determining whether or not a candidate has kept within the maximum permitted election expenditure.

---

[35] The provisions of the order do not extend to local elections in Scotland as regulations governing such elections are now the responsibility of the Scottish Parliament (with the exception of provisions relating to the franchise for Scottish local elections, which is a reserved matter under the Scotland Act 1998).

A candidate's expenses begin from the earliest of the following:

- ❖ The time he or she declares him or herself to be a candidate
- ❖ The time the agent is appointed
- ❖ The time he or she is adopted
- ❖ The time he or she is nominated

However, there is no such time set out in statute, so each case has to be decided on its merits. The main principle behind the many judicial rulings handed down over the years is that expenses incurred generally by political parties which promote the party's views, even if circulated in only one particular constituency and with which the PPC may be associated, are not election expenses. However, if the candidate is obviously identified with, for example, political literature promoting his or her candidature, then they are election expenses. Home Office Circular RPA 410 considers whether or not a candidate's use of the internet constitutes an election expense.

Section 134 of the Political Parties, Elections and Referendums Act 2000 inserts a new section (90A) into the RPA 1983 in order to bring the definition of election expenses in the RPA 1983 in line with the other provisions of the PPERA 2000 relating to campaign expenditure by political parties, controlled expenditure by third parties and referendum expenses. This means that benefits in kind given to candidates will be regarded as election expenses. The new Section 90A of the RPA 1983 defines 'election expenses' as expenses incurred for the acquisition or use of property or for the provision of services or facilities which are used for the purposes of the candidates' election. Certain expenses are exempt, including: the payment of the candidate's deposit, the publication of an article in a newspaper, magazine (other than an advertisement) or a broadcast, free mailing facilities and services provided by an individual voluntarily in his own time. New Section 90C of the RPA 1983 states that where property or goods are transferred to the candidate or his election agent free of charge or at a discount of more than 10% of the market value of the property or goods, where the difference between the market value and the value at which the goods are transferred to the candidate is more than £50, the amount must be declared as an election expense.

The Political Parties, Elections and Referendums Act 2000 inserts a new Section (Section 71A) into the Representation of the People Act 1983, relating to donations to candidates. The new Section states money or other property, provided, whether as a gift or a loan, by anyone other than the candidate or his or her election agent, for the purpose of meeting election expenses, must be given to the candidate or his or her agent. The details are set out in Schedule 16 of the PPERA 2000 (which inserts a new Schedule 2A into the RPA 1983). The provisions relating to donations are essentially the same as those relating to donations to political parties, which are also set out in the PPERA 2000.

Schedule 16 defines donations as being:

- ❖ A gift of money or other property.

- ❖ Any sponsorship provided in relation to the party (defined below).

- ❖ Any money spent (otherwise than by the candidate, his election agent or sub-agent) in paying any expenses incurred either directly or indirectly by the candidate.

❖ Any money lent to the candidate or his or her agent, otherwise than on commercial terms.

❖ The provision, otherwise than on commercial terms of any property, services or facilities for the use or benefit of the candidate (including the services of any person).

Sponsorship is defined in Section 51 as being:

❖ Any money or other property transferred to the candidate or to any person for the benefit of the candidate in order to help the candidate with meeting any 'defined expenses'.

Defined expenses is taken to mean expenses in connection with any conference, meeting or other event organised by or on behalf of the candidate, the preparation, production or dissemination of any publication by or on behalf of the candidate or any study or research organised by or on behalf of the candidate. The following are not deemed to be sponsorship: making any payment in respect of any charge for admission to any conference, meeting or other event or the purchase price of, or any other charge for access to any publication, or the making of any payment in respect of the inclusion of an advertisement in any publication where the payment is made at the commercial rate payable.

Schedule 16(5) states that where donations are made to the party for less than their market price, their value is taken to be the difference between the two. Part II of Schedule 16 defines those donors from whom donations are deemed to be permissible and those from whom donations are not acceptable. Donations cannot be accepted from anonymous donors or from those whose identity it is impossible to determine; for example, as a result of 'deception' or 'concealment'. Under the provisions of Section 54(2) foreign donations are not acceptable as the Section states the permissible donors must be any one of the following:

❖ Individuals registered in an electoral register.

❖ Companies registered under the Ccmpanies Act 1985 or the Companies (Northern Ireland) Order 1986 and incorporated within the UK or another Member State, which carry on their business in the UK.

❖ Registered parties.

❖ Trade unions entered in the list kept under the Trade Union and Labour Relations (Consolidation) Act 1992 or the Industrial Relations (Northern Ireland) Order 1992.

❖ Building societies within the meaning of the Building Societies Act 1986.

❖ Limited liability partnerships registered under the Limited Liability Partnerships Act 2000, or any corresponding Act in force in Northern Ireland, which carries on its business in the UK.

❖ Friendly societies registered under the Friendly Societies Act 1974 or a society registered under the Industrial and Provident Societies Act 1965 or the Industrial and Provident Societies Act (Northern Ireland) 1969.

❖ Any unincorporated association of two or more persons which does not fall within any of the above but which carries on its business wholly or mainly in the UK and whose main office is also in the UK.

Where a 'principal donor' gives a donation to a party along with one or more others, then each individual contribution of more than £50 is treated as a separate donation.

The Role of the Election Agent

"Work harmoniously with your agent. Don't bully him. Consult him ... If he is making the pace too hot for you ask him to ease down a little, but remember that modern elections are short and, therefore, strenuous. In the Wrekin election, 1920, I fixed up 63 meetings for the last 12 days of General Townshend's campaign, and he went through them without a murmur. He was a soldier!"

From: 'Modern Electioneering Practice', Henry James Houston & Lionel Valdar (Charles Knight & Co. Limited, 1922)

The role of the party election agent (sometimes referred to as party organiser) is often crucial to the success of an election campaign. They are frequently the unsung heroes of the electoral process, yet in recent years their numbers have been declining. The Conservative Party has traditionally employed a greater number of agents than any of the other major political parties. As Dick Leonard and Roger Mortimore point out in their comprehensive guide to elections in Britain ('Elections in Britain: A voter's guide', Palgrave, 2001) in 1966 there were 499 Conservative agents, but by 1997 this number had declined to 287. Election agents have the awesome task of making sure they are fully apprised of the latest developments in electoral law and endeavouring to ensure their candidate does not fall foul of any of them. They are responsible for election expenses and in many cases for most organisational aspects of the campaign.

Many election agents will of course, find themselves having to promote candidates for whom they have little affection and for whom success is likely to prove elusive. As our old friends Houston and Valdar point out, *"If he has to handle a crank or an eccentric personality possessing unpopular, narrow views – in a word, if his proposition is wrong – his finest efforts are likely to fail".*[36] No doubt this will strike a chord with many an election agent or organiser, in all political parties. Lionel Valdar was clearly a meticulous man and includes in his election guide a comprehensive list of the election stationery which should always be kept in stock by the election agent. Woe betide the election agent in the 1920s who ran out of 'blotting paper', 'pens and nibs', 'gum', a 'hammer', 'India rubbers', a 'list of farmers' and naturally, 'pencils in three colours'.

All candidates (except at parish and community council elections) must appoint an election agent. A candidate can be his or her own agent and if he or she does not provide the Returning Officer with the name of his or her agent he or she is deemed to have

---

[36] 'Modern Electioneering Practice', Henry James Houston & Lionel Valdar (Charles Knight & Co. Limited, 1922)

named him or herself as agent. An election agent must have an office and the address must be declared to the appropriate officer at the same time that the agent's appointment is declared. Under Section 67(1) of the 1983 Act, the agent must be named no later than the appointed time for the delivery of notices of withdrawal. Each election agent must have an office to which all notices, writs, claims, summonses, etc., can be sent. The office must be in the constituency or an adjoining one, or in a London borough or district which is partly comprised in or adjoins the constituency concerned. Where a candidate is his or her own agent, the address given on the nomination form is deemed to be the office, unless it is outside the constituency, in which case the address of the candidate's proposer is taken as the agent's office address.

The role of an election agent is an important one as he or she is responsible for ensuring that the candidate's campaign is run in accordance with the law, leaving the candidate free to concentrate on actually fighting a campaign. No payments can be made by a candidate during a campaign except by the election agent, the candidate or anyone authorised by the election agent where the expense relates to holding a public meeting or display, issuing an advertisement, publication or circular expressing the candidates views. In the case of parliamentary elections for county constituencies or European elections, an election agent can appoint a deputy, known as a sub-agent. Any sub-agent's name and address must be given in writing to the Returning Officer (or other appropriate officer) at least two days before polling day.

Under Section 73 of the RPA 1983 as amended by Schedule 18, paragraph 3 of the PPERA 2000, payments of expenses must be made by or through the candidate's election agent. Under Section 74 of the 1983 Act, as amended by the PPERA 2000, a candidate can pay any personal expenses incurred by him or her up to a level of £600. All accounts have to be sent to the agent no later than 21 days after the day on which the election result is declared. Any accounts which come in after that date cannot be paid as this would constitute an illegal practice under Section 78(3) of the Representation of the People Act 1983. All election expenses must be paid within 28 days after the day on which the result of the election is declared and anything paid after this time constitutes an illegal practice under the above section of the Representation of the People Act 1983. Disputed claims are payments which the agent refuses to pay within the 28 day period. An action for a disputed claim can be brought by the claimant. Receipts have to be kept of 'petty' expenses (stationery, etc.) and these have to be given to the agent within 14 days of the declaration of the result of the election. The candidate must also give a statement of personal expenses to the agent within 14 days.

Under Section 81 of the RPA 1983 as amended by Schedule 18 of the PPERA 2000, within 35 days of the declaration of the election result, the agent has to give to the Returning Officer a 'true return' of all election expenses. Election returns used to have to be in the form set out in Schedule 3 of the RPA 1983 (this Schedule still applied at the last general election in 2001) but under the new provisions, the Electoral Commission has prescribed a form of return in Schedule 18 to the PPERA 2000 (these regulations came into force on 1 July 2001). Under Section 88 of the RPA 1983, the acting returning officer must publish, at least 10 days after the last time for the delivery of returns and declarations, in at least two newspapers in the constituency, the time and place where they can be inspected. The returns and declarations and any accompanying documents must be kept at the acting returning officer's department for two years and must, at 'reasonable times' be open to inspection on payment of a fee of £5. Copies can be obtained at a rate of 20p per side as set out in Regulation 10 of the Representation of the People (England and Wales) Regulations 2001 (SI 2001, No. 341) and the Representation of the People (Scotland) Regulations 2001 (SI 2001, No. 497 (S.2)). After two years, the records are either returned to the candidate or destroyed. The 'Return of the Expenses of each Candidate', which used to be compiled by the Home Office and presented to the House of Commons after each general election, is now compiled by the Electoral Commission. Circular EC2 (2001) sets out the information required by the Commission.

Under Section 85 of the 1983 Act, if a candidate does not deliver the return and declarations relating to election expenses in time, he or she cannot sit or vote in the House of Commons until they have been delivered. If he or she does do so, the fine for each day on which he or she does sit in the House, is £100. A similar penalty applies to local government candidates, but the penalty is £50. Exceptions allowed under Section 86 of the 1983 Act for failure to deliver a return or declaration include the candidate's illness, the illness of death of his or her election agent, or where the person applying for relief under the Section is the election agent, the death or illness of any prior election agent, or the absence, illness or death or 'misconduct' of any sub-agent, clerk or officer of the election agent. The court may then order a return to be made in a modified form.

Under section 88 of the RPA 1983, at a parliamentary election, within 10 days after the returning officer has received all the returns, a notice is published in at least two local newspapers stating when and where returns and declarations can be inspected. Under section 89 (as amended by the PPERA 2000) returns and declarations can be inspected during the next two years, after which time they are either destroyed or returned to the candidate.

Death of a Candidate

Rule 60 of the Election Rules sets out the procedures to be followed upon the death of a candidate. Where a duly nominated candidate dies before an election result is declared, the Returning Officer has to 'countermand the poll', or if polling has begun, abandon it. The election is then begun again as if the writ had been received 28 days after the day on which the acting returning officer was informed on the death. There are no days to be discounted from the timetable and the period is therefore four weeks exactly. Similar provisions apply to local elections, where the period concerned is 35 days (The Local Elections (Principal Areas) Rules 1986 (SI 1986, No. 2214, Schedule 2, Part 6, Rule 49 and section 39(1) of the RPA 1983). The other candidates do not need to re-nominate themselves. Candidates seeking to stand for the first time would clearly need to submit nomination papers.

Polling Agents, Tellers and 'Getting the Vote Out'

Under Rule 30(1) of the Parliamentary Elections Rules, Schedule 1 Representation of the People Act 1983, Rule 24(1) of the Local Elections (Principal Areas) Rules 1986 and Schedule 2, Rule 24(1) of the Local Elections (Parishes and Communities) Rules 1986 (SI 1986, No. 2215), all candidates can appoint polling agents who are allowed to be present at the polling stations on polling day. There is no limit on the number. Polling agents should not be confused with tellers, who are party activists who have no official status at a polling station, but who are allowed to make note of voters polling card numbers in order to 'get their vote out'. By noting the electors who have already voted, they can determine which of their supporters have yet to go out and vote. Polling agents are rarely appointed now in Great Britain. At local elections, no more than four polling agents can attend any one polling station, unless the Returning Officer allows a greater number. Under Section

72(1) of the Representation of the People Act 1983, if polling agents are paid, they must be appointed by the election agent. Polling agents may not disclose any information about names of electors or proxies who have not voted and may not try and obtain information from any elector about the candidate for whom they intend to vote or have voted, nor may they attempt to discover the number on the back of the ballot paper given to an elector or persuade an elector to disclose his or her ballot paper in any way. Contravening any of these provisions (set out in Section 66 of the Representation of the People Act 1983) is an offence. Polling agents may also attempt to stop the impersonation of an elector or any attempt by an elector to vote more than once. Polling agents may mark in a copy of the electoral register, the polling card numbers of those who have voted, but they may not take this away from the station with them. Only one polling agent is allowed into a polling station on behalf of the same candidate at any one time.

Party Political Broadcasts

The allocation of Party Election Broadcasts used to be decided by the Committee on Political Broadcasting, which consisted of members of the main political parties and the BBC and ITC. The Committee had no legal status and its deliberations were not made public. In practice, the television companies issued a proposed allocation of broadcasts to the Secretary to the Government Chief Whip, who then liaised with the whips of the other political parties. A maximum of five PEBs was allocated to a single party; the Party in Government and the chief Opposition Party received parity of allocation. Any party fielding more than 50 candidates was entitled to a 5 minute broadcast.

The Committee was replaced in June 1997 by the Broadcasters' Liaison group, which liaises directly with the political parties. A consultation paper on the reform of party political broadcasting was issued jointly by the BBC, ITC, Radio Authority and S4C on 21 January 1998, which suggested reapplying the electoral support test for PEBs, abolished for the minor parties in 1996. The BBC and ITC announced in June 1999 that to qualify for a PEB, a minor party would need to contest one sixth of all seats in the election. In 1997, eight parties with no MPs were entitled to PEBs. In the local elections in 2000, the Conservatives, the Labour Party and the Liberal Democrats were all allocated three broadcasts each, while the qualifying threshold for other parties was the contesting of at least one-sixth of the seats in contention.

The consultation period ended on 31 March 1998 and on 18 September the broadcasters announced that PPBs already planned for the remainder of the year would be retained, but that a further review would be undertaken in June 1999. On 28 June 1999 the BBC and ITC announced that in future PPBs would be concentrated around particular occasions in the year (other than during elections) such as the Queen's Speech or the Budget. The following are entitled to such broadcasts: the Labour and Conservative Parties, the Liberal Democrats, the SNP and Plaid Cymru. The current rules relating to PEBs operated at the last general election and ensured that all parties with Westminster representation were entitled to at least one broadcast and in addition all parties contesting more than 50 seats were also entitled to one PEB. The allocation was as follows:

Labour Party	Five
Conservative Party	Five
Liberal Democrats	Four
Green Party	One
Socialist Alliance	One
Socialist Labour Party	One
UK Independence Party	One

Section 11 of the PPERA 2000 amends Section 36 of the Broadcasting Act 1990 to ensure that Channel 3, 4 and 5 licence holders must have regard to the views of the Commission before making rules regarding PPBs. The BBC and Sianel Pedwar Cymru are placed under a similar duty by virtue of section 107 of the PPERA 2000.

Section 144 of the PPERA 2000 substitutes a new Section 93 in the RPA 1983 which states that the broadcasting authorities must adopt a code of practice[37] with respect to the participation of candidates at parliamentary or local government elections in items about the constituency or local government area during the election period. The election period is defined as being, in the case of a parliamentary election, the period beginning with the dissolution of Parliament or when the intention to dissolve Parliament is announced by Her Majesty, if earlier. In the case of a by-election the period begins with the date of the issue of the writ for the by-election or the date on which a certificate of the vacancy is notified in the London Gazette in accordance with the Recess Elections Act 1975, if earlier. In the case of a local government election, the period begins with the last date for publication of notice of the election. In all cases the end of the period in question is the close of the poll on the day of the election.

Under the pre-existing section 93 of the RPA 1983, candidates could only take part in an election campaign programme about their constituency if all rival candidates also took part or agreed that the programme could be broadcast.

There is now no statutory requirement for all candidates to agree on a broadcast and the Code of Practice adopted by the broadcasting authorities follows the 1983 Act to some extent, but no longer requires the consent of all the candidates concerned. However, the candidates of the three main parties (four in Scotland, Wales and Northern Ireland) should be invited to participate in any programme and the broadcast should list all the candidates standing in that constituency. In the 2001 general election campaign, in Great Britain, there were 11 registered political parties, which were all eligible to have PEBs. The Labour and Conservative Parties, the Liberal Democrats, the UK Independence Party, the Socialist Labour Party and the Socialist Alliance had PEBs in England, Wales and Scotland; the Green Party did not broadcast in Scotland and Plaid Cymru, the Scottish National Party, the Scottish Socialist Party and the Pro-Life Alliance had broadcasts only in Scotland or Wales (they had candidates standing in at least one-sixth of constituencies in the relevant nations).

The Electoral Commission has said it may consider ending PEBs and allowing Party to broadcast short advertisements. The Commission is undertaking a review of PPBs and PEBs.

---

[37] The code adopted by the BBC is available at: http://www.bbc.co.uk/info/genelection/index.shtml

THE POLL

"The only way in which a candidate can really assist his cause on polling day is to keep himself in the public eye as much as possible, and to present a cheery and confident mien. It should be smiles all the way and a hearty word for everyone".

From: 'Modern Electioneering Practice', Henry James Houston & Lionel Valdar (Charles Knight & Co. Limited, 1922)

Under Rule 28 of the Parliamentary Election Rules, Schedule 1, Representation of the People Act 1983, poll cards must be sent to all electors, apart from postal and proxy voters (who have elected to vote by post) and overseas voters. The form which the card must take is set out in Schedule 3 to the Representation of the People Regulations 2001 (in Wales, the bilingual versions sct out in the Schedule to the Representation of the People (Welsh Forms) Order 1986 must be used) and must contain the name of the constituency, the elector's name and address and electoral registration number, the date and hours of polling and the location of the relevant polling station. On the back of the card voters are advised that they do not need to take the poll card with them to the polling station. Its production is not required in order to vote. In the case of an election which is only a Parish or Community Council election, poll cards are only sent out if the Returning Officer is requested to do so by the Parish Council, in which case they must be sent out no later than noon on the 19th day before polling day.

Polling takes place between 7am and 10pm in the case of parliamentary and European Parliamentary elections and between 8am and 9pm in the case of local elections. Where elections are combined, the longer hours apply.

More than one election can take place on the same day; for example, local government elections and a general election. Where local government elections are combined with a general election or European Parliamentary elections, any parish or community council elections must be postponed for three weeks (the Elections Act 2001 (Supplemental Provisions) (No. 2) Order 2001, brought in under the Elections Act 2001, which postponed the local elections in England, Wales and Northern Ireland until 7 June 2001, also ensured that any parish council by-elections could be held on the same day as the 2001 General Election (7 June). The Order disapplied the provisions of section 16(1) of the Representation of the People Act 1985 which states that where a general election and parish council elections fall on the same day, the latter should be postponed for three weeks).

Schools and public rooms can be used free of charge as polling stations (not Sixth Form colleges as set out in Home Office Circular, Representation of the People Act 373). All polling stations must have compartments in which electors can vote free from observation from others (Rule 25, Elections Rules, Schedule 1, RPA 1983). Section 18(2)(a) of the RPA 1983 as amended by paragraph 4(1)(a) of Schedule 4 to the RPA 1985 requires District and London Borough Councils (County and County Borough Councils in Wales) where possible, to designate as polling places only venues which are accessible to people with disabilities.

Under Rule 29 of the Election Rules, ballot boxes have to be constructed so that once inserted, ballot papers can only be retrieved by unlocking the boxes. Before polling beings, the presiding officer must show the empty ballot box to those present, so that they can verify that it is empty. The box is then locked and the presiding officer places his or her seal on it so that it can only be opened by breaking the seal. It must also be possible to ensure that they can be sealed up again at the close of the poll. Ballot boxes can be made of any material and can be any size or shape, provided they are fire resistant. They must each have a distinctive number stamped on them. Under the same Rule, the Returning Officer must provide each polling station with 'materials to enable voters to mark the ballot papers' (in most cases a blunt pencil attached to a piece of string).

A notice (as set out in the Appendix to the Parliamentary Elections Rules), which gives direction to voters has to be placed both inside and outside all polling stations.[38] Each polling station must now be provided with at least one large version of the ballot paper to be displayed inside the station for the assistance of partially sighted voters (Rule 29 of the Election Rules, RPA 1983 as amended by the RPA 2000). A notice is placed inside the ballot booth stating: 'Vote for one candidate only (for some elections a specific number of candidates may be stated). Put no other mark on the ballot paper, or your vote may not be counted'. Rule 25 of the Election Rules (RPA 1983) states that each polling station must be provided with as many compartments as necessary to ensure that voters can vote without being observed by another (it is not obligatory to provide a curtain or screen to ensure greater secrecy).

The Role of the Presiding Officer and Poll Clerks

Under Rule 26 of the Election Rules, there must be a presiding officer at each polling station (no one who has been employed by a candidate in relation to the election may be employed as a presiding officer) and as many polling clerks as necessary. They are paid, except at parish and community council elections, where they 'may' be paid. Attendance at a particular polling station may prevent a presiding officer or polling clerk from voting at their allotted polling station, in which case, the acting returning officer may authorise them to vote at any polling station, by virtue of signing a 'certificate of employment'. Alternatively, they can vote by post or proxy. Some of the duties of presiding officers are set out in statute and some have become customary over the years. These are set out below:

Duty	Statutory Provision
Showing empty ballot boxes to those in the polling station before the election, sealing it so that it can only be opened by breaking the seal	Rule 34 Parliamentary Election Rules and Local Election Rules
Placing voting booths in a suitable place in polling station	
Posting notice of directions for guidance of voters inside and outside polling station	Rule 23 (4) Local Elections Rules and Parliamentary Elections Rules, Schedule 1, Representation of the People Act 1983
Posting notice in voting booths as to maximum number of candidates for which electors can vote	Rule 23 (5) Local Elections Rules and Parliamentary Elections Rules, Schedule 1, Representation of the People Act 1983
Ensuring that everyone present at polling station has right to be there and to exclude anyone without authority to be present	Rule 26 Local Elections Rules and Parliamentary Elections Rules, Schedule 1, Representation of the People Act 1983
Ensuring that ballot papers are marked with the official mark and are placed in the ballot box	Rule 31 Local Elections Rules and Parliamentary Elections Rules, Schedule 1, Representation of the People Act 1983

---

[38] A Welsh language version can also be used at polling stations in Wales.

Assisting those who cannot see or read to mark ballot paper. Rule 39 of the Parliamentary Election Rules in Schedule of the 1983 RPA has now been replaced by Section 13(3) of the RPA 2000 which states that if a voter makes an application to the presiding officer on the grounds of blindness or other physical incapacity or inability to read, to vote with the assistance of another person – a companion – the voter must make a declaration either orally or in writing to the effect that they cannot vote without assistance. A person can assist a disabled voter to vote if he or she is the father, mother, brother, sister, husband, wife, son or daughter of the voter, is 18 years of age or over and is entitled to vote as an elector at the election.	Rule 32 Local Elections Rules and Parliamentary Elections Rules, Schedule 1, Representation of the People Act 1983
Ensuring secrecy of the ballot	Rule 25 Local Elections Rules and Parliamentary Elections Rules, Schedule 1, Representation of the People Act 1983 and Section 66
Ensuring the electoral register is marked when a ballot paper has been issued	Rule 31 Local Elections Rules
Ensuring the counterfoils of ballot papers are marked with the number of the voter as it appears on the electoral register	Rule 31 Local Elections Rules
Closing the poll, sealing the ballot boxes, putting marked copy of electoral register and counterfoils in appropriate packages and delivering ballot box and packages to the Returning Officer at the count	Rule 37 Local Elections Rules

The costs of administering general elections at local level are met by central government; however, some elements of funding are discretionary. Fees paid for election duties are subject to income tax. Rates for the 2001 General Election in Great Britain were set out in The Parliamentary Elections (Returning Officers' Charges) Order 2001 (SI 2001, No. 1736) and are set out (in summary) below:

Maximum recoverable amounts for services of a returning officer	
Returning officer's duties	£2,000
Returning officer's duties, increase for combined polls	£300
Returning officer's duties, increase payable where he or she is responsible for between three and six constituencies	£250
Returning officer's duties, increase payable where he or she is responsible for more than six constituencies	£400
Maximum amount payable in case of uncontested election	£408.11
Expenses of returning officers (maximum recoverable amounts)	
Payments to presiding officers at polling stations	£135
Increase payable when presiding officer is at polling station in constituency in London Borough	£70
Increase payable when presiding officer is at polling station in constituency adjacent to London Borough	£35
Increase payable to one presiding officer where more than one polling place is situated at one polling station	£7.50
Increase payable to presiding officer when there are combined polls	£35
Polling clerks	£80
Increase payable when polling clerk is at polling station in constituency in London Borough	£70
Increase payable when polling clerk is at polling station in constituency adjacent to London Borough	£35
Increase payable to polling clerks when there are combined polls	£20

Maximum amount payable to pay those employed in: preparing and issuing poll cards; issuing and counting postal ballot papers; assisting at the count and those providing "clerical or other assistance for the purposes of the election"	£9,500
Increase payable where a recount is called	£450
Increase payable where there are combined polls (increase in maximum amount payable for each constituency)	£1,300
Maximum amount payable in case of uncontested election	£1007.97

These rates effectively meant that a presiding officer and a polling clerk could expect £135 and £80 respectively, for a 15 hour period, with higher rates being paid in the London area and in those areas where combined polls were necessary as a result of the delay in the date of the local elections. A lump sum payment was made for staff present at the count (£9,500 per constituency and £10,800 in the case of combined polls) and £450 was payable for a recount. Part C of the Order sets out those expenses which can be claimed by the local authority, but for which there is no maximum amount recoverable; for example, travelling expenses, the costs of printing ballot papers, poll cards, etc., the costs involved in providing ballot boxes and conveying them to and from the polling stations.

The equivalent rates for Northern Ireland are set out in The Parliamentary Elections (Returning Officer's Charges) (Northern Ireland) (Amendment) Order 2001 (SI 2001, No. 1659) which amends the earlier 1997 order (SI 1997, No. 774). These rates are set out below. The returning officer for each constituency in Northern Ireland is the Chief Electoral Officer (section 26, RPA 1983).

Maximum amount payable at an uncontested election	£1,007.97
Payments to presiding officers at polling stations	£112.28
Increase payable to one presiding officer where more than one polling place is situated at one polling station	£7.45
Polling clerks	£77.32
Amount payable to pay those employed in preparing and issuing poll cards	£1.55 for every 100 cards or fraction thereof
Maximum amount payable to pay those employed in issuing and counting postal ballot papers; assisting at the count and those providing "clerical or other assistance for the purposes of the election"	£4,460.87
Maximum amount payable to pay those employed in issuing and counting postal ballot papers; assisting at the count and those providing "clerical or other assistance for the purposes of the election" where the number of entries in the register exceeds 60,000	£4,460.87 plus £48.39 for every 1,000 entries over 60,000
Maximum amount payable to pay those employed in issuing and counting postal ballot papers; assisting at the count and those providing "clerical or other assistance for the purposes of the election"	£4,460.87 plus £42.93 for every 100 voters (or faction thereof) entitled to vote by post
Increase payable where a recount is called	£387.48

Part B of the Order sets out those expenses which can be claimed by the local authority, but for which there is no maximum amount recoverable; for example, returning officers' and acting returning officers' travelling expenses, the costs of printing ballot papers, poll cards, etc., the costs involved in providing ballot boxes and conveying them to and from the polling stations. The acting returning officer has to submit accounts to the Secretary of State for the payment of any charges within 12 months of the result of the election.

Only the following are entitled to be present in a polling station during polling hours:

- ❖ Candidates and their election agents
- ❖ Polling agents appointed by candidates to attend that polling station
- ❖ Poll clerks
- ❖ The constable on duty (where necessary)
- ❖ Companions of voters with disabilities

Only one polling agent per candidate can be allowed into the polling station at any one time. The presiding officer must issue a ballot paper to anyone whose name appears on the electoral register. Under Rules 38 and 39 of the Election Rules (RPA 1983) as amended by the section 13 of the RPA 2000, voters who are blind, have another disability which renders voting without assistance difficult, or who are unable to read, can either ask for the help of the presiding officer or can vote with the help of a companion. Where a voter requests the assistance of the presiding officer, he or she then marks the voter's ballot as directed by the voter (Rule 38). The presiding officer has to complete a statement of the number of voters who have voted with his or her assistance. The alternative method of voting for an elector with a disability is to vote with the help of a qualified companion (Rule 39). The voter's companion has to make a written declaration to confirm that he or she is qualified to assist the voter and has not already assisted more than one person with disabilities to vote. The companion of a disabled voter must be an elector themselves or be the father, mother, brother, sister, husband, wife, son or daughter of the voter and be over 18 years of age.

Under common law, a person can be disqualified from voting, if they appear to the presiding officer to be an 'idiot' or 'lunatic'. Clarification of the law in this area and the end to the use of such vague terminology is clearly long overdue. A voter, perhaps with a learning difficulty, could easily appear to be confused, but nevertheless be perfectly capable of casting a vote with assistance.

Under normal circumstances, polls cannot be combined in Northern Ireland, but 2001 was an exception because of the outbreak of Foot and Mouth Disease. As a result, the local elections scheduled for 16 May were postponed until 7 June 2001. This necessitated an amendment to the 1997 Order to increase the payments to presiding officers and others. Section 5 of the Elections Act 2001 increased the amount payable to a presiding officer in the event of a combined poll by £67.25 and the amount payable to one presiding officer at a polling place at a polling station was increased by £3.02. The amount payable to poll clerks was increased by £34.80. The increases took effect regardless of whether the 1997 order was subsequently amended (which it was, by The Parliamentary Elections (Returning Officer's Charges) (Northern Ireland) (Amendment) Order 2001 (SI 2001, No. 1659)). The costs of local elections are met by the local authorities themselves.

A SECRET BALLOT?

Under Section 66 of the Representation of the People Act 1983, ballots for parliamentary, local and European elections are supposedly secret - in fact they are not. At the polling station, the elector is given a ballot paper on which is printed a serial number (also printed on the counterfoil retained by the electoral official). The elector will have previously given his or her name and address and preferably handed over his or her registration card.

The electoral official then ticks off the person's name on the electoral register, gives him or her a ballot paper and then writes his or her electoral registration number on the counterfoil of the ballot paper . It is therefore possible, although illegal under the Representation of the People Act 1983, to trace the way in which an individual elector voted. However, the counterfoils are placed in packets which are then sealed and these may only be opened by a court order. The aim of the current system is to prevent voter impersonation and fraud by allowing votes to be traced. Under Rule 20 of the Elections Rules, Schedule 1, RPA 1983, the official mark must be kept secret and a seven year period must elapse between the use of the same official mark at elections in the same constituency (five years for local government elections). Postal ballot papers must have a different official mark from other ballot papers. The official mark used for postal ballot papers is different from the mark used on other ballot papers.

The ballot paper (set out in an Appendix to the Election Rules) must contain the names and descriptions (and pictorial descriptions, if any) for which the candidates are standing. The names and descriptions of the candidates must be the **same** as those on the nomination papers. Under Rule 19 of the Election Rules, ballot papers must be capable of being folded up, have a number printed on the back and have a counterfoil with that same number printed on it. The words 'vote for one candidate only' must be printed on local and parliamentary election ballot papers (or 'vote for no more than ... candidates' in cases of local elections where wards elect more than one councillor). The order of the names on the ballot paper must be the same as in the statement of nominated candidates. The exact specifications for the design of the ballot paper are set out in the Appendix of Forms in the RPA 1983.

The acting returning officer has to ensure that each polling station has a sufficient number of ballot papers (essentially, this is enough for each of those electors registered to vote at that polling station plus some extra in case of spoilt ballot papers) and enough tendered ballot papers, which must be a different colour. The Guidance for Acting Returning Officers in England and Wales 2001 helpfully includes a list of all the items which acting returning officers should ensure are provided for all polling stations.

BALLOT BOXES	RELEVANT PARTS OF ELECTORAL REGISTER	ABSENT VOTERS LIST
LIST OF PROXIES	LIST OF POSTAL PROXIES	BALLOT PAPERS
TENDERED BALLOT PAPERS	STAMPING INSTRUMENT	VOTING DEVICE FOR BLIND & PARTIALLY SIGHTED VOTERS
STATUTORY QUESTIONS	DECLARATION FORMS FOR COMPANIONS OF VOTERS WITH DISABILITIES	FORM OF LIST OF TENDERED VOTERS
FORM OF LIST OF VOTES MARKED BY PRESIDING OFFICER	FORM OF LIST OF VOTERS WITH DISABILITIES ASSISTED BY COMPANIONS	FORM OF STATEMENT OF NUMBER OF VOTES MARKED BY PRESIDING OFFICER
FORM OF BALLOT PAPER ACCOUNT	DIRECTION FOR GUIDANCE OF VOTERS	ENLARGED VERSION OF BALLOT PAPER FOR DISPLAY AS NOTICE
VOTING COMPARTMENT NOTICES	POLLING STATION NOTICES	POLLING SCREENS
SEALING WAX AND TAPER (OR PLASTIC SEALS)	PENCILS FOR USE BY VOTERS	WRITING PAPER, BLOTTING PAPER AND ENVELOPES
ENVELOPES IN WHICH TO PLACE POSTAL BALLOT PAPERS RETURNED TO POLLING STATION	ENVELOPES FOR MAKING UP PACKETS	*The guidance also suggests that presiding officers avail themselves of a plentiful supply of paper clips, drawing pins, scissors, a ruler and tape or string!*

Tendered Ballot Papers, Impersonation and Plural Voting

Under Rule 36 of the Parliamentary Elections Rules, if a candidate, his or her agent or polling agent, informs the presiding officer that he or she suspects a person of impersonating another voter ('personation', as it is termed in the relevant legislation), he or she can ask the presiding officer (before and not after the elector concerned has voted) to ask the elector whether or not they are the person they claim to be, as set out in the register of electors and whether or not they have already voted. If they declare themselves to be the person whose entry appears in the register, they must be allowed to vote. Where the candidate, agent or polling agent concerned, agrees to substantiate the charge of personation in court, the presiding officer can order a police officer to arrest the person concerned, provided the polling agent signs a formal declaration requiring the person to be removed to policy custody. The elector in question, cannot, however, be prevented from voting.

Under Section 60 of the 1983 Act, anyone who *"commits, or aids, abets, counsels or procures the commission of the offence of personation"*, anyone who *"votes in person or by post as some other person, whether as an elector or as proxy, and whether that other person is living or dead or is a fictitious person"* is guilty of a corrupt practice. Anyone who votes in person or by post as proxy *"for a person whom he knows or has reasonable grounds for supposing to be dead or to be a fictitious person"* or when he knows or has reasonable grounds for believing that his appointment as proxy is no longer in force is guilty of a corrupt practice.

Under Rule 40 of the Election Rules, if, at the polling station, a person who appears on the electoral register and who is not registered as an absent voter (or who is named as a proxy, but is not entitled to vote by post as proxy) applies for a ballot paper after someone else has voted in person either as elector or proxy, that person is given a 'tendered ballot paper' which must be a different colour from other ballot papers and which is given to the Presiding Officer rather than being put into the ballot box. The voter's name and electoral number is written on the ballot paper. In the case of a proxy voter, the name of the proxy voter is written on the ballot paper, but the electoral number of the elector. The reason for allowing someone to vote in this way is that a mark next to a voter's name on the electoral register could have resulted from prior impersonation or from a fault on the part of a polling clerk. In this way, an elector who has been impersonated is not denied a vote, *although that vote is not counted.* In reality, tendered ballot papers are simply a means of allowing those who have been the victim of personation, an opportunity to make their mark on a ballot paper. Their votes are not actually counted. However, if the result of the election was challenged on an election petition, tendered ballot papers could be scrutinised. Where an elector, who should not have voted on the grounds of legal incapacity, is discovered to have voted, his or her vote can be rejected. If an election petition is brought after an election and a candidate is shown to have used bribery, treating or undue influence to persuade someone to vote, votes corresponding to the number of electors bribed will be deducted from his or her total. If anyone legally incapable of voting because of a previous conviction for corrupt or illegal practices, votes, their vote would be considered void and the vote of anyone found guilty of a corrupt or illegal practice at that election, would also be considered void. If an election result is challenged by an election petition the vote of someone who had impersonated another voter can be struck off. However, it is difficult to prove personation. In the case of Thompson v Dann (3 November 1994) when a proxy tried to vote he was told that the elector in question had already voted. The elector had not voted. The proxy therefore completed a tendered ballot paper. The defeated candidate felt the disputed vote should be discounted, but the successful candidate argued that it should count because it had not been proved that the vote had been cast by someone who had intentionally impersonated the elector. Both votes counted making the election results tied. Lots had to be drawn. The unsuccessful candidate was then elected.

Spoilt Ballot Papers

If a voter inadvertently spoils a ballot paper, he or she can be given a fresh one, but the original one, although cancelled, is not destroyed. At the close of the poll the presiding officer must include such papers in the total number of spoilt papers and must place them in a separate packet. Spoilt ballot papers must not be taken out of the polling station.

At the Close of Polling

After the close of the poll, under Rule 40, the Presiding Officer has to do the following:

- ❖ Seal each ballot box, but ensure the key is attached.

- ❖ Put the unused and spoilt ballot papers into a separate packet and seal them.

- ❖ Put the tendered ballot papers together into a separate packet and seal them.

- ❖ Put the marked copies of the electoral register and list of proxies into a packet and seal them.

- ❖ Put the counterfoils of the used ballot papers including spoiled ballot papers and certificates of employment into a separate packet and seal them.

- ❖ Put the tendered votes list, the list of blind voters assisted by companions, the list of votes marked by the presiding officer, a statement of the number of voters whose votes were marked by the presiding officer under the headings 'physical incapacity' and 'unable to read' and the declarations made by companions of blind voters into a packet and seal them.

All the above are then sent to the Returning Officer along with a 'ballot paper account' made by the Presiding Officer. This shows the number of ballot papers issued to his or her polling station and the number used under the following headings: ballot papers issued, unused ballot papers, spoilt ballot papers and tendered ballot papers. In the case of European Parliamentary elections, ballot papers are delivered to the verifying officer rather than the Returning Officer.

COMBINED POLLS

A poll at a general election can be combined (as it was in 2001) with local government elections or with elections to the European Parliament. Where an elector has applied for an absent vote at a local government election, before the date of a general election is known, that application is deemed to be for both elections. When two or more polls are combined, postal ballot papers must be different colours for different elections and postal ballot envelopes marked to indicate the colour of the ballot paper to be placed inside it. Only one declaration of identity is required however, to cover all the ballot papers to be returned.

Where a parliamentary general election or by-election and a European Parliamentary general election or by-election are combined, the acting returning officer for the parliamentary election has responsibility for the smooth running of both elections. Where a general election and an ordinary local election are combined, the acting returning officer for the parliamentary election has takes responsibility, but where a parliamentary and local election are combined, although there is no legal requirement to do so, the acting returning officer for the parliamentary election and the returning officer for the local election may decide amongst themselves who should take on the job. Where polls are combined, the acting returning officer is usually referred to as 'the primary returning officer'. When the polls are combined, the Election Rules contained in the RPA 1983 are modified by Regulation 100 of the Representation of the People Regulations 1986 (SI 1986, No. 1081). The same ballot box is used for the ballot papers for all the elections taking place on that day. Staff at the polling station should ask voters whether they want ballot papers for all the elections taking place that day. Voters are quite entitled to vote in only one election and not the other(s). A voter could also decide to vote in one election, return later in the day and vote in the other. Why anyone should wish to do this is hard to determine. The electoral register must be clearly marked to show which ballot papers were issued to voters. Where a local election is combined with either a parliamentary or European parliamentary election, the polling hours are between 7.00am and 10.00pm.

At the count, where the primary returning officer is the acting returning officer for the parliamentary election, only the counting agents for the parliamentary election can attend the separation of ballot papers (into ballot papers for the parliamentary election and whichever other election has taken place). Where the primary returning officer is the returning officer for a local government election, the acting returning officer for the parliamentary election counts the votes after the ballot papers for the parliamentary election have been separated from the ballot papers for the other election by the primary returning officer delivered to him. Only the counting agents for the local government election are permitted to attend the separation of the ballot papers and the verification of the ballot paper account. In reality, the primary returning officer frequently allows those counting agents who are theoretically not allowed to attend the separation and verification, to be present provided they are unlikely to impair the proceedings. Where the acting returning officer for the parliamentary election is the primary returning officer, he or she must open each ballot box in the presence of the parliamentary counting agents and record separately the number of ballot papers used in all the elections concerned. Each ballot paper account is then verified. The postal ballot papers for each election are then counted (where the issuing and reception of postal ballot papers for all the elections taking place have been combined). The ballot papers for the parliamentary election are then separated from those relating to the other election(s) and made up into packets and sealed in separate containers. These are then delivered to the returning officer for the local or European Parliamentary election along with the ballot paper accounts and a copy of the statement of the result of their verification. Packets containing the unused and spoilt ballot papers, tendered ballot papers and counterfoils of the used ballot papers and the certificates of employment are also delivered to the returning officer for the local or European Parliamentary election. The count for the parliamentary election then proceeds in the usual way.

Where the parliamentary acting returning officer is not the primary returning officer, the acting returning officer must open the containers containing the ballot papers after they have been delivered by the primary returning officer, count the postal ballot papers that have been returned, record the number counted (where the proceedings on issue and receipt were not combined) and then mix together postal and ordinary ballot papers before counting the votes in the usual manner. After the count the primary returning officer forwards to the Clerk of the Crown the tendered votes list, the list of voters with disabilities, the list of votes marked by the presiding officer and related statements, the declarations made by the companions of voters with disabilities and the packets containing the marked copies of the electoral register and the list of proxy voters.

THE COUNT

The count is where the candidates finally learn their fate; for some this will mean jubilation and for others, humiliation. The count is usually held in a central venue in the town or county in which the constituency is situated. It is quite usual for more than one count to take place in the same venue; for example, the counts for the three Croydon constituencies took place in 2001 in the Fairfield Halls in Croydon. Only those permitted to do so by the Returning Officer, under the Election Rules, can actually attend the count, but there are usually supporters, campaigners, well-wishers, etc., milling around outside the rooms where the counts are taking place, listening to the news from other constituencies and watching on television, the results from other parts of the country as they are declared. This is all very exciting for the supporters of the winning candidate(s), but there is nothing worse for the losers than to be surrounded by their opponents, cheering and clapping and generally intent on celebrating late into the night.

Under Rule 44 of the Election Rules states that every candidate (and his or her respective spouse) and his or her election agent has a right to attend the count and to appoint counting agents who may also attend the count on his or her behalf (Rule 30). The Returning Officer may limit the number of counting agents, but this must be the same for each candidate.[39] Under Rule 30, this number is the number of the Returning Officer's staff employed at the count (excluding the Returning Officer), divided by the number of candidates. Notice, in writing of counting agents at both parliamentary and European Parliamentary elections have to be given by the candidate to the Returning Officer before or on the second day before polling day (no later than the fifth day before polling day for local elections). Counting agents are usually given seats opposite the counting assistants. The Returning Officer may also appoint others to attend the count provided they will not interfere with the counting of votes (for example, partners as well as husbands and wives are usually allowed to attend). Everyone attending the count is given a copy of the secrecy provisions of Section 66 (2) and (6) of the Representation of the People Act 1983. Sufficient counting assistants (employed by the acting returning officer to count the votes) are usually appointed on a ratio of around one to every 1,500 electors on the electoral register. It is up to the acting returning officer to decide whether or not to allow the Press to attend the count, or whether just to admit them for the declaration of the result.

At the count, the Returning Officer opens each ballot box and takes out the ballot papers in the presence of the counting agents (although if the latter are not present when the count begins, it does not delay the start of the count). Each ballot box is opened and the number of ballot papers counted are recorded to ensure the number tallies with the number recorded by the Presiding Officer. Each ballot paper account has to be verified and postal ballot papers must be counted and recorded. Each ballot paper account is

---

[39] There is no limit to the number of 'counting assistants', as opposed to 'counting agents' who can be employed by the acting returning officer – a ratio of one counting assistant to every 1,500 electors on the register is suggested by the 'Guidance for Acting Returning Officers in England and Wales, 2001' (available at: www.elections.dtlr.gov.uk/index.htm). Counting assistants should be given a copy of the rules relating to secrecy at the count (section 66 (2) and (6) of the RPA 1983).

verified by comparing it with the number of ballot papers recorded, the number of unused and spoilt ballot papers and the tendered votes list. Packets containing unused and spoilt ballot papers and the tendered votes list must be opened and then resealed. A final statement is written up with the results of the verification, which the election agents can copy. Votes cannot be counted until, in the case of postal ballot papers, they have been mixed with the ballot papers from at least one ballot box, and in the case of ballot papers from a ballot box, they have been mixed with the ballot papers from at least one other ballot box. This is to ensure that it is not possible to determine how the voters in one polling district have voted. Counting begins when the Returning Officer can mix the ballot papers from one ballot box with those from another (so it is not necessary to wait for all the ballot boxes to arrive, provided one is kept to mix with the final one delivered). In some areas, the distances which ballot boxes have to travel to the count are fairly considerable, delaying the time at which a result can be declared. There is always a race to see which constituency can be the first to declare. Tendered ballot papers are not counted. As the votes are counted, the ballot papers must be kept face upwards to prevent anyone seeing the numbers printed on the back. The ballot papers are sorted into piles for each candidate and are then counted into bundles of 100. The counting agents may not touch any of the ballot papers but can point out any irregularities. Were a counting assistant is concerned about the validity of a ballot paper, it is put to one side for the Returning Officer to adjudicate upon after all the votes have been counted. He or she does this in the presence of the candidates and their agents. If the Returning Officer rejects a ballot paper; for example, if it is spoilt, a counting agent can object and have the words 'rejection objected to' marked on the paper (Rule 47(3) Parliamentary Election Rules, Schedule 1, Representation of the People Act 1983). At the end of the count, the number of votes cast for each candidate is recorded by the chief counting assistant, who gives the result to the Returning Officer, who then informs the candidates and their agents in private.

The count in Northern Ireland takes place the next day rather than overnight.

Void and Rejected Ballot Papers

The following ballot papers are considered void under the terms of Rule 47 of the Election Rules:

- ❖ Those without an official mark.
- ❖ Those on which votes have been cast for more than one candidate (applies to first past the post elections where only one candidate is to be elected).
- ❖ Those on which anything is written or marked which could identify the voter (except the number on the back of the paper).
- ❖ Those unmarked or void for uncertainty in any way.

The Returning Officer has to draw up a statement of the numbers in the above categories.

At a local government election a ballot paper would be void if an elector had voted for more candidates than the elector is entitled to vote for.

The following can be counted provided the voter's intention is clear:

- ❖ Those on which the vote is marked other than in the correct place.
- ❖ Those marked by a mark other than a cross.
- ❖ Those with more than one mark (Rules 27(2)).

Some examples might be[40]:

1	RUDGE **Barnaby Rudge** 21 Acacia Avenue Purley CR8 5BW Conservative	X	*(Emblem goes here)*	X
2	TWIST **Oliver Twist** 19 Manor Park Avenue Kenley CR8 5AP Liberal Democrat		*(Emblem goes here)*	
3	COPPERFIELD **David Copperfield** 31 Purley Park Rise Purley CR9 1AW Labour		*(Emblem goes here)*	

1	RUDGE **Barnaby Rudge** 21 Acacia Avenue Purley CR8 5BW Conservative	*(Emblem goes here)*	X
2	TWIST ~~Oliver Twist~~ 19 Manor Park Avenue Kenley CR8 5AP Liberal Democrat	*(Emblem goes here)*	
3	~~COPPERFIELD~~ David Copperfield 31 Purley Park Rise Purley CR9 1AW Labour	*(Emblem goes here)*	

---

[40] The form of the ballot paper is set out in the RPA 1983, Schedule 1, Part VI, Appendix of Forms.

1	RUDGE Barnaby Rudge 21 Acacia Avenue Purley CR8 5BW Conservative	(Emblem goes here)	√
2	TWIST Oliver Twist 19 Manor Park Avenue Kenley CR8 5AP Liberal Democrat	(Emblem goes here)	
3	COPPERFIELD David Copperfield 31 Purley Park Rise Purley CR9 1AW Labour	(Emblem goes here)	

A full consideration of the cases on which these and other decisions were based can be found in Schofields. Where a ballot paper is rejected under Rule 47, the acting returning officer must write 'rejected' on it and his or her decision is final, unless reviewed on an election petition.

A candidate or election agent can request a recount. For example, a candidate will often demand a recount if he or she is within a few votes of losing a deposit, or where the result is extremely close. Where two candidates have an equal number of votes, and any recount has taken place, under Rule 49 of the Parliamentary Election Rules, the Returning Officer must decide between the candidates by lot. Whichever candidate wins is then deemed to have received one additional vote.

Declaring the Result

Once the result is determined in a parliamentary, European or local government election, the Returning Officer must declare the result. It is usually the returning officer rather than the acting returning officer who performs this duty, provided this has been set out in writing beforehand. In some cases, the Mayor, rather than the returning officer makes the declaration; for example, in Croydon, the Mayor rather than the returning officer (the Chief Executive) reads out the results of the three parliamentary constituencies in the borough.

After the public declaration, the acting returning officer must 'return' the name of the successful candidate(s) to the Clerk of the Crown, or in the case of a European Parliamentary election, to the Secretary of State, or in the case of a local government election, to an officer of the council concerned. In the case of a parliamentary election, under Rule 51 the Returning Officer must endorse on the writ a certificate (as set out in the Election Rules). The writ along with the certificate is delivered to the postmaster of the principal post office of the constituency, who must send it first class, free of charge to the Clerk of the Crown, bearing the words, 'Election Writ and Return'. Under Rule 52, the Clerk of the Crown must then enter the name of the Member in a book, which is kept at the Crown Office.

After the count, the Returning Officer must inform the Clerk of the Crown of the name of the Member duly elected, by endorsing on the writ a certificate, which is set out in the

Appendix to the Election Rules (RPA 1983). The writ should reach the Clerk of the Crown before midday on the Sunday after the election. The acting returning officer returns the candidates' deposits immediately after the election. Lost deposits are sent to the Treasury.

The acting returning officer must put counted and rejected ballot papers into separate packets which must then be sealed. He does not open sealed packets of tendered ballot papers or the packets of counterfoils or copies of the register of electors and list of proxies. Under Rule 55 (and Regulation 91 of the 2001 Regulations) the following packets are then forwarded to the Clerk of the Crown.

❖ Uncounted ballot papers, including the following:

rejected ballot papers;

unused ballot papers, both ordinary and tendered, along with their counterfoils and the spoilt ballot papers, and

used, tendered ballot papers.

❖ Ballot paper accounts.

❖ Tendered votes list, list of voters with disabilities assisted by companions, list of votes marked by presiding officers and relevant statements and declarations made by companions of voters with disabilities.

❖ Marked copies of absent voters list, list of postal proxies, list of spoilt postal ballot papers and list of lost postal ballot papers.

❖ Marked copies of the register and lists of proxies.
❖ Counterfoils of issued ballot papers, including those for spoilt ballot papers and certificates of employment.

❖ Sealed packets containing the following:

counterfoils of issued postal ballot papers;

contents of receptacles for declarations of identity and votes rejected;

postal ballot paper envelopes and postal ballot papers marked 'rejected';

spoilt postal ballot papers and declarations of identity and ballot paper envelopes accompanying them; and

unopened covering envelopes to postal ballot papers received after close of poll or returned as undelivered.

All the above must bear a description of the contents, date of election and the name of the constituency.

Acting returning officers must also return the following:

- ❖ The statement of ballot papers rejected and not counted
- ❖ The verification of the ballot paper accounts
- ❖ The statement as to postal ballot papers

Details of the way in which the above should be sent to the Lord Chancellor's Office are set out in the Guidance for Acting Returning Officers in England and Wales 2001. If these are sent by post, a separate letter detailing the contents must also be sent. A copy of the receipt from the Post Office, showing date and time, must be retained by the Post Office. On delivery of the aforementioned to the Clerk of the Crown, he or she issues a receipt and keeps the documents for a year before destroying them. Under Rule 58 of the Election Rules, in Scotland documents are retained by the sheriff clerk of the sheriff court comprising the constituency, whereas, in Northern Ireland they are sent to the Clerk of the Crown for Northern Ireland. After a European Parliamentary election the Returning Officer retains the documents referred to above for a year before destroying them.

After a parliamentary election the Returning Officer must publish in two or more newspapers and send to election agents, notice of the time and place at which candidates' returns and declarations concerning election expenses can be inspected. These are retained for two years (one year in the case of European Parliamentary elections and parish and community council elections) at the end of which they are either destroyed or, if the candidate so requests, returned to the candidate. Returns and declarations can be inspected on payment of a fee of £5 as set out in the Representation of the People Regulations 2001 (SI 2001, No. 341) and copies of returns cost 20p for each side of each page.

PARLIAMENTARY CONSTITUENCY BOUNDARIES

There are four Boundary Commissions in the UK: one each for England, Wales, Scotland, and Northern Ireland. Their role is to review the boundaries and number of parliamentary constituencies. Since their establishment in 1944 (House of Commons (Redistribution of Seats) Act 1944), there have been four reviews, in 1955, 1974, 1983 and 1995. The rules under which their reviews are carried out are set out in the Parliamentary Constituencies Act 1986. Their reports are presented to Parliament as draft Orders in Council, which then require the approval of both Houses of Parliament. The Boundary Commission Act 1992 specified that there must be a review of constituency boundaries every eight to 12 years. As well as general reviews, the Boundary Commissions may undertake special reviews; i.e. in 1990 the electorate in Milton Keynes had increased to 101,839 and the existing constituency was divided into two as a consequence. The Speaker is the ex-officio Chairman of all four Commissions. The Deputy Chairmen of the English and Welsh Commissions are High Court Judges. There are two other members of each Commission, usually a judge, barrister or solicitor. The Deputy Chairman is unpaid, but the other two members receive some remuneration. Assistant Commissioners are appointed to chair local enquiries.

Composition of House of Commons	Number of Seats
England	529
Scotland	72
Wales	40
Northern Ireland	18
TOTAL	659

The Parliamentary Constituencies Act 1986 states that the number of constituencies shall not be substantially greater or less than 613 for England, Wales and Scotland combined. There are minimum figures set out for Scotland and Wales (71 and 35 respectively). In Northern Ireland there cannot be fewer than 16 or more than 18 constituencies. This effectively means that Scotland, Wales and Northern Ireland are over-represented, in that order. The Rules for the Redistribution of Seats are contained in Schedule 2 of the 1986 Act. Rule 8 states that the electoral quota (the approximate figure for the number of voters in any one constituency) should be the total electorate of England divided by the existing number of constituencies. Any additional seats created under rules 5 and 6 in one review are included in the divisor for calculating the quota in the next review. As a result the number of constituencies has increased after recent reviews. The electoral quota for the fifth general review, which began in February 2000 is 69,934. The Scotland Act 1998 amended rule 1 of the Rules for Redistribution of Seats contained in Schedule 2 of the 1986 Act by repealing the reference to the minima of 71 Scottish constituencies. It also stipulated that in future the Boundary Commission for Scotland apply the English electoral quota. This will have the effect of reducing the number of Scottish MPs in the Westminster Parliament by 15. However, the Commission could still take into account 'special geographical' features. This impacts on the Scottish Parliament as the Constituency MSPs are directly related to the number of Scottish MPs at Westminster. Orkney and Shetland are guaranteed two separate MSPs, irrespective of any reduction in the number of Scottish MPs at Westminster. There is also provision in the Scotland Act for the number of Regional seats to be reduced if the number of Constituency seats were to be reduced, so that the proportion of 56:73 can be maintained if possible. So, if the number of Constituency seats fell to 60, the number of Regional List seats would fall to 46. As the number of European Regions has to be eight, some Regions would have six Regional List Members and some would have five. The Commission has to ensure that Regions elect the same number of Regional List members, but where they differ, this should only be by one.

The Boundary Commissions attempt to ensure that there are similar numbers of electors within each constituency - that a vote in one Constituency should be of equal value to a vote in another - whilst attempting to respect local boundaries. The 'electoral quota' is obtained by dividing the electorate of the given area; e.g., England, by the number of constituencies. The Commissions then attempt to ensure that the electorate of any constituency is as near to the electoral quota as possible.

The number of electors on the register at the beginning of a review forms the basis of the Commissions' calculations; unfortunately, these numbers are frequently out of date by the time the Commissions' proposals actually take effect. The start of a general review, the 'enumeration' date, is the date on which a notice of the review is published in the London Gazette. The Boundary Commissions are guided by the Rules for Redistribution of Seats set out in Schedule 2 of the 1986 Act. The Rules state that every attempt should be made to ensure that constituency electorates remain as close as possible to the electoral quota, that English and Welsh Constituencies do not cross county or London borough boundaries, that Scottish Constituencies do not cross local authority boundaries and that Northern Ireland Constituencies are contained within ward boundaries. This is not always possible as the most recent boundary reviews demonstrate. The Commissions may take special geographical features into account when conducting their reviews as well as any local 'inconveniencies', which would be caused by redrawing the boundaries. The smallest unit used in constructing constituency boundaries is the district ward (electoral divisions in the Isle of Wight) and do not divide wards between constituencies. The Commissions also recommend the names of proposed constituencies.

The Boundary Commissions do not undertake a consultation exercise before making their recommendations, but must take into consideration any representations resulting from the publication of their proposals. Their proposals must be published in at least one newspaper in each constituency and must be available for inspection by the public at least one address in each constituency. Objections and 'counter proposals' should be submitted within one month. They may hold local enquiries where they consider this would be appropriate and are obliged to hold an enquiry where more than 100 electors in a constituency object (or if a local authority in the relevant area objects) to the proposals. Once an enquiry has been held, a report is produced. The Commission may or may not revise its original recommendations in the light of the representations it has received. If it does revise its proposals and produces a new report, objections may be made to the new proposals, but another enquiry need not be held, unless the Commission feels this to be necessary. If a second enquiry is held, the procedures set out above are followed again.

In most cases, the conclusions of local enquiries are simply adopted by the three working Commissioners when they meet once a month. This can lead to divergent decisions being made in different parts of the country with similar problems being resolved in a wide variety of ways. This lack of consistency is one of the problems of the current procedure.

Only the Home Secretary has the power, under Parliamentary Constituencies Act 1986, to make amendments to the Order containing the Boundary Commissions' proposals, if it is rejected by Parliament. Draft Orders in Council must be approved by both Houses, but cannot be amended by either, before being submitted to the Queen for signature. The Parliamentary Constituencies Act 1986 also contains a so-called 'ouster clause', which excludes the jurisdiction of the courts in relation to any Orders brought in under the Act. The Order has no effect until the dissolution of the Parliament during which it was approved (i.e., it has no effect until the next General Election).

The last set of boundary reviews in 1995 did not bring good news for many sitting Conservative MPs and resulted in what was known as the 'chicken run'. A number of MPs whose majorities were threatened by the boundary commission's redrawing of constituency boundaries, sought selection elsewhere. Some, however, failed to gain re-election despite finding a supposedly safer seat – Rt Hon Norman Lamont (now Lord Lamont) swapped Kingston-upon-Thames for Harrogate and John Watts moved from Slough to Reading East, but both failed to be returned to Parliament in the 1997 General Election. Others were more successful: Sir George Young Bt MP left Ealing Acton for the safer climes of Hampshire North West; Hon Nicholas Soames MP, moved from Crawley to Mid Sussex; Nick Hawkins MP, decided Surrey Heath was a safer bet than Blackpool South and Peter Bottomley MP left South East London's Eltham and moved to Worthing West on the south coast.

The four Boundary Commissions began work on the last boundary reviews between February, 1991 and March, 1993. England gained five seats, Wales two and Northern Ireland one. In general terms, rural areas gained at the expense of urban constituencies. Greater London lost 10 seats and some of the new constituencies created by the Commission cut across the boundaries of some London Boroughs. England now has 529 seats, Wales, 40, Scotland 72 and Northern Ireland 18.

The Electoral Commission, established under Part I of the Political Parties, Elections and Referendums Act 2000, will eventually take on the functions of the former Boundary Commissions and the local Government Commission (LGC) for England and the Local Government Boundary Commission for Wales. The transfer will not take place until after the four Parliamentary Boundary Commissions have completed their fifth general reviews, although the LGC may merge with the Commission in April 2002. Section 14 of the PPERA 2000 sets out the main functions of the Electoral Commission in relation to establishing the boundaries of parliamentary constituencies and local government areas. The Commission must establish four Boundary Committees: for England, Scotland, Wales and Northern Ireland. Each Boundary Committee has to consist of a chairman, who must be one of the Electoral Commissioners and two other members who must be either Electoral Commissioners or Deputy Electoral Commissioners. Section 14(3)(b) provides for that number to be increased to four other members when the functions of a Local Government Boundary Commission are transferred to a Boundary Committee. Subsection 6 provides for the following to be appointed as assessors to the Boundary Committees:

❖ In the case of the Boundary Committee for England and the Boundary Committee for Wales, the Registrar General for England and Wales and the Director General of Ordnance Survey.

❖ In the case of the Boundary Committee for Scotland, the Registrar General of Births, Deaths and Marriages for Scotland and the Director General of Ordnance Survey.

❖ In the case of the Boundary Committee for Northern Ireland, the Registrar General of Births and Deaths in Northern Ireland, the Commissioner of Valuation for Northern Ireland and the Chief Electoral Officer for Northern Ireland.

Section 16 of the Act provides for the functions of the existing boundary commissions to be transferred to the Electoral Commission. Section 18 of the Act provides for the transfer, by order, of the functions of the Local Government Commission for England to the Electoral Commission. The Local Government Commission was set up under the Local Government Act 1992 to review local government areas in England. Section 19 gives Scottish Ministers the power to transfer the functions of the Local Government Boundary Commission for Scotland to the Electoral Commission, Section 20 transfers the functions of the Local Government Boundary Commission for Wales to the Electoral Commission.

More information about the Boundary Commissions can be found at: www.statistics.gov.uk/pbc/.

BY-ELECTIONS

By-elections are held in order to fill vacancies in the House of Commons arising from the death of a Member, an MP's retirement from the House (known as 'taking the Chiltern Hundreds'), a Member's elevation to the peerage or declaration of bankruptcy, or on the occasion of an MP being declared of unsound mind under the Mental Health Act 1983. Technically, any Member of the House of Commons can 'move the writ' for a by-election and on occasion this has been used as a delaying tactic by MPs attempting to prevent a particular item of business from being reached, but in practice, such writs are usually moved by the Chief Whip of the Party which held the vacated seat. Technically, any such motion is an 'order of the House' to the Speaker to make out his warrant for the issue of a writ for the election of a new member to fill a vacancy' (Erskine May 'Parliamentary Practice', 22nd Edition, page 286[41]). In 1973 a Speaker's Conference recommended a

[41] Erskine May's Parliamentary Practice is the 'bible' of parliamentary procedure. In addition to the Standing Orders of the House of Commons, it is the definitive source of guidance on parliamentary

time limit of three months within which the writ for a by-election should be moved (Cm 5500, December 1973). Technically, as the motion for a new writ is a matter of privilege, no notice has to be given by a Member of his or her intention to move the writ. Members may also move amendments to such a motion. On 21 Februrary 1990, the House agreed that if a writ was moved on a Friday when Private Members' business had precedence, and was opposed, the motion to move the writ would lapse enabling debate to proceed with Private Members' Bills. Once a motion to move the writ has been voted on and defeated, the same motion, relating to the same constituency, could not be moved again in the same Session of Parliament.

If a seat becomes vacant during a parliamentary recess, the Speaker can issue a warrant for a writ under certain circumstances. Under the Recess Election Act 1975, if the seat is vacated either because a Member is elevated to the peerage, or because he or she has become bankrupt, the writ can be moved during a recess, provided two MPs certify the seat is vacant and six days notice is given in the London Gazette. However, the warrant cannot be issued, if the House is scheduled to return within that time. If a Member dies during the recess, the warrant to issue the writ cannot be made unless notification of the death was brought to the Clerk of the Crown's office 15 days before the end of the last sitting of the House. Nor could the warrant be issued if after taking into account the six days notice which needs to be made in the London Gazette, the House would be sitting again. A by-election cannot take place during a recess in those cases where a Member has resigned or been detained under the Mental Health Act 1959 as amended by the Mental Health (Amendment) Act 1982. In the latter case, where an MP has been detained on the grounds of mental illness, a by-election can only take place if two psychiatrists declare, after visiting the MP on two occasions, six months apart, that the said MP is indeed suffering from some form of mental illness. Where an MP becomes bankrupt, he or she has six months grace, but if after that time a Certificate of Bankruptcy is issued to the Speaker by the Court, the seat will be declared vacant and a by-election called. Where a Member resigns (takes the 'Chiltern Hundreds'[42]) during a recess, the seat is vacated, but no writ can be issued until the House re-assembles).

A writ issued for a by-election would be superseded by the calling of a General Election (although this is not set out in statute) as a Member could not be elected to a Parliament which did not exist! If a by-election was due to be held on a day between the announcement of a General Election and the date of Parliament's dissolution, a Returning Officer could decide to let the by-election go ahead, particularly if the House was sitting on

---

practices and procedural devices. It is now in its 22nd edition, having first been published in 1844. Quite clearly, it is no longer edited by its originator, Thomas Erskine May, himself a Clerk in the House of Commons, but by Sir Donald Limon KCB, Clerk of the House of Commons and W R McKay CB, the Clerk Assistant. The latest edition, the 22nd was published in 1997 by Butterworths. The first edition was apparently described by the Times as 'a popular work ... a compact and compendious volume'. To describe it as popular today, might be something of an overstatement, but compendious it certainly is. It is a vital reference work for anyone seriously interested in following the minutiae of parliamentary life.

[42] MPs technically cannot resign their seats in Parliament. In order to evade this restriction, any MP wishing to resign accepts an'office of profit under the Crown', legally obliging him or her to resign and allowing a by-election to be called. There are certain offices which cannot be held by Members of the House of Commons (these are set out in the House of Commons Disqualification Act 1975) and two are reserved for those wishing to resign. These are the office of Steward or Bailiff of Her Majesty's three Chiltern Hundreds of Stoke, Desborough and Burnham and the office of the Steward of the Manor of Northstead. The offices are given by the Chancellor of the Exchequer and are awarded alternately in order to allow two MPs to resign at the same time. Those granted the offices retain them until another MP wishes to retire.

the day of the by-election. The Speaker appoints a 'Speaker's Panel' as soon as possible after taking office, consisting of no more than seven and no less than three Members of the House of Commons, who can exercise the Speaker's powers under the Act at any time when there is no Speaker or the Speaker is not in the country. Appointments remain in force until the dissolution of the Parliament in which they are made.

BY-ELECTION TIMETABLE

Day	Procedure	Timing
0	Issue of writ	As soon as possible after the issue of the warrant for the writ
1	Receipt of writs by returning officers	The day after the writ is issued
3	Notice of the Election	No later than 4pm on second day after the writ has been received
6 - 8	Delivery of candidates' nomination papers and delivery of notices of candidates' withdrawal	Between 10am and 4pm on any day after date of publication of notice of election, but no earlier than 3rd day after and not later than the 7th day after that on which writ was received.
	Making of objections to nomination papers	Objections to nomination papers handed in up to 4pm on the day before the last day for delivery, must be made between 10am and noon on the morning of the last day of delivery, but objections to papers handed in between 4pm on the day before the last day for delivery and 4pm on the last day, can be objected to until 5pm on that day. Under Rule 15(2) Where a Returning Officer thinks a candidate may be disqualified for nomination under the Representation of the People Act 1981 (under the provisions of this Act, anyone sentenced to more than one year's imprisonment is disqualified from membership of the House of Commons during the period of imprisonment) objections can be made between 10am and 4pm on the day after the last day for delivery of nomination papers.
	Publication of statement of persons nominated	At close of time for making objections to nomination papers
	Last day of receipt of absent voting applications	5pm on 6th day before polling day
	Last day for postal voters to apply for replacement for lost ballot paper	4th day before polling day
	Last day for appointment of polling and counting agents	2nd day before polling day
	Last day for replacement of lost or spoilt ballot papers	5pm on day before polling day
15-19	Polling Day	Between 7am and 10pm on a day set by the Returning Officer, no earlier than the 8th day, nor later than the 10th after the last day for delivery of nomination papers

ELECTION OFFENCES

This section covers 'corrupt' and 'illegal' practices, other election offences, as defined in the RPA 1983 (as amended), and the ways in which an election result can be challenged. Unlike other sections in this Chapter, this section also refers to provisions covering local as well as parliamentary elections. The provisions relating to election offences are applied to elections to the Scottish Parliament, the Welsh Assembly and the Northern Irish Assembly by means of regulations, which are considered in the Chapters relating to those bodies. The Greater London Assembly is considered a local authority for the purposes of legislation relating to election offences.

Corrupt Practices

The distinction between 'corrupt' and 'illegal' practices in electoral law is now rather blurred. The distinction used to be between corrupt acts which were perpetrated with malicious intent and illegal ones which were illegal as a result of being prohibited in statute rather than being carried out with intent, or by default. The penalties for those found guilty of corrupt and illegal practices, as set out in the RPA 1983, have recently been amended by the PPERA 2000 and are considered below in the section entitled: 'Penalties for Corrupt and Illegal Practices.'

Bribery and Treating

Bribery is a statutory offence under section 113 of the RPA 1983. This states that a person is guilty of bribery if he or she:

❖ gives any money[43] to, or 'procures any office' for any voter or any other person on behalf of any voter or any other person, in order to induce any voter to vote or refrain from voting; or, does so after a person has voted or not voted, or does so in order to induce someone to procure the vote of another person or does so in order to try and secure the election of a particular candidate.

Accepting such a bribe, either before or after an election, is also an offence under section 113 of the 1983 Act.

At common law, treating is considered corrupt if it can be demonstrated that it had such a corrupt influence on the election that it could not be considered a free election. If proven, it invalidates the election result. Section 114 of the RPA 1983 specifically states that treating is a corrupt practice if *"either before during or after an election, directly or indirectly"* a person *"gives or provides, or pays wholly or in part the expense of giving or providing, any meat, drink, entertainment or provision to or for any person (a) for the purpose of corruptly influencing that person or any other person to vote or refrain from voting; or, (b) on account of that person having voted or refrained from voting, or being about to vote or refrain from voting"*. The recipient of such treating would also be considered to have committed a corrupt practice.

---

[43] References to giving money are taken to mean giving, lending, agreeing to lend, offering, promising or promising to, or trying to procure money or 'valuable consideration'.

Undue Influence

'Undue influence' is a corrupt practice as defined by section 115(2) of the RPA 1983. This defines a person as being guilty of using undue influence if he or she:

❖ *(a) "directly or indirectly, by himself or by any other person on his behalf, makes use of or threatens to make use of any force, violence or restraint, or inflicts or threatens to inflict, by himself or by any other person, any temporal or spiritual injury, damage, harm or loss upon or against any person in order to induce or compel that person to vote or refrain from voting, or on account of that person having voted or refrained from voting"* or

❖ *(b) "if, by abduction, duress or any fraudulent device or contrivance, he impedes or prevents the free exercise of the franchise of an elector or proxy for an elector, or so compels, induces or prevails upon an elector or proxy for an elector either to vote or to refrain from voting."*

The section goes on to state that the use of *"abduction, duress or any fraudulent device or contrivance"* to impede or prevent someone from voting constitutes undue influence. It is not always necessary for the use of undue influence to be successful for a corrupt practice to have been committed. In the case of R v Rowe, ex parte Mainwaring (4 All ER 821, CA 1992) the Liberals in Tower Hamlets sent out mock Labour Party leaflets, entitled 'Labour News', on which the Liberal agent's name was printed in small letters. In the three wards where the leaflets were delivered, the Liberals won by small majorities and were challenged by the defeated Labour candidates who alleged undue influence under section 115(2)(b) of the RPA 1983. The Local Government Election Commissioner decided against the Labour candidates on the basis that although some electors might have been taken in, the election had not been impeded. On judicial review, this was held to be incorrect and it was said that there had been a deliberate attempt to try and confuse Labour voters. The Liberals then appealed and the Court of Appeal held that the leaflet was a 'fraudulent device' (R v Local Government Election Commissioner, ex parte Mainwaring and others) but that it was not possible to show 'beyond reasonable doubt' that voters had been 'impeded' in voting. The appeal was therefore allowed.

Personation

'Personation' (Impersonating another elector) is a corrupt practice under Section 60 of the Representation of the People Act 1983. This includes *intentionally* purporting to be another elector, or their proxy (whether that person is alive or dead or is indeed fictitious) either by voting in person, or by post. Anyone voting by proxy (either in person or by post) for a person he or she knows, or has reasonable grounds for supposing, to be dead or to be a fictitious person, or, when he or she knows, or has reasonable grounds for supposing that his appointment as proxy is no longer in force, is guilty of the offence of personation. Under section 168(1)(a)(i) of the RPA 1983, someone convicted on indictment of impersonating a voter, is liable to imprisonment for a term of up to two years or a fine or both or, under section 168(1)(b), on summary conviction to a term of imprisonment of up to six months, or a fine not exceeding the statutory maximum, or both.

False Statements in Nomination Papers

Under section 65A of the RPA 1983 as amended by the RPA 2000, a person is guilty of a corrupt practice if he or she includes in any document submitted to the returning officer in connection with the election, a false statement concerning any candidate's name or address. It is also a corrupt practice to forge the signature of a proposer, seconder or backer of any candidate on a nomination paper. This applies both to local and parliamentary elections.

Illegal Practices

Displaying Election Notices

Under section 109(1) of the RPA 1983, it is an offence to pay an elector to display an election notice promoting a particular candidate, unless it is their *"ordinary business"*; for example, a company providing poster sites. The person in receipt of the payment is guilty of an offence only if he or she knew the practice to be prohibited under the Act.

Providing Money for Illegal Purposes

Under section 112 of the RPA 1983, where someone *"knowingly provides money"* for any payment which is contrary to the provisions of the Act, or for any expenses incurred in excess of the maximum amount allowed under the Act, or for replacing any money expended in any such payment or expenses, except where permitted under section 167 of the Act, they are guilty of making an illegal payment.

Inducing a Candidate to withdraw from an Election

Under section 107 of the RPA 1983, a payment made to a candidate to induce him or her to withdraw from an election is an illegal payment. The candidate who agrees to withdraw from the election is also guilty of having accepted an illegal payment.

Illegal Employment of Canvassers

Under section 111 of the RPA 1983, the illegal offence of employing canvassers carries a penalty on summary conviction of a fine up to level 3 on the standard scale.

False Statements Concerning Candidates

Under section 106(5) of the RPA 1983, the following are illegal practices:

❖ Publishing a false statement about a candidate's personal character or conduct, unless there were reasonable grounds for believing it *(the candidate who publishes the statement is not liable where the offence is committed by his or her agent and the candidate has not authorised it).*[44]

---

[44] The candidate about whom such a statement has been made can seek an injunction in the High Court or County Court preventing any repetition of the allegations, providing there is prima facie proof they are false.

❖ Publishing a false statement that a candidate has withdrawn from the election *(a candidate making such a statement is not liable where this offence is committed "by his agent other than his election agent").*

Disrupting a Meeting

Under Section 97(1) of the RPA 1983, it is an illegal practice to disrupt an election meeting (special provisions apply in Northern Ireland) – heckling the speaker, however irritating, does not constitute disruption.

Voting Offences

Under Section 61 of the 1983 Act as amended by the 1985 Act, the following are offences:

❖ Voting or attempting to vote (either in person or by post) either as an elector or as a proxy if subject to a legal incapacity to vote at a parliamentary or local government election.

❖ Applying for a proxy vote if subject to a legal incapacity to vote at a parliamentary or local government election.

❖ Applying for a proxy vote if the proxy is subject to a legal incapacity to vote at a parliamentary or local government election.

❖ Voting as a proxy for a person subject to a legal incapacity to vote at a parliamentary or local government election.

❖ Voting more than once in the same constituency at a general election or more than once in the same electoral area at a local government election (unless as a proxy). *

❖ Voting in more than one constituency at a general election or in more than one ward/electoral area in a local government area in which there is more than one ward/electoral area being contested. *

❖ Voting as a proxy for an elector who already has a proxy in place in another constituency at a general election or in another electoral area at a local government election. *

❖ Voting as a proxy for the same elector more than once in the same constituency at a general election or more than once in the same electoral area at a local government election. *

❖ Voting as a proxy for the same elector in more than one constituency at a general election or in more than one electoral area in a local government election. *

❖ Voting in person as proxy for an elector at a parliamentary or local government election when entitled to vote by post as proxy.

❖ Voting in person as proxy at a parliamentary or local government election knowing the elector has already voted.

❖ Voting as an elector in person at a parliamentary or local government election when already entitled to vote by post.

❖ Voting as an elector in person at a parliamentary or local government election, knowing that a person appointed to vote as proxy has already either voted by person or by post.

❖ Applying for a proxy vote without cancelling a previous appointment of a proxy, which is still in force in that or another constituency at a parliamentary election, or electoral area at a local government election.

❖ Voting as proxy for more than two people who are not the proxy's husband, wife, parent, grandparent, brother, sister, child or grandchild at a parliamentary or local government election.

not applicable to elections to the Greater London Assembly (see below)

The following offences were added to section 61 of the RPA 1983 by Schedule 3, paragraph 10 of the Greater London Authority Act 1999 and relate specifically to elections to the GLA:

❖ Voting more than once at the same election for the Mayor of London.

❖ Voting more than once at the same election of the London members of the Assembly at an ordinary election.

❖ Voting more than once in the same Assembly constituency at the same election of a constituency member of the Assembly.

❖ Voting in more than one Assembly constituency at the same ordinary election.

❖ Voting in any Assembly constituency at an ordinary election, or an election of the Mayor of London, under section 16 of the Greater London Authority Act 1999 (a by-election), when a proxy has already been appointed to vote in another constituency.

❖ Voting more than once at the same election for Mayor of London.

❖ Voting more than once at the same election of the London members of the Assembly at an ordinary election.

❖ Voting more than once in the same Assembly constituency at the same election of a constituency member of the London Assembly.

❖ Voting in more than one Assembly constituency at the same ordinary election.

It is also an offence to 'knowingly induce' someone to commit any of the offences set out above. A candidate would be considered to have committed an illegal practice if his or her agent had attempted to induce someone to commit any of the above offences. A candidate would not be liable for an illegal practice as set out above, if the offence had been perpetrated by his agent(s), unless the agent(s) had knowingly induced a person to commit one of the above offences.

Offences Related to Election Expenses

Unauthorised expenses may constitute either corrupt or, in some cases, illegal practices.

Section 73 of the RPA 1983, as amended by the PPERA 2000, states that no payment in respect of election expenses can be made by a candidate during an election, except by that candidate's agent. To make such a payment constitutes an *illegal* practice. The section does not apply to candidates' personal expenses. New section 74A of the RPA 1983, as inserted by the PPERA 2000, states that in additional to personal expenses, expenses incurred *"by or on behalf of a candidate otherwise than for the purpose of the candidate's election"* do not fall within the remit of section 73. However, only candidates, their agents, or those authorised in writing by agents, may incur election expenses and incurring, aiding, abetting, or procuring anyone else to incur election expenses is a *corrupt* practice under Section 75(5) of the 1983 Act. Where an officer of an association is accused of such an offence, it is a defence under the Act if the offence took place without his or her consent or knowledge. Section 75 of the RPA 1983 was amended by the Greater London Authority Act 1999 to cover the expenses of candidates standing as London Members as well as individual candidates. Section 75 states that no expenses in connection with *"promoting or procuring the election of a candidate"* may be incurred by anyone other than the candidate, his or her election agent and those authorised in writing by the election agent, where that expenditure relates to holding public meetings, issuing advertisements or publications or presenting the views of the candidate to the electorate (this does not restrict newspapers or broadcasters from reporting the election). Claims for expenses must be submitted within 21 days after the day on which the result of the election Is declared. Anyone who *"incurs, or aids, abcts, counsels or procures any other person to incur any expenses in contravention"* of the section is guilty of an *illegal* practice, but a candidate is not liable if the offence was committed by an agent without his consent.

Section 76 of the RPA sets out the limits on candidates' election expenses in parliamentary and local elections. Spending in excess of the specified amounts constitutes an *illegal* practice.

Under section 81 of the RPA 1983 (as amended by the Greater London Authority Act 1999 and the PPERA 2000) candidates' returns must be submitted within 35 days after the day on which the election result is declared (70 days in the case of the election of London Mayor and the London members of the GLA). Knowingly making a false declaration of election expenses is a corrupt practice under section 82(6) of the RPA 1983.

Section 84 of the RPA 1983 states that the failure to send in either a return (section 81) or a declaration of expenses under section 82 constitutes an illegal practice. Under section 85, where an elected candidate fails to deliver a return and declaration of expenses within the period allowed, he or she incurs a penalty of £100 for each day he or she continues to sit and vote in the House of Commons (£50 in the case of a local authority). Under section 85A of the RPA 1983 as amended by the Greater London Authority Act 1999, failure to send in a return and declaration in the case of the election of London Mayor would result in the candidate in question being disqualified from either being elected or being Mayor.

In summary, the following are election expenses:

❖ Failure on the part of a candidate or election agent to make a return or declaration of election expenses is an illegal practice.

❖ Spending over the maximum permitted limit.

❖ With exceptions for personal expenses, making payments through someone other than the election agent.

❖ Providing money for election expenses, other than to the candidate or his or her agent.

❖ Paying election expenses outside the permitted time limit.

If a candidate or his or her election agent has not complied with statutory provisions relating to election expenses, either the candidate or agent can apply to the High Court or election court or County Court to gain exemption from any penalties. The DPP must be notified. Relief can be granted on the grounds of illness or where the candidate is the applicant, the illness, absence, misconduct or death or his or her agent, sub-agent or officer. Relief can also be granted if an omission relating to election expenses was due to a 'reasonable cause'. Where a candidate can show that any act or omission on the part of his or her election agent was done without the sanction of the candidate and that he or she attempted to prevent it, relief is granted to the candidate, but the candidate will usually have to send in a modified return within a set period of time (section 86, RPA 1983).

Forgery and Perjury

Forging official papers, such as ballot papers or nomination papers is an offence under the Forgery and Counterfeiting Act 1981. Making a false statement in answer to the questions which the Presiding Officer at a polling station is entitled to make (for example, asking electors whether they are the person stated on the electoral register), is an offence of perjury under the Perjury Act 1911. Making a false declaration of election expenses is also an offence under the 1911 Act. On summary conviction a fine can be imposed up to level 5 on the standard scale. Other instances of forgery or using a false instrument can result on summary conviction in a fine up to the statutory maximum, or a term of up to six months' imprisonment or both and on indictment to a fine, or 10 years imprisonment, or both.

Broadcasting from Outside the UK

Under Section 92 of the RPA 1983, it is an illegal practice to broadcast any party political material designed to influence voting in a UK election, from a broadcasting station outside the UK.

Imitation Poll Cards

It is an illegal practice under section 94 of the RPA 1983 to issue any poll card or document which so closely resembles a poll card that it is *calculated to deceive* the electors.

Other Election Offences

Offences Relating to Declarations

Under Section 62 of the 1983 Act, it is an offence to make a declaration of local connection, under Section 7B of the Act (as amended by the RPA 2000), or a service declaration, under Section 15, if subject to a legal incapacity to vote. It is also an offence to make a false statement in such a declaration. It is an offence to attest a patient's declaration or a service declaration if not authorised to do so. It is also an offence to attest a service declaration, when not authorised to do so or knowing it contains a false statement. The penalty, on summary conviction, is a fine not exceeding level 5 on the standard scale.

Breach of Official Duty

Under section 63 of the RPA 1983, if any of the following officers are in breach of their official duties, *"without reasonable cause"*, they are liable, on summary conviction to a fine not exceeding level 5 on the standard scale. However, no such official is liable to any penalty at common law and cannot be sued for damages. The following officials are:

* Clerk of the Crown, or Clerk of the Crown for Northern Ireland

* Any Sheriff Clerk, Registration Officer, Returning Officer or Presiding Officer

* Any other person whose duty it is to be responsible after a local government election for the used ballot papers and other documents (including returns and declarations)

* Any Postmaster

* Any deputy of any of the above or anyone appointed to assist (or who in the course of his or her employment does assist) a person mentioned above

Election Literature

Schedule 18, paragraph 14 of the PPERA 2000 substituted a new section for the existing section 110 of the RPA 1983. Under the provisions of the section, all election material had to include the name and address of the printer, promoter and publisher. The Schedule also contained detailed provisions on where those names and addresses should appear on any publications. Section 143 of the PPERA 2000 included similar provisions for all national election material (there were no such provisions in the RPA 1983). On summary conviction this would have attracted a fine up to level 5 on the standard scale. However, after a Commencement Order enacted the new measures included in the PPERA 2000, several political parties complained that they had already printed a large amount of election material, which would, as a result or the Order, be redundant. As a result, the Government decided to delay the implementation of the aforementioned measures.

As the Political Parties, Elections and Referendums Act 2000 (Commencement No 1 & Transitional Provisions) Order 2001 (SI 2001, No. 222) had already implemented the relevant sections of the PPERA 2000, new legislation was required. The result was the Elections Publications Act 2001, which deferred the introduction of the measures in the

PPERA 2000. The effect of section 1 of the Elections Publications Act was to undo the commencement of section 143 and paragraph 14 of Schedule 18 to the PPERA 2000 and to restore Section 110 of the RPA 1983. These sections of the PPERA 2000 were therefore deemed not to have come into effect. As a result of the Elections Publications Act, no specific imprint requirements applied to national election material. However, the provisions of the Newspapers, Printers and Reading Rooms Repeal Act 1869 still applied under which *"any paper or book whatsoever which shall be meant to be published or dispersed"* is required to have the name and address of the printer imprinted on the front (in the case of a single page document) or on the first or last page (in the case of longer documents). This allowed publication of material that complied either with the old section 110 in the RPA 1983 or the new provisions in PPERA 2000. This led to some confusion about whether an imprint on a publication was legal or not. Section 2 of the Elections Publications Act 2000 allowed the Secretary of State to re-commence, by order, section 143 and paragraph 14 of Schedule 18 to the PPERA 2000.

Nomination Papers, Ballot Papers and Ballot Boxes

Under Section 65 of the 1983 Act the following are offences:

❖ Fraudulently defacing or destroying nomination papers, ballot papers, the official mark on a ballot paper, a declaration of identity or an official envelope used in postal voting.

❖ Supplying ballot papers without authorisation.

❖ Putting papers other than ballot papers into a ballot box.

❖ Taking a ballot paper out of the polling station or (without authority) destroying, taking, opening or interfering with any ballot box or ballot papers.

If any of the following officers is found guilty of any of the above offences it can result on indictment in a term of up to two years imprisonment, or a fine, or both, or on summary conviction, in imprisonment for a term of up to six months, or a fine up to the statutory maximum[45] or both. The officers concerned are: a returning officer, verifying officer, presiding officer or clerk. If another other person is convicted of any of these offences he or she faces possible imprisonment on summary conviction, of a term of up to six months, or a fine up to level 5 on the standard scale, or both.

Secrecy

Returning officers, presiding officers, clerks, candidates and election agents must, when present at the polling station, attempt to ensure the secrecy of the ballot. They must not, under Section 66 of the RPA 1983:

❖ Reveal the name of an elector or proxy who has or has not applied for a ballot paper or voted at a polling station.

❖ Reveal the number on the register of electors of any elector who, or whose proxy, has or has not applied for a ballot paper or voted at a polling station.

---

[45] As set out in Section 32(9) of the Magistrates' Court Act 1980

❖ Reveal any information relating to the official mark on the ballot paper.

❖ Attempt to discover the number on the back of any ballot paper at the count.

❖ Attempt to communicate to anyone any information obtained at the count as to the candidate for whom any vote is given on any ballot paper.

❖ Attempt to intervene when a voter is voting.

❖ Attempt to discover which candidate a voter is about to or has voted for (at a polling station).

❖ Communicate any information as to the candidate for whom an elector has voted.

❖ Communicate any information as to the number on the back of the ballot paper given to any voter.

❖ Induce a voter to show his ballot paper after it has been marked.

Those attending the issue or receipt of postal votes must not do any of the following:

❖ Communicate any information about the number on the back of any ballot paper.

❖ Communicate any information relating to the official mark.

❖ Attempt to discover for which candidate any given voter has voted.

No one assisting a disabled person to vote must communicate to anyone else, any information about the candidate for whom that voters intends to vote, or has voted, or any information about the number on the back of the ballot paper.

Anyone contravening section 66, is liable on summary conviction to a fine not exceeding level 5 on the standard scale or up to 6 months' imprisonment.

Electoral Register

Part III of the Representation of the People (England and Wales) Regulations 2001[46], sets out the powers available to registration officers in gathering information needed to compile the electoral register. Anyone failing to comply with such requests for information is liable on summary conviction to a fine not exceeding level 3 on the standard scale.

Falsely Acting as Agent

The following may not act as election agents (Section 99 Representation of the People Act 1983):

---

[46] The same provisions are applied to Scotland by the Representation of the People (Scotland) Regulations 2001 (SI 2001, No. 497 (S. 2)) and to Northern Ireland by the Representation of the People (Northern Ireland) Regulations 2001 (SI 2001, No. 400).

> ❖ Returning officers
> ❖ Officers and clerks appointed under the Election Rules

Canvassing

Under section 100 of the RPA 1983, police officers may not canvass or attempt to persuade voters to vote for particular candidates. The penalty is a fine not exceeding level 3 on the standard scale, on summary conviction.

Publication of Exit Polls

Under section 66A of the RPA 1983 as inserted by Schedule 6, paragraph 6 of the RPA 2000, the publication of exit polls before the close of polling is an offence, liable on summary conviction to a fine not exceeding level 5 on the standard scale or to imprisonment for a term not exceeding six months.

Penalties for Corrupt and Illegal Practices

Election Petitions

Except for the provisions of the House of Commons Disqualification Act 1975, the only way to unseat a successful candidate in a parliamentary election is by means of an parliamentary election petition, as set out in Part III of the 1983 Act. Since 1888, election petitions have been heard, in England, by the Election Court - basically a Divisional Court of the Queen's Bench Division of the High Court (consisting of two judges), by the High Court of Justice in Northern Ireland and the Court of Session in Scotland. The Election Court has the power to order a recount, disqualify a candidate from membership of the House of Commons and declare the runner-up the winner, declare the election void or declare that there have been 'corrupt or illegal practices'.

Section 121 of the RPA 1983 states that a parliamentary election petition can be presented by one of the following:

> ❖ A voter or someone who had the right to vote at the election concerned
> ❖ A person claiming to have had a right to be elected or returned at the election
> ❖ A person alleging to have been a candidate at the election

A parliamentary election petition is presented to the High Court, the Court of Session or the High Court of Northern Ireland in the form set out in the Election Petition Rules 1960[47]. Three copies of the petition must also be presented, one of which is sent to the Returning Officer of the constituency concerned, where it is published. An election petition is not tried by a jury but by two judges, who are collectively referred to as the 'election court'. The trial has to take place in the constituency where the election

---

[47] The Election Petition Rules 1960 (SI 1960, No. 543), were amended by The Election Petition (Amendment) Rules 1999 (SI 1999, No. 1352 (L. 14)) which govern the form, content and manner of presentation of election petitions. The amended order was necessary to take into account the implementation of the Civil Procedure Rules 1998. The Rules are made by the Civil Procedure Rule Committee (the 'authority' referred to in section 182 of the RPA 1983) and the power conferred on them to make such rules, is exercisable by statutory instrument and is treated as if conferred on a Minister of the Crown.

concerned took place, unless the High Court specifies it should be held elsewhere. Notice of the trial must be given 14 days before the trial date. A shorthand writer from the House of Commons (Gurneys) must attend the trial to record the evidence. When an election petition is presented, the petitioner must 'give security' for costs up to an amount not exceeding £5,000 in the case of a parliamentary election and £2,500 in the case of a local election (section 136(2) RPA 1983). Within five days the petitioner must send a copy of the petition to the respondent (usually the candidate whose election is disputed or the Returning Officer).

The petition must be presented within 21 days of the election; however, if the petition alleges a 'corrupt' payment of money has been made since the election, the time limit is 28 days after the date of the alleged payment. Where an election petition relates to an allegation of an illegal practice it can be presented within 21 days after the day specified in Section 122(3)(a) of the RPA 1983 or where the petition relates to a payment of money or some other act, within a period of 28 days after the date on which the illegal practice was said to have occurred. The day specified in Section 122(3)(a) is the 10th day after the end of the time allowed for the delivery to the returning officer of the return of election expenses, or the day on which the Returning Officer actually receives the return and declarations as to election expenses, or where the return and declarations are received on different days, the last of those days, or where there is a valid excuse for failing to make the return and declarations, the day when the excuse is allowed. If the petition relates to an act said to have been carried out after the specified day, then the petition can be presented within 28 days. The provisions above also apply to cases of expenses having been paid without proper authorisation by an election agent.

Local elections can also be questioned by means of an election petition. Such a petition may be presented by either four or more voters (or those who could have voted) or by a person alleging to have been a candidate at the election. The petition must be presented within 21 days of the election unless it alleges that a payment or money or other reward has been made or promised since the election by an elected candidate, in which case the time limit is 28 days. Where the petition relates to a similar payment, which is an illegal rather than a corrupt practice the time limit is 28 days. Where the petition relates to election expenses, the petition can be presented within 14 days of the day on which the return and declaration as to election expenses is received (where the return and declaration are received on different days, the last of those two days) or within 14 days of the day on which an authorised excuse for failing to make a proper return or declaration was allowed (where the excuse for failing to make a proper return is allowed on a different day from the excuse for failing to make a proper declaration, the last of those two days). The above provisions apply to cases of expenses having been paid without proper authorisation by an election agent. A local election petition is tried by a Commissioner (in Scotland by a sheriff principal) appointed by the judges on the rota for the trial of parliamentary election petitions. The time and place of the trial of an election petition must be given in the case of a parliamentary election, within 14 days, or in the case of a local election, within seven days.

Under section 144 of the RPA 1983, at the conclusion of the trial of an election petition relating to a parliamentary election, if the judges cannot agree, the Member in question is deemed to have been duly elected, but if they agree that the Member concerned was not properly elected, although they differ on other matters, the Member concerned is deemed not to have been duly elected. The Speaker of the House of Commons has to be notified of the election court's decision by a 'certificate'. The court's decision is then entered in the Journal of the House of Commons. Under Section 144(7) of the Representation of the

People Act 1983, the House of Commons must then decide whether to confirm the result, or issue a writ for a new election. Where the Election Court has determined that the runner-up should have been elected, the Clerk of the Crown must substitute the new name on the return[48].

At the conclusion of the trial of a local election petition, the election court determines whether or not the person concerned is duly elected or whether the election was void. Where a charge is made in the election petition of a corrupt or illegal practice having been committed, a report is made to the High Court stating whether or not such practices have occurred. A petitioner cannot withdraw an election petition without leave of the election court and where a petition is withdrawn, the petitioner is liable to pay the costs of the respondent.

The provisions of the RPA 1983 relating to corrupt and illegal practices have recently been amended by the PPERA 2000. Part III of the amended RPA 1983 sets out the penalties for corrupt and illegal practices and the methods by which an election result can be challenged. Section 158 of the 1983 Act states that if a corrupt practice other than treating or undue influence was committed with the knowledge and consent of a candidate, he or she is treated as having been found personally guilty. If an illegal practice is found to have been committed with the knowledge and consent of a candidate at a parliamentary election, he or she is treated as having been found personally guilty of the offence. Where a candidate is found guilty 'by his agent' of any corrupt or illegal practice, he or she is not deemed to be guilty if he or she can demonstrate that the offences were committed against the express orders of the candidate or election agent and that they took all reasonable steps to prevent the commission of the offence, that they were relatively trivial and that in all other respects the election was free from any corrupt or illegal practices. If as a result of an election petition, an election court finds a candidate guilty of *undue influence, treating* or any *illegal practice* as a result of actions carried out by 'his agents' (party workers) and the candidate can prove that no corrupt or illegal practice was committed at the election by the candidate or his or her election agent and the offences were committed in opposition to the order and without the sanction of the candidate or agent and they took reasonable measures to prevent the corrupt or illegal practice from taking place and that the election was free from corrupt or illegal practices in all other respects then the candidate is not considered to be guilty of the offence.

Candidates can apply to the High Court or election court (where the application relates to election expenses, a County Court) to exempt an illegal practice, payment, hiring or employment from being considered as such if the act was committed in innocence. The Director of Public Prosecutions must be notified. It the candidate can demonstrate that the act in question was committed inadvertently or accidentally, the court can allow it to be exempted from the 1983 Act.

Under Section 159, sub-section (2) of the RPA 1983 (prior to its amendment by Schedule 17, paragraph 7 of the PPERA 2000) where any candidate was elected and subsequently

---

[48] a 'return' is basically an entry in the 'Return Book' listing the names of those Members 'returned' to serve in Parliament after the General Election – hence the title 'Returning Officer' – the local council official whose task it is to ensure that candidates nominations are valid and whose moment of fame comes on election night when he or she is called to read out the relevant constituency's election results.

found to be personally guilty of a corrupt or illegal practice, the election was declared void and the candidate in question could not sit in the House of Commons or stand for election to that particular constituency at any subsequent election, for a period of 10 years if found personally guilty and for seven years if 'reported guilty by his agents'. Under Section 160, he or she could not stand as a candidate in another constituency for five years and could not vote in any constituency for five years.

Section 159(1) of the RPA 1983 states that where a candidate who has been elected is reported by an election court either personally guilty or guilty by his agents of any corrupt or illegal practice, then his election is declared void. Schedule 17 (8) of the PPERA 2000 omits section 159(2) and amends section 159 (3) of the RPA 1983 and so that it relates solely to local government elections in Scotland.

Section 160 of the RPA 1983 is amended by Schedule 17 of the PPERA 2000 to ensure that a candidate or other person reported personally guilty of a corrupt or illegal practice cannot be elected to the House of Commons or hold any elective office (if he or she is already an MP or holding such an office, he or she must vacate the seat or office from the date of the report of the election court) for the period of time set out below. The period referred to above is the period beginning with the date of the report of the election court and ending in the case of a person reported personally guilty of a corrupt practice, five years after the date, or in the case of a person reported guilty of an illegal practice, three years after that date. Anyone found personally guilty under sections 60 and 61 of the RPA 1983 (personation and voting offences) is also prevented from being registered as an elector or voting at any parliamentary or local government election for the period set out above.

If an MP is found guilty of a corrupt practice, for example failing to submit election returns, his or her election is considered 'void' under Section 160 of the RPA 1983 as amended. If a candidate who has been elected sits as an MP or councillor and votes, he or she is liable to a fine of £100 for each day on which he or she sits and votes (£50 in the case of local authorities). This is applied to Northern Ireland by section 48 of the Electoral Law Act (Northern Ireland) 1962. The provisions in the PPERA 2000 do not encompass Northern Ireland, but similar provisions were extended to Northern Ireland by the Local Elections (Northern Ireland) (Amendment) Order 2001 (SI 2001, No. 417).

Under Section 164 of the Representation of the People Act 1983, where an election court decides that corrupt or illegal practices have been so extensive as to have affected the result, the successful candidate's election is considered void. If a candidate is elected and is then found by an election court to be guilty (or if found to be guilty by virtue of his or her election agent's actions) then the election is void. An election is also void if an elected candidate is found to be disqualified from being a candidate. These provisions apply to all elections. If a candidate engages an agent whom he or she knows to be subject to an incapacity to vote at the election by reason of his having been convicted or reported of any corrupt or illegal practice under the 1983 Act, the candidate is deemed to be incapable of being elected. Under Section 166, if a parliamentary candidate is proved to be personally guilty, or guilty on his or her agent's behalf, or bribery, treating or undue influence, the number of votes corresponding to those proved to have been bribed, treated or unduly influenced are struck off. If anyone guilty of a corrupt or illegal practice or illegal payment, employment or hiring votes at an election, their vote is void. If anyone subject to an incapacity to vote at an election as a result of corrupt or illegal practices, votes at an election, his or her vote is considered void.

Where someone is convicted of a voting offence under Section 61 of the RPA 1983, of making unauthorised expenses (section 75(5), RPA 1983), broadcasting from outside the UK (section 92(1), RPA 1983) or imitating poll cards (section 94(1), RPA 1983) the court can mitigate or remit any incapacities (set out in section 173 of the RPA 1983) which might result on conviction. Where an election agent is late in sending in and paying claims (sections 78(1) and (2) RPA 1983) but the candidate did not know then the candidate's election is not void and he or she is not liable to any incapacity under the Act.

Under section 168 of the RPA 1983, anyone convicted on indictment of a corrupt practice, other than 'personation' (impersonating a voter) is liable to a term of imprisonment of up to one year or a fine or both. Anyone summarily convicted of a corrupt practice is liable to a term of imprisonment of up to six months or a fine or both.

Section 136 of the PPERA 2000 substitutes a new Section 173 in the RPA 1983 which has the effect of bringing the consequences of conviction for illegal practices into line with the those for corrupt practices. Under the pre-existing section 173, a person convicted of a corrupt practice could not sit in the House of Commons or hold any public or judicial office, but a person convicted of an illegal practice was not subject to the same penalties. The new section 173 states that a person convicted of a corrupt or illegal practice (as set out in Sections 60 (personation) and 61 (voting offences) of the RPA 1983) will, for the period of time set out below, be incapable of being registered as an elector or voting at any parliamentary election in the UK or any local government election in Great Britain. Anyone convicted of any other corrupt or illegal practice will be barred from being elected to the House of Commons or holding any elective office for the period set out below. The period of time referred to above is five years in the case of a corrupt practice and three years in the case of an illegal practice, except where (if at any time within that period) a court determines on appeal that the conviction should not be upheld, the relevant period referred to above ends on the date the conviction is quashed. Where an MP has to vacate his or her seat as a result of such a conviction, he or she must do so at the end of the period prescribed by law within which notice of appeal may be given, or an application for leave to appeal may be made by him or her in respect of the conviction or, if (at any time within that period) that period is extended, the end of the extended period or the end of the period of three months beginning with the date of the conviction, whichever is the earlier. If before the time mentioned above, notice of appeal is given, or an application for leave to appeal is made the person concerned must vacate his or her seat or office in question, at the end of the period of three months beginning with the date of the conviction unless such an appeal is dismissed or abandoned at an earlier time (in which case he or she must vacate his or her seat at that time) or if at any time within that period of three months the court determines on appeal that the conviction should not be upheld (in which case he or she would not vacate the seat). Where a seat or office is vacated no subsequent decision by a court that that conviction should not be upheld entitles the person concerned to resume the seat or office in question. In the period between the date of the person's conviction and the person concerned vacating the seat or office in question or the date on which the court determines the conviction should not be upheld, the person concerned is suspended from performing any of his or her functions as an MP or any of the functions of the office in question. The above provisions do not apply to elections to the Northern Ireland Assembly or to local elections in Northern Ireland. However, similar provisions relating to Northern Ireland were brought into effect by The Local Elections (Northern Ireland) (Amendment) Order 2001 (SI 2001, No. 417) which amended the Electoral Law Act (Northern Ireland) 1962.

Section 173A of the RPA 1983, as inserted by section 136 of the PPERA 2000, states that any convicted of a corrupt practice cannot hold any public or judicial office in Scotland for a period of five years and if he or she already holds such an office, he or she must vacate it from the date of the conviction. These provisions are in addition to those in sections 168 and 173.

ELECTION FRAUD IN NORTHERN IRELAND

The Electoral Fraud (Northern Ireland) Bill (introduced in the House of Commons on 28 June 2001) is an attempt to combat fraud in Northern Ireland elections. The provisions in the bill stem from the report, 'Vote Early, Vote Fairly', produced by the Elections Review, a body set up by the Secretary of State for Northern Ireland in July 1997 to consider election fraud in Northern Ireland. The Review was itself a response to allegations of widespread personation, made by the SDLP in the aftermath of the 1996 local elections.

The bill will provide the Chief Electoral Officer for Northern Ireland with new powers to combat fraud. The bill requires a canvas form and an application for voter registration to be signed by and include the date of birth of each of the persons to whom the form or application relates. It provides for an electoral identity card to be issued to anyone entitled to vote who does not have other satisfactory proof of identity. Presiding officers at polling stations will have the power to ask an elector's date of birth applying for a ballot paper. In Northern Ireland, under the provisions of the Elections (Northern Ireland) Act 1985, voters must present identity documents at the polling station before being given a ballot paper. There had been some concerns that among the documents specified (a driving licence, passport, social security payment book, medical card or, under certain conditions, a marriage certificate) only a passport and Northern Ireland driving licence contained photographs. Once a voter has identified himself, the presiding officer issues a ballot paper. If a candidate or his election or polling agent believes that the voter is not who he or she claims to be, he or she may require the presiding officer to ask if the voter in question is who they claim to be and if they have already voted in the election other than as a proxy voter. If the presiding officer is satisfied with the answer, the ballot paper is held to be acceptable unless the candidate, or his election or polling agent, accuses the voter of personation. Under the provisions of the bill, the presiding officer will be able to ask a voter (who is not a proxy) his or her date of birth. Under Clause 1 of the Bill electors will have to state their date of birth on the form for the annual canvass as well as stating name and address. The signature and date of birth will not appear on the electoral register but the information will be used in the electoral office and at polling stations in order to make checks against the name of an elector when they apply for a postal or proxy vote or when they arrive at the polling station to vote. A voter will have to sign an application to vote by post or proxy and the signature will have to correspond with the signature provided on registration. The bill also amends section 10 and 10A of the Representation of the People Act 1983 and the parliamentary election rules in Schedule 1 to the Act. The eventual aim is to allow only photographic ID including the new electoral-ID card proposed by the bill, a passport or Northern Ireland driving licence. The bill will also re-introduce the provision for those with disabilities to show identification. This rectifies the anomaly which resulted from the introduction of section 13 of the Representation of the People Act 2000 which amended the Elections (Northern Ireland) Act 1985. Under the 1985 Act blind voters had to produce documents to identify themselves. The 2000 Act provided for those with other physical disabilities to be given assistance in voting, but did not include reference to identifying documents. This bill rectifies that omission.

CHAPTER THREE – LOCAL GOVERNMENT ELECTIONS

THE STRUCTURE OF LOCAL GOVERNMENT

Local Government in England and Wales

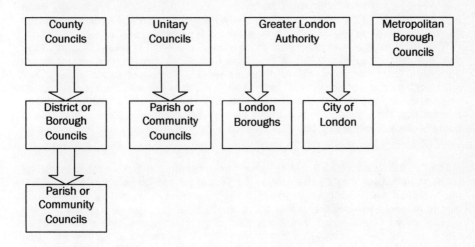

Principal Local Authorities in England and Wales

For the purposes of electoral law, 'principal' councils in England and Wales are County Councils, District Councils, including Metropolitan and Unitary Authorities, London Boroughs and County Borough Councils. Parish and Community Councils are not considered principal authorities. The first major step in the establishment of elected local government in urban areas was the Municipal Corporations Act 1835 which extended the municipal franchise to all ratepayers. The Local Government Act 1888 created County Councils for the whole of England and Wales; however, boroughs with a population of more than 50,000 were given the status of 'County Boroughs' and were independent from the County Council. Other boroughs were known as 'Non-County Borough Councils'.

Under the Local Government Act 1894, the urban and rural sanitary authorities set up under the Public Health Acts of 1872 and 1875, were renamed as Urban District Councils and Rural District Councils. The Local Government Act 1972 introduced two-tier metropolitan government in six areas: West Midlands, Merseyside, Greater Manchester, West Yorkshire, South Yorkshire and Tyne & Wear. They lasted only until 1986, when under the Local Government Act 1985, they were abolished along with the Greater London Council.

In 1972, outside the metropolitan areas, two tier County and District Councils were introduced. Some districts applied for Royal Charters in order to be called 'Boroughs'. The Act caused a considerable amount of consternation as traditional counties such as Rutland and Westmorland disappeared. Anonymous councils called 'Avon', 'Cleveland' and 'Dyfed' were created. These councils were almost universally unpopular. Several cities and large towns, which had previously been County Boroughs became 'District Councils' under the aegis of County Councils.

The Local Government Act 1992 established the Local Government Commission for England, the successor to the former local government boundary commissions (set up under the Local Government Act 1972). One of the Commission's main roles was also to conduct a rolling review of local government structure in England. In Wales, the review was overseen, not by a Commission, but by the Secretary of State for Wales. The result was the creation of 22 unitary authorities in April 1996, under the Local Government (Wales) Act 1994. In England, the Commission made recommendations to the Secretary of State, who had the final decision on any proposed reforms. The review process was to be completed by the end of 1994. Although the Government's preference was for unitary authorities, there was no central edict that all areas should adopt such a system. Not surprisingly a public relations battle ensued between County Councils keen to cling to their existing powers and District Councils eager to expand theirs. The result of the 1992 reforms was confusion. In some areas the two-tier structure of County and District Councils was left unchanged, but in others Unitary Authorities were to exist alongside both County and District Councils.

In London, the Metropolitan Board of Works was established in 1855. This became the London County Council in 1889 and then the Greater London Council in 1965. The GLC was abolished in 1986 and was replaced by a number of residuary bodies. There was no elected authority covering the capital and surrounding area of Greater London until the creation of the Greater London Authority (GLA) under the Greater London Authority Act 1999, the first elections to which took place in 2000. As for the 32 London Boroughs themselves, under the Local Government Act 1972, each borough is divided into wards. The number of councillors to be elected in each ward is set out in Orders made under Part IV of the Act

Parish Councils

Underneath the County, District and Unitary Authorities are the Parish Councils, some of which are known as Town Councils. In Wales, Parish Councils are called Community Councils. Under the Local Government Act 1972, there is a Parish Council for:

❖ Each parish or group of parishes, which had a Parish Council before 1 April 1974, when the Local Government Act 1972 came into force.

❖ Each parish, which immediately before the coming into force of the 1972 Act was a borough in a rural district.

❖ Each parish, which immediately before the coming into force of the 1972 Act was co-extensive with a rural district.

❖ Parishes established by Schedule I, Part 4, paragraph 1 of the Local Government Act 1972.

❖ Each parish, to which was added part of another parish, under Schedule 1, Part 4, paragraph 2 of the Local Government Act 1972 and which immediately before its enactment, had no Parish Council.

❖ Each parish set up under Schedule 1, Part 5 of the Local Government Act 1972 (this part of the Act provided for new parishes by reference to previous urban districts and boroughs).

A District Council can make Orders under the Local Government Act 1972 to create new Parish Councils, to create groups of parishes under one Parish Council, to dissolve groups of parishes, etc. These powers are set out in Sections 9 to 12 of the Act. Under the Act, if a parish does not have a parish council, the District Council use an Order to establish one, if the population includes 200 or more local government electors, or, where the population is between 150 and 200 such electors, if a parish meeting passes a resolution to this effect. Section 16 of the 1972 Act states that orders made by District Councils must stipulate the number of Parish Councillors, which must be at least five.

In Wales, under Section 27(2) of the Local Government Act 1972, there must be a Community Council for:

❖ Each community co-extensive with the area of a rural parish existing before 1 April 1974 that had a separate parish council.

❖ Each group of communities whose areas were co-extensive with those of rural parishes existing immediately before 1 April 1974 and which were grouped under a common parish council.

❖ Any other community which the Secretary of State stipulated should have a Community Council in Orders made under sub-sections (3) or (4) of Section 27(2) of the 1972 Act.

County and Former County Areas Consisting of Unitary Authorities

Avon	Bath & North East Somerset Bristol City North Somerset South Gloucestershire
Berkshire	Bracknell Forest Borough Newbury Reading Borough Slough Windsor & Maidenhead Royal Borough Wokingham
Cleveland	Hartlepool Middlesbrough Redcar & Cleveland Stockton-on-Tees
Herefordshire	Herefordshire Council
Humberside	East Riding of Yorkshire Kingston upon Hull City North East Lincolnshire North Lincolnshire
Isle of Wight	Isle of Wight Council

Metropolitan Borough Councils in Former Metropolitan County Areas

Greater Manchester	Bolton
	Bury
	Manchester City
	Oldham
	Rochdale
	Salford City
	Stockport
	Tameside
	Trafford
	Wigan
Merseyside	Knowsley
	Liverpool City
	St Helens
	Sefton
	Wirral
South Yorkshire	Barnsley
	Doncaster
	Rotherham
	Sheffield City
Tyne & Wear	Gateshead
	Newcastle upon Tyne City
	North Tyneside
	South Tyneside
	Sunderland
West Midlands	Birmingham City
	Coventry City
	Dudley
	Sandwell
	Solihull
	Walsall
	Wolverhampton
West Yorkshire	Bradford City
	Calderdale
	Kirklees
	Leeds City
	Wakefield City

Greater London Boroughs (excluding Corporation of London)

Barking & Dageham	Haringey	Merton
Barnet	Harrow	Newham
Bexley	Havering	Redbridge
Brent	Hillingdon	Richmond upon Thames
Bromley	Hounslow	Southwark
Camden	Islington	Sutton
Croydon	Royal Borough of	Tower Hamlets
Ealing	Kensington and Chelsea	Waltham Forest
Enfield	Royal Borough of Kingston	Wandsworth
Greenwich	upon Thames	Westminster City
Hackney	Lambeth	
Hammersmith & Fulham	Lewisham	

County Councils with Partial Two-Tier Systems

County Councils	District or Borough Councils	Unitary Authorities
Bedfordshire	Mid Bedfordshire District Council Bedford Borough Council South Bedfordshire District Council	Luton
Buckinghamshire	Aylesbury District Council Chiltern District Council South Buckinghamshire District Council Wycombe District Council	Milton Keynes
Cambridgeshire	Cambridge City Council East Cambridgeshire District Council Fenland District Council Huntingdonshire District Council South Cambridgeshire District Council	Peterborough City
Cheshire	Chester City District Council Congleton Borough Council Crewe & Nantwich Borough Council Ellesmere Port & Neston Borough Council Macclesfield Borough Council Vale Royal Borough Council	Halton Borough Warrington Borough
Derbyshire	Amber Valley Borough Council Bolsover District Council Chesterfield Borough Council Derbyshire Dales District Council Erewash Borough Council High Peak Borough Council North East Derbyshire District Council South East Derbyshire District Council	Derby City
Devon	East Devon District Council Exeter City District Council Mid Devon District Council North Devon District Council South Hams District Council Teignbridge District Council Torridge District Council West Devon District Council	Plymouth Torbay
Dorset	Christchurch Borough Council East Dorset District Council North Dorset District Council Purbeck District Council West Dorset District Council Weymouth & Portland Borough Council	Bournemouth Poole
Durham	Chester-le-Street District Council Derwentside District Council Durham City District Council Easington District Council Sedgefield District Council Teesdale District Council Wear Valley District Council	Darlington
East Sussex	Eastbourne Borough Council Hastings Borough Council Lewes District Council Rother District Council Wealden District Council	Brighton & Hove

County Councils	District or Borough Councils	Unitary Authorities
Essex	Basildon District Council Braintree District Council Brentwood Borough Council Castle Point District Council Chelmsford Borough Council Colchester Borough Council Epping Forest District Council Harlow District Council Maldon District Council Rochford District Council Tendring District Council Uttlesford District Council	Southend-on-Sea Borough Thurrock Borough
Hampshire	Basingstoke & Dean Borough Council East Hampshire District Council Eastleigh Borough Council Fareham Borough Council Gosport Borough Council Hart District Council Havant Borough Council New Forest District Council Rushmoor District Council Test Valley Borough Council Winchester City District Council	Portsmouth City Southampton City
Kent	Ashford Borough Council Canterbury City District Council Dartford Borough Council Dover District Council Maidstone Borough Council Sevenoaks District Council Shepway District Council Swale Borough Council Thanet District Council Tonbridge and Malling Borough Council Tunbridge Wells Borough Council	Medway Towns
Lancashire	Burnley Borough Council Chorley Borough Council Fylde Borough Council Hyndburn Borough Council Lancaster City District Council Pendle Borough Council Ribble Valley Borough Council Rossendale Borough Council South Ribble Borough Council West Lancashire District Council Wyre Borough Council	Blackburn with Darwen Borough Blackpool Borough
Leicestershire	Blaby District Council Charnwood Borough Council Harborough District Council Hinckley and Bosworth Borough Council Melton Borough Council North West Leicestershire District Council Oadby & Wigston Borough Council	Leicester City Rutland

County Councils	District or Borough Councils	Unitary Authorities
Nottinghamshire	Ashfield District Council Bassetlaw District Council Broxtowe Borough Council Gedling Borough Council Mansfield District Council Newark and Sherwood District Council Rushcliffe Borough Council	Nottingham City
North Yorkshire	Craven District Council Hambleton District Council Harrogate Borough Council Richmondshire District Council Ryedale District Council Scarborough Borough Council Selby District Council	City of York
Shropshire	Bridgnorth District Council North Shropshire District Council Oswestry Borough Council Shrewsubry & Atcham Borough Council South Shropshire District Council	Wrekin
Staffordshire	Cannock Chase District Council East Staffordshire Borough Council Lichfield District Council Newcastle-under-Lyme Borough Council South Staffordshire District Council Stafford Borough Council Staffordshire Moorlands District Council Tamworth District Council	Stoke on Trent City
Wiltshire	Kennet District Council North Wiltshire District Council Salisbury District Council West Wiltshire District Council	Swindon

County Councils with Complete Two-Tier Systems

County Councils	District or Borough Councils
Cornwall	Caradon District Council Carrick District Council Kerrier District Council North Cornwall District Council Penwith District Council Restormel Borough Council
Cumbria	Allerdale District Council Barrow-in-Furness Borough Council Carlisle City District Council Copeland Borough Council Eden District Council South Lakeland District Council
Gloucestershire	Cheltenham Borough Council Cotswold District Council Forest of Dean District Council Gloucester City District Council Stroud District Council Tewkesbury Borough Council

County Councils	District or Borough Councils
Worcestershire	Bromsgrove District Council
	Malvern Hills District Council
	Redditch District Council
	Worcester City District Council
	Wychavon District Council
	Wyre Forest District Council
Hertfordshire	Broxbourne Borough Council
	Dacorum Borough Council
	East Hertfordshire District Council
	Hertsmere Borough Council
	North Hertfordshire District Council
	St Albans City Council
	Stevenage Borough Council
	Three Rivers District Council
	Watford Borough Council
	Welwyn Hatfield District Council
Lincolnshire	Boston Borough Council
	East Lindsey District Council
	Lincoln City District Council
	North Kesteven District Council
	South Holland District Council
	South Kesteven District Council
	West Lindsey District Council
Norfolk	Breckland District Council
	Broadland District Council
	Great Yarmouth Borough Council
	King's Lynn & West Norfolk Borough Council
	North Norfolk District Council
	Norwich City District Council
	South Norfolk District Council
Northamptonshire	Corby Borough Council
	Daventry District Council
	East Northamptonshire District Council
	Kettering Borough Council
	Northampton Borough Council
	South Northamptonshire District Council
	Wellingborough Borough Council
Northumberland	Alnwick District Council
	Berwick-upon-Tweed Borough Council
	Blyth Valley Borough Council
	Castle Morpeth Borough Council
	Tynedale District Council
	Wansbeck District Council
Oxfordshire	Cherwell District Council
	Oxford City District Council
	South Oxfordshire District Council
	Vale of White Horse District Council
	West Oxfordshire District Council
Somerset	Mendip District Council
	Sedgemoor District Council
	South Somerset District Council
	Taunton Deane Borough Council
	West Somerset District Council

County Councils	District or Borough Councils
Suffolk	Babergh District Council
	Forest Heath District Council
	Ipswich Borough Council
	Mid Suffolk District Council
	St Edmundsbury Borough Council
	Suffolk Coastal District Council
	Waveney District Council
Surrey	Elmbridge Borough Council
	Epsom and Ewell Borough Council
	Guildford Borough Council
	Mole Valley District Council
	Reigate & Banstead Borough Council
	Runnymede Borough Council
	Spelthorne Borough Council
	Surrey Heath Borough Council
	Tandridge District Council
	Waverley Borough Council
	Woking Borough Council
Warwickshire	North Warwickshire Borough Council
	Nuneaton and Bedworth Borough Council
	Rugby Borough Council
	Stratford-on-Avon District Council
	Warwick District Council
West Sussex	Adur District Council
	Arun District Council
	Chichester District Council
	Crawley Borough Council
	Horsham District Council
	Mid Sussex District Council
	Worthing Borough Council

Local Authorities in Wales *(all unitary authorities)*

Blaenau Gwent County Borough Council	Monmouthshire County Council
Bridgend County Borough Council	Neath Port Talbot County Borough
Caerphilly County Borough Council	Council
Cardiff County Council	Newport County Borough Council
Carmarthenshire County Council	Pembrokeshire County Council
Ceredigion County Council	Powys County Council
Conwy County Borough Council	Rhondda Cynon Taff County Borough
Denbighshire County Council	Council
Flintshire County Council	City & County of Swansea Council
Gwynedd Council	Torfaen County Borough Council
Isle of Anglesey County Council	Vale of Glamorgan Council
Merthyr Tydfil County Borough Council	Wrexham County Borough Council

Local Government in Scotland

Local Authorities in Scotland *(all unitary authorities)*

Aberdeen City Council	Inverclyde Council
Aberdeenshire Council	Midlothian Council
Angus Council	Moray Council
Argyll & Bute Council	North Ayrshire Council
Clackmannanshire Council	North Lanarkshire Council
Dumfries & Galloway Council	Orkney Council
Dundee City Council	Perth & Kinross Council
East Ayrshire Council	Renfrewshire Council
East Dunbartonshire Council	Scottish Borders Council
East Lothian Council	Shetland Council
East Renfrewshire Council	South Ayrshire Council
City of Edinburgh Council	South Lanarkshire Council
Falkirk Council	Stirling Council
Fife Council	West Dunbartonshire Council
City of Glasgow Council	Western Isles Council
Highland Council	West Lothian Council

Local Government in Northern Ireland

Local Authorities in Northern Ireland

The reorganisation which took place in Northern Ireland in 1973, under the provisions of the Local Government (Boundaries) Act (Northern Ireland) 1971 and the Local Government Act (Northern Ireland) 1972, resulted in the creation of 26 District Councils. Article 2(3) of the Local Government (Boundaries) Order (Northern Ireland) 1992 constituted new wards for each local government district in Northern Ireland. The Secretary of State then appointed a Commissioner under Article 3(1) of the District Electoral Areas Commissioner (Northern Ireland) Order 1984 (SI 1984, No. 360). The Commissioner was charged with recommending how wards should best be grouped together into electoral areas for the purpose of local government elections. The 1993 Order gave effect to those recommendations. The numbers of councillors to be elected from each of the district electoral areas within the various District Councils are set out in the District Electoral Areas (Northern Ireland) Order 1993 (SI 1993, No. 226).

Antrim District Council	Down District Council
Ards District Council	Dungannon District Council
Armagh District Council	Fermanagh District Council
Ballymena District Council	Larne District Council
Ballymoney District Council	Limavady District Council
Banbridge District Council	Lisburn District Council
Belfast City Council	Magherafelt District Council
Carrickfergus District Council	Moyle District Council
Casltereagh District Council	Newry & Mourne District Council
Coleraine District Council	Newtonabbey District Council
Cookstown District Council	North Down District Council
Craigavon District Council	Omagh District Council
Londonderry City District Council	Strabane District Council

LOCAL GOVERNMENT BOUNDARIES

The Local Government Act 1992 established the Local Government Commission for England, the successor to the former local government Boundary Commission for England (set up under the Local Government Act 1972). The Commission conducted periodic reviews of local government electorates. Its responsibilities have now been taken on by the Electoral Commission set up under the Political Parties, Elections and Referendums Act 2000.

THE ELECTORAL CYCLE IN LOCAL GOVERNMENT

Although all local government councillors are elected for a four-year term of office, the timing of elections follows different patterns depending on the type of local government authority concerned.

Type of Authority	Electoral Cycle
County Councils (Sections 6, 7 & 26 Local Government Act 1972)	Elections every four years (1973 and thereafter) on first Thursday in May or other day as fixed by Secretary of State by an order made no later than 1 February in preceding year to one in which order is to take effect (Section 37 Representation of the People Act 1983) Whole Council retires at same time on fourth day after election day (successors take up office on this day) One councillor returned for each electoral division (Section 6 Local Government Act 1972)
London Boroughs (excluding City of London)[1] (Section 8 and Schedule 2 Local Government Act 1972 and London Councillors Order 1976, SI 213)	Elections every four years on first Thursday in May (1974 and every four years thereafter) with councillors retiring on fourth day after election day (when successors take up office) Whole Council retires at same time Wards return up to three councillors

---

[1] The Corporation of London is the local authority for the City of London and is currently undertaking a major review of its franchise. A private bill, the City of London (Ward Elections) Bill, is currently progressing through Parliament. The City's current 25 wards would remain in place but a review of their boundaries is being proposed. Voters in the wards elect the 112 members of the Court of Common Council, which meets once a month and has a number of committees (non-party political). Elections are held each year in December (all seats are elected at this time). Wards return between four and 12 members depending on the size of the electorate. Candidates must be freemen of the City. The Court of Aldermen is presided over by the Lord Mayor and meets about nine times a year. Each ward elects one alderman (they automatically become Justices of the Peace upon election). There are 25 aldermen and they also sit on the Court of Common Council.

Type of Authority	Electoral Cycle
Metropolitan Borough/District Councils (Section 7 Local Government Act 1972 *as amended*)	Elections held in every three out of four years, on first Thursday in May, with one third of the council (one councillor in each ward) retiring each year on fourth day after election day (successors take up office on this day) Wards return a number of councillors divisible by three County Council elections are held in the fourth year
District and Borough Councils in two-tier areas (Sections 6, 7 & 26 Local Government Act 1972)	Elections held either in every three out of four years, on first Thursday in May, with one third of the council (one councillor in each ward) retiring each year or whole council retires at same time, with elections midway between County Council elections Wards return number of councillors set out in order under paragraph 3 of Schedule 3 of the 1972 Act County Council elections are held In the fourth year, where one third of councillors retire at any one time. However, the council can ask the Secretary of State for a system of whole council elections or for election by thirds, provided the council has agreed by a two-thirds majority to such a change. No similar change can be made for 10 years after.
Unitary Authorities	Elections either held in every three out of four years, with one third of the council (one councillor in each ward) retiring each year or whole council retires at same time, with elections midway between County Council elections Wards return number of councillors set out in Part II of the Local Government Act 1992 Special arrangements apply in areas where there is still a County Council
Parish Councils & Community Councils (Sections 16 & 35 Local Government Act 1972)	Elections every four years on first Thursday in May, with all councillors retiring at same time on fourth day after election day (when successors take up office)

THE ELECTORAL TIMETABLE IN LOCAL ELECTIONS

The timetable for local elections is set out in Part I of Schedule 2 of the Local Elections (Principal Areas) Rules 1986.

Proceeding	Time
Publication of notice of election	Not later than the 25th day before the date of election
Delivery of nomination papers	Not later than noon on the 19th day before the day of election
Publication of statement as to persons nominated	Not later than noon on the 17th day before the day of election
Delivery of notices of withdrawals of candidature	Not later than noon on the 16th day before the day of election
Notice of poll	Not later than the 6th day before the day of election
Polling	Between 8am and 9pm on the day of election

The following days are disregarded when calculating the relevant number of days in the above timetable: Saturday or Sunday, Christmas Eve, Christmas Day, Maundy Thursday, Good Friday or a bank holiday or a day appointed for 'public thanksgiving or mourning'. A bank holiday is any day which is a bank holiday under the Banking and Financial Dealings Act 1971 in England and Wales.

The Impact of Foot and Mouth Disease on the 2001 Local Elections

The outbreak of foot and mouth disease in the UK in 2001 resulted in the decision to delay the local elections scheduled to take place on Thursday 3 May in England and Wales (Section 37 of the RPA 1983) and Wednesday 16 May in Northern Ireland (Electoral Law Act (Northern Ireland) 1962, as amended by Local Elections (Northern Ireland) Order 1985). 34 English county councils and 11 unitary authorities were due to hold elections on 3 May and 26 Northern Ireland district councils were due for election on 16 May. New legislation was required to delay the elections, as under the provisions of Section 137 of the RPA 1983, local elections could only be deferred if a decision was taken a year in advance of the elections themselves.

Under the provisions of the Elections Act 2001, the local elections were postponed until 7 June and sitting councillors remained in office until that date. The Act also ensured that no by-elections were held to fill casual vacancies during the period of the deferral. By-elections due to have been held during the period of the deferral were postponed until 7 June. The Act also ensured that valid nominations remained valid until the new election day, to obviate the need for candidates to submit new nomination papers. However, candidates had until 15 May to withdraw existing nomination papers and until 10 May to submit new ones. The Act also allowed candidates to spend 50 per cent more on their election campaigns in recognition of the fact that some election literature would have carried the original election date and would therefore be redundant. The Act also gave the Secretary of State the power to compensate local authorities and candidates for additional expenditure incurred as a result of the deferral of the elections. The Act covered local elections in England, Wales and Northern Ireland, but not Scotland (now the remit of the Scottish Parliament). The Act did not cover by-elections for the Scottish Parliament, Welsh Assembly, Northern Ireland Assembly or European Parliament. The Act brought Northern Ireland legislation into line with the rest of the UK by providing that the polls for local elections and a General Election could be combined on the same day (even though local elections are held using the Single Transferable Vote system).

ELECTORAL CHANGES

Under Section 13 of the Local Government Act 1992, the Local Government Commission has the power to undertake periodic reviews of local councils with a view to recommending electoral changes. Where the Secretary of State feels the changes should proceed he/she can make an order giving effect to the recommendations. For example The District of Tandridge (Electoral Changes) Order 1999 (SI 1999, No 2480), which came into force on 10 October 1999, in time for the local elections on 4 May 2000, abolished the existing ward structure of the borough and divided it into 20 wards (set out in the order). Paragraph 3 of the order states that elections are to be 'by thirds' but that 'elections of councillors for all wards of the district shall be held simultaneously on the ordinary day of election of councillors in 2000'. The order then goes on to state that for any ward electing more than two councillors, the first to retire should be the councillor elected by the smallest number of votes and the second to retire, the councillor with the next smallest number (where a ward is not contested the order stipulates that the person to retire in each year 'shall be determined by lot'). All councillors serve for four years. Schedule 1 sets outs the wards and the number of councillors and Schedule 2 the order of retirement of councillors. For example, in the Whyteleafe ward, two councillors are elected, one of whom retires in 2002 and one in 2004. The Council passed a resolution to move permanently to four-yearly elections of all councillors, but the request was rejected by the Secretary of State, despite the fact that 78 per cent of the 400 members of the Council's Residents' Panel supported the change.

The Local Government Act 2000 gives the Secretary of State power to specify by order that a particular type of electoral system be applied to a county council, district council or London borough. Section 85 sets out three possible options for the cycle of local government elections.

❖ Whole council elections with all councillors being elected every four years.

❖ Two-halves elections, with one half of the total number of councillors being elected every two years for a four-year term.

❖ Elections by thirds, with one third of the total number of councillors being elected in three out of four years (with councillors having a four-year term of office).

Part II of the Local Government Act 2000 deals with new political structures for local authorities, some of which have already been adopted in 'shadow' form by some councils. Three possible models are set out in the Act, on which local authorities must consult (there is a further structure open to smaller district councils set out in Sections 31 and 32 of the Act). In some cases, local authorities will be required to hold a referendum where certain of the new options are proposed. Until now, local authority decision-making has been based on a combination of a full council and committee system in which all councillors participate. Section 11 sets out the three possible options for local authorities to adopt.

❖ A directly elected mayor and a cabinet executive appointed by the mayor (where the executive numbers no more than 10).

❖ An executive leader, elected by a full council, with an executive appointed either by the leader or the council (where the executive may not number more than 10).

❖ A directly elected mayor, with an officer of the authority appointed by the council as council manager.

The alternative arrangements for smaller district councils are set out in Section 23 of the Act and can take one of the following forms:

❖ A structure not involving an executive of the authority
❖ A structure involving committees or sub-committees

Under Section 25 of the Act, all local authorities (except those to which Section 31 applies) must consult on new executive arrangements before coming forward with proposals. A copy of the proposals must then be sent to the Secretary of State who can, by order, direct the authority to put the new structure into effect. Some forms of executive government will require a referendum, in which case the authority will have to put forward alternative proposals, which could be implemented if their original proposals were to be rejected in a referendum. These forms are those where a local authority proposes a mayor and cabinet executive or a mayor and council manager or where the Secretary of State prescribes any of the following systems in regulations and states that a referendum is required.

❖ An executive where all or some of the members are elected by the local government electors to a specified post in the executive.

❖ An executive where all or some of the members are elected by the electors but not to any specific post.

Where a local authority receives a petition from 5% of its electors to hold a referendum on a type of decision making structure which requires a referendum under the Act, the Secretary of State can set out in regulations the date on which a referendum must be held.[2] Under the provisions of Section 45, a local authority may only hold one referendum in any five-year period. Those eligible to vote in a referendum are the same as those entitled to vote in ordinary local government elections.

The Local Authorities (Conduct of Referendums) (England) Regulations 2001 (SI 2001, No. 1298) sets out in detail the form of words to be used in a referendum under the Act, the wording of ballot papers and also contains provisions to allow a local authority to conduct such a referendum entirely by using postal ballots. The regulations are extremely lengthy and detailed (the internet version runs to 94 pages) and contain numerous modifications and amendments to the RPA 1983, RPA 2000, the Local Elections (Principal Areas) Rules 1986 and the RPA (England and Wales) Regulations 2001.

A number of local authorities have recently held referendums on elected mayors. In October 2001, in Hartlepool, Middlesbrough, North Tyneside and Lewisham, proposals for elected mayors were all endorsed, but in Sedgefield, Brighton and Hove, they were fairly decisively rejected. Watford and Doncaster have already decided to hold mayoral elections.

Sections 42 to 44 and Schedule 2 of the Act set out the voting method for electing a directly elected mayor. The system to be used is the Supplementary Vote (SV) system (unless there are only two candidates). Electors have two votes: a first and a second preference. Where one candidate receives more than half of the first preference votes, he or she is duly elected. However, if this is not the case, all candidates are eliminated except the two with the highest number of first preference votes. The second preference votes of the eliminated candidates are then added to the votes for the two remaining candidates. If the two remaining candidates both have the same number of votes, the returning officer must decide between by lots.

The Local Authorities (Elected Mayors) (Elections, Terms of Office and Casual Vacancies) (England) Regulations 2001 (SI 2001, No. 2544) sets out the dates on which an election for mayor could be held. Two dates are possible: either the first Thursday in May or the third Thursday in October – whichever is first after the three-month period beginning on the day on which a referendum was held. The mayoral term of office depends on the type

---

[2] Further details on petitions are set out in the Local Authorities (Referendums) (Petitions and Directions) (England) Regulations 2000 (SI 2000, No. 2852), which came into effect on 16 November 2000, and which were amended by the Local Authorities (Referendums) (Petitions and Directions) (England) (Amendment) Regulations 2001 (SI 2001, No. 760), which came into effect on 1 April 2001.

of local authority. In the case of metropolitan and non-metropolitan, not within a county council area, whose councillors are elected by thirds, the second mayoral election would, after a statutory 23-month period, be in the next year after the year in which there would not normally be local government elections in their area. Other councils must hold a second mayoral election on the ordinary day for the election of councillors, not later than either the fifth or sixth year after the first mayoral election, depending on whether the election was in May or October. If the first election was held in May, the second would have to be held no later than the fifth year following and if held in October, the sixth year following.

Where a vacancy for mayor occurs, an election would have to be held within 35 days, unless it occurs within six months before the day on which the mayor was to have retired, in which case a new mayor would be elected at the normal time.

WHO CAN BE A CANDIDATE?

Under the provisions of Sections 79 and 80 of the Local Government Act 1972 (as amended by the Local Government (Changes to the Franchise and Qualification of Members) Regulations 1995 (SI 1995, No. 1948) anyone wishing to stand as a candidate in a local government election must be:

❖ A citizen of Britain, the Commonwealth, the Republic of Ireland or another EU Member State; and

❖ be properly nominated and be at least 21 years of age (on the day of his or her nomination and the day of the poll).

He or she must also fulfil the following criteria. These are, that he or she should:

❖ be a local government elector for the local authority area for which he or she wishes to be elected[3], or;

❖ for the past 12 months preceding nomination day and election day, have occupied land or premises in that area, or;

❖ have had his or her principal place of work in that area for the past 12 months, or;

❖ for the whole of the 12 months prior to both nomination day and election day, lived in that area, or, in the case of Parish Councils, lived in, or within 4.8 kilometres of the Parish concerned.

Similar provisions are applied in Scotland under the Local Government (Scotland) Act 1973.

---

[3] This requirement continues for the period of the person's term of office. The requirement to be a registered elector refers to the local authority area as a whole not to a particular ward.

WHO CANNOT BE A CANDIDATE?

The following are ineligible to stand as candidates in local government elections:

❖ **Aliens** (anyone who is not a British Citizen, a citizen of the Republic of Ireland, a citizen of the Commonwealth or a citizen of the European Union) *(section 79, Local Government Act 1972, as amended).*

❖ Anyone **under 21** years of age *(section 79(1) Local Government Act 1972).*

❖ Anyone declared **bankrupt** or who has made a composition or arrangement with his creditors *(section 80(1)(b) Local Government Act 1972)* except *(as set out under Section 81)* where the bankruptcy order is annulled or where the person concerned is discharged from bankruptcy).

❖ Anyone who has been disqualified as a councillor.

❖ Anyone who is a **paid officer** of the authority for which he or she wishes to stand *(section 80, Local Government Act 1972).*

❖ Anyone who is a paid officer of any local authority in a **'politically restricted post'** as set out in Section 2 of the Local Government and Housing Act 1989 (politically restricted posts include chief executives, statutory chief officers[4], non-statutory chief officers[5], deputy chief officers[6], monitoring officers, assistants to political groups[7], those earning more than a specified amount[8] and employed by the authority whose duties involve giving advice to decision makers or speaking on behalf of the authority).

❖ Any councillor who has been disqualified by virtue of having been **surcharged** under section 19 of the Local Government Finance Act 1982 which states that some items of expenditure may be deemed 'contrary to law' (an example might be the case of a local authority which set a council tax beyond the limits laid down by central government) and the amount in question was more than

---

[4] 'Statutory chief officer' as defined under Section 2(6) of the Local Government and Housing Act 1989, means the Chief Officer appointed under Section 88 of the Education Act 1944, the Chief Officer of a Fire Brigade, the Director of Social Services or Chief Social Work Officer, the person responsible for the administration of the local authority's financial affairs.

[5] A non-statutory chief officer includes a person 'for whom the head of the authority's paid service is directly responsible' (Section 2(7)(a) of the Local Government and Housing Act 1989), a person who must report directly to the head of the authority's paid service or anyone who reports directly to the local authority themselves or is directly accountable to the authority themselves or one of its committees or sub-committees (does not include those whose duties are primarily secretarial or clerical).

[6] Under Section 2(8) of the Local Government and Housing Act 1989, a deputy chief officer is someone who with respect to most of his or her duties, reports directly or is directly accountable to one or more of the statutory or non-statutory chief officers (does not include those whose duties are primarily secretarial or clerical).

[7] A political appointment is defined in Section 9(2)(c) of the Local Government and Housing Act 1989 as being one of 'nor more than three posts which a relevant authority have decided to create for the purposes of this section'.

[8] Under Section 2(2)(a) of the Local Government and Housing Act 1989, the annual rate of salary above which a local government official may not stand for election, can be altered by regulations made by the Secretary of State; for example, the Local Government (Politically Restricted Posts) (No.2) Regulations 1990 which link the salary level to point 44 of the NJC Scale.

£2,000, can be disqualified for a specified period. Where a local authority fails to include a sum of more than £2,000 in its accounts, the councillor in question may be disqualified for five years.

❖ Anyone *convicted* of an offence carrying a sentence of imprisonment of not less than three months (without the option of a fine) may not stand as a candidate for five years and anyone so convicted after his or her election, would be disqualified *(section 80, Local Government Act 1972, extended to local elections in Northern Ireland by Section 9 of the Elected Authorities (Northern Ireland) Act 1989).*

❖ Under the provisions of sections 159 and 160 of the RPA 1983 as amended by Schedule 17 of the PPERA 2000, anyone held by an election court to have committed a *corrupt* or *illegal* practice cannot vote in any local government election or hold an elective for five years in the case of a corrupt practice and three in the case of an illegal practice.[9]

Similar provisions are applied in Scotland under the Local Government (Scotland) Act 1973.

WHO CAN BE DISQUALIFIED FROM BEING A COUNCILLOR?

Under Section 92 of the Local Government Act 1972, any local government elector may bring an action against a councillor who should be disqualified on any of the grounds set out above, within six months of the earliest date when the councillor concerned first 'acted' or 'claimed to be entitled to act' as a councillor. Once a candidate has been elected as a councillor, he or she can be disqualified under Section 92 if he or she fails to be qualified as councillor, fails to make the relevant declaration of acceptance (as set out in Section 83 of the 1972 Act), resigns (as defined in Section 84 of the 1972 Act) or fails to attend meetings (as set out in Section 85 of the 1972 Act). Both the Magistrates Court and the High Court can impose financial penalties on a disqualified councillor, but only the High Court can declare the seat vacant.

Under Section 86 of the 1972 Act, where a councillor becomes disqualified **other than** by an order from the High Court after a finding of unlawful expenditure, surcharge, conviction or a finding of corrupt or illegal practices (i.e., those disqualifications in bold, but not italicised, above) the local authority must declare the seat vacant. If a councillor is disqualified as a result of a conviction or as a result of a court order following a finding of unlawful expenditure, he or she may appeal. If convicted by a Magistrates Court the period for an appeal is 21 days (the Crown Court may extend this[10]), if convicted by the Crown Court the period is 28 days (the Court of Appeal may extend the period[11]), if convicted under Section 19 of the Local Government Finance Act 1982 by the County Court or High Court, the period allowed is four weeks[12]. A vacancy occurs (where the disqualification results from conviction or a Court order following unlawful expenditure)

---

[9] Section 159 of the RPA 1983 as amended by Schedule 17 of the PPERA 2000 a candidate at a local government election in Scotland who is found personally guilty or guilty by his agents of any corrupt or illegal practice may not be a councillor in any local authority in Scotland for 10 years in the case of a corrupt practice, for three years if found guilty by his agents of a corrupt practice and during the period for which he or she was elected serve, if found personally guilty or guilty by his agents, of an illegal practice. A councillor found guilty as above would have to vacate the office immediately.
[10] Crown Court Rules 1982 SI 1982 No 1109 Rule 7
[11] Criminal Appeals Rules 1968 SI 1968 No 1262 Rule 1
[12] Order 59 Rule 4(1) Rules of the Supreme Court

after the period for an appeal has expired (or the date when the appeal was abandoned) or where the councillor's disqualification arises for another reason, on the date the High Court or local authority declares that he or she has vacated the seat.

Under Section 85 of the Local Government Act 1972, if a councillor does not attend any meeting for six months, he ceases to be a member of the council, unless the council approved the absence before the end of the six-month period. 'Attendance' means attendance at committees, sub-committees or at meetings where he or she was to act as a representative of the authority. Where a councillor ceases to be a member of the council in this way, the authority has to declare the office vacant (vacancy occurs from the date on which they make the declaration).

A councillor's term of office is for four years, beginning on the fourth day after the day of the election and ending on the fourth day after the day of election (Section 26 Local Government Act 1972). As far as by-elections are concerned the term of office begins immediately after the election. Under Section 89 of the 1972 Act, when a councillor resigns or is disqualified, the election to fill the vacancy takes place within 35 days of the office being declared vacant. However, where a vacancy occurs within six months before the day on which the councillor whose office has become vacant would under ordinary circumstances have retired anyway, an election is not held. The exception is where failure to hold a by-election would result in the total of vacancies on the council exceeding one third of the total number of members.

WHO CAN VOTE?

The Representation of the People Act 2000 amends the RPA 1983 by substituting a new Section 2 which provides for a 'rolling register' of local government electors. The new Section is set out below.

2   (1)   A person is entitled to vote as an elector at a local government election in any electoral area if on the date of the poll he –

    (a)   is registered in the register of local government electors for that area;

    (b)   is not subject to any legal incapacity to vote (age apart);

    (c)   is a Commonwealth citizen, a citizen of the Republic of Ireland or a relevant citizen of the Union; and

    (d)   is of voting age (that is, 18 years or over).

    (2)   A person is not entitled to vote as an elector -

    (a)   more than once in the same electoral area at any local government election; or

    (b)   in more than one electoral area at an ordinary election for a local government area which is not a single electoral area

A person is (under the new Section 4 of the RPA 1983 as set out in Section 4 of the RPA 2000) entitled to be registered in the register of local government electors for any for any electoral area if on the relevant date he is:

❖   Resident in that area

❖   Is not subject to any legal incapacity to vote (age apart)

❖ Is either a qualifying Commonwealth citizen, a citizen of the Republic of Ireland or a relevant citizen of the Union

❖ Is of voting age

Anyone who will become 18 in the period of 12 months beginning with the next 1 December, following the relevant date, may be entered in the register along with the date on which he or she is to become 18. He or she cannot vote until that date. The relevant date is the date on which an application for registration is made or in the case of someone making a declaration as an overseas voter, the date on which that declaration was made. Peers (regardless of whether or not they continue to sit in the House of Lords) may also vote.

The following cannot vote:

❖ Foreign nationals (other than citizens of EU Member States).

❖ Offenders detained under mental health legislation *(full details of the provisions relating to how non-offenders in mental institutions, those on remand and the homeless can vote by making a 'declaration of local connection' can be found in the preceding chapter).*

❖ Those convicted of an offence and detained in prison or a special hospital (not those on remand).

❖ Those found guilty of corrupt electoral practices for five years and those found guilty of illegal practices for three years.

❖ British voters overseas.

Under Section 61(2) of the Representation of the People Act 1983, a person may not vote more than once in the same electoral area (electoral division, ward or parish), except where a person is voting as both elector and proxy.

THE ROLE OF THE ELECTORAL REGISTRATION OFFICER

Every Unitary Authority, London Borough Council, Metropolitan Borough Council and Shire District or Borough Council in a two-tier area (not the County Council) has to have an Electoral Registration Officer, whose task it is to compile the electoral register. A form is sent to each home in the area and completion of the form is compulsory. Before the enactment of the Representation of the People Act 2000, the place of residence on 10 October each year was the key to being included on the register. The draft register was open for inspection until 16 December and mistakes could be rectified. The register came into effect on the following 16 February (this could be altered if there was to be a general election). Anyone changing their address after 10 October could not be registered at their new address until the register was next updated.

The Representation of the People Act 2000 provides for 'rolling registration' so that those who have just moved home can have a new address added to the register at the beginning of the month. The register cannot be altered once the final date for nominations for an election has passed. Under the Act, there will be two versions of the electoral register: a full version, open to public inspection and used for elections but copies of which will only be supplied to certain categories of people prescribed in regulations and an edited version, which can be sold to anyone, which will exclude the names of those who do not wish their names to be included.

ELECTORAL PROCEDURE

The notice of election must be published at least 25 days before the election. Nomination papers for candidates must be handed in by noon, 19 days before the election. Under Rule 4 of the Local Election Rules as set out in Schedule 2, of the Local Elections (Principals Areas) Rules 1986 (SI 1986, No. 2214), nomination papers must bear the candidate's name and those of a proposer and seconder and eight other people eligible to vote in the area. Nominations do not have to be set out on the form supplied by the returning officer, although they usually are (the layout of the form is set out below). Where a poll is abandoned or where there are no valid nominations, the Returning Officer orders a new election to be held within 35 days (Section 39, Representation of the People Act 1983). The provisions of the PPERA 2000 relating to the descriptions which candidates may use on nomination papers are applied to local elections *(the registration of political parties is covered in Chapter Nine).*

Form of nomination paper	Rule 4
*ELECTION OF COUNCILLORS/A COUNCILLOR for the .... *electoral division/ward of the *county/district/London borough/county borough of	
*Delete whichever is inappropriate	
We, the undersigned, being local government electors for the said *electoral division/ward do hereby nominate the under-mentioned person as a candidate at the said election.	

Candidate's surname	Other names in full	Description (if any)	Home address in full

Signatures	Electoral number (see note 3) Distinctive letter(s)	Number
Proposer	....	....
Seconder..	....	....
We, the undersigned, being local government electors for the said *electoral division/ward, do hereby assent to the foregoing nomination Signatures		
1..	....	....
2..	....	....
3..	....	....
4..	....	....
5..	....	....
6..	....	....
7..	....	....
8..	....	....

Under Rule 6 of the aforementioned regulations, candidates must give their consent to nomination in writing in the form set out below, on or within one month before the last date for the delivery of nomination papers. The form must be signed by one witness.

Form of candidate's consent to nomination

Front of form

I *(name in full)* ....
of *(home address in full)* ....
....
hereby consent to my nomination as a candidate for election as –
*Delete whichever is   *councillor for .... electoral division/ward of the
inappropriate   *county/district/London borough/county borough of ....

I declare that on the day of my nomination I am qualified and that, if there is a poll on the day of election, I will be qualified to be so elected by virtue of being on that day or those days a Commonwealth citizen or a citizen of the Republic of Ireland, or a citizen of another Member State of the European Community, who has attained the age of 21 years and that

*Delete whichever is   *(a) I am registered as a local government elector for the area of
inappropriate   the *county/district or London borough/county borough named
                          above in respect of *(qualifying address in full)* ....
                          ....
                          and my electoral number (see Note below) is ....; or
                          *(b) I have during the whole of the 12 months preceding that day
                          or those days occupied as owner or tenant the following land or
                          other premises in that area *(description and address of land or
                          premises)*..; or
                          *(c) my principal or only place of work during those 12 months
                          has been in that area at *(give address of place of work and, where
                          appropriate, name of employer)*..............................; or
                          *(d) I have during the whole of those twelve months resided in
                          that area at *(give address in full)* ....
                          ....

I declare that to the best of my knowledge and belief I am not disqualified from being elected by reason of any disqualification set out in section 80 of the Local Government Act 1972, a copy of which is printed overleaf and I do not hold a politically restricted post, within the meaning of Part I of the Local Government and Housing Act 1989, under a local authority, within the meaning of that Part.

Signed ....
Date ....

Signed in my presence
Signature of witness ....
Name and address of witness ....
(CAPITAL LETTERS)
Note – A person's electoral number is his number in the register to be used at the election (including the distinctive letter of the parliamentary polling district in which he is registered) except that before publication of the register his number (if any) in the electors' lists for that register shall be used instead.

The form to be used in local elections in Northern Ireland is set out in The Local Elections (Northern Ireland) Order 1985 (SI 1985, No. 454) (see below)

ELECTION OF DISTRICT COUNCILLORS

District of ....

District Electoral Area ....

Day of election ....

We, the undersigned, being electors in the above-mentioned district electoral area do hereby nominate the under-mentioned person as a candidate at the said election.

Candidate's surname	Other names in full	Description (if any)	Home address in full

Signatures	Electoral number (see note 3)
Proposer	....
Seconder...	....
We, the undersigned, being electors for the above-mentioned district electoral area do hereby assent to the foregoing nomination	
1..	....
2..	....
3..	....
4..	....
5..	....
6..	....
7..	....
8..	....

ELECTION OF DISTRICT COUNCILLORS

I (name in full) ....

of (home address in full) ....

....

hereby consent to my nomination as a candidate for election as councillor for the ....
district electoral area in the district of ....

I declare that I have attained the age of 21 years and that I am a Commonwealth citizen, or a citizen of the Republic of Ireland, or a citizen of another Member State of the European Community and

continued overleaf ....

154

*Delete whichever is
inappropriate

*(a) I am a local elector for the district of the council; or
*(b) during the whole of the period of twelve months preceding
the day of the poll: -
*(i) I have occupied as owner or tenant land in that district, or
*(ii) resided in that district: or
*(c) my principal or only place of work during that twelve months
has been in that district.

I further declare that to the best of my knowledge and belief I am not disqualified from being elected by reason of any disqualification contained in section 4 of the Local Government Act (Northern Ireland) 1972, a copy of which is printed overleaf.

I declare that, if elected, I will not by word or deed express support for or approval of –
(a)   any organisation that is for the time being a proscribed organisation specified in Schedule 2 to the Northern Ireland (Emergency Provisions) Act 1978; or
(b)   acts of terrorism (that is to say, violence for political ends) connected with the affairs of Northern Ireland.

Signed ....

Date ....

Signed in my presence
Signature of witness ....
Name and address of witness ....
(in CAPITAL LETTERS)

A list of all the candidates nominated must be published by noon on the 17th day before the election and if any candidate wishes to withdraw before an election it must be no later than 16 days before the election.   Under Rule 10 of the Regulations, a candidate can withdraw his candidature in writing provided that notice of withdrawal has been attested by one witness, or if the candidate is not in the UK at the time, signed by his proposer. Any candidate found to be standing in more than one electoral area in the same local government area; for example, in more than one ward in a district council election, must stand down in all but one area and if he or she does not do so, he or she is deemed to have withdrawn his or her candidate in all the areas in which he or she was standing as a candidate. Provisions as to the layout of ballot papers, the presence of the official mark, the conduct of the campaign, voting procedure, voting by blind and disabled persons, the counting of votes etc., contained in the Parliamentary Election Rules in Schedule 1 of the 1983 Act, are applied to local elections by Part III of Schedule 2 of the Local Elections (Principal Areas) Rules 1986 as amended by the following regulations:

The Local Elections (Principal Areas) (Amendment) Rules (SI 1987, No. 261)
The Local Elections (Principal Areas) (Amendment) Rules (SI 1990, No. 158)
The Local Elections (Principal Areas) (Amendment) Rules (SI 1998, No. 578)
The Local Elections (Principal Areas) (Amendment) Rules 1999 (SI 1999, No. 394)
The Local Elections (Principal Areas) (Amendment) Rules 2001 (SI 2001, No. 81) *(applies the new provisions relating to voting by blind and disabled voters to local elections – see previous chapter for further details)*

Under Rule 24 of the aforementioned Local Election Rules, each candidate can appoint polling agents to attend polling stations on polling day. No more than four are permitted in any one polling station at a time. All candidates are entitled to apply to have counting agents at the election count. The number of counting agents allowed to each candidate is the number obtained by dividing the number of clerks employed at the count by the number of candidates. Notice of polling or counting agents must be made five days before the election. Polling stations are open from 8am to 9pm for local elections. Under Section 37 of the 1983 Act, local government elections take place on the first Thursday in May or another day set out by the Secretary of State in an order made no later than 1 February in the year preceding the year in which the order is to take place.

Under the Representation of the People Act 2000, local authorities were permitted to experiment with times and places of voting in the May 2000 elections. 40 authorities ran pilot schemes including electronic voting, total postal voting, early voting and Saturday voting. These pilots may lead to permanent changes to electoral law.

ELECTION EXPENSES

There are legal limits on the maximum amount candidates may spend on election expenses. Exceeding those limits is an election offence. At a local government election (excluding elections to the Greater London Authority) the maximum is £242 with an additional 4.7 pence for each entry in the register of electors to be used at that election (Representation of the People (Variation of Limits of Candidates' Expenses) Order 2001 (SI 2001, No 535). Similar provisions apply to local elections in Northern Ireland under the Local Elections (Northern Ireland) (Amendment) Order 2001 (SI 2001, No. 417) (which amends the Electoral Law Act (Northern Ireland) 1962) where the respective limits are £242 and 4.8 pence. Where there are joint candidates at a local election, the amounts are reduced by a quarter for each of the joint candidates or if there are more than two joint candidates, by one third.[13] Joint candidates are defined as being two or more candidates who appoint the same election agent or who by themselves or by any agent, employ or use the services of the same committee rooms, publish joint addresses, etc. The candidate's agent sends a return of the candidate's expenses to the Returning Officer and failure to do so is an election offence. In the case of parish and community councils, sections 72 to 72 and 78 to 89 of the RPA 1983 do not apply.

TAKING AND RESIGNING OFFICE

All newly elected councillors must make a declaration of acceptance in a manner set down in an order made under Section 83 of the Local Government Act 1972.[14] The form of declaration is set out in The Local Elections (Principal Areas) (Declaration of Acceptance of Office) Order 1990 (SI 1990 No. 932) which relates to principal authorities and The Local Elections (Parishes and Communities) (Declaration of Acceptance of Office) Order 1990 (SI 1990, No. 2477) which relates to parish councils (the Welsh language forms are set out in the Local Elections (Declaration of Acceptance of Office) (Welsh Forms) Order 1991 (SI 1991, No, 1169)).

---

[13] The same provisions are applied to local elections in Northern Ireland under section 42 of the Electoral Law Act (Northern Ireland) 1962

[14] Section 30(2) of the Local Government and Housing Act 1989 amended Section 83 of the Local Government Act 1972 to stipulate that the form of declaration be set out in an order made by the Secretary of State.

The declaration is as follows:

"I, ..., having been elected to the office of (description of office inserted here) declare that I take that office upon myself, and will duly and faithfully fulfil the duties of it according to the best of my judgement and ability.

I undertake to be guided by the National Code of Local Government Conduct in the performance of my functions in that office"

The National Assembly for Wales (which can institute secondary but not primary legislation) has recently amended the declaration to be made by community councillors. Part III of the Local Government Act 2000 establishes a new 'ethical' framework for local government in Wales and section 51 of the Act requires county, county borough and community councils to adopt a code of conduct which is expected of members and co-opted members. Section 52(2) of the Act states that the form of declaration of acceptance of office prescribed by order under section 83 of the Local Government Act 1972 may include an statement that in performing their functions as councillors, members will observe the code of conduct of the relevant council for the time being under section 51 of the 2000 Act. The Local Elections (Declaration of Acceptance of Office) (Amendment) (Wales) Order 2001 (Welsh SI 2001, No. 2963 (W.245)) amends the three orders in force under section 83 of the 1972 Act so that where a council has adopted a code of conduct under section 51 of the 2000 Act, declarants will undertake to observe the council's code of conduct for the time being under that section.

This declaration has to be made within two months from the day of election and must be delivered to a designated officer within the local authority. If this is not done, the office becomes vacant at the end of the two-month period (section 87(1)(a) Local Government Act 1972). In the case of Parish and Community Councils, councillors must make the declaration before, or at, the first Parish or Community Council meeting after his or her election. If the Council concerned permits it, this can be done at a later meeting. Under Section 83 of the aforementioned Act, if this is not done, the seat becomes vacant.

A local councillor may resign at any time by giving a 'written notice' to the relevant officer of the local authority concerned or the Chairman of the Parish or Community Council. The resignation is effective from the time at which the notice is received and no special form is required. A councillor ceases to be qualified to continue in office, if his or her only qualification to be a councillor was inclusion on the electoral register and, for whatever reason, his or her name did not appear on the electoral register. This is not the same as being 'disqualified' as a councillor. When a councillor ceases to be qualified a vacancy occurs.

When, on an election petition, a local government election is declared void, a vacancy is said to occur on the date of the report or certificate of the election court. Where an election is not held when it should have been, the High Court can order an election on a day appointed by them. In the case of elections to Parish or Community Councils, where difficulties arise other than those set out above, the relevant District or Borough Council or Unitary Council in Wales (or where parishes are grouped, the District, Borough or Unitary Council with the majority of voters) can, under Section 39(4) of the Representation of the People Act 1983, do whatever is necessary to hold a proper election.

BY-ELECTIONS IN LOCAL GOVERNMENT

A candidate elected in a local government by-election, serves out the term of the person originally elected, unless he or she fails to sign the declaration of acceptance of office, he or she resigns, dies in office, ceases to be qualified as a councillor (is no longer included on the electoral register, when his or her only qualification to be a councillor was that he or she was included on the register), he or she fails to attend meetings (this includes committees and sub-committees) for six months (section 85, Local Government Act 1972)[15], he or she becomes disqualified or the election is declared void. Where a councillor is believed to be disqualified, under the provisions of section 89 of the Local Government Act 1972, proceedings against a him or her can be instituted by any local government elector. Where a Councillor is disqualified, a vacancy is declared and a by-election called.

A by-election is held either within 35 days of the High Court or the local authority concerned declaring the seat to be vacant (for example, where a councillor was disqualified or where an election was held to be void) or within 35 days from the date on which written notice of the vacancy was given to the authority by two local government electors for the area concerned. If no such request is made there is no by-election.

However, under the provisions of Section 89 of the Local Government Act 1972, when a councillor resigns or dies within six months before the day on which the councillor in question would have retired anyway, the seat remains vacant until that election, unless by not holding a by-election, total vacancies on the council would be more than one third of the entire number of council members. The six month period relates to the date on which the vacancy arose not the date on which a by-election is requested; i.e., if a councillor died at the beginning of September and a by-election was not requested by two electors until late November, the by-election would have to take place within 35 days because the vacancy occurred before the six-month cut off point.

If the poll at an election is abandoned or no one remains validly nominated to fill the vacancy in question then a by-election must be held within 35 days after the day on which the election should have taken place. Under section 21 of the RPA 1985 certain conditions apply where there are insufficient valid nominations remaining to fill all the vacancies at an ordinary election of parish or community councillors. Provided there is a quorum for meetings, the new councillors may co-opt people to fill the vacancies. Under the Local Elections (Parishes and Communities) Rules 1986 (SI 1986, No. 2215), a vacancy is filled if ten electors request a by-election in writing (this has to be given to a district or borough council official) within 14 days of the notice of the vacancy. The election has to be held on a day within 60 days from the day on which the notice was given. If there is no such request then the Parish or Community Council concerned may co-opt someone. Where a vacancy arises within six months before an ordinary election, there is no by-election and the position is filled by co-option.

Under the provisions of the 1972 Act, where the day "on which anything is required or permitted to be done" is a Saturday, Sunday, Christmas Eve, Christmas day, Maundy Thursday, Good Friday or bank holiday the day is taken to mean the first day thereafter which is itself not one of the days so mentioned.

---

[15] Where failure to attend is approved by the local authority before the end of the sixth month period, the seat is not vacated.

PARISH COUNCILS

Proceeding	Time
Publication of notice of election	Not later than the 25th day before the date of election
Delivery of nomination papers	Not later than noon on the 19th day before the day of election
Publication of statement as to persons nominated	Not later than noon on the 17th day before the day of election
Delivery of notices of withdrawals of candidature	Not later than noon on the 16th day before the day of election
Notice of poll	Not later than the 6th day before the day of election
Polling	Between 8am and 9pm on the day of election

The following days are disregarded when calculating the relevant number of days in the above timetable: Saturday or Sunday, Christmas Eve, Christmas Day, Maundy Thursday, Good Friday or a bank holiday or a day appointed for 'public thanksgiving or mourning'. A bank holiday is any day which is a bank holiday under the Banking and Financial Dealings Act 1971 in England and Wales.

The Rules governing the election of parish councillors are almost identical to those governing the election of councillors to principal authorities (district councils, London boroughs, etc) as set out in the Local Elections (Principal Areas) (Amendment) Rules 1986 (SI 1986, No. 2214) and subsequent orders, although nominations (as set out under Rule 5(1) of the Local Elections (Parishes and Communities) Rules 1986 (SI 1986, No. 2215) require only a proposer and seconder. The Local Elections (Parishes and Communities) Rules 1986 (SI 1986, No. 2215) have been modified subsequently by the following:

The Local Elections (Parishes and Communities) (Amendment) Rules 2001
(SI 2001, No. 80)[16]
The Local Elections (Parishes and Communities) (Amendment) Rules 1999
(SI 1999, No. 395)
The Local Elections (Parishes and Communities) (Amendment) Rules 1998
(SI 1998, No. 585)
The Local Elections (Parishes and Communities) (Amendment) Rules 1990
(SI 1990, No. 157)
The Local Elections (Parishes and Communities) (Amendment) Rules 1987
(SI 1987, No. 260)

The Elections Act 2001 (Supplemental Provisions) (No. 2) Order 2001, brought in under the Elections Act 2001, which postponed the local elections in England, Wales and Northern Ireland until 7 June 2001, also ensured that any parish council by-elections could be held on the same day as the 2001 General Election (7 June). The Order disapplied the provisions of section 16(1) of the Representation of the People Act 1985 which states that where a general election and parish council elections fall on the same day, the latter should be postponed for three weeks.

---

[16] The provisions of the PPERA 2000 are applied to local elections by means of The Local Elections (Parishes and Communities)(Amendment) Rules 2001 (SI 2001, No. 80)

PILOT SCHEMES

Section 10 of the Representation of the People Act 2000 contained provisions allowing local authorities in England and Wales to run pilot schemes of different types of voting at local elections. Under Section 10(1) local authorities can submit proposals for such schemes to the Secretary of State who can approve them either with or without modifications. The Secretary of State can then make the necessary orders to enable such pilot schemes to take place. Section 10(2) enables pilot schemes to use voting methods which differ from those set out in the Representation of the People Acts; for example, they may differ in 'when, where and how voting' takes place, how the votes are counted. Under Section 10(3) voting can take place on more than one day and at places other than polling stations. Any local authorities running pilot schemes are obliged to prepare a report on the scheme afterwards containing an assessment of its success or otherwise in terms of turnout, etc. A number of local authorities ran pilot schemes in the local elections in 2000 and the reports of their relative success or otherwise have been published on the Home Office website (www.homeoffice.gov.uk). For example, in Amber Valley Borough Council, postal voting on demand was made available in two wards; Heanor West, which in 1998 had the lowest turnout (21 per cent) in the Borough and Duffield in which turnout had fallen to 42 per cent in 1999. All households in these wards received a poll card which had a return section on which the elector could apply for a postal vote. In Heanor West, applications for postal votes increased by 162 per cent and in Duffield by 84 per cent. However, in Heanor West turnout increased from 21 per cent in 1998 to 28 per cent in 2000, but in Duffield turnout actually fell, from 42 per cent in 1999 to 39 per cent.

Blackpool Borough Council (a unitary authority) piloted an early voting scheme which allowed electors to vote between 8.00am and 9.00pm on Tuesday 2 May and on Wednesday 3 May between 8.00am and 2.00pm. Results of a questionnaire completed by those taking part in the pilot revealed that 81 voters would not have been able to vote on Thursday and 49 might not have voted. However, some of these might well have opted for a postal vote had this been available. 396 electors voted early (0.35 per cent). Overall, turnout at the election was 28.75 per cent, a decline of 13.6 per cent from 1995 (in 1997 local elections in Blackpool were combined with the General Election). In Chester, a mobile polling station was established by the Town Hall from Tuesday 25 April to Friday 28 April at which electors could vote from 9.00am to 5.00pm. Turnout increased by one percent, from 36 per cent in 1999 to 37 per cent in 2000, as a result. In Leeds City Council, an early voting scheme increased turnout by only 0.2 per cent on 1999.

In Bolton Metropolitan Borough Council three wards were chosen in which to pilot all postal voting. As a result of the pilot, in Bromley Cross ward turnout increased from 31.6 per cent in 1999 to 45.75 per cent in 2000, in Farnworth, turnout increased from 15.1 per cent in 1999 to 26.67 per cent in 2000 and in Smithills, from 29.1 per cent in 1999 to 45.52 per cent in 2000. Increases of 14.1 per cent, 11.6 per cent and 13.42 per cent respectively. In Doncaster Borough Council, in the Conisbrough Ward, turnout increased as a result of all postal voting from 24.49 per cent in 1999 to 40.12 per cent in 2000. Average turnout across the borough was 25.49 per cent.

In Broxbourne, the council conducted a pilot using a semi-automated counting scheme. In the four largest wards; Wormley, Turnford, Cheshunt Central, Cheshunt North and Hoddesdon North, bar codes were printed on the ballot papers against the name of each candidate in order to expedite counting.

In Watford, a mobile ballot box enabled electors at residential care homes and sheltered accommodation to vote at their place of residence rather than at a polling station. A ballot box was taken to the homes on 4 or 5 May 2000. Although some residents decided to exercise their right to vote at a polling station, the initiative was popular and turnout was 55.57 per cent (not counting residents who participated in the council's early voting pilot and those who retained postal/proxy votes). Watford also experimented with weekend voting, allowing voting in 12 wards on Saturday 6 and Sunday 7 May, but this does not appear, by the council's own admission, to have enticed vast numbers of new voters out to vote.

Under Section 11 of the Representation of the People Act 2000, if the Secretary of State believes that in the light of a report on pilot voting procedures in any local authority, it would be desirable to apply such measures to all local authorities on a permanent basis he can do so by order under Section 11(2). Such orders must make the same provisions for all elections of a particular type although such an order can exempt a particular local government area.

LOCAL ELECTIONS IN SCOTLAND

Local Government in Scotland has undergone two radical changes in the post-war period; one in 1975 and the other in 1994. In 1975 the existing structure of cities, burghs and counties was abolished and replaced by a system of regions and districts, with three all-purpose authorities for the Western Isles, Orkney and Shetland (Local Government (Scotland) Act 1973). Nine regions were created: Borders, Dumfries & Galloway, Strathclyde, Lothian, Central, Fife, Tayside, Grampian and Highland. There were 53 district authorities. Under the Local Government etc (Scotland) Act 1994, the two-tier system was replaced by 29 unitary authorities. The Act set out provisions governing local elections in Scotland. However, since the passage of the Scotland Act 1998 local elections in Scotland are now the responsibility of the Scottish Parliament and the relationship between local authorities and the new Parliament is currently being considered by the latter's Local Government Committee.

Section 5 of the 1994 Act stated that the first local elections (other than to the councils of the Orkney Islands, Shetland Islands and Western Isles) should take place on 6 April 1995, the next elections in 1999 and in every third year thereafter. Each local government area is divided into electoral wards and each ward returns one councillor. Under Section 6 of the Act, elections are held on the first Thursday in May or a day fixed by the Secretary of State by order made by statutory instrument not later than 1st February in the year preceding the year in which it is to take effect.

The Scottish Executive has indicated its intention to legislate to bring the cycle for local elections into line with those for the Scottish Parliament. This would delay local elections until 2003. The Parliament's Local Government Committee is currently considering the Draft Local Government (Timing of Elections) (Scotland) Bill. The possible introduction of proportional representation in local elections remains controversial. Two recent reports have recommended this. The McIntosh Commission on Local Government Reform ('The Report of the Commission on Local Government and the Scottish Parliament, June 1999) and the Kerley Report ('Renewing Local Democracy', June 2000) the latter of which recommended the adoption of STV. The McIntosh Commission (under the chairmanship of Neil McIntosh CBE) recommended that any PR system needed to preserve the councillor-ward link, ensure fair provision for independent candidates, provide for geographical diversity and ensure a close fit between council wards and natural communities. It argued that three systems be given particular attention: AMS, STV and AV-top-up (as recommended by the Jenkins Commission - 'The Report of the Independent Commission on the Voting System', October 1998, Cm 4090). The Scottish Local

Government (Elections) Bill was introduced in the Scottish Parliament on 4 October 2001 and would bring the local electoral cycle into line with elections to the Scottish Parliament, so that both elections would be held every four years. Local elections scheduled for 2002 would be postponed until 2003. Section 4 of the Bill would allow local authorities (where orders had been made by Ministers) to run pilot schemes to encourage voting in local elections; for example, allowing voting to take place over more than one day an in places other than polling stations.

Section 42 of the RPA 1983 states that the Election Rules set out in Schedule 1 of the Act are applied to local elections in Scotland by rules made by the Secretary of State. These are the Scottish Local Election Rules 1986 (SI 1986, No. 2213 (S 163)) as amended by the Scottish Local Elections Amendment Rules 1990 (SI 1990, No. 262 (S. 25)), the Scottish Local Elections Amendment (No. 2) Rules 1999 (SI 1999, No. 492 (S.34)) and the Local Government (Transitional and Consequential Provisions and Revocations) (Scotland) Order 1996 (SI 1999, NO. 739 (S.72)). Local elections in Scotland are also affected by the provisions of the Representation of the People (Scotland) Regulations 2001 (SI 2001, No. 497); Parts I to IV apply to Scotland, but Part V, which concerns the issue and receipt of postal ballot papers does not.

The majority of the provisions of the Scottish Local Election Rules 1986 (SI 1986, No. 2213 (S 163)) 1986 (as amended) are the same as those contained in the Local Elections (Principal Areas) Rules 1986 (SI 1986, No. 2214) and as a result, only where procedures in Scotland differ markedly from those in England and Wales, have they been referred to below.

TIMETABLE FOR LOCAL ELECTIONS IN SCOTLAND

Proceeding	Time
Publication of notice of election	On or within seven days before the fifth Tuesday before polling day
Delivery of nomination papers	Not later than 4.00pm on the fourth Tuesday before polling day
Delivery of notices of withdrawals of candidature	Not later than 4.00pm on the third Thursday before polling day
Notice of poll	Not later than the Thursday before polling day
Polling	Between 8am and 9pm on the day of election

Where a vacancy arises the by-election must take place within three months on a day set by the returning officer and the timetable above applies subject to any modifications necessary to secure completion of the proceedings before the date fixed for the by-election. In the timetable above the following days are disregarded:

- ❖ Saturdays and Sundays
- ❖ Christmas Eve, Christmas Day, Maundy Thursday, Good Friday or a bank holiday as defined as a bank holiday in Scotland under the Banking and Financial Dealings Act 1971
- ❖ A day appointed for public thanksgiving or mourning

Local elections in Scotland were modified by Schedule 5 of the Scottish Parliament (Elections etc) Order 1999 (SI 1999, No 787), which relates to occasions where Scottish parliamentary elections are on the same day as local government elections.

LOCAL ELECTIONS IN NORTHERN IRELAND

The law governing local elections in Northern Ireland is primarily set out in the Electoral Law Act (Northern Ireland) 1962 as amended by the Local Elections (Northern Ireland) Order 1985 (SI 1985, No. 454) (there have been other, subsequent, amendments to the 1962 Act and the 1985 order and where appropriate, these are detailed below). Local elections in Northern Ireland take place on the third Wednesday in May. The Elected Authorities (Northern Ireland) Act 1989 was amended by the Representation of the People Act 2000 and the subsequent Representation of the People (Northern Ireland) Regulations 2001 (SI 2001, No. 400). Schedule 3 of the RPA 2000 made a number of amendments to Schedule 1 to the Elected Authorities (Northern Ireland) Act 1989, which applies the provisions of the RPA 1983 to local elections. This has the effect of ensuring that the measures contained in the RPA 2000 relating to rolling registration, declarations of local connection and service declarations are all applied to local elections in Northern Ireland. These measures were outlined in Chapter Two on parliamentary elections.

Schedule 1 of the Elected Authorities (Northern Ireland) Act 1989 applies the following provisions of the RPA 1983 (as recently amended by the RPA 2000) to local elections in Northern Ireland. References to the registration officer in the RPA 1983 are taken as being references to the Chief Electoral Officer for Northern Ireland. Only the main provisions of the Schedule are set out below.

Section 3(1) and (2) (disenfranchisement of offenders in prison, etc.), section 3A(1) and (4) to (7).	This disqualifies prisoners from voting as well as offenders detained in mental hospitals.
Section 4(2) to (6).	This has the effect of ensuring that in Northern Ireland, voters must have been resident for three months before being eligible to be on an electoral register. The normal provisions of not being subject to any legal incapacity to vote, being a qualifying Commonwealth, Irish or EU citizen also apply. Overseas electors cannot vote in local government elections.
Sections 5, 6, 7A to 7C	Section 6 of the RPA 1983 allows merchant seamen to be considered as resident and therefore to vote. Sections 5, 7 and 7A to 7C extend the provisions of the RPA 2000 (now incorporated into the RPA 1983) which allow homeless people, those detained in mental hospitals who are not offenders, those in custody on remand and those who have made a declaration of local connection, to vote.
Sections 9, 10, 10A and 13 to 13B	This applies the new provisions relating to 'rolling registration' to local elections in Northern Ireland.
Sections 14 to 17 (service qualifications and service declarations)	This implements the new provisions relating to service declarations as set out in the RPA 2000 to local elections in Northern Ireland. Under Schedule 1 (7) and (8) of the RPA 2000, Section 15 of the RPA 1983 is amended to make service declarations valid for one year, as opposed to indefinitely, as at present. There will no longer be any difference between declarations made by members of the armed forces and their spouses and those made by others with a service qualification.
Sections 49 and 50 (effect of registers and of misdescription)	These sections ensure that anyone on the electoral register can vote, even if they are NOT legally qualified to vote. In order to vote, an elector only needs to be included on the electoral register; however, this does not mean that it is not an offence to vote if not legally entitled to.
Section 53 and in Schedule 2, paragraphs 1(2) to (5), 3, 3A, 4 to 11A and 13	These provisions, amended by the RPA 2000, allow certain matters pertaining to registration to be set out in secondary

	legislation. It also makes it an offence (punishable on summary conviction by a fine not exceeding level 3 on the standard scale) not to give the Chief Electoral Officer the information required for the purpose of his or her registration duties.
Section 54(2) to (4) (expenses of registration)	This section states that expenses incurred by the Chief Electoral Officer are to be paid from funds provided by Parliament.
Section 56(1) and (3) to (5), 58(2) and 59	These sections deal with registration appeals (section 58 of the RPA 1983 was amended by paragraph 15 of Schedule 1 of the RPA 2000) and applies the provisions relating to such appeals to Northern Ireland (in a way which is applicable to the legal system there).
Section 62 and 180A	This extends the provisions of new section 62 of the RPA 1983, as inserted by paragraph 17 of Schedule 1 of the RPA 2000, to Northern Ireland, making it an offence to make a declaration of local connection when not authorised to do so or to attest a service declaration when not authorised to do so, punishable on summary conviction by a fine not exceeding level 5 on the standard scale.
Section 4(2), a reference to parliamentary electors is to be read as 'local electors for any district electoral area' and for the words 'subsection (1) above', 'subsection (3) below' is substituted. In section 4(4)(a) the reference to any enactment includes an enactment comprised in Northern Ireland legislation. In section 7B references to the UK are to be read as references to Northern Ireland. In section 9, for subsection (1)(b) there is substituted (b) a register of local electors for each district.	The effect of new section 4(2) of the RPA 1983 as substituted by the RPA 2000 is that electors must have been resident in Northern Ireland for three months in order to be entitled to vote. The provisions on the left ensure that this also applies to local electors.

Section 3 of the Elected Authorities (Northern Ireland) Act 1989 states that a person is not validly nominated as a candidate in a local election unless he or she has made a declaration stating that he or she will not support terrorism.[17]   The penalty for breaching the terms of the declaration is disqualification.

Schedule 1 of the 1985 Order substituted a new schedule for Schedule 5 of the 1962 Act. This schedule contained the Local Election Rules. The main provisions of those Rules are set out in the following paragraphs.

---

[17] The declaration against terrorism as set out in Part I of Schedule 2 to the Elected Authorities (Northern Ireland) Act 1989 is inserted into the form, 'Candidate's consent to nomination' as set out in Schedule 5 to the Electoral Law Act (Northern Ireland) 1962. A similar declaration has to be made where a candidate stands in a by-election.

Proceeding	Time
Publication of notice of election	Not later than the 25th day before the date of election
Delivery of nomination papers	Between 10am and 5pm on the 17th and 16th days before election day
Delivery of notices of withdrawals of candidature	Within the time for the delivery of nomination papers at the election
Objections to nomination papers	Within the time allowed for the delivery of nomination papers and on the 16th day before election day for an hour after as well
Publication of statement of persons nominated	After nominations have closed or as soon as possible after objections have been made
Polling	Between 7am and 10pm on the day of election

The timetable for local authority by-elections is set out below.

Proceeding	Time
Publication of notice of election	Within 21 days from the date on which a casual vacancy is deemed to have occurred under section 11(5) of the 1962 Act
Delivery of nomination papers	Between 10am and 5pm on two consecutive days, the second of which must not be earlier than the 4th day, nor later than the 7th day after the day of publication of the notice of election
Delivery of notices of withdrawals of candidature	Within the time for the delivery of nomination papers at the election
Objections to nomination papers	Within the time allowed for the delivery of nomination papers and on the 16th day before election day for an hour after as well
Publication of statement of persons nominated	After nominations have closed or as soon as possible after objections have been made
Polling	Between 7am and 10pm on the day of election (fixed by the Chief Electoral Officer, or deputy returning officer, and which must be no earlier than the 18th day nor later than the 21st day after the last day for the delivery of nomination papers)

For the purposes of the above tables, the following days are disregarded: Saturday and Sunday, Christmas Eve, Maundy Thursday or any public holiday.

A candidate's nomination paper must state the candidate's full name, home and address and if desired, a description, consisting of either a description of no more than six words in length or the word 'independent'. Under the provisions of paragraph 5A of Schedule 1 of the 1985 Order (as inserted by the Local Elections (Northern Ireland) (Amendment) Order 2001 (SI 2001, No. 417), a nomination paper may not include a description of a candidate which is likely to lead voters to associate the candidate with a registered political party unless the party is a qualifying party in relation to the district electoral area and the description is authorised by a certificate issued by or on behalf of the registered nominating officer of the party and received by the returning officer before the last time for the delivery of nomination papers. A person is guilty of a corrupt practice if he or she fraudulently pretends to be authorised to issue a certificate on behalf of a registered political party's nominating officer. A registered political party is one registered under Part II of the PPERA 2000 and a registered party is a qualifying party in relation to a district electoral area if the party is registered in the Northern Ireland register under Part II of the Act.

A candidate must give his or her consent to nomination in writing on or within one month before the last day for delivery of nomination papers and this must be attested by one witness and delivered at the time for delivery of nomination papers.

A candidate's nomination paper requires a proposer and seconder and must be supported by eight other electors (all of whom must live in the relevant electoral area). Candidates must give their consent to be nominated in writing within one month before the last day for the delivery of nomination papers and this consent must be attested by one witness. The following can attend the delivery of nomination papers: the candidates or their election agents, proposers or seconders (where a candidate is acting as his or her own election agent, he or she can name another person to attend in place of an agent). If a candidate subsequently decides to withdraw from the election, he or she must do so in writing and this must be attested by one witness (this can be done by a candidate's proposer if the candidate is not in Northern Ireland at the time).

Ballot papers are marked with the official mark. There has to be an interval of at least seven years between the use of the same official mark in elections for the same district area. A different mark must be used for postal ballot papers. Ballot papers can now include party emblems. The provisions of the Schedule 1 of the 1985 Order (Schedule 5 of the 1962 Act) have been amended to take account of the new provisions of the RPA 2000 relating to disabled voters. Rule 26 of Schedule 5 accordingly states that each polling station should have one large version of the ballot paper which must be displayed inside the polling station to assist blind or partially sighted voters. There must also be a 'device' to assist blind or partially sighted voters cast their vote without assistance. The device was described in Chapter 2 on parliamentary elections.

Candidates can appoint polling agents to attend polling stations and one counting agent to attend the count. Names and addresses must be given by the candidate to the returning officer before 5pm on the second day before the day of the poll. The presiding officer can allow certain people to attend the polling station. The following may attend as of right: candidates and election agents, polling agents, clerks, police on duty, companions of disabled voters. Only one polling agent can attend a polling station at any one time on behalf of the same candidate. Police officers and those employed by the returning officer can vote at polling stations other than the one to which they have been allocated on production of a certificate.

Before the polls open, the returning officer and presiding officers, every clerk authorised to attend either a polling station or the count and all candidates and election agents attending polling stations or the count and anyone else permitted to attend the count, must sign a declaration of secrecy. Candidates, election agents, those allowed to attend the count must make the declaration before the count.

In contrast to elections in Great Britain, electors in Northern Ireland are required to produce some evidence of identity before they can vote. An elector must produce one of a number of specified documents before he or she can be given a ballot paper. Under the provisions of the Elections (Northern Ireland) Act 1985, voters must present identity documents at the polling station before being given a ballot paper. Provisions relating to local elections are set out in Rule 34 of Schedule 5 in the Electoral Law Act (Northern Ireland) 1962 (as inserted by Schedule 1, Part III, Article 34 of the Local Elections (Northern Ireland) Order 1985 (SI 1985, No. 454). Rule 32 of Schedule 5 states that before a ballot paper is issued, an elector can be asked the following questions:

❖ "Are you the person registered in the register of electors for the election as follows"? (the relevant entry from register is then read out)

❖ "Have you already voted on your own behalf either here or elsewhere in this or any other district electoral area at this election"?

Where the elector is voting as proxy, the questions are:

❖ "Are you the person whose name appears as ... in the list of proxies for this election as entitled to vote as proxy on behalf of ..."?

❖ "Have you already voted as proxy on behalf of ... either here or elsewhere in this or any other district electoral area at this election"?

The following additional question may also be asked:

❖ "Are you the husband (wife), parent, grandparent, brother (sister), child or grandchild or ..."?

If the answer to that question is 'no', then the following question is asked:

❖ "Have you at this election already voted in this district electoral area on behalf of two persons of whom you are not the husband (wife), parent, grandparent, brother (sister), child or grandchild"?

A candidate, his or her election agent or polling agent can challenge a voter on the grounds of personation provided he undertakes to substantiate the accusation in court. The presiding officer can then order that voter's arrest, although that person may still vote.

The specified documents, one of which must be produced by each voter, are: a current driving licence, a current passport, a current social security payment book, a medical card or a marriage certification (where the voter is a woman married within two years ending with the day of the poll concerned), a British seaman's card or a national insurance card. Under new section 36 of Schedule 5 (as inserted by the Local Elections (Northern Ireland) (Amendment) Order 2001 (SI 2001, No. 417) a voter who is blind or has another disability or who is unable to read can vote with the assistance of a companion, who must make a written declaration stating that he or she has not previously assisted more than one voter with a disability to vote. A person (over 18 years of age) who is entitled to vote at the election, or the father, mother, brother, sister, husband, wife, son or daughter of the voter concerned may act as a companion. Provisions relating to tendered ballot papers are similar to those which apply in England, Wales and Scotland.

At the close of the poll, the presiding officer must put together the following packets and deliver them to the returning officer. He or she must also include a 'ballot paper account' showing the number of ballot papers issued, the number unused, spoilt and also the number of tendered ballot papers.

❖ Unused and spoilt ballot papers.

❖ Tendered ballot papers.

❖ Marked copies of the register of electors and of the list of proxies.

❖ Counterfoils of the used ballot papers and the certificates as to employment on duty on the day of the poll.

❖ The tendered votes list, the list of disabled voters, the list of votes marked by the presiding officer, a statement of the number of voters whose votes have been marked by the presiding officer (on the grounds of disability) and the declarations made by disabled voters' companions.

❖ Marked copies of the register of electors and list of proxies.

The proceedings at the count differ from local elections in England, Wales and Scotland in that the Single Transferable Vote (STV) is used. Those who can attend the count include the returning officer and his or her clerks, the candidates, the election agents, the counting agents, the police on duty and those given permission to attend by the returning officer. Before the count, the returning officer opens each ballot box and counts and records the number of ballot papers (ballot papers are kept face upwards). Each ballot paper account is verified in the presence of the election agents and is compared with the number of ballot papers recorded by the returning officer, the number of unused and spoilt ballot papers returned to him and the tendered votes list. The packets containing unused, spoilt and the tendered votes list are opened and then resealed. The postal ballot papers are then counted before being mixed with the other ballot papers. The following ballot papers are rejected:

❖ Those without the official mark.

❖ Those on which the figure '1'(indicating a first preference) is not placed so as to indicate a first preference for a candidate (the word 'one' instead of the figure '1' would be considered acceptable).

❖ Those on which the figure '1' is placed against more than one candidate.

❖ Those on which anything identifying the voter is written.

❖ Those which are unmarked.

❖ Those which are considered 'void' for uncertainty.

Rejected ballot papers are marked with the word 'rejected' and any election agent can object, in which case the words 'rejection objected to' are written on the ballot paper. A statement of rejected ballot papers (under the headings above) is made by the returning officer. The returning officer's decision is final but can be challenged on an election petition.

The count then takes place in various stages. In the first stage the ballot papers are sorted according to the candidates' first preference votes. The numbers of first preferences accorded to each candidate are then recorded. The quota is then obtained by firstly, dividing the number of valid ballot papers by the number of members to be elected plus one, then adding one. Where one candidate's votes exceeds the quota, the returning officer then transfers his or her second preferences.

All the ballot papers on which that candidate appears as a first preference are then sorted into piles according to the next available preference (the second preference). Some of those ballot papers will be non-transferable, i.e., the voter will only have expressed a first preference. These second preference votes are then transferred to the relevant candidates. However, these second preferences do not have the same value as a first preference. They are given a 'transfer value', which reduces the value of each vote transferred so that the value of all such votes does not exceed the surplus and is calculated by dividing the surplus of the candidate from whom the votes are being transferred by the total number of the ballot papers on which those votes are given (i.e., the candidate's surplus votes are divided by the total number of their first preferences) – the calculation being made to two decimal places.

If at the end of the process any candidate has votes exceeding the quota, those surplus ballot papers are then counted into piles according to the next preference (some votes will again be non-transferable). These transferred votes have a value which is either the value calculated by the method set out above or the value at which the vote was received by the candidate from whom it is being transferred, whichever is the less. This process continues until either there is no candidate with surplus votes or all the places have been filled. However, votes are not transferred where any surplus is less than the difference between the total vote at that point credited to the continuing candidate with the lowest recorded vote and the vote of the candidate with the next lowest recorded vote or less than the difference between the total votes of the two or more continuing candidates credited at that stage of the count with the lowest recorded total number of votes and the candidate next above such candidates.

If at any stage of the count, two or more candidates have surpluses, the transferable ballot papers of the one with the largest surplus is transferred first. Where the surpluses of two or more candidates are equal, the votes of the candidate with the highest recorded votes at the earliest preceding stage at which they had unequal votes are transferred first. If the votes for two or more candidates were equal at all stages of the count, the returning officer must decide between them by lot. When votes are transferred to a candidate their value is added to the previous total of votes for that candidate. When there are no candidates remaining with surplus votes, the candidate with the lowest vote is eliminated and his or her second preferences transferred. In some cases the second preference will be for a candidate already elected, in which case the vote is transferred to the next available preference. The transfer value is the value at which the vote was received by the candidate who has been eliminated. If after this process any candidate has a surplus it is dealt with in the manner set out above.

Where the total of the votes of the two or more lowest candidates together with any un-transferred surpluses is less than the number of votes for the next lowest candidate, the returning officer excludes those candidates. If two or more such candidates have the same number of votes, the one with the lowest number of votes at the earliest stage of the count at which they had an unequal number of votes, is eliminated. Where the number of continuing candidates is equal to the number of vacancies remaining unfilled the continuing candidates are elected. Where only one vacancy remains and the votes of any one continuing candidate are equal to or greater than the total of votes credited to another candidate together with any surplus not transferred, the candidate is deemed elected. Candidates can request recounts of any of the stages outlined above.

After the result has been declared, the counted and rejected ballot papers are sealed up in separate packets. These along with the ballot paper accounts, statements of rejected ballot papers, the result of the verification of the ballot paper accounts, the tendered votes list, the lists of disabled voters, the lists of votes marked by the presiding officer and the declarations made by companions of disabled voters, the counterfoils and certificates of those on duty on the day of the poll and the marked copies of the registers and lists of proxies are forwarded in separate packets to the relevant council.

If a candidate dies before the result of the election is declared the notice of the poll is countermanded or if polling has begun, the poll is abandoned. The proceedings then start again as if it were a by-election (fresh nominations are not required).

An Appendix to Schedule 1 to the 1985 Regulations sets out the format of the following forms: nomination papers, the candidate's consent to nomination, the ballot paper itself, the declaration of identity required for postal voting, the elector's official poll card, the proxy's official poll card, the directions for the guidance of voters, the form of certificate of employment and the declaration to be made by a disabled voter.

Absent Voters

The provisions relating to absent voting in Northern Ireland have been amended frequently. The provisions contained in Schedule 2 to the Local Elections (Northern Ireland) Order 1985 (SI 1985, No. 454) were replaced by Article 5(5) (effectively substituting a new Schedule 2 for the previous one in the 1985 Order) of the Local Elections (Northern Ireland) Order 1987 (SI 1987, No. 168). These new provisions were then subsequently amended by the Local Elections (Northern Ireland) (Amendment) Order 1990 (SI 1990, No. 595), but were then further amended by the Local Elections (Northern Ireland) (Amendment) Order 1997 (SI 1997, No. 867) and later, the Local Elections (Northern Ireland) (Amendment) Order 1998 (SI 1998, No. 3150). The details below refer to the absent voting provisions as amended by all of the above.

To be eligible for an absent vote at local elections for an indefinite period, a person must be one of the following:

❖ Registered as a service elector

❖ Unable to go in person to a polling station

❖ Unable to vote unaided on the grounds of disability at a polling station

❖ Unable to get to a polling station for occupational or employment reasons (or those of his or her spouse)

❖ Unable to get to a polling station without making a journey by air or sea

To be eligible for an absent vote at a particular local election, an elector must be able to show that he or she would be unable to get to the polling station allotted to him or her. Proxy voters can also vote by post at local elections for an indefinite period of for a particular election. An application for a postal or proxy vote must be signed and attested by a UK resident of at least 18 years of age, who knows the applicant but is not related to him[18] and who has not attested 'any other application in respect of the election for which the application he attests is made'. A medical practitioner could attest more than one application to vote by post or proxy on the grounds of ill health for a particular election.

---

[18] One person is deemed to be related to another if he is the husband, wife, parent, grandparent, brother, sister, child or grandchild of the other.

Where an application for either a postal or proxy vote is on the grounds of disability, it must be attested and signed by one of the following (except where the application is registered blind or in receipt of the mobility component of the disability living allowance, in which case they automatically qualify):

❖ A registered medical practitioner (who is treating the applicant)

❖ A registered nurse[19] (who is treating the applicant)

❖ A Christian Science practitioner (who is treating the applicant)

❖ The person registered under the Registered Homes (Northern Ireland) Order 1992 as 'carrying on' the residential care home or nursing home in question

❖ The warden of accommodation provided for pensioners or people with disabilities

❖ The officer in charge of accommodation under Article 15 of the Health and Personal Social Services (Northern Ireland) Order 1972

The person attesting the application must state that he or she has seen the applicant in connection with the circumstances that have rendered a postal vote necessary on the grounds of illness.

Where an application is on the grounds of employment it must be attested and signed where the person concerned is self-employed, by a UK resident aged 18 or over who knows the person concerned and is not related to him or her or where the applicant is an employee, by his or her employer.

Applications to vote by post or proxy at a particular election on the grounds of ill health, which could not reasonably have been foreseen, can be delivered to the Chief Electoral Officer after 5pm on the 14th day before the election (the standard closing date) (17 May in the case of the 2001 district council elections) but must be delivered before 5pm on the 6th day before the election (30 May in the case of the 2001 elections). This is also the deadline for applications from police constables and those employed by returning officers, who by virtue of the fact that they will be employed to assist with the election, will not be able to vote at their normal polling station.

Applications to vote by post or proxy indefinitely, applications from postal voters to vote by proxy and from proxy voters to vote by post, applications to appoint proxies indefinitely and applications by proxies to vote by post indefinitely must all be received by the Chief Electoral Officer by 5pm on the 14th day before polling day.

Applications to vote by post or proxy at a particular election, applications from postal voters for ballot papers to be sent to different addresses or to vote by proxy instead at a particular election, applications to appoint a proxy for a particular election, applications from proxies to vote by post at a particular election and applications from proxies voting by post to ballot papers to be sent to different addresses for a particular election must be received by the Chief Electoral Officer before 5pm on the 14th day before polling day.

---

[19] A registered nurse is one who comes within the meaning of section 10(7) of the Nurses, Midwives and Health Visitors Act 1979

Applications from those registered as postal and proxy voters indefinitely and those proxy voters registered as voting by post indefinitely, to be removed from those registers must be received before 5pm on the 14th day before polling day. This is also the deadline for the cancellation of a proxy's appointment.

The lists of proxy and postal voters are available for inspection after 5pm on the 14th day before polling day and a copy is made available to candidates or their agents. Postal voters are denoted on the register by the letter 'A'. Part II of Schedule 2 to the 1985 Regulations sets out the format of the forms for applications for absent voting for an indefinite period or for a particular election, the forms to be used for declarations by medical practitioners, etc.

Under Article 6(7) of the of the Local Elections (Northern Ireland) Order 1985 (SI 1985, No. 454) (as amended by the Local Elections (Northern Ireland) (Amendment) Order 1987 (SI 2001, No. 168), where a local elector, who is not entitled to an absent vote, but cannot reasonably be expected to attend the polling station allotted to him or her on the grounds of his or her employment "either as a constable or by the returning officer, on the day of the poll", he or she can vote at any polling station within the relevant district electoral area.

The regulations governing the issuing and counting of postal ballot papers are similar to the provisions which apply in Great Britain and are set out in Part III of Schedule 2 to the Local Elections (Northern Ireland) Order 1985 (SI 1985, No. 454).

The absent voting forms set out in Part II of Schedule 2 to the Local Elections (Northern Ireland) Order 1985 (SI 1985, No. 454) were revoked by Article 5(6) of the Local Elections (Northern Ireland) (Amendment) Order 1987 (SI 1987, No. 168) because the Order set out the contents of applications to vote by post or proxy but did not prescribe the forms as such.

The absent voting system in Northern Ireland has been, and some would claim still is, open to abuse. The report 'Vote Early, Vote Fairly – Administering Elections in Northern Ireland' (Report of the Elections Review 1998)[20] refers to concerns expressed by the Chief Electoral Officer that up to half of all absent vote applications for the 1997 local government elections were suspicious. It appeared that many forms in the same ward had been photocopied with the name of the ward and the date of the elections applied for, included in the photocopy. In other wards, the handwriting on several forms appeared to be identical, apart from the applicant's signature. There were also reported cases of health workers signing several blank postal ballot application forms, which were completed at a later stage by people they were not treating and may not even have known. This, despite the warning on the form that *"a fine of up to £5,000 can be incurred by anyone who on this application makes a statement he or she knows to be false, or signs an application when not authorised to do so, or signs an application which he or she knows contains a false statement"*.

The 'Vote Early, Vote Fairly' report also suggested that the photocopying of absent voting application forms be prohibited and that applications forms be numbered, watermarked and / or bar-coded. The report also suggested that the use of correction fluid be disallowed and that the involvement of any other individual in the completion of the form be declared with the applicant signing to say that they had sanctioned the other person's involvement. The report also suggested that consideration be given to the introduction of

---

[20] Available at: www.nics.gov.uk/nio_old/press/981021z-nio.htm

a computer-generated application form, which could print individually marked forms with each applicant's name and address and the reason for application prior to its being sent to the applicant for completion.

The law relating to local elections in Northern Ireland is set out not in the RPA 1983 but in Section 2 of the Elected Authorities (Northern Ireland) Act 1989, which applies the provisions as those set out in the 1983 Act to local elections in Northern Ireland. Part 1 of Schedule 1 of the 1989 Act set out those provisions of the RPA 1983 which apply to local elections in Northern Ireland (with some amendments). Schedule 3 of the RPA 2000 amends the aforementioned 1989 Act to take into account the new provisions relating to rolling registration. Schedule 3 (3) of the RPA 2000 amends Part I, Schedule I of the 1989 Act to reflect the changes made by Section 1 of the RPA 2000 to Section 2 of the RPA 1983. The effect is to ensure that those in mental hospitals (apart from offenders) and those on remand are able to vote. The Chief Electoral Office oversees elections and the administration of registration and elections lies with the staff of the Electoral Office as opposed to local authorities. The franchise for local elections in Northern Ireland is set out in section 1 of the Elected Authorities (Northern Ireland) Act 1989 as amended by Schedule 3 of the RPA 2000 and consists of those who are:

❖ Resident there on the qualifying date and have been resident in Northern Ireland during the whole of the period of three months ending on that date.

❖ Are not subject to any legal incapacity to vote, and are aged 18 years or over on the date of the poll.

Under Section Three of the 1989 Act, all candidates must sign a declaration against terrorism, as set out in Part I of Schedule 2. This states that the candidate will not express support for any organisation proscribed under Schedule 2 of the Northern Ireland (Emergency Provisions) Act 1978 or for acts of terrorism *"connected with the affairs of Northern Ireland"*. Under Section 6 of the Act, any candidate who is elected as a councillor breaches the terms of his or her declaration if at any subsequent time he or she expresses support for terrorism at a public meeting. He or she would be disqualified for a five-year period.

The provisions of the RPA 2000 relating to proxy and postal voting do not extend to Northern Ireland. The rules governing absent voting in Northern Ireland are contained in the Representation of the People (Northern Ireland) Regulations 2001 (SI 2001, No. 400) which concerns parliamentary elections, the Electoral Law Act (Northern Ireland) 1962 and the Local Elections (Northern Ireland) Order 1985 (SI 1985, No. 454) as subsequently amended by the Local Elections (Northern Ireland) Order 1987 (SI 1987, No. 168) and the Local Elections (Northern Ireland) Order 1997 (SI 1997, No. 867).

The Legislation Relating to Corrupt and Illegal Practices in Northern Ireland

The provisions in the RPA 1983 concerning corrupt and illegal practices are applied, with some modifications, to Northern Ireland UK Parliamentary elections and elections to the Northern Ireland Assembly by Order in Council. *These provisions do not apply to local elections in Northern Ireland. The provisions relating to corrupt and illegal practices and other electoral offences as they relate to local government elections in Northern Ireland are set out primarily in the Electoral Law Act (Northern Ireland) 1962 as subsequently amended by the Local Elections (Northern Ireland) (Amendment) Order 1987 (SI 1987,*

No. 168) and the Local Elections (Northern Ireland) (Amendment) Order 2001 (SI 2001, No. 417). References in the 1962 Act to 'Parliament' are not to the UK Parliament but to the Parliament at Stormont, which existed prior to direct rule. The following section details the provisions of the 1962 Act, as amended, which relate to local elections.

A local election in Northern Ireland can be questioned on the grounds that the person elected was at the time of the election disqualified from standing or was not duly elected or on the grounds that the election was avoided by corrupt or illegal practices. A local election petition questioning a local election can be presented by four or more people who voted as electors or who had the right to do so at the election or by a candidate at the election. A local election petition must be presented within 21 days after the day on which the election was held, unless the petition makes an allegation of corrupt or illegal practices alleging a payment of money or other reward to have been made or promised by a candidate elected at the election, or on his account since the election, in which case it can be presented within 28 days after the date of the alleged payment.

If an election court finds that a corrupt or illegal practice has been committed with the knowledge and consent of a candidate he or she is treated as having been found personally guilty of that corrupt or illegal practice. If a candidate is found personally guilty or guilty by his agents of any corrupt or illegal practice his election is void. Section 96 (3) and (4) of the 1962 Act were recently amended by Article 7 of the Local Elections (Northern Ireland) (Amendment) Order (SI 2001, No. 417). A candidate found personally guilty of a corrupt practice (personation) or an illegal practice (other voting offences as set out in paragraph 4 of Schedule 9 to the 1962 Act) cannot, for a period of five years in the case of a corrupt practice and three years in the case of an illegal practice, be registered as an elector or vote in any local election in Northern Ireland or hold any election office (if he or she is already holding such an office, it must be vacated). Under section 98, where corrupt or illegal practices are deemed to have been so extensive as to have affected the result of the election, the election is declared void and the candidate's election is deemed void. Under section 99, if a local election candidate or his agent personally engages as a canvasser or agent any known to be subject to an incapacity to vote on the grounds of having been convicted or reported guilty of any corrupt or illegal practice, the candidate is deemed incapable of being elected.

Electoral misdemeanours are set out in Schedule Nine to the Electoral Law Act (Northern Ireland) 1962. Corrupt practices are set out in Part I, illegal practices in Part II and electoral offences in Part III. In the case of local elections, a corrupt practice is an indictable offence but a person charged with a corrupt practice can be tried summarily is he so consents. A person charged with an illegal practice is tried summarily. A person charged with an electoral offence other than the offence set out in paragraph 26(2) of Schedule Nine is tried summarily and anyone to whom section III(2A)(c)(i) applies charged with the offence in paragraph 26(2) of Schedule Nine can be tried either way. A person convicted of a corrupt practice at a local election is liable to (in the case of conviction on indictment) in the case of a corrupt practice under paragraph 4 of Schedule 9 or paragraph 8 or 9 of Schedule 9 in relation to the offence in paragraph 4, to imprisonment for a term not exceeding one year, or to a fine or both. In the case of someone found guilty on summary conviction, the penalty is imprisonment for a term not exceeding six months or to a fine not exceeding the statutory maximum or to both. In the case of a local election a person found guilty of an illegal practice is liable to a fine not exceeding level five on the standard scale. Under section 111(2A) of the 1962 Act as amended by the Local Elections (Northern Ireland) (Amendment) Order 1987, a person found guilty of an electoral offence is liable in the case of an offence under paragraphs 24, 24A, 25, 28, 29, 30, 31 or 32A of Schedule 9 to a fine not exceeding level 5 on the standard scale; in the case of an offence under paragraph 26(1) or 33 of Schedule 9, on summary conviction to a fine not exceeding level 3 on the standard scale and in the case of an offence under paragraph 26(2) of Schedule 9 (i) if the person guilty of the offence is the Chief Electoral Officer or any person to whom functions are delegated by him under this Act, a presiding officer or a clerk appointed to assist in taking the poll, counting the votes or assisting at the proceedings in connection with the issue or receipt of postal ballot papers, on conviction on indictment to a fine, or to imprisonment for a term not exceeding two years, or to both or on summary conviction to a fine not exceeding the statutory maximum or to imprisonment for a term not exceeding six months, or to both; (ii) if the person guilty of the offence is any other person, on summary conviction to a fine not exceeding level 5 on the standard scale or to imprisonment for a term not exceeding six months, or to both; in the case of an offence under paragraph 27 of Schedule 9, on summary conviction to a fine not exceeding level 5 on the standard scale or to imprisonment for a term not exceeding six months and in the case of an offence under paragraph 32 of Schedule 9 on summary conviction to a fine not exceeding level four on the standard scale.

Section 112(1) of the 1962 Act as amended by the Local Elections (Northern Ireland) (Amendment) Order 2001 (SI 2001, No. 417) states that a person convicted of a corrupt practice under paragraph 4 of Schedule 9 (personation) or an illegal practice (under paragraph 12A of Schedule 9 (other voting offences), cannot for the period of five years in the case of a corrupt practice and three in the case of an illegal practice, be registered as an elector or vote at any local election in Northern Ireland or hold any elective office (if already holding such an office they must vacate it). If an appeal against conviction was successful, then the period above would end at the time of the successful appeal. Where a person has to vacate an office, this must be done at the end of the period prescribed in law within which notice of appeal may be given, or an application for leave to appeal may be made by him in respect of the conviction, or if that period is extended, the end of the extension period or the end of the period of three months beginning with the date of the conviction, whichever is the earlier. If, before the times mentioned above, notice of appeal is given, or an application for leave to appeal is made by a person in respect of the conviction, he or she must vacate the office in question at the end of the period of three months beginning with the date of the conviction unless the appeal is dismissed or abandoned at an earlier time (in which case the person concerned must vacate the office at that time) or unless at any time within that period of three months the court determines on appeal that the conviction should not be upheld (in which case he or she does not vacate the office concerned). Where a person has already vacated an office, no later ruling of a court that the conviction should not be upheld entitles him or her to resume the office. If a person convicted of a corrupt or illegal practice has already been elected he or she is suspended from performing any function of that office from the date of the conviction until either the date on which the office is vacated or the date on which the court determines the conviction should not be upheld.

In computing any period of time involved in a local election campaign or the questioning of any election campaign, the following days are disregarded, Saturday and Sunday, Christmas Eve, Maundy Thursday or any public holiday.

Schedule 9 (as subsequently amended) lists what are considered to be electoral misdemeanours. As far as local elections are concerned, corrupt practices are bribery, treating, undue influence, personation, making a false statement in a nomination paper (inserted by the Local Elections (Northern Ireland) (Amendment) Order 2001 (SI 2001, No. 417), making false declarations as to election expenses, incurring unauthorised expenses, attempting to conspire or commit a corrupt practice or aiding and abetting the commission of a corrupt practice. The following are illegal practices: disrupting an election meeting during the election campaign; failure to deliver any statement, return or declaration required under sections 41, 46 and 47 of the 1962 Act (election returns and declarations of expenses); the making of payments in contravention of section 39(1) and (4) (payments other than by the election agent); payments to anyone other than advertising agents to exhibit election posters; the publication of a false statement alleging that a candidate has withdrawn from the election; the publication of false statements about candidates; the payment of expenses in contravention of section 42 (payments in excess of the maximum amount which candidates are permitted to spend at local elections); payments in contravention of 43(1) and (2) (claims for election expenses must be submitted within 21 days after the election and paid within 28) and attempting or conspiring, or aiding, abetting or counselling or procuring the commission of any of the above illegal practices.

As far as postal or proxy voting is concerned paragraph 12A of Schedule 9 (as inserted by the Local Elections (Northern Ireland) (Amendment) Order 1987) states that a person is guilty of an illegal practice if he votes in person or by post (whether as an elector or as a proxy) or applies to vote by proxy or by post as an elector, if he or she knows that he or she is subject to a legal incapacity to vote at the election or if he applies for the appointment of a proxy knowing that the person to be appointed is subject to a legal incapacity to vote, if he votes whether by post or in person as proxy for someone knowing that he or she is subject to a legal incapacity to vote. Legal incapacity to vote does not include being below voting age if the person concerned will be 18 on polling day. It is an illegal practice to vote more than once in the same district electoral area at any local election or in more than one district electoral area at an election or in any district electoral area where he has appointed a proxy for another district electoral area. It is an illegal practice to vote in person if entitled to vote by post or to vote in person knowing that a proxy has already voted on his behalf. It is also an illegal practice to vote as proxy for the same elector more than once in the same district electoral area or in more than one district electoral area or if he votes in person as proxy for an elector at a local election knowing that the elector has already voted in person. It is also an illegal practice to vote in any district electoral area as proxy for more than two people of whom one is not the husband, wife, parent, grandparent, brother, sister, child or grandchild. Inducing anyone to do any of the above is also an illegal practice.

Electoral offences are listed in Part III of Schedule 9 and include the following:

- ❖ Making a service declaration when not entitled to do so or in the knowledge that he is subject to a legal incapacity or knowing that it contains a false statement.

- ❖ Attesting a service declaration knowing that he is not authorised to do so or knowing that it contains a false statement.

- ❖ Making a false statement in any declaration or form used in connection with proxy or postal voting.

- ❖ Fraudulently defacing or destroying a nomination paper or ballot paper, voters declaration or official envelope used in postal voting.

- ❖ Supplying a ballot paper without due authority.

- ❖ Putting into a ballot box anything other than a ballot paper.

- ❖ Taking out of the polling station any ballot paper.

❖ Destroying, concealing, losing, taking or opening any ballot box or ballot papers or any papers or documents of any kind then in use or intended to be used for the purposes of the election or any ballot paper account or marked copy of a register prepared or used for the purposes of the election or any unused ballot papers.

A person attending a polling station is guilty of an electoral offence, if, before the poll is closed, he or she communicates to anyone any information regarding the name of an elector or proxy who has or has not applied for a ballot paper or voted at a polling station or the number on the register of any elector who, or whose proxy, has or has not applied for a ballot paper or voted at a polling station. Anyone attending the count is guilty of an electoral offence if he attempts to discover the number on the back of any ballot paper or if he communicates any information obtained in a polling station concerning the candidate for whom an elector has or is about to vote or the number on the back of the ballot paper issued to that voter. It is also an offence to induce a voter to show how he has voted after he has marked his ballot paper, or to act as a companion to a disabled voter and then to disclose how that person has voted or the number on the back of the ballot paper. Anyone attending the issue and receipt of postal ballot papers if guilty of an offence if he or she communicates before the poll is closed, any information gained regarding the number on the back of any ballot paper or the number on the back or at the receipt of ballot papers attempts to discover how any particular voter has voted. Under section 27A of Schedule 9 (as inserted by the Local Elections (Northern Ireland) (Amendment) Order 2001 (SI 2001, No. 417) the publication, before the poll has closed, of any exit poll is guilty of an electoral offence. It is an electoral offence to publish election material which does not include the name and address of the publisher and printer.

The following are illegal payments: payments in excess of any maximum amounts set out in the 1962 Act, payments made to induce a candidate to withdraw from an election, payments made to canvassers. Any returning officer or any officer or clerk appointed under the Act, who acts as an agent of a candidate is guilty of an electoral offence. If the Chief Electoral Officer, any presiding officer or anyone to whom they have delegated functions or any postmaster or his deputy, without reasonable cause, act in breach of their official duty, they are guilty of an electoral offence. Including in a register of electors the name of anyone not qualified to be included is an electoral offence as is negligently failing to include someone. Giving false information in connection with the preparation of the register is also guilty of an electoral offence.

CHAPTER FOUR – EUROPEAN PARLIAMENTARY ELECTIONS

THE EUROPEAN ELECTIONS

The date of elections to the European Parliament is governed by Article 10(2) of the 'Act Concerning the Election of the Representatives of the European Parliament by Direct Universal Suffrage', annexed to the decision of the Council of the European Communities (20 September, 1976). Elections take place every five years. Article 9 states that elections to the European Parliament in all Member States must fall within the same period starting on a Thursday morning and ending on the following Sunday. The precise date of the poll is set by the Secretary of State by order under Section 3D of the European Parliamentary Elections Act 1978 (as substituted by Section 1 of the European Parliamentary Elections Act 1999). The timetable for European parliamentary elections is set out in Schedule 1 of the European Parliamentary Elections Regulations 1999 (SI 1999, No. 1214), which makes modifications to the provisions of Schedule 1 of the Representation of the People Act 1983.

Procedure	Timing
Publication of Notice of Election	Not later than the 25th day before the date of the poll
Delivery of nomination papers and list of candidates of registered parties	Between the hours of 10am and 4pm on any day after the date of the publication of the notice of election but not later than the 19th day before the date of the poll
Delivery of notices of withdrawals of candidature	Within the time for the delivery of nomination papers at the election
The making of objections to nomination papers or list of candidates of registered parties	During the hours allowed for delivery of nomination papers on the last day for their delivery and one hour following (until 5pm) except that on that final afternoon objections can only be made to nomination papers delivered within 24 hours of the last time for the delivery of nomination papers. Where such a nomination paper is delivered no objection can be made to the particulars of the registered party or candidate on the party's list or individual candidate unless the objection is made at, or just after the time of, the delivery of the nomination paper. Under Rule 15(2) where a Returning Officer thinks an individual candidate may be disqualified for nomination under the Representation of the People Act 1981 (under the provisions of this Act, applied to European elections by Schedule 1 of the European Parliamentary Elections Act 1978) anyone sentenced to more than one year's imprisonment is disqualified from membership of the European Parliament during the period of imprisonment) objections can be made between 10am and 4pm on the day after the last day for delivery of nomination papers.
Publication of statement of parties and individual candidates nominated	At the close of the time for making objections to nomination papers or list of candidate of registered parties or as soon afterwards as any objections are disposed of
Polling	Between 7am and 10pm on the day of the poll

Until the recent enactment of the European Parliamentary Elections Act 1999, elections to the European Parliament were conducted in single member constituencies using the First Past The Post system (the Single Transferable Vote in Northern Ireland) and the rules governing these elections were set out in the European Parliamentary Elections Act 1978 and the European Parliamentary Elections Regulations 1986.

The Government first introduced the European Parliamentary Elections Bill on 29 October 1997. However, the House of Lords would not give way on its amendments to the bill and it eventually ran out of parliamentary time. It was therefore reintroduced in the 1998/99 Session, gaining Royal Assent and paving the way for the 1999 European Elections on 10 June 1999 to be held using a regional list system of PR.

The Government intends consolidating the provisions of the European Parliamentary Election Acts of 1978, 1993 and 1999 and a consolidation bill was introduced to this effect in the 1999/2000 Session of Parliament; however, as the Joint Committee on Consolidation Bills pointed out in their Second Report (HL 80-I/HC 604-I, Session 1999/2000) published on 5 July 2000, the bill was drafted on the assumption that the provisions of the Political Parties, Elections and Referendums Bill would be enacted.

The Political Parties, Elections and Referendums Act 2000 does in fact amend the existing legislation relating to European Parliamentary Elections and the amendments are set out below. The Government has introduced a consolidation bill in the House of Lords (on 23 July 2001) in order to reflect the amendments contained in the Political Parties, Elections and Referendums Act 2000. As this bill has only just been introduced, the references below are to existing legislation, primarily the European Parliamentary Elections Act 1999.

Under the provisions of Section 2 of the 1999 Act, the total number of MEPs remains at 87 (71 from England, eight from Scotland, five from Wales and three from Northern Ireland). England is divided into nine regions based on the regions currently covered by the Government Offices of the Regions (except for the combination of Merseyside and the North West). Scotland, Wales and Northern Ireland each constitute single regions. Northern Ireland retains its current electoral system – the Single Transferable Vote.

Under the Act, the responsibility for any realignment of European boundaries or revision of the number of seats per region passed from the Boundary Commissions to the Secretary of State, who must seek to ensure that the ratio of electors to MEPs is the same in all regions in England. Under the provisions of paragraph 4 of Schedule 2 to the European Parliamentary Elections Act 1978 (as amended by both the European Parliamentary Elections Act 1999 and the RPA 2000) the Secretary of State must consider *"as soon as possible after 1 May in each pre-election year"* whether the ratio of electors to MEPs is, as far as is possible, the same in each electoral region in England.

The electoral system for England, Wales and Scotland is set out in Section 3 of the Act. MEPs are elected from a 'closed' regional list; i.e., voters may choose either a party or an Independent candidate, but cannot vote for an individual 'named' candidate from a political party. The order in which candidates are elected depends on the order in which their own party has placed them on its list. A candidate's placing on his or her party list is crucial to his or her success. For example, in the last European Elections on 10 June 1999, London returned 10 MEPs and the Labour Party received 399,466 votes; this meant that only the first four candidates on its list were returned. Carole Tongue, an existing Labour MEP, who was placed fifth on the list, was therefore not elected.

The d'Hondt formula is used to allocate seats (see Appendix A for an explanation of this formula). The deposit is £5,000 for each list of candidates and a party needs more than one fortieth of the vote to avoid its forfeiture. In Northern Ireland the deposit is £1,000 and candidates need to gain one quarter of the quota in order to avoid forfeiture (in Northern Ireland, elections to the European Parliament are held using the Single Transferable Vote, hence forfeiture of the deposit is related to the quota rather than total votes cast).

WHO CAN BE A CANDIDATE?

Under paragraph 5(1) of Schedule 1 of the European Parliamentary Elections Act 1978, anyone who is 21 year of age and who is a citizen of the European Union may stand as a candidate in their Member State of residence, even if they are not registered as an elector in the UK (European Parliamentary Elections (Changes to the Franchise and Qualification of Representatives) Regulations 1994) and Schedule 1((5)(3)(e) of the European Parliamentary Elections Act 1978. Members of Parliament may also be MEPs, unless disqualified under the House of Commons (Disqualification) Act 1975. Lords of Appeal in Ordinary (Law Lords) may not be MEPs. A citizen of an EU member state cannot, however, be an MEP if he or she is disqualified through a criminal law or civil law decision under the law of the Member State of which he or she is a national.

The following can be candidates, as set out in Schedule 1(5)(3) of the European Parliamentary Elections Act 1978:

❖ Peers (except Law Lords)

❖ Ordained ministers of any religious denomination

❖ Those disqualified by virtue of holding an office mentioned in Section 4 of the House of Commons Disqualification Act 1975 (stewardship of the Chiltern Hundreds, etc.)

❖ Those holding any of the offices described in Part II or Part III of Schedule 1 to the House of Commons Disqualification Act 1975 which are designated in an order by the Secretary of State as non-disqualifying offices in relation to the European Parliament

The following may not stand as candidates[1]. These include:

❖ A member of the Government of a Member State

❖ A member of the European Commission

❖ A Judge, Advocate-General or Registrar of the Court of Justice of the European Union

❖ A member of the Court of Auditors of the European Union

❖ A member of the Consultative Committee of the European Coal and Steel Community or member of the Economic and Social Committee of the European Economic Community and of the European Atomic Energy Community

---

[1] As set out in Article 6(1) of the Act relating to the election of representatives of the European Parliament annexed to the decision of the Council of the European Communities (20 September 1976).

❖ A member of any committees or other bodies set up under the Treaties establishing the European Coal and Steel Community, the European Economic Community and the European Atomic Energy Community to manage the Communities' funds or carry out administrative tasks

❖ A member of the Board of Directors, Management Committee or staff of the European Investment Banks

❖ An active official servant of the institutions of the European Communities

It is an offence under the European Parliamentary Elections (Changes to the Franchise and Qualification of Representatives) Regulations 1994 to stand as a candidate in a European Parliamentary election in the UK and in another Member State.

Under Article 5 of the European Parliamentary Elections Regulations 1999 the following are illegal practices:

❖ Being nominated as an individual candidate in more than one electoral region

❖ Being nominated as an individual candidate in an electoral region and at the same time being nominated as a party list candidate in that or another electoral region

❖ Being nominated in more than one party's list in the same electoral region

❖ Being nominated in a party's or parties' lists for more than one region

Under Part III, Article 10 of the Regulations, a party standing in more than one electoral region must appoint a national election agent. Under Article 12 (1) a national election agent can appoint a deputy agent to act in a particular electoral region. The names of all such deputy agents have to be given to the returning officer no later than the second day before the day of the poll.

WHO CAN VOTE?

Under the provisions of the 1999 Act, anyone entitled to vote in a parliamentary election (this therefore includes British nationals overseas) may vote in the European Parliamentary elections with the addition of peers (new Section 3 of RPA 1985 as substituted by RPA 2000) and other EU nationals who fulfil the residency criteria.[2] Under the aforementioned provisions, peers living overseas may vote in European Parliamentary elections. This includes life and hereditary peers. Any EU citizen wishing to vote in a European Parliamentary election must complete a registration form in addition to the form

---

[2] Although Ireland is a Member State of the European Union, Irish citizens retain their existing voting rights as Irish citizens rather than as EU nationals. Under the provisions of Schedule 2 of the Representation of the People Act 2000 and the Holders of Hereditary Peerages (Overseas Electors) (Transitional Provisions) Order 2001 (2001, 84), peers overseas retain a right to vote. The SI was necessary because of the removal of the qualifying date for entry on the electoral register and its replacement with rolling registration based on previously having been on the register of parliamentary electors within the last 20 (soon to be reduced to 15) years. Peers could not previously have been on the parliamentary register so references to the parliamentary register have been altered to refer to the local government register, to enable them to continue to participate in elections to the European Parliament even if living overseas.

pertaining to local government elections. Under the provisions of the European Parliamentary Elections (Franchise of Relevant Citizens of the Union) Regulations 2001 (SI 2001, No. 1184) EU nationals are only entitled to vote in EU elections in Northern Ireland if they have been resident there for the whole of the three month period ending on the qualifying date for that election. The provisions of the RPA 2000 concerning declarations of local connection also apply to EU citizens who wish to vote in European Parliamentary elections. New Section 7C of the RPA 1983 states (as modified by the schedule to the 2001 Regulations) that where a person's declaration of local connection is in force when he applies for registration, he is regarded for the purposes of section 4 of the 2001 Regulations as being resident on the date of the declaration or in the case of Northern Ireland, as being resident during the whole of the period of the three months ending with that date.

A European citizen who is a member of the armed forces or the husband or wife of such a member has a service qualification and can make a service declaration. Where practicable, the register of European electors, must in the same way as the register of local government electors, be combined with the register of parliamentary electors and names of EU citizens marked with a letter 'U'. EU citizens may be appointed as proxies at European Parliamentary elections. An overseas elector who registers to vote in the Member State where he or she lives, cannot then vote in European Parliamentary elections in the UK. It is an offence to vote in more than one Member State, or in more than one electoral area in a European Parliamentary election.

EUROPEAN PARLIAMENTARY ELECTIONS

Region	Parliamentary and local government areas included	No. of MEPs
EAST MIDLANDS Conservative – 285,662 Labour – 206,756 Liberal Democrat – 92,398 UK Independence Party – 54,800 Green – 38,954 Alternative Labour List supporting Left Alliance – 17,409 Pro Euro Conservative Party – 5,528 Socialist Labour Party – 5,528 Natural Law Party – 1,525 MEPs ELECTED: two Conservative, two Labour and two Liberal Democrats	44 Parliamentary Constituencies in counties of Derbyshire, Leicestershire, Lincolnshire, Northamptonshire & Nottinghamshire & unitary authorities of Leicester, Nottingham, Derby & Rutland	6
EASTERN Conservative – 425,091 Labour – 250,132 Liberal Democrat – 118,822 UK Independence – 88,452 Green – 61,334 Liberal Party – 16,861 Pro Euro Conservative – 16,340 British National – 9,356 Socialist Labour – 6,143 Natural Law – 1,907 MEPs ELECTED: four Conservative, two Labour, one Liberal Democrat and one UK Independent	56 Parliamentary Constituences in counties of Bedfordshire, Cambridgeshire, Essex, Hertfordshire, Norfolk & Suffolk & unitary authorities of Luton, Peterborough, Southend-on-Sea and Thurrock	8

Region	Parliamentary and local government areas included	No. of MEPs
LONDON Labour – 399,466 Conservative – 372,989 Liberal Democrat – 133,058 Green – 87,545 UK Independent – 61,741 Socialist Labour – 19,632 British National – 17,960 Liberal – 16,951 Pro Euro Conservative – 16,383 Architect, Human Rights Peace in Europe – 4,851 Independent – Anti Value Added Tax – 2,596 Humanist – 2,586 Hemp Coalition – 2,358 Natural Law – 2,263 Weekly Worker – 846 MEPs ELECTED: four Labour, four Conservative, one Liberal Democrat and one Green	74 Parliamentary Constituencies in the London Boroughs & the City of London	10
NORTH EAST Labour – 162,573 Conservative – 105,573 Liberal Democrat – 52,070 UK Independence Party – 34,063 Green – 18,184 Socialist Labour – 4,511 British National – 3,505 Pro Euro Conservative – 2,926 Socialist Party GB – 1,510 Natural Law – 826 MEPs ELECTED: three Labour and one Conservative	30 parliamentary constituencies in counties of Durham, Northumberland, Tyne and Wear & unitary authorities of Darlington, Hartlepool, Middlesbrough, Redcar and Cleveland & Stockton-on-Tees	4
NORTH WEST Conservative – 360,027 Labour – 350,511 Liberal Democrat – 119,376 UK Independence Party – 66,779 Green – 56,828 Liberal Party – 22,640 British National – 13,587 Socialist Labour – 11,338 Pro Euro Conservative – 9,816 Anti Corruption Pro-Family Christian Alliance – 2,251 Natural Law – 2,114 English Independent Humanist – 1,049 Weekly Worker – 878 MEPs ELECTED: five Conservative, four Labour and one Liberal Democrat	76 parliamentary constituencies in counties of Cheshire, Cumbria, Greater Manchester, Lancashire & Merseyside & unitary authoriites of Blackburn, Blackpool, Halton & Warrington	10

Region	Parliamentary and local government areas included	No. of MEPs
SOUTH EAST Conservative – 661,931 Labour – 292,146 Liberal Democrat – 228,136 UK Independence – 144,514 Green – 110,571 Pro Euro Conservative – 27,305 British National – 12,161 Socialist Labour – 7,281 Natural Law – 2,767 Independent Open Democracy for Stability – 1,857 Independent Making a Profit in Europe – 1,400 MEPs ELECTED: five Conservative, two Labour, two Liberal Democrat, one UK Independent, one Green	83 parliamentary constituencies in counties of Buckinghamshire, East Sussex, Hampshire, Kent, Oxfordshire, Surrey & West Sussex & unitary authorites of Bracknell Forest, Brighton and Hove, Isle of Wight, Medway Towns, Milton Keynes, Portsmouth, Reading, Slough, Southampton, West Berkshire, Windsor and Maidenhead & Wokingham	11
SOUTH WEST Conservative – 434,645 Labour – 188,362 Liberal Democrat – 171,498 UK Independence – 111,012 Green – 86,630 Liberal – 21,645 Pro Euro Conservative – 11,134 British National – 9,752 Socialist Labour – 5,741 Natural Law – 1,968 MEPs ELECTED: four Conservative, one Labour, one Liberal Democrat and one UK Independent (now sits as Independent)	51 parliamentary constituencies in counties of Cornwall, Devon, Dorset, Gloucestershire, Somerset & Wiltshire & unitary authorities of Bath and North East Somerset, Bournemouth, Bristol, North Somerset, Plymouth, Poole, South Gloucestershire, Torbay and Swindon & Isles of Scilly	7
WEST MIDLANDS Conservative – 321,719 Labour – 237,671 Liberal Democrat – 95,769 UK Independence – 49,621 Green – 49,440 MEP Independent Labour – 36,849 Liberal – 14,954 BNP – 14,344 Pro Euro Conservative – 11,144 Socialist Labour – 5,257 EDP English Freedom – 3,066 Natural Law – 1,647 MEPs ELECTED: four Conservative, three Labour and one Liberal Democrat	59 parliamentary constituencies in counties of Herefordshire, Shropshire, Staffordshire, Warwickshire, West Midlands, Worcestershire & unitary authorities of Stoke-on-Trent & The Wrekin	8

Region	Parliamentary and local government areas included	No. of MEPs
YORKSHIRE AND HUMBERSIDE Conservative – 272,653 Labour – 233,024 Liberal Democrat – 107,168 UK Independence – 52,824 Green – 42,604 Alternative Labour List supporting Left Alliance – 9,554 British National – 8,911 Pro Euro Conservative – 8,075 Socialist Labour – 7,650 Natural Law – 1,604 MEPs ELECTED: three Conservative, three Labour and one Liberal Democrat	56 parliamentary constituencies in counties of North Yorkshire, South Yorkshire & West Yorkshire & unitary authorities of Kingston upon Hull, East Riding of Yorkshire, North East Lincolnshire & North Lincolnshire and York	7
SCOTLAND Labour – 283,490 Scottish Nationalist – 268,528 Conservative – 195,296 Liberal Democrat – 96,971 Green – 57,142 Scottish Socialist – 39,720 Pro Euro Conservative – 17,781 UK Independence – 12,459 Socialist Labour – 9,385 British National – 3,729 Natural Law – 2,087 Accountant for Lower Scottish Taxes – 1,632 MEPs ELECTED: three Labour, two SNP, two Conservative and one Liberal Democrat	72 parliamentary constituencies	8
WALES Labour – 199,690 Plaid Cymru – 185,235 Conservative – 142,631 Liberal Democrat – 51,283 UK Independence – 19,702 Green – 16,146 Pro Euro Conservative – 5,834 Socialist Labour – 4,283 Natural Law – 1,621 MEPs ELECTED: two Labour, two Plaid Cymru and one Conservative	40 parliamentary constituencies	5
NORTHERN IRELAND Ian Paisley (Democratic Unionist) – *elected* Jim Nicholson (Ulster Unionist) – *elected* John Hume (Social Democratic and Labour) – *elected* James Anderson (Natural Law) David Ervine (Progressive Unionist) Robert McCartney (UK Unionist) Mitchel McLaughlin (Sinn Fein) Sean Neeson (Alliance) MEPs ELECTED: one DUP, one UUP and one SDLP elected by STV	18 parliamentary constituencies	3

ELECTION EXPENSES

Under the provisions of Schedule 9, Part II of the Political Parties, Elections and Referendums Act 2000, where a party stands for election in only one electoral region in England, the limit on election expenses is £45,000 multiplied by the number of MEPs to be returned for that region. Where a party stands for election in two or more electoral regions in England, the limit is £45,000 multiplied by the total number of MEPs to be returned for those regions taken together. Where a party stands for election in Scotland or Wales or one or more candidates stand for election in Northern Ireland, the limit is £45,000 multiplied by the number of MEPs to be returned for that part of the UK. The relevant period during which limitations on expenditure apply is the four-month period ending with the date of the election.

Area	Number of Constituencies	Maximum Expenditure
East Midlands	6	£270,000
Eastern	8	£360,000
London	10	£450,000
North East	4	£180,000
North West	10	£450,000
South East	11	£495,000
South West	7	£315,000
West Midlands	8	£360,000
Yorkshire & the Humber	7	£315,000
Total for England	71	£3,195,000
Total for Scotland	8	£360,000
Total for Wales	5	£225,000
Total for GB	84	£3,780,000
Total for Northern Ireland	3	£135,000

THE ELECTORAL PROCESS

The European Parliamentary Elections Regulations 1999 apply the majority of provisions of the Parliamentary Election Rules contained in Schedule 1 of the Representation of the People Act 1983 to European Parliamentary Elections. The modifications to the Parliamentary Election Rules are set out in Schedule 1 of the European Parliamentary Elections Regulations 1999. The following Sections of the Representation of the People Act 1983 are applied to European Parliamentary Elections with some modifications. Only the major modifications have been set out in detail below.

Sections of the Representation of the People Act 1983
applied to European Parliamentary Elections

Sections & Rules Applied Without Modifications
Sections 24(2) (returning officers), 50 (effect of misdescription), 54 (payment of expenses of registration), 57 (registration appeals), 60 (personation), 80 (election agent's claim), 94 (imitation poll cards), 98 (premises not affected for rates), 100 (illegal canvassing), 109 (payments to exhibit election notices), 110 (printer's name on publications), 111 (paid canvassing), 112 (payments for illegal purposes), 114 (treating), 115 (undue influence), 116 (rights of creditors), 119 (computation of time), 123 (election court) 124 & 125 (judges' expenses), 136 (security for costs), 137 (petition at issue), 141 (duty to answer questions), 143 (expenses of witnesses), 147 (withdrawal of petition), 154 (costs of petition), 155 (refusal to pay costs), 167 (application for relief from finding of corrupt or illegal practices), 168 (prosecutions for corrupt practices), 170 (convictions), 176 (time limits for prosecutions), 179 (offences by associations), 181 (DPP), 182 (rules of procedure), 183 (costs), 184 (service of notices), 186 (computation of time), 203 (local government provisions), 204 (application to Scotland)   Schedule 1, Rules 20 (official mark), 24 (postal ballot papers), 25 (polling stations), 33 (keeping order at polling stations), 34 (sealing of ballot boxes), 37 (voting procedure), 38 (votes marked by presiding officer), 39 (voting by disabled people), 40 (tendered ballot papers), 41 (spoilt ballot papers), 42 (adjournment of poll in case of riot)

Sections Applied With Modifications	
Section Number	**Modification(s)**
18	Polling districts and polling stations to be the same as those used for parliamentary elections except where 'special circumstances' dictate otherwise.
23, 29, 30	References to 'returning officer' to include reference to 'local returning officer'.
49	*(minor amendments to wording of section on registration)*
52	*(minor amendments to wording of section on registration)*
56	*(minor amendments to wording of section on registration)*
61	*(minor amendments to section on voting offences)*
63	*(minor amendments to wording of section on breach of official duty of returning officers)*
65, 66	*(minor amendments to wording of sections on tampering with nomination papers and section on requirement of secrecy)*
67, 68, 69, 70, 73	*(minor amendments to wording of sections on election agents; for example, substituting 'individual candidate' for 'candidate')*
74	The amount of a candidate's allowable personal expenses in a European election to be £900 as opposed to £600 for a Parliamentary election.
75	Section 75(1)(ii) of the 1983 Act allows expenditure other than by the candidate or her agent up to a level of £5 - the amount in a European election is £5,000 per electoral region.
76	This Section of the 1983 Act sets out the levels of election expenses for European elections, the amount is £45,000 multiplied by the number of MEPs to be returned for that electoral region (see Chapter Nine on campaign expenditure for more details).
78, 79	States that claims against registered parties in respect of election expenses should be sent in within 21 days after the result is declared.
81	This Section of the 1983 Act stipulates that election returns should be sent in within 35 days after the election result is declared - in European elections, the time limit is 50 days for individual candidates or for parties whose candidates have stood for election in only one electoral region; or registered parties whose candidates have stood for election in more than one electoral region, the time limit is 70 days after the election result is declared.

Sections Applied With Modifications	
Section Number	**Modification(s)**
82, 84, 86, 87	*(minor amendments to ensure that references to a candidate are construed as references to 'an individual candidate')*
88	Modifications to the section on the publication and inspection of returns and declarations.
89	Under Section 89 of the 1983 Act, election returns or declarations relating to parliamentary elections must be retained by the appropriate officer for two years, but in the case of European elections, this period is 12 months.
91	Section 91 allows candidates in parliamentary elections to send one free election address to all residents in the constituency - the modifications in the European Parliamentary Elections Regulations 1999 extend this right to candidates and nominating officers of registered parties.
92, 95, 97, 99	*(minor modifications to sections on broadcasting from outside UK, use of schools for meetings, disturbances at meetings and officials not acting for candidates)*
106, 107	*(minor amendments to sections on sections relating to false statement about candidates and corrupt withdrawal from candidature)*
113	*(minor amendments to section on bribery)*
117, 118	*(minor amendments to interpretation clauses)*
120, 121, 122	*(minor amendment of sections on presentation of election petitions, stipulating that a petition must be presented within 21 days after the day on which the election result was declared)*
139, 140	*(minor amendment of sections on election petitions which state that the trial of an election petition shall continue despite the fact that the respondent is no longer an MEP)*
144, 146	*(minor amendments to sections on conclusion of trial of election petition and on special cases determined by High Court)*
157	*(minor amendments on section on appeals)*
160	Modification of section on those reported guilty of corrupt and illegal practices – this section has recently been amended by the PPERA 2000 – *see Chapter Two for more details.*
169	Modification of section on prosecutions for illegal practices, so that these are tried on indictment rather than summarily.
174, 175	*(minor amendments to sections on mitigation and on illegal payments)*
178	*(minor amendments to section on prosecution of offences committed outside the UK)*
180	*(minor amendment to section on evidence 'by certificate' of holding election)*
185	*(minor amendments to interpretation clause)*
200, 202	*(minor amendments to interpretation sections)*
Election Rules (Schedule 1 of the RPA 1983)	
Rule 1	(Timetable applied with modifications – see timetable set out above).
Rule 2	Omits sub-section which refers to election commencing afresh by reason of candidate's death.
Rule 5	This modification stipulates that the returning officer send a copy of the notice of election to the local returning officer for each parliamentary constituency wholly or partly contained in the electoral region concerned and that each local returning officer publish the copy of the notice.
Rules 6, 6A	Inserts a new Rule 6B which sets out rules governing the nomination papers of party list candidates. The number of candidates in a list cannot exceed the number of MEPs to be elected in that particular electoral region.
Rules 8, 8A	Inserts new Rule 8A which states that candidates (both individual and list candidates) must make a declaration setting out nationality and home address and stating that he or she is not standing as a candidate for election in another Member State. A certificate made by the relevant authorities in the

Sections Applied With Modifications	
Section Number	**Modification(s)**
	candidate's Member State, must state that he or she is not disqualified from standing as a candidate in that Member State.
Rule 9	This concerns the deposit which is £5,000 for an individual candidate or a party's list of candidates.
Rules 10, 11	States that individual and list candidates and agents can attend the delivery of nomination papers. Take away the right of candidates' partners to attend in the case of European elections.
Rule 12	This relates to the validity of nomination papers and inserts new subsections 2A and B, which state that a party's list will be declared invalid if the number of candidates in the list exceeds the overall number of MEPs to be elected. Where a candidate's details are not correct or the relevant declarations and certificates have not been made available, then the name of that candidate will be deleted from the list.
Rules 13, 14	Allows the nominating officer of a registered party to withdraw that party's nomination and allows individual candidates to withdraw nominations. Deletes Rule 13(2) which allowed candidates outside the UK at the time to withdraw candidature.
Rule 15	Confines the disqualification under the Representation of the People Act 1981 (prisoners) to individual not list candidates.
Rule 17	States that where the number of list or individual candidates is the same or less than the number of seats to be filled, they are duly elected.
Rules 18, 19	Amends the rules relating to the design of the ballot paper
Rules 21, 22, 23	*(minor amendments to Rules on prohibition on disclosure of vote, use of schools and notice of poll)*
Rules 26, 28	*(minor amendments to sections on appointment of presiding officers and clerks and issue of poll cards)*
Rule 29	Substitutes the words, 'Put only one cross on the ballot paper' in place of 'Vote for one candidate only in paragraph 5 of Rule 29.
Rule 30	Makes some amendments to the provisions relating to the appointment of polling and counting agents and states that the election agent or sub-agent of a registered party or an individual candidate or some authorised by his or her agent can appoint polling and counting agents.
Rules 31 and 32	*(minor amendments to sections on requirement of secrecy and admission to polling station)*
Rules 35, 36	*(minor amendments to sections on questions to be put to voters and challenging a voter*
Rules 43, 44 and 45	Adds a new Rule 43A to the effect that no one other than the returning officer, local returning officer and his clerks, candidates, election agents and counting agents can attend the verification of the ballot paper accounts unless given permission by the local returning officer. Under 43B each ballot box is opened at the verification of ballot paper accounts and the number of ballot papers it contains verified against the ballot paper account. The provisions are similar to those set out in Rule 45 of the Parliamentary Election Rules, which relate to the count itself. The verification of accounts and the count are separate procedures in European parliamentary elections by virtue of the fact that under Rule 44, the counting of votes only becomes permissible until the close of polling in the Member State whose electors are the last to vote within the period of Thursday to Sunday in June in the last year of the five year period of the parliament (Decision of the Council of the European Community (76/787/ECSC, EEC, Euratom) Article 3). Candidates' partners cannot attend the count. At the count, the local returning officer mixes all the ballot papers together before they are counted.

Sections Applied With Modifications	
Section Number	**Modification(s)**
Rule 46, Rule 47	A new paragraph 2A is added to Rule 47 to state that ballot paper on which someone has marked for a particular candidate on a party's list as well as the party, is treated as a vote for that party.
Rule 48	Rule 48A states that the local returning officer must show the number of votes given for each party and individual candidate. Under Rule 48B the returning officer receives notification from the local returning officers of the number of votes cast for the parties and individual candidates and must then calculate the total number votes given to each registered party and individual candidate in all the parliamentary constituencies within the electoral region. Once the total number of votes is known then the seats can be allocated.
Rule 49	This substitutes a new rule to the effect that if, in the case of the last seat to be allocated, two or more registered parties or individual candidates have an equal number of votes and that number is greater than the number of votes of any other party or candidate, one vote is added to the votes of each party of individual candidate having such an equal number and the rules in subsections (3) to (7) of Section 3 of the 1978 Act are applied again. These subsections state that the first seat is allocated to the party of individual candidate with the greatest number of votes, the second and subsequent seats are allocated in the same way, except that the number of votes given to a party to which one or more seats have already been allocated are divided by the number of seats allocated plus one (in allocating the second or any subsequent seat votes given to a party to which there has already been allocated a number of seats equal to the number of names on the party's list of candidates and an individual candidate to whom a seat has already been allocated). If this still results in an equality of votes, the returning officer has to decide between the parties/individual candidates by lot.
Rule 50	This relates to the declaration of results and states that the returning officer must prepare a statement setting out the total number of valid votes, the number of votes which each party or candidate had after the d'hondt formula had been applied and the names of those candidates duly elected.
Rule 53	A party or individual candidate's deposit is lost if they fail to secure more than one-fortieth of the total number of votes polled.
Rules 54, 55	Rather than sending ballot papers, etc., to the Clerk of the Crown, these are retained by the returning officer.
Rules 56 and 57	This substitutes 'local returning officer' for 'Clerk of the House of Commons' in Rule 56 of the Parliamentary Election Rules and relates to the orders for the production of ballot papers, etc., in relation to election petitions, etc.

An annex to Schedule 1 of the European Parliamentary Elections Regulations 1999 details the layout of the various forms required in European elections, including the ballot paper itself. Schedule 2 sets out the modifications which are required to give effect to certain provisions in subordinate legislation; however, some of the regulations listed have been superseded; for example, in the case of The Representation of the People Regulations 1986 (SI 1986, No. 1081), the whole Regulations except 1, 4 and 97 to 100 have been repealed by the Representation of the People (England and Wales) Regulations 2001 (SI 2001, No. 341). The Schedule to the European Parliamentary Elections (Franchise of Relevant Citizens of the Union) Regulations 2001 (SI 2001, No. 1184) lists those sections of the RPA 1983 and various regulations brought in under the Act which relate to registration of electors for European Parliamentary elections. The provisions which apply are listed below. The European Parliamentary Elections (Franchise of Relevant Citizens of the Union) Regulations 2001 (SI 2001, No. 1184) revoke Regulations 7 to 14 and 17 and 18 of the European Parliamentary Elections (Changes to the Franchise and Qualification of Representatives) Regulations 1994 (SI 1994, No. 342) and provide for the registration of EU citizens who are resident here (who are not Commonwealth citizens or citizens of the Irish Republic) as European Parliamentary electors. The Regulations were necessary given the introduction of 'rolling registration' under the RPA 2000.

RPA 1983 - Sections Applied Without Modifications
Sections 9(2), (3), (4), (7), (8) (register of electors), 50 (effect of misdescription), 57 (registration appeals), 58 (registration appeals, Northern Ireland),
RPA 1983 - Sections Applied With Modifications
(These sections are all modified in order to apply the new provisions relating to rolling registration to the provisions of the RPA 1983 as they relate to elections to the European Parliament – they have the effect of inserting references to section 4 of the European Parliamentary Elections (Franchise of Relevant Citizens of the Union) Regulations 2001 where appropriate. Section 4 of these regulations sets out the entitlement of EU citizens to be registered as European Parliamentary electors.)
Sections 5, 6, 7, 7A, 7B, 7C, 9, 13, 13A, 13B, 52, 54, 56, 62, 63, 202
Part II of The Representation of the People (England and Wales) Regulations 2001 (SI 2001, No. 341) - Sections Applied Without Modifications
(These sections apply the new provisions relating to rolling registration to the provisions of the RPA 2001 Regulations as they relate to elections to the European Parliament.)
Regulations 3, 5, 6, 7, 8, 11, 27, 28, 29, 30, 31, 32, 38, 39, 41
Part II of The Representation of the People (England and Wales) Regulations 2001 (SI 2001, No. 341) - Sections Applied With Modifications
Regulations 24, 36, 40
The Representation of the People (Scotland) Regulations 2001 (SI 2001, No. 497(S.2)) – Sections Applied Without Modifications
Regulations 3, 5, 6, 7, 8, 11, 24, 27, 28, 29, 30, 31, 32, 38, 39, 41
The Representation of the People (Scotland) Regulations 2001 (SI 2001, No. 497 (S.2)) – Sections Applied With Modifications
Regulations 24, 36, 40
The Representation of the People (Northern Ireland) Regulations 2001 (SI 2001, No. 400) – Sections Applied Without Modifications
Regulations 3, 5, 6, 7, 8, 11, 27, 28, 29, 30, 31, 32, 36, 38, 39, 41
The Representation of the People (Northern Ireland) Regulations 2001 (SI 2001, No. 400) – Sections Applied With Modifications
Regulations 24, 36, 40

THE COUNT

The count cannot begin until the close of polling in the Member State whose electors are the last to vote within the 'specified period' (between Thursday morning and the following Sunday). The Returning Officer must appoint verifying officers to verify the ballot paper accounts. The following may attend the verification: the Returning Officer, the verifying officer and his clerks, candidates, election agents and counting agents and anyone else permitted to attend by the verifying officer. The ballot boxes containing postal ballots are opened and the papers counted and the number recorded. The other ballot boxes are then opened and the number of papers counted and recorded and the ballot paper accounts verified. Tendered ballot papers are not counted. The ballot papers must be kept face downward. The verification officer must verify the ballot paper accounts by comparing them with the numbers of ballot papers earlier recorded. A statement is then written up and a copy given to the counting agents.

BY-ELECTIONS

Part IV of the European Parliamentary Elections Regulations 1999 sets out the detailed provisions governing by-elections to fill vacancies between elections.

Under Article 16 of the European Parliamentary Elections Regulations 1999, where the MEP concerned was an individual candidate, a by-election is held, within six months. There is no by-election if the vacancy occurs within six months of the next European Parliamentary elections. Under Article 17, where the MEP who has vacated his or her seat is a party list member, then the highest placed person on the list (after the MEP who has resigned/died, etc.) is contacted to ask if he or she is willing to take up the vacancy. If not, then the procedure is repeated, with the next highest placed candidate being asked to fill the vacancy. When a candidate does agree to fill the vacancy, he or she must set out this agreement in writing and deliver a certificate signed by or on behalf of the relevant party's nominating officer stating that he or she may be returned as that party's MEP.

ELECTION PETITIONS

Special election petition rules apply in the case of European Parliamentary elections; namely, the following:

❖ The European Parliamentary Election Petition Rules 1979 (1979, No. 521) – *as amended by:*

❖ The European Parliamentary Election Petition (Amendment) Rules 1988 (SI 1988, No. 557)

❖ The European Parliamentary Election Petition (Amendment) Rules 1999 (SI 1999, No. 1398 (L. 15))[3]

These are similar to the Election Petition Rules 1960 (SI 1960, No. 543), as amended by The Election Petition (Amendment) Rules 1999 (SI 1999, No. 1352 (L. 14)) which govern the form, content and manner of presentation of election petitions. The amended order was necessary to take into account the implementation of the Civil Procedure Rules 1998. The Rules are made by the Civil Procedure Rule Committee (the 'authority' referred to in section 182 of the RPA 1983) and the power conferred on them to make such rules, is exercisable by statutory instrument and is treated as if conferred on a Minister of the Crown.

Complete results of the 1999 European elections (both in the UK and in other Member States) can be found on the BBC excellent website, at the following address:

http://news.bbc.co.uk/hi/english/static/euros_99/northern_ireland/ni.stm

---

[3] These Rules were necessary in order to take account of the implementation of the Civil Procedure Rules 1998

CHAPTER FIVE – ELECTIONS TO THE SCOTTISH PARLIAMENT

THE SCOTTISH PARLIAMENT

The Scottish Parliament was established under the Scotland Act 1998. It consists of 129 members, 73 of whom are directly elected on a constituency basis (using the same constituencies as those used for elections to the Westminster Parliament, but with the addition of an extra seat for Orkney and Shetland) and 56 of whom are additional members, seven being elected from each of eight European constituencies (as set out in the Parliamentary Constituencies (Scotland) Order 1996 (SI 1996, No. 1926)) using a proportional list-based system.

Detailed provisions governing the conduct of elections to the Scottish Parliament are contained in the Scottish Parliament (Elections etc) Order 1999 (SI 1999, No 787). Schedule 2 of the SI (as amended by the Scottish Parliament (Elections etc.) (Amendment) (No. 2) Order 2001 (SI 2001, No. 1748 (S.10)) and the Scottish Parliament (Elections etc.) (Amendment) Order 2001 (SI 2001, No. 1399 (S 5)) contains the Scottish Parliamentary Election Rules.

Rules governing elections to the Scottish Parliament, to the Scottish Constituencies of the House of Commons, and to the European Parliament are reserved matters under Part II of Schedule 5 the Scotland Act 1998 (Head B3. Elections). The Franchise in local government elections in Scotland is also a reserved matter, although other provisions governing local elections are now the responsibility of the Scottish Parliament. Section 12 of the Scotland Act 1998 states that the Secretary of State may make provisions (by order) relating to the conduct of elections to the Scottish Parliament, including provisions concerning the registration of electors and election expenses.

MEMBERS OF THE SCOTTISH PARLIAMENT

73 Constituency MSPs	56 Additional Members
73 MSPs elected using the first-past-the-post system with one MSP being elected per Constituency	7 MSPs elected from each of the 8 regions (the old European Parliamentary Constituencies) giving a total of 56 Additional Members. Electors within each Constituency, within each region, have two votes, one for the Constituency Member and one regional vote for a party. Where a party gains, for example, 40 per cent of the regional votes but has already gained 40 per cent of the Constituency seats, it is not be entitled to any Additional Members (the reason for having a list is to 'top-up' parties who have gained votes, but not seats). Account is taken of the number of Constituency seats gained within the European Parliamentary Constituency area. The number of regional votes cast for each party within the European Constituency are counted. The number of regional votes cast for each party are divided by the number of Constituency MSPs gained in the Parliamentary Constituencies contained within the relevant region, plus one. The party with the highest total after these calculations have been made gains the first additional member. The remainder of the additional Members are allocated in the same way except that the additional Members themselves are included in the calculations for the Party for which they were elected.

THE EIGHT SCOTTISH ADDITIONAL MEMBER REGIONS & RESULTS OF 1999 ELECTIONS

Region	Constituencies
Central Scotland Labour – 129,822 Scottish Nationalist – 91,802 Conservative – 30,243 Independent (Canavan) – 27,700 Liberal Democrat – 20,505 Socialist Labour – 10,956 Green – 5,926 Scottish Socialist – 5,739 Scottish Unionist – 2,886 Pro-Life – 2,567 Scottish Families & Pensioners – 1,373 Independent (Nizumo) – 248 Natural Law – 719 Labour won nine constituencies, therefore the regional list seats were allocated as follows: one Conservative, one Liberal Democrat and five SNP	Airdrie and Shotts - Labour Coatbridge and Chryston - Labour Cumbernauld and Kilsyth - Labour East Kilbride - Labour Falkirk East - Labour Falkirk West - Independent Hamilton North and Bellshill - Labour Hamilton South - Labour Kilmarnock and Loudon - Labour Motherwell and Wishaw - Labour
Glasgow Labour – 112,588 Scottish Nationalist – 65,360 Conservative – 20,239 Scottish Socialist – 18,581 Liberal Democrat – 18,473 Green – 10,159 Socialist Labour – 4,391 Scottish Unionist – 2,283 Pro-Life – 2,357 Communist – 521 Humanist – 447 Natural Law Party – 419 Socialist Party GB – 309 Independent Choice – 221 Labour won all 10 Glasgow constituencies and therefore the regional list seats were allocated as follows: one Conservative, one Liberal Democrat, four SNP and one Scottish Socialist	Glasgow Anniesland - Labour Glasgow Baillieston - Labour Glasgow Cathcart - Labour Glasgow Govan - Labour Glasgow Kelvin - Labour Glasgow Maryhill - Labour Glasgow Pollock - Labour Glasgow Rutherglen – Labour Glasgow Shettleston - Labour Glasgow Springburn - Labour

Region	Constituencies
Highlands and Islands Scottish Nationalist – 55,933 Labour – 51,371 Liberal Democrat – 43,226 Conservative – 30,122 Green – 7,560 Independent (Noble) – 3,522 Socialist Labour – 2,808 Highlands & Islands Alliance – 2,607 Scottish Socialist – 1,770 Scottish Peoples Mission – 1,151 Independent (International) – 712 Natural Law – 536 Independent (Robertson) – 354 The Liberal Democrats won five of the constituencies in this region and therefore the regional list seats were allocated as follows: three Labour, two Conservative and two SNP	Argyll and Bute – Liberal Democrat Caithness, Sutherland and Easter Ross – Liberal Democrat Inverness East, Nairn and Lochaber - SNP Moray - SNP Orkney – Liberal Democrat Shetland – Liberal Democrat Ross, Syke and Inverness West – Liberal Democrat Western Isles - Labour
Lothians Labour – 99,908 Scottish Nationalist – 85,085 Conservative – 52,067 Liberal Democrat – 47,565 Green – 22,848 Socialist Labour – 10,895 Scottish Socialist – 5,237 Liberal – 2,056 Witchery Tour – 1,184 Pro-Life – 898 Civil Rights – 806 Braveheart – 557 Natural Law Party – 564 Socialist Party GB – 388 Independent Voice for the Scottish People – 256 Independent (Independent) – 145 Anti-Corruption, Mobile Home Scandal, Roads – 54 Labour won all but one Edinburgh constituency and therefore the regional lists seats were allocated as follows: two Conservative, three SNP, one Green and one Liberal Democrat	Edinburgh Central - Labour Edinburgh East and Musselburgh - Labour Edinburgh North and Leith - Labour Edinburgh Pentlands - Labour Edinburgh South - Labour Edinburgh West – Liberal Democrat Linlithgow - Labour Livingston - Labour Midlothian - Labour
Mid Scotland and Fife Labour – 101,964 Scottish Nationalist – 87,659 Conservative – 56,719 Liberal Democrat – 38,896 Green – 11,821 Scottish Socialist – 3,044 Socialist Labour – 4,266 Pro-Life – 735 Natural Law – 558 Labour won six of the constituencies in this region and as a result the regional list seats were allocated as follows: three Conservative, three SNP and one Liberal Democrat	Central Fife - Labour Dunfermline East - Labour Dunfermline West - Labour Kirkcaldy - Labour Fife North East – Liberal Democrat Tayside North - SNP Ochil - Labour Perth - SNP Stirling - Labour

Region	Constituencies
North East Scotland Scottish Nationalist – 92,329 Labour – 72,666 Conservative – 52,149 Liberal Democrat – 49,843 Green – 8,067 Socialist Labour – 3,557 Scottish Socialist – 3,016 Independent (Watt) – 2,303 Independent (Sleaze Buster) – 770 Natural Law – 736 Labour won four of the constituencies in this region and the regional list seats were therefore allocated as follows: four SNP and three Conservative	Aberdeen Central - Labour Aberdeen North - Labour Aberdeen South – Liberal Democrat Angus - SNP Banff and Buchan - SNP Dundee East - Labour Dundee West - Labour Gordon – Liberal Democrat Aberdeenshire West and Kincardine – Liberal Democrat
South of Scotland Labour – 98,836 Scottish Nationalist – 80,059 Conservative – 68,904 Liberal Democrat – 38,157 Socialist Labour – 13,887 Green – 9,468 Liberal – 3,478 Scottish Socialist – 3,304 UK Independent – 1,502 Natural Law – 775 As Labour won six of the constituencies in this region, the regional list seats were allocated as follows: four Conservatives and three SNP	Ayr - Labour Carrick, Cumnock and Doon Valley - Labour Clydesdale - Labour Cunninghame South - Labour Dumfries - Labour East Lothian - Labour Galloway and Upper Nithsdale - SNP Roxburgh and Berwickshire – Liberal Democrat Tweeddale, Ettrick and Lauderdale – Liberal Democrat
West of Scotland Labour – 119,663 Scottish Nationalist – 80,417 Conservative – 48,666 Liberal Democrat – 34,095 Green – 8,175 Scottish Socialist – 5,944 Socialist Labour – 4,472 Pro-Life – 3,227 Independent People in Parliament – 2,761 Scottish Unionist – 1,840 Natural Law – 589 Independent Labour Keep Scottish Water Public – 565 Labour won all constituencies in this region and as a result the regional list seats were allocated as follows: four SNP, two Conservative and one Liberal Democrat	Clydebank and Milngavie - Labour Cunninghame North - Labour Dumbarton- Labour Eastwood - Labour Greenock and Inverclyde - Labour Paisley North - Labour Paisley South - Labour Strathkelvin and Bearsden - Labour West Renfrewshire - Labour

FIXED TERMS

The Parliament has a fixed four-year term and section 2(2) of the Scotland Act 1998 states that elections to the Parliament should take place on the first Thursday in May. The Presiding Officer (the Speaker of the Scottish Parliament) can propose a dissolution before this time provided he or she has the agreement (on a division) of at least two thirds of MSPs (Members of the Scottish Parliament) or if it is not possible to agree on the appointment of a First Minister.[1]

At the end of its fixed four-year term, the Parliament is dissolved at the beginning of a 'minimum' period (which is set out in the Scottish Parliament (Elections etc) Order 1999 (SI 1999, No. 787) under Section 12(1) of the Act) which is a period of 25 days and meets again after the election, within a period of seven days beginning immediately after the day of the poll (this seven day period does not include Saturdays, Sundays, Christmas Eve, Christmas Day, Good Friday, a bank holiday in Scotland or a day appointed for public thanksgiving or mourning).

Where the Presiding Officer proposes a day for the election which is not more than one month earlier nor more than one month later than the first Thursday in May, the Queen may dissolve the Parliament (by proclamation under the Scottish Seal) stipulate that the election be held on that day and that Parliament return within a seven day period beginning immediately after election day. Where the day proposed by the Presiding Officer is within the six-month period ending with the day on which the next fixed-term election to the Parliament would ordinarily be held, that election is not held. The first elections to the Scottish Parliament were on 6 May 1999.

THE FIRST MINISTER

The provisions relating to the election of First Minister of the Scottish Parliament are set out in Part II of the Scotland Act 1998. The Scottish Executive comprises the First Minister, other Ministers (appointed under section 47 of the Act) and the Lord Advocate and the Solicitor General for Scotland. The First Minister is appointed by the Queen from among the Members of the Scottish Parliament. After the resignation of Henry McLeish as First Minister (and Leader of the Labour Party in the Scottish Parliament) Jack McConnell was confirmed on 17 November 2001, as the new Leader of the Scottish Labour Party. He was unopposed and his leadership was affirmed in a ballot of the party's MSPs and its 29-strong Scottish Executive (he needed to gain more than 50 per cent of the votes and in the event won, 97.23 per cent). At the time of writing, it seemed clear that Mr McConnell would be elected as First Minister by the Scottish Parliament on 22 November 2001.

THE ELECTORAL TIMETABLE

The timetable for elections to the Scottish Parliament is set out in Schedule 2 (the 'Election Rules') to the Scottish Parliament (Elections etc) Order 1999 (SI 1999, No. 787) as amended by The Scottish Parliament (Elections etc.) (Amendment) (No. 3) Order (SI 2001, No. 1748 (S. 10)).

---

[1] The Presiding Officer can propose the dissolution if the period during which the Parliament must nominate a First Minister ends without a nomination being made; i.e., 28 days (Section 46, Scotland Act 1998).

Proceeding	Time
Publication of notice of election	Not earlier than the 28th day before the date of the poll and not later than the 21st day before the date of the poll.
Delivery of nomination papers	Not later than 4pm on any day after the date of the publication of the notice of election but not later than the 16th day before the date of the poll.
Making objections to nomination papers	During the hours allowed for delivery of nomination papers on the last day for their delivery and the hour following (5pm) although no objection can be made to a nomination paper in the afternoon of the last day, except to a nomination paper delivered within 24 hours of the last time for delivery and in the case of such a nomination paper, no objection may be made to a candidate unless made at or immediately after the time of the delivery of the nomination paper. These provisions do not apply to objections made under Rules 20 or 21. Rules 20 and 21 relate to candidates disqualified under the provisions of the Representation of the People Act 1981 (candidates serving prison sentences of more than one year) and state that where a candidate is objected to for this reason, that objection must be made between 10am and 4pm on the day after the last day for the delivery of nomination papers.
Delivery of notices of withdrawals of candidature	Within the time for the delivery of nomination papers.
Publication of statement of persons nominated	At the close of the time for making objections to nomination papers or as soon afterwards as any objections are disposed of.
Polling	Between 7am and 10pm on polling day.

The following days are disregarded when computing the timetable above:

❖ Saturdays and Sundays
❖ Christmas Eve, Christmas Day, Good Friday, Easter Monday
❖ Bank holidays in Scotland (as set out in the Banking and Financial Dealings Act 1971)
❖ Days appointed for public thanksgiving or mourning

There are no legislative provisions to combine elections to the Scottish Parliament with Westminster elections. In the 2001 General Elections, by-elections in Banff and Buchan and Strathkelvin and Bearsden were held on the same day as the General Election, but were held in 'parallel'.

BY-ELECTIONS

Under Section 9 of the Scotland Act 1998, where a constituency seat becomes vacant, a by-election must take place within three months (at a time fixed by the Presiding Officer). The notice of the by-election must be between 28 and 14 days before the date of the poll and the delivery of nomination papers no later than 4pm on any day after the day on which the notice of the election is published, but before the 11th day before the date of the by-election.[2]   Otherwise, the timetable is the same as the one set out in the table in the section above. However, when the last possible date for a by-election would fall within the three month period ending with the day on which the next set of fixed term elections are due to be held, there is no by-election.

---

[2] Rule 1 of the Scottish Parliament (Elections, etc.) Order 1999, which contains the timetable for elections to the Scottish Parliament was amended by the Scottish Parliament (Elections etc.) (Amendment) (N. 3) Order (SI 2001, No. 1748 (S. 10)).

Where a vacancy occurs amongst the MSPs elected from the Regional List, where the candidate is an individual candidate, the seat remains vacant until the next election. Section 10 of the 1998 Act is modified by Article 88 of the Scottish Parliament (Elections etc) Order 1999 (SI 1999, No 787). Where the vacancy occurs amongst regional list candidates, the next highest eligible candidate on the relevant Party list takes the seat. The candidate may decline to take the seat in which case the returning officer has to contact the next highest candidate on the list. If there is no eligible candidate left on the list the seat is left vacant until the next full Election.

WHO CAN STAND AS A CANDIDATE?

MPs, peers (but not Lords of Appeal in Ordinary), EU citizens who are resident and Ministers of Religion are eligible to stand for election to the Scottish Parliament. The effect of the Disqualifications Act 2000 is that members of the Irish legislature may also stand for election to the Scottish Parliament.

The following may not stand for election to the Scottish Parliament:

❖ Those disqualified from membership of the House of Commons under the provisions of paragraphs (a) to (e) of section 1(1) of the House of Commons (Disqualification) Act 1975[3]

❖ Those disqualified from membership of the House of Commons for any other reason (for example, anyone under 21, someone found guilty of corrupt electoral practices, prisoners)

❖ Those disqualified under the provisions of the Scottish Parliament (Disqualification) Order 1999 (SI 1999, No. 680) (some office-holders are only disqualified from being MSPs for particular constituencies or particular regions)[4]

❖ Lords of Appeal in Ordinary (the 'Law Lords')

If someone who is disqualified from being a Member of the Scottish Parliament is elected, the election is void and he or she must vacate the seat in question. Where an elected Member becomes disqualified by virtue of mental illness (section 141 of the Mental Health Act 1983) or bankruptcy (section 427 of the Insolvency Act) he or she may not participate in any proceedings of Parliament until such time as his or her seat is vacated.

---

[3] Judges, civil servants, members of the armed forces, members of police forces and members of foreign legislatures (with the exception of members of the Irish legislature).

[4] Part I of the order lists office-holders disqualified from standing as candidates in any constituency or region and these include members of a range of authorities including, for example, the Gaming Board for Great Britain, the National Radiological Protection Board, Scottish Natural Heritage, the UK Ecolabelling Board and for reasons which seem unclear, the Sea Fish Industry Authority. Part II of the order lists those office-holders who are disqualified from standing for particular constituencies and regions; for example, Her Majesty's Lord-Lieutenant for the city of Aberdeen may not stand for election to any constituency comprising the whole or part of the city in which he or she holds office or for which he or she is appointed or any region comprising the whole of part of the city in which he or she holds office or for which he or she is appointed.

The following restrictions apply to those standing as candidates:

❖ A person may not be a candidate to be a constituency member in more than one constituency.

❖ A party may not submit a list of candidate for the regional seats consisting of more than 12 names.

❖ Party lists may not include anyone who is included in any other list for that or any other region.

❖ Party lists may not include anyone who is an individual candidate standing for election as a regional member for that or any other region.

❖ Party lists may not include anyone who is a constituency candidate for a constituency not in that region.

❖ Party lists may not include anyone who is a constituency candidate for another party in that region.

❖ No one can stand as an individual candidate to be a regional member if he or she is included in a party's regional list for that or any other region.

❖ No one can stand as an individual candidate to be a regional member if he or she is standing as a individual candidate for another region.

❖ No one can stand as an individual candidate to be a regional member if he or she is a candidate to be a constituency member for a constituency not in that region.

❖ No one can stand as an individual candidate to be a regional member if he or she is a candidate of a registered party to be a constituency member for a constituency included in that region.

WHO CAN VOTE?

The franchise for Scottish Parliamentary elections is the same as the franchise for local government elections. Those entitled to vote as electors in a local government area within the constituency who are also registered at an address in the constituency and are over 18 years of age, are entitled to vote. This includes peers resident in Scotland as well as EU nationals and excludes UK residents overseas. Except for the cases stated above, the same disqualifications apply to voting in elections to the Scottish Parliament, as apply to parliamentary elections (for example, prisoners and those guilty of corrupt electoral practices cannot vote).

THE ELECTORAL REGISTER

The new system of 'rolling registration' was extended to elections to the Scottish Parliament by The Scottish Parliament (Elections, etc.) (Amendment) Order 2001 (SI 2001, No. 1399 S.5)). A description of the new provisions is contained in Chapter Two on parliamentary elections. Under Schedule 1 of the Scottish Parliament (Elections etc) Order 1999 (SI 1999, No 787) as amended by the aforementioned 2001 Order, the relevant constituency MSP is entitled to one copy of that part of the electoral register which relates to a particular constituency and the relevant regional MSP is entitled to the part of the register which relates to that region.

The registration officer must also supply, free of charge, one copy of the relevant part of the register, to anyone who requires it for use *"in connection with his own or some other person's prospective candidature for return as a constituency member for that constituency"*. Candidates or their election agents are entitled to one copy of the relevant part of the register. Individual prospective candidates standing as regional member and prospective candidates on regional party lists are entitled to one copy of the register for that region. Individual candidates for return as regional members or their election agents or the agent for a registered party submitting a list are also entitled to one copy of the part of the register for that region.

THE ELECTORAL SYSTEM

The method of electing Members of the Scottish Parliament is the Additional Member System. Electors within each constituency, within each region, have two votes, one for a Constituency Member and one for a party list (or individual regional candidate).

Where a party gains, for example, 40 per cent of the regional votes but has already gained 40 per cent of the Constituency seats, it is not be entitled to any Additional Members (the reason for having a list is to 'top-up' parties who have gained votes, but not seats). Account is taken of the number of Constituency seats gained within the European Parliamentary Constituency area. The number of regional votes cast for each party within the European Constituency is counted. The number of regional votes cast for each party is then divided by the number of Constituency MSPs gained in the Parliamentary Constituencies contained within the relevant region, plus one (essentially the 'd'hondt allocation formula' – explained in Appendix A). The party with the highest total after these calculations have been made gains the first additional member. The remainder of the additional Members are allocated in the same way except that the additional Members themselves are included in the calculations for the party for which they were elected.

The Scotland Act allows the number of Scottish MPs at Westminster to be reduced, if necessary, following a review by the Boundary Commission. This will allow them to apply the 'English' rather than the 'Scottish' quota, thereby reducing the number of Scottish Constituencies. However, the Commission could still take into account 'special geographical' features. This impacts on the Scottish Parliament as the Constituency MSPs are directly related to the number of Scottish MPs at Westminster.

Orkney and Shetland are guaranteed two separate MSPs, irrespective of any reduction in the number of Scottish MPs at Westminster. There is also provision in the Act for the number of Regional seats to be reduced if the number of Constituency seats were to be reduced, so that the proportion of 56:73 can be maintained if possible. So, if the number of Constituency seats fell to 60, the number of Regional List seats would fall to 46. As the number of European Regions has to be eight, some Regions would have six Regional List Members and some, five. The Boundary Commission has to ensure that Regions elect the same number of Regional List members, but where they differ, this should only be by one. The next review must be between 2002 and 2006.

APPLYING THE D'HONDT FORMULA IN SCOTLAND*

Region with 9 Constituency Members and 7 Additional Members
(* = elected)

	Seats gained in constituency section	Votes gained in Region	1st round (votes ÷ aggregate of 1 + seats gained) (= d'hondt divisor 1)	2nd round (votes ÷ aggregate of 1 + seats gained) (= d'hondt divisor 2)	3rd round (votes ÷ aggregate of 1 + seats gained) (= d'hondt divisor 3)	Regional Seats gained
Labour	7 *(as Labour has 36% of the regional vote and approximately 80% of the seats – it is not entitled to any additional members)*	400,000	400,000 ÷ 7 + 1 = 50,000 (no seat gained in 1st round, so aggregate unchanged in next round)	400,000 ÷ 7 + 1 = 50,000 (no seat gained in 2nd round, so aggregate unchanged in next round)	400,000 ÷ 7 + 1 = 50,000	
Conservative	2	300,000	300,000 ÷ 2 + 1 = 100,000* (no seat gained in 1st round, so aggregate unchanged in next round)	300,000 ÷ 2 + 1 = 100,000*	300,000 ÷ 2 + 2 = 75,000*	3
Liberal Democrat	0	200,000	200,000 ÷ 0 + 1 = 200,000* (gains 1 seat – added to aggregate in next round)	200,000 ÷ 1 + 1 = 100,000*	200,000 ÷ 1 + 2 = 66,666	2
SNP	0	200,000	200,000 ÷ 0 + 1 = 200,000* (gains 1 seat – added to aggregate in next round)	200,000 ÷ 1 + 1 = 100,000*	200,000 ÷ 1 + 2 = 66,666	2

*It should be remembered that the Party with the highest average after each round gains a seat, NOT the Party with the highest average in each round – so for example, after round 1, the Conservatives do not gain an Additional Member, but, after round 3, they win three regional seats. There would be no point in continuing with another round as no Party could achieve a higher average than has already been achieved and as a result, all the seats are allocated after only three rounds.

THE ELECTORAL PROCESS

Declarations of Local Connection and Service Declarations

The provisions of the RPA 2000 relating to declarations of local connection and service declarations are applied to elections to the Scottish Parliament by amendments to Schedule 3 of the Scottish Parliament (Elections etc) Order 1999 (SI 1999, No 787), contained in the Scottish Parliament (Elections etc.) (Amendment) Order 2001 (SI 2001, No. 1399 (S.5)). An explanation of both declarations of local connection and service declarations can be found in Chapter Two.

Proxy Voters

Part II, Article 8 of the Scottish Parliament (Elections etc) Order 1999 (SI 1999, No 787) as amended by the Scottish Parliament (Elections etc.) (Amendment) Order 2001 (SI 2001, No. 1399 (S.5)) states that where a person applies to a registration officer to vote by proxy at Scottish parliamentary elections for, either a definite or indefinite period, the application should be granted, provided, in the case of proxy voters, they fulfil certain conditions (which are set out in Schedule 3 of the amended order). These conditions are that:

❖ He or she will be registered as a service voter.

❖ He or she cannot go in person to their allotted polling station by reason of his or her occupation or that of his or her spouse or by reason of attendance on an educational course.

❖ He or she cannot get to a polling station to vote as a result of *"blindness or other physical incapacity"*.

❖ He or she cannot get to a polling station without making a journey either by sea or air.

Where an application is made on the grounds of physical incapacity that application has to be attested and signed by a registered medical practitioner, or a registered nurse[5] or Christian Science practitioner (they must be treating the person concerned for the relevant physical incapacity) or where the applicant is resident in a home, the warden or person in charge of that accommodation[6] or premises[7]. Where the application is based on a person blindness and the applicant is registered with a local authority as blind or where the application states that the applicant is (under section 73 of the Social Security Contributions and Benefits Act 1992) in receipt of the higher rate of the mobility component of a disability living allowance, then those facts alone are sufficient to qualify for a proxy vote, without the need for attestation.

---

[5] A registered nurse is someone who is a nurse within the meaning of section 10(7) of the Nurses, Midwives and Health Visitors Act 1979.

[6] A 'home' is defined as an establishment within the meaning of section 61 of the Social Work (Scotland) Act 1968 or section 59(2) of the Social Work (Scotland) Act 1968.

[7] Such premises are defined as being those *"provided for persons of pensionable age or physically disabled persons, and for which there is a resident warden"*.

Where an application is based on occupation, education or employment the application must be attested and signed where the person is self-employed by someone over 18 years of age, who knows the person concerned and is not related to him or her, in the case of an employed person the employer or another employee to whom this function has been delegated and in the case of a student, by the director or tutor of the course or by the principal or head of that institution or another employee to whom the function has been dedicated. A relative of the applicant is taken to be one of the following: husband, wife, parent, grandparent, brother, sister, child or grandchild.

No one can act as a proxy, if he or she is subject to any legal incapacity to vote, is not, or will not be 18 on the date of the poll, is neither a Commonwealth citizen or a citizen of the Republic of Ireland or an EU citizen. No one can vote as a proxy in any constituency at the same Scottish parliamentary election on behalf of more than two electors of whom that person is not the husband, wife, grandparent, brother, sister, child or grandchild.

The following applications must be received by the registration officer by 5pm on the sixth day before polling day:

❖ Applications to vote by post or proxy for an indefinite period
❖ Applications to vote by post or proxy for a particular period
❖ Applications to appoint a proxy for an indefinite period
❖ Applications to appoint a proxy for a particular period
❖ Applications by proxies to vote by post

The following applications must be received by 5pm on the 11th day before polling day unless there are good reasons why the person concerned cannot be reasonably be expected to vote in person at his local polling station (in which case the time limit is 5pm on the sixth day before polling day).

❖ Applications by absent voters to alter their mode of voting (e.g., from post to proxy)
❖ Applications to change from a proxy to a postal vote
❖ Applications by a postal voter for a ballot paper to be sent to a different address
❖ Applications to vote by proxy instead of by post at a particular election
❖ Applications from a postal proxy voter for ballot papers to be sent to a different address at a particular election

The following applications must also be received by 5pm on the 11th day before polling day:

❖ Applications from those registered as postal or proxy voters and those registered as their proxies to be removed from the relevant records.

❖ Applications to cancel proxies' appointments and applications from those registered as postal proxies applying to be removed from the register.

Ballot papers for those wishing to vote by post or proxy at a particular election and those proxies wishing to vote by post cannot be issued until after 5pm on the 11th day before the date of the poll. In all other cases, ballot papers can be sent out as soon as practicable after the application to vote by post has been granted.

The following days are disregarded when calculating time limits: Saturdays and Sundays, Christmas Eve, Christmas Day, Easter Monday, Good Friday, bank holidays in Scotland.

Under Part III, paragraph 34 of the Election Rules as set out Schedule 2 of the Scottish Parliament (Elections etc) Order 1999 (SI 1999, No 787) ballot papers and declarations of identity must be sent out in the manner of Form P (included in the Appendix to the regulations) as amended by The Scottish Parliament (Elections etc.) (Amendment) Order 2001 (SI 2001, No. 1399 (S.5)).

Under paragraphs 3 and 4 of Schedule 4 of the Scottish Parliament (Elections etc) Order 1999 (SI 1999, No 787) as amended by the 2001 Order (SI 2001, No. 1399) only the constituency returning officer and his staff may be present when postal ballot papers are issued, but on receipt of postal ballot papers the following may also be present:

❖ Constituency candidates or their election agents (or another person appointed by the candidate to attend in his or her agent's place).

❖ The regional returning officer.

❖ Individual candidates standing for return as regional members or their election agents (or another person appointed by the candidate to attend in his or her agent's place).

❖ Registered parties' election agents or the nominating officers of those parties (or another person authorised by the agent or nominating officer to attend in his or her place).

Constituency and individual candidates and election agents of registered parties can also appoint one or more agents (up to a number specified by the constituency returning officer) to be present.

Each postal ballot issued has to be stamped with the official mark. The name and number of the elector as set out in the electoral register is called out and the number marked on the counterfoil and a mark placed in the absent voters or postal proxies voters list against that elector to denote that a ballot paper has béen issued to them. The number of the postal ballot paper is then marked on the declaration of identity, which is sent out with the ballot paper. The elector is sent two envelopes: the covering envelope, marked 'B' and a small one, marked 'A', the ballot paper envelope. The covering envelope is for the return of both the ballot paper (or ballot papers) and the declaration of identity. Envelope A must have the number of the ballot paper marked on it. Spoilt ballot papers must be returned by 5pm on the day before polling day if a replacement ballot is to be issued. Where a postal voter has not received his postal ballot paper by the third day before the day of the poll, he can apply for a replacement (evidence of identity is required), which can be issued before 5pm on the day before polling day. A list is then kept of lost ballot papers, containing the number of both the lost paper and its replacement.

Postal ballot papers can be returned by hand to a polling station in the relevant constituency at any time up until the close of the poll or can be returned by hand or by post to the constituency returning officer up until the close of poll.

The constituency returning office has to give at least 48 hours notice in writing to constituency candidates, individual regional candidates and election agents for each registered party, of the time and place of opening of the postal voters' ballot boxes. The returning officer may also specify the number of agents a candidate can appoint to attend.

The returning officer must provide a separate ballot box for the reception of the covering envelopes ('the postal voters ballot box') and another for the reception of the postal ballot papers ('the postal ballot box'). The name of the constituency or electoral area must be clearly written on each. The following 'receptacles' (as they are called in the regulations) must also be provided: one for rejected votes, one for declarations of identity, one for ballot paper envelopes and one for rejected ballot paper envelopes. When the covering envelopes are returned, they are placed unopened in a postal voters' ballot box. As long as there is one such postal voters' ballot box available for the reception of covering envelopes up until the close of the poll, the other such boxes can be opened. The last such box is opened at the count.

When a postal voters' ballot box is opened the constituency returning officer counts and records the number of covering envelopes and then opens each one. Where the covering envelope does not contain the declaration of identity separately, the ballot paper envelope is opened to see whether the declaration is inside. Where a covering envelope does not contain both the declaration and a ballot paper envelope (or where there is no envelope, a ballot paper) the covering envelope is marked 'provisionally rejected' and is placed in the 'receptacle' for rejected votes. Where the constituency returning officer is not satisfied that a declaration of identity has been properly signed and authenticated by a witness, it is marked 'rejected', attached to the relevant ballot paper envelope or ballot paper and placed in the receptacle for rejected votes. Any of the 'agents' present can object to his decision, in which case the words 'rejection objected to' are added.

If the number on the declaration of identity tallies with the number on the ballot paper, the declaration is placed in the receptacle for declarations of identity and the ballot paper envelope in the one for ballot paper envelopes. Where the numbers do not tally, the ballot paper envelope and declaration of identity are put in the box for rejected votes. When the ballot paper envelopes are opened, where the number on the ballot paper tallies with the number on the ballot paper envelope the ballot paper is placed in the postal ballot box. Where the numbers do not tally, the ballot paper is attached to the ballot paper envelope and placed in the receptacle for rejected votes. Where a ballot paper envelope does not contain a ballot paper it is placed with the other rejected ballot paper envelopes.

The constituency returning officer has to keep two separate lists of rejected postal ballot papers: the first lists the numbers of those postal ballot papers not accompanied by a valid declaration of identity and the second lists the numbers of those postal ballot papers not received with any declaration of identity. The lists are checked up until the close of poll to see whether either the relevant declaration or ballot paper has subsequently been received. If either is received the vote can be counted. After the count, the rejected votes, declarations of identity, rejected ballot paper envelopes and lists of spoilt and lost postal ballot papers are sealed in individual packets and sent to the sheriff clerk. Covering envelopes received after the close of the poll, postal ballot envelopes returned as undelivered and too late to be readdressed and spoilt ballot papers returned too late for another to be issued are put in a separate packet, sealed and forwarded to the sheriff clerk.

THE ELECTION CAMPAIGN

Nominations

A candidate's consent to nomination is required one month before the day fixed as the last day for the delivery of constituency nomination papers. The consent must be attested by one witness and delivered along with his or her nomination paper and must state the candidate's date of birth and must contain a statement that he or she is, to his or her knowledge, not disqualified for membership of the Scottish Parliament. Under Part II of Schedule 2 (the 'Election Rules') of the Scottish Parliament (Elections etc) Order 1999 (SI 1999, No. 787) each candidate standing as a constituency candidate must be nominated in the manner set out in Form J in the Appendix to the regulations.

The nomination must be signed by the candidate and by a witness (who must include their name and address). The nomination must state the candidate's full names (with surname first), home address and any description of the candidate not exceeding six words in length. Form K is used for individual candidates standing as regional members. In the case of a regional party list, Form L is used and the list is submitted by the party's nominating officer, or other person who has been so authorised in writing.

The regional list must set out the full names and home addresses (in full) of each candidate included in the list and must be accompanied by a statement of the names by which the candidates will be described on the ballot paper. Candidates can withdraw their nominations but a withdrawal must be signed by the candidate and attested by one witness and delivered to the returning officer. A registered party can withdraw the candidature of any or all of the candidates in a regional list by a notice signed by the party's nominating officer and attested by one witness.

Where a constituency candidate dies before the election result is declared, under Part VI, paragraph 70 of the Election Rules, set out in Schedule 2 of the Scottish Parliament (Elections etc) Order 1999 (SI 1999, No 787) the election (or polling where this has begun) is abandoned and proceedings begun again as if publication of notice of the election had been given 28 days after the day on which the death occurred. Those already nominated do not need to be re-nominated. Where an individual candidate standing as a regional member or a candidate on a party list dies, the election continues as normal (unless the death has rendered the election uncontested).

Only those nominated as candidates, party nominating officers, election agents (and where a candidate is his or her own agent, another person nominated by them to attend) may be present at the delivery of nomination papers.

The Deposit

Under Part II, paragraph 10 of the Election Rules, the deposit for constituency candidates, individuals standing as regional members and a party submitting a regional list, is £500. Where a constituency candidate does not poll more than one twentieth of the total number of votes cast for all candidates, his or her deposit is lost. Where an individual candidate standing for election as a regional member or a registered party does not receive one twentieth of all the votes cast for all registered parties and individual and candidates in all the constituencies included in the region and has not been allocated a seat under Section 8 of the 1998 Act, the deposit is lost.

Ballot Papers

Under Part III of the Elections Rules, ballot papers for the election of constituency members must be set out in the manner of Form N in the Appendix to the regulations. The ballot paper must have a number printed on the back (this is also printed on the counterfoil). The ballot paper for regional members must contain the names of the individual candidates and the registered parties standing, with the names of their candidates. Regional ballot papers must be in the manner set out in Form O in the Appendix and must be a different colour from the constituency ballot papers. The official mark on the ballot paper can only be used once every seven years at an election for a Scottish parliamentary election in that constituency. A different official mark must be used for postal ballot papers.

Poll Cards and Polling Stations

Under Part III, paragraph 36 of the Election Rules, the form of the official poll card is set out in Form Q in the Appendix to the regulations and the proxy's poll card in Form R. Under Part III, paragraph 37 of the Election Rules, a guidance notice (as set out in Form S in the Appendix) must be displayed both inside and outside each polling station. A notice in the manner of Form T must also be displayed (this is similar to the guidance to voters which is displayed in parliamentary elections and is reproduced in Appendix B). In each compartment in the polling station there must be a notice stating:

> "Vote once only on each ballot paper by marking an X. Put no other mark on each ballot paper issued or your vote may not be counted".

Under Part III, paragraph 38 of the Election Rules, each constituency candidate, individual candidate standing for election as a regional member and the election agent of each registered party can appoint polling agents to attend the polling stations and counting agents to attend the count. The returning officer can limit the number of counting agents. Each constituency candidate must be allowed the same number of counting agents. The number is obtained by dividing the number of clerks employed at the count by the number of candidates standing as constituency members. The same applies to individual candidates and registered parties. The names and addresses of those appointed as polling and counting agents must be given to the returning officer no later than the fifth day before polling day.

Under Part III, paragraph 40 of the Election Rules, only certain people, other than electors, can attend a polling station and these are:

- ❖ Candidates
- ❖ Election agents
- ❖ Polling agents
- ❖ Clerks
- ❖ Constables on duty
- ❖ Companions of disabled voters

No more than one polling agent can be admitted at the same time to a polling station on behalf of the same candidate or registered party. Police officers employed during the election to attend particular polling stations can vote other than at their allotted polling station provided they have a certificate of employment as specified in Form U in the Appendix of Forms.

When a ballot paper is issued to a voter under the procedures set out in paragraph 45 of Part III of the Election Rules, it must be stamped with the official mark, the name and number of the elector as it appears in the register must be called out, the number of the elector must be marked on the counterfoil and a mark placed in the register of electors against the number of the elector to denote that a ballot paper has been received by them, but without showing the particular ballot paper which has been issued. Rule 45 also states that a voter could ask for only a constituency ballot paper, only a regional ballot paper, or both, but in the absence of any evidence to the contrary, the voter is presumed to want both ballot papers.

The new provisions of the RPA 2000 relating to blind and partially sighted voters are applied to elections to the Scottish Parliament by amendments to Schedule 2, Rule 37 of the Scottish Parliament (Elections etc) Order 1999 (SI 1999, No 787) (set out in The Scottish Parliament (Elections etc.) (Amendment) Order 2001 (SI 2001, No. 1399 (S.5))). These provisions relate to the new device designed to enable blind voters to vote without assistance from the presiding officer (the device is described in Chapter Two). Under rule 46 of Part III of the Election Rules, the presiding officer at the polling station can, if a voter is blind or has another physical disability which makes it difficult for his or her to vote, or who cannot read (in the presence of polling agents) mark the ballot paper in the manner directed by the voter. The name and number of any voter who has voted in this way is then placed on the 'list of votes marked by the presiding officer'.

Rule 47 is amended to allow anyone who if blind or has another physical incapacity or who cannot read, to vote with the assistance of a companion. The voter has to declare, either orally or in writing, that he is unable to vote without assistance. Where a person votes with the assistance of a companion, the companion must have made a written declaration and must not have previously assisted more than one disabled person to vote at the election. A person is qualified to assist a disabled voter if he or she is registered as an elector for that election, or is the father, mother, brother, sister, husband, wife, son or daughter of the blind voter and is 18 years of age. The name of electors and their companions who vote in this way must be entered in a list of 'voters with disabilities assisted by their companions'. The declaration is set out in Form V and is made at the time when the elector applies to vote.

Under paragraph 48 of Part III of the Election Rules, where someone claims to be a particular elector who is not on the absent voters list or where someone claims to be a proxy voter (who does not have a postal vote) and tries to vote after another person of that name and address has already voted, the person concerned is entitled to vote (as they could be the legitimate voter). However, they are given a 'tendered ballot paper', which is a different colour from other ballot papers. It is not put into the ballot box, but is given to the presiding officer and endorsed by him or her with the name of the voter and his or her electoral number and is then put into a separate packet. The name and number of the voter is then entered on the register of electors and entered on the 'tendered votes list'.

At the close of polling, the presiding officer must seal the ballot boxes and must then place the following into separate packets:

- ❖ Unused and spoilt constituency ballot papers

- ❖ Tendered constituency ballot papers

- ❖ Unused and spoilt regional ballot papers

- ❖ Tendered regional ballot papers

- ❖ Marked copies of the register of electors and list of proxies

- ❖ Counterfoils of the used constituency ballot papers and the certificates of employment (i.e., police officers on duty at the polling station who have voted there rather than at their own polling station)

- ❖ Counterfoils of the used regional ballot papers

- ❖ The tendered votes list, the list of blind voters assisted by companions, the list of votes marked by the presiding officer, a statement of the number of voters whose votes have been marked by the presiding officer under the headings 'physical incapacity' and 'unable to read' and the declarations made by the companions of disabled voters

Marked copies of the register of electors and list of proxies must be placed in one packet – this may not be the same as the one for counterfoils of used constituency or used regional ballot papers. The packets have to be accompanied by a statement by the presiding officer, referred to as the 'ballot paper account' (one for constituency ballot papers and another for regional ballot papers) which shows the number of ballot papers initially given to him or her and an account under different headings of the ballot papers issued, not otherwise accounted for, unused, spoilt and tendered.

The Count

Under paragraph 52 of Part III of the Election Rules, only the following may be present at the count:

- ❖ The constituency and regional returning officers
- ❖ The candidates
- ❖ The election agents
- ❖ The counting agents
- ❖ Others expressly permitted by the constituency returning officer to attend

At the count, the constituency returning officer opens each ballot box in the presence of the counting agents and counts and records separately the number of constituency ballot papers in each box and the number of regional ballot papers in each box. The ballot paper accounts then have to be verified and the constituency postal ballot papers and regional postal ballot papers counted. Counting may not begin until the constituency postal ballot papers have been mixed with constituency ballot papers from at least one ballot box and until the constituency ballot papers from one ballot box have been mixed with constituency ballot papers from at least one other ballot box. The same applies to regional postal and regional ballot papers. Tendered ballot papers are not counted.

As ballot papers are being counted and votes being counted, ballot papers must be kept face upwards to prevent anyone seeing the numbers printed on the back. The constituency returning officer must verify each ballot paper account by comparing it with the number of ballot papers recorded by him and the unused and spoilt ballot papers in his possession and the tendered votes list. He or she must draw up a statement as to the result of the verification, which any election agent may copy.

The following ballot papers would be rejected under paragraph 56 of Part III:

- ❖ Those not bearing the official mark

- ❖ In the case of a constituency ballot paper, one on which votes are given for more than one candidate

- ❖ In the case of regional ballot papers, those on which votes are given for more than one registered party or individual candidate or for both a registered party and an individual candidate

- ❖ Those on which anything is written or marked which could identify the voter (except the number printed on the back)

- ❖ Those which are unmarked or void for uncertainty

Some ballot papers are not deemed to be void if the intention of the voter is clear; for example, where the mark on the ballot paper is not in the proper place, where the mark is not a cross, where there is more than one mark. Where a ballot paper is rejected, the constituency returning officer must write 'rejected' on the offending ballot paper and add 'rejection objected to' if an objection is made by a counting agent. A statement is then drawn up showing the number of ballot papers rejected under the following headings:

- ❖ No official mark

- ❖ Constituency ballot paper marked for more than one candidate

- ❖ Regional ballot paper marked for more than one party's regional list or individual candidate or for both a registered party and an individual candidate

- ❖ Includes a mark identifying the voter

- ❖ Unmarked

The constituency returning officer's decision is final, but can be challenged by means of an election petition.

If after the count, 'an equality of votes' exists between any candidates, the constituency returning officer must decide between them by lot (paragraph 58, Part III, Election Rules). Once the total of votes cast for regional members in any given constituency is known, the constituency returning officer draws up a statement showing the number of votes given for each registered party and each individual candidate standing as a regional list candidate and informs the regional returning officer of the result. The regional returning officer receives the statements form all the constituency returning officers in that region. The following can attend the calculation and allocation of regional seats:

- ❖ The regional returning officer and his or her clerks
- ❖ Candidates on registered party lists
- ❖ Individual candidates standing for election as regional members
- ❖ Election agents of individual candidates or registered parties
- ❖ Nominating officers of registered parties
- ❖ Other specifically permitted by the regional returning officer

As set out in paragraph 62 of Part III of the Election Rules, the regional returning officer calculates the total number of regional votes given for each registered party and each individual candidate in all the constituencies included in the region by adding together the votes given for that registered party or individual candidate. The seats are then allocated in accordance with Sections 7 and 8 of the 1998 Act (see before). Section 8(7) of the Act is amended by the provisions of paragraph 63 of Part III of the Election Rules to provide for the situation where an equality of votes would result in more than the correct number of seats being allocated, in which case the regional returning officer has to decide by lot.

After the election, the constituency returning officer must forward to the sheriff clerk of the sheriff court district comprising the constituency (or if the constituency comprises the whole or part of more sheriff court districts than one, the sheriff clerk of any one of those sheriff court districts) the following:

- ❖ The packets of constituency ballot papers

- ❖ The packets of regional ballot papers

- ❖ The ballot paper accounts and statements of rejected ballot papers and statements of the result of the verification of the ballot paper accounts

- ❖ The tendered votes list, the lists of blind voters assisted by companions, the lists of votes marked by the presiding officer and the related statements and the declarations made by the companions of blind voters

- ❖ The packets of counterfoils and certificates as to employment on duty on polling day

- ❖ The packets containing the marked copies of registers and lists of proxies.

The sheriff clerk must retain the documents for a year. Documents except ballot papers, counterfoils and certificates of employment are open to public inspection.

Election Agents

Under the provisions of Part III, Article 30 of the Scottish Parliament (Elections, etc) Order 1999 (SI 1999, No 787), the following must appoint an election agent:

- ❖ Each candidate standing for election as a constituency member
- ❖ Each individual candidate standing for election as a regional member
- ❖ Each registered party which has submitted a regional list

A candidate can name him or herself as election agent. The election agent is responsible for payments made on behalf of candidates and all payments, except those under £20, must 'be vouched for by a bill stating the particulars and by a receipt' (Part III, Article 36, Scottish Parliament (Elections etc) Order 1999 (SI 1999, No 787)). Where list candidates are concerned, no payments can be made other than by the election agent of that party or by the nominating officer of the party that has put forward the list. Under Article 38, candidates can pay any personal expenses incurred in relation to the election provided these do not exceed £600 (in the case of a candidate standing as a constituency member who is not a regional list candidate as well) and £900 in the case of a candidate standing as a regional list candidate, regardless of whether or not he is also standing as a constituency candidate. Candidates must send to their agent a written statement of personal expenses paid. No expenses in relation to holding public meetings, issuing advertisements, publications, etc, can be incurred by anyone other than the candidate or his or her election agent and those authorised in writing by the election agent.

A return of these expenses, accompanied by a declaration, must be sent to the returning officer within 21 days after the date on which the election result is declared (the form in which these must be presented is set out in form A and B in the Appendix to the Scottish Parliament (Elections etc) Order 1999 (SI 1999, No 787). Copies of all such returns and declarations must be sent to the Secretary of State 21 days after the date on which the election result is declared. Anyone who makes, or 'aids, abets, counsels or procures any other person' to make any expenses in contravention of the provisions set out above or who knowingly makes a false declaration is guilty of a corrupt practice. Failure to deliver a declaration is an illegal practice. Where such corrupt or illegal practices have been committed by an election agent, a candidate is not liable and his or her election is not considered void, if the act was committed without his consent. Similar provisions apply under Article 40 in relation to regional list candidates. Expenses incurred by list candidates cannot be incurred by anyone other than candidates on the list, the nominating officer of the party concerned, the election agent of the registered party, or another person 'in accordance with arrangements for which the nominating officer is responsible'. The relevant return and declaration must be set out in the manner of forms C and D, which are contained in the Appendix to the regulations.

Article 41 limits candidates' election expenses. In the case of candidates standing as constituency members or individual candidates standing as regional members and their agents, election expenses are limited to a maximum amount as set out below:

❖ For a constituency candidate in a constituency coterminous with a parliamentary constituency which is a county constituency - £5,483, with an additional 6.2p for each entry in the register of electors to be used at that election (in a by-election, the limit is £100,000).

❖ For a constituency candidate in a constituency coterminous with a parliamentary constituency which is a burgh constituency - £5,483, with an additional 4.6p for each entry in a register of electors to be used at that election (in a by-election, the limit is £100,000).

❖ For a constituency candidate for the constituencies of the Orkney Islands or Shetland Islands - £5,483, together with an additional 6.2p for each entry in the register of electors to be used at that election (in a by-election, the limit is £100,000).

❖ For an individual candidate for return as a regional member, the total of the maximum amounts (calculated in accordance with the rules in 1 to 3 above) for a single candidate standing as a constituency member in each constituency within that region.

These maximum amounts do not include the candidates' personal expenses.

Under Schedule 9, Part II of the Political Parties, Elections and Referendums Act 2000, the limit applying to campaign expenditure in Scottish parliamentary elections is £12,000 for each constituency contested plus £80,000 for each region contested (the maximum if all 73 constituencies and all eight regions are contested is therefore, £1,516,000) and the relevant period to which the limitations apply is the four-month period ending on the date of the election, except where an extraordinary general election is called, in which case the period begins with the date when the Presiding Officer proposes a date for the election and ends with the date of the election. The limits on expenditure replace those set out in Article 42 of the Scottish Parliament (Elections, etc) Order 1999 (SI 1999, No. 787).

Claims for payments from constituency candidates or individual regional list candidates must be sent to the election agent within 21 days of the date on which the election result of declared, otherwise they cannot be paid. All election expenses must be paid within 28 days after that date. Payments made in contravention of these regulations constitute an illegal practice. Where payments are made illegally in this way by an election agent without the 'sanction or connivance' of the candidate (Article 43) the candidate's election is not considered void. Where a claim is sent in after 21 days, the claimant, constituency candidate or individual regional list candidate or his or her respective election agent, can apply to the Court of Session or to a sheriff court for leave to pay such a claim.

Under Article 46, in the case of candidates standing for election as constituency members and individual candidates standing as regional members, returns of election expenses must be sent to the returning officer within 35 days after the day on which the election result is declared (the form this should take is set out in Form E in the regulations). Candidates' election agents must also send in a declaration as set out in Form G in the Appendix, and candidates themselves must also send in a declaration within seven days of the delivery of the agent's declaration. If the candidate is out of the country, the time limit is 14 days. Making a false declaration constitutes a corrupt practice.

Under Article 52, a candidate who fails to send in a declaration and election returns cannot sit or vote in the Scottish Parliament and is subject to a penalty of £100 for each day on which they try to do so. Applications for exemptions from the above regulations relating to returns and declarations can be made to the Court of Session, an election court or a sheriff court by a candidate or an election agent, on the grounds of the illness of either one of them, or, where the applicant is the candidate, on the grounds of the 'absence, death, illness or misconduct' of the election agent. An agent could also apply on the basis of the absence, death or illness of any prior election agent, the candidate or any sub-agent.

Returns and declarations can be inspected by the public on payment of a fee (currently £1.50, plus 15p for each page copied) and are retained for two years.

Election Addresses and Broadcasts

Each constituency candidate and each individual candidate standing as a regional member and each nominating officer of each registered political party which has submitted a regional list is entitled to send a free election address to each elector. It is an illegal practice under Article 59 of the regulations to broadcast election material designed to 'influence persons to give or refrain from giving their votes' in a Scottish parliamentary election, from outside the UK. Under Article 75, all election material must carry the name and address of the printer and publisher.

Hiring Rooms

Under Article 61, candidates standing for election as constituency members are entitled to the free use of school rooms in which to hold meetings (not including independent schools). Under Article 62, individual candidates standing as regional members and registered parties with regional lists are entitled to the free use of school rooms.

ELECTION OFFENCES

Bribery and Treating

Under Article 78 of the aforementioned 1999 Order, anyone found guilty of the following is guilty of bribery, which is a corrupt practice under the regulations:

❖ Giving money or procuring any office to or for any voter, or to or for any other person, on behalf of any voter, or to or for any other person in order to induce any voter to voter or refrain from voting.

❖ Doing any of the above as a result of a voter having voted or refrained from voting.

❖ Doing any of the above in order to induce that person to procure or endeavour to procure a particular result, or to induce a voter to vote in a particular way.

A voter is guilty of bribery if before or during a Scottish parliamentary election, he or she, either *"directly or indirectly"* by himself, or by another on his behalf, receives, agrees to receive, or contracts for, any money, gift, loan or 'valuable consideration', office, place or employment for himself or another, for voting or agreeing to vote, or for refraining or agreeing to refrain from voting. A person, regardless of whether or not they are a voter, is guilty of bribery if after a Scottish parliamentary elections he or she directly or indirectly alone, or by someone else on his or her behalf, receives any money or 'valuable consideration' on account of any person having voted or refrained from voting or having induced any other person to vote or refrain from voting.

Under Article 79, treating is an offence and someone is guilty of treating if, before, during or after a Scottish parliamentary election, they provide *"any meat, drink, entertainment"* for the purpose of 'corruptly influencing' someone to vote or refrain from voting, or as a payment for someone having voting or refrained from having voted. The recipient of such treating is also guilty of an offence.

Undue Influence

Under Article 80 of the regulations, undue influence is a corrupt practice and a person is guilty of undue influence if he or she uses *"force, violence or restraint, or inflicts or threatens to inflict, by himself or by any other person, any temporal or spiritual injury, damage, harm or loss upon or against any person in order to induce or compel that person to vote or refrain from voting, or on account of that person having voted or refrained from voting"*. It is also undue influence for someone to use abduction, duress or any fraudulent device of contrivance to impede or prevent someone from voting freely.

Personation

Impersonating a voter either by post or in person, either as an elector or as a proxy is an election offence.

False Statements Relating to Candidates

Under Article 71 of the Order, anyone who makes a false statement concerning the 'personal character' or conduct of any candidate is guilty of an illegal practice, unless he or she can demonstrate that there were reasonably good grounds for making such a statement and that they believed it to be true. A candidate would not liable and his or her election would not declared void if such a statement were to be made by an agent, other than the candidate's election agent, without the candidate's knowledge. Under Article 72, anyone who attempts to 'corruptly' induce another candidate to withdraw from being a candidate, in return for payment or promise of payment, is guilty of an illegal payment and the candidate who so withdraws from the election is also guilty of having accepted an illegal payment.

Other Voting Offences

Under Article 26 it is an offence for an elector to vote in the knowledge that he or she is subject to a legal incapacity to vote (including being under 18 years of age on polling day). It is an offence to vote more than once in any constituency at a poll for the return of a constituency member of the Scottish Parliament and more than once at a poll for the return of a regional member. It is an offence to vote in person if entitled to a postal vote, to vote in person knowing that a proxy has been appointed or to appoint a new proxy without cancelling a previous proxy. A person is also guilty of an offence if he or she votes as proxy for the same elector more than once in the same constituency or in more than one constituency. It is also an offence to vote in person as proxy if entitled to a postal vote or to vote as proxy knowing the elector has already voted in person. These offences constitute illegal practices. A candidate's election would not be void if any of the above offences were to be committed by his or her election agent.

Tampering with Nomination Papers, Imitating Poll Cards, etc.

Under Article 28, it is an offence to deface or destroy a nomination paper, ballot paper or the official mark on any ballot paper or any declaration of identity or official envelope used in connection with postal voting. It is also an offence to supply ballot papers to anyone without proper authority, to open or interfere with (without proper authority) any ballot box. It is an offence to forge a nomination paper, a ballot paper or the official mark on a ballot paper. It is also an offence to sign a nomination paper (this includes nomination papers for regional lists) as candidate or nominating officer for a registered political party, knowing it contains any false statements. Anyone found guilty of such offences is liable on summary conviction to a fine not exceeding the amount specified as level 5 on the standard scale or to imprisonment for a term not exceeding three months or both.

It is an illegal practice under Article 60 of the regulations to produce election material that so closely resembles a poll card as to deceive the elector.

Secrecy

Under Article 29, anyone who does not maintain the secrecy of the ballot or who attempts to influence a voter when voting, or who attempts to discover for which candidate or party an elector has voted, is guilty of an offence and is liable on summary conviction to a fine not exceeding the amount specified as level 5 on the standard scale or to imprisonment for a term not exceeding three months.

Disorderly Conduct

Under Article 63, anyone at a public meeting during an election campaign who acts in a 'disorderly manner' in an attempt to disrupt the meeting is guilty of an illegal practice.

Illegal Canvassing

Canvassing by police officers is an offence under Article 65 of the regulations and can lead on conviction to a fine not exceeding level 3 on the standard scale. It is also an offence under Article 74 to pay an elector to display an election notice unless that is their ordinary line of business as an advertising agent. Under Article 76, it is illegal to employ paid canvassers.

LEGAL PROCEEDINGS

Article 85 of The Scottish Parliament (Elections etc) Order 1999 (SI 1999, No 787) as amended by The Scottish Parliament (Elections etc.) (Amendment) Order 2001 (SI 2001, No. 1399 (S.5)) stipulates that certain provisions of the RPA 1983 relating to legal proceedings are to be applied to Scottish parliamentary elections. Those provisions that relate to elections in Scotland are set out in Schedule 6 of the regulations. The sections of the RPA 1983 that apply to elections of constituency members are: sections 120 to 123, sections 125 and 126, sections 136 to 141, sections 143 and 144, sections 146 and 147, sections 154 to 170, sections 173 to 176, sections 178 to 118, sections 183 to 186. These sections deal with elections petitions and the penalties for corrupt and illegal practices. These are considered in detail in Chapter Two. These apply with certain modifications to make them relevant to the Scottish Parliament; for example, substituting 'Clerk of the Scottish Parliament' for 'Speaker' and reducing the penalty for those found guilty on summary conviction of a corrupt practice under section 168 from a term of imprisonment of six months and / or a fine not exceeding the statutory maximum, to a sentence of three months, and a fine specified as level 5 on the standard scale.

The following sections of the 1983 Act apply with modifications to the elections of regional members of the Scottish Parliament: sections 120 to 123, sections 125 and 126, sections 136 and 137, sections 139 to 141, sections 143 and 144, sections 146 and 147, sections 154, 155 and 157, section 160, sections 167 to 170, sections 174 to 176, sections 178 to 181, sections 183 to 186. Modifications include the amendment under section 122 that elections petitions must be presented within 21 days after the result has been declared. In section 160, subsections 1 to 3 are removed and subsection 4 is amended so that the words 'reported by an election court personally guilty' are replaced by 'convicted'. After 'corrupt practice', 'or a candidate convicted of an illegal practice' is inserted. In section 168, which relates to prosecutions for illegal practices, three months is substituted for six months and in section 169 those found guilty of illegal practices are liable in the case of illegal practices under articles 41 and 42 of the Order on conviction on indictment to a fine and on summary conviction to a fine not exceeding the amount specified as level 5 on the standard scale.

COMBINATIONS OF POLLS

Schedule 5 of The Scottish Parliament (Elections etc) Order 1999 (SI 1999, No 787) sets out the modifications of the Elections Rules that are necessary when elections to the Scottish Parliament are combined with local government elections.

CHAPTER SIX – ELECTIONS TO THE WELSH ASSEMBLY

THE WELSH ASSEMBLY

The composition of the National Assembly for Wales is set out in Schedule 1 of the Government of Wales Act 1998. The National Assembly consists of 60 members, 40 Constituency Members (elected from the existing parliamentary constituencies in Wales) and 20 elected using the Additional Member System from the five former European parliamentary constituencies (renamed Assembly electoral regions in the Act) as set out in the European Parliamentary Constituencies (Wales) Order 1994, SI: 428. Each Assembly electoral region returns four Members (see below).

WELSH ADDITIONAL MEMBER REGIONS & 1999 ELECTION RESULTS

Region	Constituencies
North Wales Labour - 73,673 Conservative - 41,700 Liberal Democrat - 22,130 Plaid Cymru - 69,518 Green - 4,667 Natural Law - 917 United Socialist - 828 Communist - 714 Rhuddian - 1,353 Two Conservative, one Liberal Democrat and one Plaid Cymru candidate were therefore elected	Alyn and Deeside - Labour Caernarfon - Plaid Cymru Clwyd West - Labour Clwyd South - Labour Conwy - Plaid Cymru Delyn - Labour Wrexham – Labour Vale of Clwyd - Labour Ynys Mon - Plaid Cymru
Mid and West Wales Labour - 53,842 Conservative - 36,622 Liberal Democrat - 31,683 Plaid Cymru - 84,554 Socialist Labour - 3,019 Natural Law - 705 Independent (Turner) - 1214 Two Conservative, one Labour and One Plaid Cymru candidates were therefore elected	Brecon and Radnorshire - Liberal Democrat Carmarthen East & Dinefwr - Plaid Cymru Carmarthen West & Pembrokeshire South - Labour Ceredigion - Plaid Cymru Llanelli - Plaid Cymru Meirionnydd Nant Conwy - Plaid Cymru Montgomeryshire - Liberal Democrat Preseli Pembrokeshire - Labour
South Wales West Labour - 70,625 Conservative - 20,993 Liberal Democrat - 18,527 Plaid Cyrmu - 50,757 Green - 4,082 Natural Law - 676 United Socialist - 1,257 Peoples' Representative - 204 Two Plaid Cymru, one Conservative and one Liberal Democrat were therefore elected	Aberavon - Labour Bridgend - Labour Gower - Labour Neath - Labour Ogmore - Labour Swansea East - Labour Swansea West - Labour

South Wales Central	Cardiff Central - Liberal Democrat
Labour - 79,564	Cardiff North - Labour
Conservative - 34,944	Cardiff South and Penarth - Labour
Liberal Democrat - 30,911	Cardiff West - Labour
Plaid Cymru - 58,080	Cynon Valley - Labour
Green - 5,336	Pontypridd - Labour
Socialist Labour - 2,822	Rhondda - Plaid Cymru
Natural Law - 665	Vale of Glamorgan - Labour
Communist - 652	
United Socialist - 602	
Independent (Philips) - 378	
Independent (Mathias - 1,524	
Two Conservative and two Plaid Cymru candidates were therefore elected	
South Wales East	Blaenau Gwent - Labour
Labour – 83,953	Caerphilly - Labour
Conservative – 33,947	Islwyn – Plaid Cymru
Liberal Democrat – 24,757	Merthyr Tydfil and Rhymney - Labour
Plaid Cymru – 49,139	Monmouth - Conservative
Green – 4,055	Newport East - Labour
Socialist Labour – 487	Newport West - Labour
	Torfaen - Labour
Two Plaid Cymru, one Conservative and One Liberal Democrat were therefore elected	

THE ELECTORAL PROCESS

Electors have two votes – one for a Constituency MP and one for a registered Party or independent candidate (Part I, section 4, Government of Wales Act 1998). The elections follow the same procedure as the elections to the Scottish Parliament and employ the d'Hondt allocation formula (an example of how the formula is applied is contained in the preceding chapter). The Assembly sits for a fixed four-year term and elections are held on the first Thursday in May. However, the Secretary of State can order the poll at be held on a day a month earlier or later than the first Thursday in May. The Assembly electoral region members, as opposed to the Assembly constituency members are elected from a closed list.

TIMETABLE FOR ELECTIONS

The timetable for elections is set out in Schedule 5 to the National Assembly for Wales (Representation of the People) Order 1999 (SI 1999, 450).

Proceeding	Time
Publication of notice of election	Not later than the 25th day before the date of the election.
Delivery of nomination papers	Daily between 10am and 4pm, after the day on which the notice of election is published, but before the 19th day before polling day and, additionally, between 10am and 12 noon on the 19th day itself.

Making objections to nomination papers	During the hours allowed for delivery of nomination papers on the last day for their delivery and the hour following, although no objection can be made to a nomination paper in the afternoon of the last day, except to a nomination paper delivered within 24 hours of the last time for delivery and in the case of such a nomination paper, no objection may be made to a candidate unless made at or immediately after the time of the delivery of the nomination paper. These provisions do not apply to objections made under paragraph 18(2). Paragraph 18(2) relates to candidates disqualified under the provisions of the Representation of the People Act 1981 (candidates serving prison sentences of more than one year) and states that where a candidate is objected to for this reason, that objection must be made between 10am and 4pm on the day after the last day for the delivery of nomination papers.
Delivery of notices of withdrawals of candidature	Not later than noon on the 17th day before the day of the election.
Publication of statement of persons nominated	Not later than noon on the 16th day before the day of election
Polling	Between 7am and 10pm on polling day.

In computing any period of time the following are disregarded:

- ❖ Saturday and Sunday
- ❖ Christmas Eve, Christmas Day, Maundy Thursday, Good Friday
- ❖ A day which is a bank holiday under the Banking and Financial Dealings Act 1971
- ❖ A day appointed for public thanksgiving or mourning

BY-ELECTIONS

Where there is a vacancy in an Assembly constituency seat, a by-election is held within three months of the occurrence of the vacancy[1] (or, where it is not notified to the Presiding Officer until one month later, three months after the date when it is notified), unless that date would fall within the three-month period preceding an ordinary election, in which case it is not held. Where the vacancy is for an Assembly electoral region member and the member who has vacated the seat was elected from the list of a registered political party, the regional returning officer must choose the next highest candidate on that party's list (unless that person is no longer a member of that party). Where the member vacating the seat was an individual candidate the seat remains vacant until the next ordinary elections to the Assembly.

WHO MAY STAND AS A CANDIDATE?

MPs, peers, EU citizens who are resident and Ministers of Religion are eligible to stand for election to the National Assembly. The effect of the Disqualifications Act 2000 is that members of the Irish legislature may also stand for election to the National Assembly.

---

[1] The vacancy is taken to have occurred on a date determined under the standing orders of the Assembly.

Those disqualified from standing as candidates are:

- ❖ Anyone disqualified from being a member of the House of Commons under paragraphs (a) to (e) of Section 1(1) of the House of Commons Disqualifications Act 1975; i.e., judges, civil servants, members of the armed forces, members of police forces and members of foreign legislatures (with the exception of members of the Irish Legislature).

- ❖ Anyone holding any of the offices designated by Order in Council as offices disqualifying someone from being a member of the Assembly.[2]

- ❖ Anyone holding the office of Auditor General for Wales or the office of Welsh Administration Ombudsman.

- ❖ Anyone disqualified from being a member of a local authority under section 17(2)(b) or 18(7) of the Audit Commission Act 1998; i.e., members of local authorities who have incurred unlawful expenditure.

- ❖ Anyone disqualified from being a member of the House of Commons other than under the House of Disqualifications Act 1975 (for example, anyone under 21 years of age, someone found guilty of a corrupt electoral practice, prisoners).

- ❖ A person who holds office as lord-lieutenant, lieutenant or high sheriff or any area in Wales (but only from being an Assembly member for an Assembly constituency or Assembly electoral region wholly or partly included in that area).

If someone who is disqualified from being a member of the National Assembly is elected, the election is void and he or she must vacate the seat in question. Where an elected Member becomes disqualified by virtue of mental illness (section 141 of the Mental Health Act 1983) or bankruptcy (section 47 of the Insolvency Act) he or she may not participate in any Assembly proceedings until such time as his or her seat is vacated.

The following restrictions also apply to candidates:

- ❖ No one may stand as a candidate in more than one Assembly constituency

A regional list submitted by a registered political party for election in an Assembly electoral region must not contain more than 12 names and must not contain any of the following:

- ❖ A person who is included on any other list submitted for that or any other Assembly electoral region.

- ❖ A person who is an individual candidate to be an Assembly member for that or any other Assembly electoral region.

- ❖ A person who is a candidate to be the Assembly member for an Assembly constituency, not in that Assembly electoral region.

---

[2] A draft of the statutory instrument containing the Order in Council must be laid before and approved by a resolution of each House of Parliament, unless it is an Order in Council varying or revoking a previous Order in Council which the Assembly has resolved the that Secretary of State should recommend the making of such an Order in Council.

❖ A person who is a candidate for Assembly member for an Assembly constituency included in the Assembly electoral region but who is not a candidate of that party.

No one may be an individual candidate for an Assembly electoral region if he or she is:

❖ Included on a list submitted by a registered political party for that or another Assembly electoral region.

❖ Is an individual candidate to be an Assembly member for another Assembly electoral region.

❖ Is a candidate to be an Assembly member for an Assembly constituency, which is not included in the Assembly electoral region.

❖ Is a candidate of any registered political party to be the Assembly member for an Assembly constituency in that Assembly electoral region.

WHO CAN VOTE?

Section 10 of the Government of Wales Act 1998 states that those entitled to vote in elections to the National Assembly are those entitled to vote at local government elections in an electoral area included in the Assembly constituency, who are registered in the register of local government elections. This includes those entitled to vote in Parliamentary elections, with the addition of peers and EU nationals but with the exception of overseas voters. A person is not entitled to vote more than once in the election for a constituency member or more than once in the election for regional members in the same Assembly constituency or vote in more than one Assembly constituency.

PROXY VOTERS

Electors may apply for proxy votes for an indefinite period under Part I, Article 8 of the National Assembly for Wales (Representation of the People) Order 1999 (SI 1999, No. 450).[3] Those who may apply include the following:

❖ Service voters.

❖ Those no longer resident at an address in that area.

❖ Those who cannot reasonably be expected to go in person to a polling station by reason of blindness or other physical incapacity.

❖ Those who cannot be expected to go in person to a polling station because of their occupation or employment or that of their spouse.

❖ Those who cannot get to a polling station except by making an air or sea journey.

---

[3] The National Assembly for Wales (Representation of the People) Order 1999 (SI 1999, No.450) will need to be amended to take into account the new provisions relating to absent voting contained in the RPA 2000.

The following may apply to vote by post or proxy at a particular election:

❖ Those whose circumstances on polling day are likely to mean that they cannot reasonably be expected to vote in person and they fulfil the criteria set out in Schedule 2.

A proxy voter may not act as proxy on behalf of more than two people of whom he is not the husband, wife, parent, grandparent, brother, sister, child or grandchild. A proxy voter may also apply for a postal vote.

Under Schedule 2, paragraph 3, where an application is made on the grounds of physical incapacity that application has to be attested and signed by a registered medical practitioner, or a registered nurse or Christian Science practitioner (they must be treating the person concerned for the relevant physical incapacity)[4] or where the applicant is resident in a home, the warden or person in charge of that accommodation.

Under paragraph 4, where an application is based on occupation or employment the application must be attested and signed where the person is self-employed by someone over 18 years of age, who knows the person concerned and is not related to him or her or in the case of an employed person the employer or another employee to whom this function has been delegated. A relation is taken as being husband, wife, parent, grandparent, brother, sister, child or grandchild.

An elector, who appears in the register of electors, can also apply for an absent vote at a particular election if their circumstances on polling day mean that they cannot 'reasonably' be expected to vote in person on health grounds. Applications must be received by the registration officer between 5pm on the 11th day before polling day but before 5pm on the sixth day before polling day.

The registration officer must keep a list of those who have applied for postal or proxy votes indefinitely and those whose applications are for a particular election. A list of proxy voters is also kept. No one can act as a proxy if he or she is subject to any legal incapacity to vote, is not, or will not be 18 on the date of the poll, is neither a Commonwealth citizen or a citizen of the Republic of Ireland or an EU citizen. No one can vote as a proxy in any constituency at the same Assembly parliamentary election on behalf of more than two electors of whom that person is not the husband, wife, grandparent, brother, sister, child or grandchild.

Under paragraph 8, applications to vote by post or proxy for an indefinite period must be received by the registration officer before 5pm on the 11th day before the date of the poll. Applications to vote by post or proxy at a particular election must also be received by this deadline except where the application for an absent vote is on health grounds in which case the deadline is before 5pm on the sixth day before polling day. The following days are disregarded when calculating time limits: Saturdays and Sundays, Christmas Eve, Christmas Day, Maundy Thursday, Good Friday, bank holidays in Wales. Copies of the lists of postal and proxy voters must be supplied free of charge to candidates standing as

---

[4] However, this is not necessary where the applicant is registered as blind by a local authority or where the application states that the applicant is in receipt of the higher rate of the mobility component of the disability living allowance.

constituency members or their election agents and individual candidates standing as regional members or nominating officers of parties submitting regional lists.

Under paragraph 5 of Schedule 3, only the following may be present when postal ballot papers are issued:

❖ The constituency returning officer and his or her clerks

❖ Constituency candidates or their election agents

❖ The regional returning officer

❖ Individual candidates standing for return as regional members or their election agents

❖ Registered parties' election agents or the nominating officers of those parties

Constituency and individual candidates can also appoint one or more agents (up to a number specified by the constituency returning officer) to be present.

Under the provisions of paragraph 8, Schedule 3, each postal ballot issued has to be stamped with the official mark. The name and number of the elector as set out in the electoral register is called out and the number marked on the counterfoil and a mark placed in the absent voters or postal proxies voters list against that elector to denote that a ballot paper has been issued to them. The number of the postal ballot paper is then marked on the declaration of identity, which is sent out with the ballot paper. The elector is sent two envelopes: the covering envelope, marked 'B' and a small one, marked 'A', which is the ballot paper envelope. The Covering envelope is for the return of both the ballot paper (or ballot papers) and the declaration of identity. Envelope A must have the number of the ballot paper marked on it along with the words 'Ballot paper envelope' in English and Welsh. If a postal voter inadvertently spoils the ballot paper, it can be returned to the constituency returning officer along with the declaration of identity and the two envelopes. If all these documents are returned, a new ballot paper can be issued provided it is not too late for a new ballot paper to be issue and returned before the close of the poll.

Postal voters' ballot boxes must be opened by the constituency returning officer and provided one at least is available until the close of poll, the others can be opened beforehand. Constituency candidates and individual candidates standing as regional members and agents for registered parties must be given not less than 48 hours notice in writing of the time and place of opening of the postal voters' ballot boxes.

When the postal voters' ballot boxes are opened, the constituency returning officer must ensure that a covering envelope contains both a declaration of identity and a ballot paper envelope, or if there is no ballot paper envelope, a ballot paper. Under paragraph 17 of Schedule 2, if the covering envelope does not contain both a declaration of identity and a ballot paper envelope (or ballot paper as the voter might not have put this in the ballot paper envelope), the covering envelope is marked 'rejected' and is put along with any contents into the box for rejected votes. A declaration of identity must have been signed by the voter and attested and signed by a witness – if not, it is rejected and is put along with the relevant ballot paper envelope into the box for rejected votes.

Where the number of the declaration of identity tallies with the number on the ballot paper envelope the declaration is put in the box for declarations of identity and the ballot paper envelope (or ballot paper) is put into the box for ballot paper envelopes. Where the numbers do not tally, the ballot paper envelope and declaration of identity are put in the box for rejected votes. The only reason for opening the ballot paper envelope should be to determine whether a ballot paper envelope contains a declaration of identity or in cases where the number on the ballot paper envelope differs from that on the declaration of identity, whether the number on the declaration agrees with the number on the ballot paper. When the ballot papers are opened, ballot papers the numbers of which are the same as the number on the ballot paper envelopes are placed in one 'receptacle' and those where the numbers do not tally are rejected.

ELECTORAL REGISTER

Under the provisions of Schedule 1 of the National Assembly as contained in the National Assembly for Wales (Representation of the People) Order 1999 (SI 1999, 450) the registration officer must supply free of charge four copies of the electoral register to prospective candidates. Assembly members are entitled to one copy of that part of the register which relates to their constituency or region.

NOMINATIONS

Under Part II, Schedule 5, paragraph 9 of the National Assembly for Wales (Representation of the People) Order 1999 (SI 1999, 450) a candidate's consent to nomination is required one month before the day fixed as the last day for the delivery of constituency nomination papers. The consent must be attested by one witness and delivered along with his or her nomination paper and must state the candidate's date of birth and must contain a statement that he or she is, to his or her knowledge, not disqualified for membership of the Assembly.

Under paragraph 4 of Part II of Schedule 5 each candidate standing as a constituency candidate must be nominated in the manner set out in the form (in English and Welsh) in the Appendix to the regulations. The nomination must be signed by the candidate and by a witness (who must include their name and address) to the candidate's signature. It must state the candidate's full names (with surname first), home address and any description of the candidate not exceeding six words in length. In the case of a regional party list, the list is submitted by the party's nominating officer or person authorised in writing. Different forms are required for constituency candidates, those standing as individuals in regional areas and party lists submitted by nominating officers. These are set out in the Appendix to the regulations.

The regional list must set out the full names and home addresses in full of each candidate included in the list and must be accompanied by a statement of the names by which the candidates will be described on the ballot paper. Candidates can withdraw their nominations but a withdrawal must be signed by the candidate and attested by one witness and delivered to the returning officer. A registered party can withdraw the candidature of any or all of the candidates in a regional list by a notice signed by the party's nominating officer and attested by one witness.

Where a constituency candidate dies before the election result is declared, under paragraph 65 of Part VI of Schedule 5 of the regulations, the election (or polling where this has begun) is abandoned and proceedings begun again as if publication of notice of the election had been given 28 days after the day on which the death occurred. Those already nominated do not need to be re-nominated. Where an individual candidate standing as a regional member or a candidate on a party list dies, the election continues as normal (unless the death would render the election uncontested).

THE DEPOSIT

Under paragraph 10 of Part II of Schedule 5 of the regulations, the deposit for constituency candidates, individual candidates at regional elections and regional lists is £500. Under paragraph 60 of Part IV of Schedule 5 of the regulations, a constituency candidate or an individual candidate in a region or a party list loses his or her deposit if he, she or they fail to gain one twentieth of the total number of votes polled by all the candidates in the case of a constituency election or all individual candidates and registered parties in the case of a regional election.

THE ELECTION CAMPAIGN

Ballot Papers

Under Part III of Schedule 5 of the regulations, ballot papers for the election of constituency members must be in the manner set out in the Appendix to the regulations. It must have a number printed on the back, which is also printed on the counterfoil. The ballot paper for regional members must contain the names of the individual candidates and the registered parties standing, with the names of their candidates. Regional ballot papers must be in the manner set out in the form in the Appendix and must be a different colour form the constituency ballot papers. The official mark on the ballot paper can only be used once every seven years. A different official mark must be used for postal ballot papers.

Poll Cards and Polling Stations

The form of the ordinary elector's and a proxy's poll card is set out in the Appendix to the regulations (paragraph 33, Part III, Schedule 5 of the regulations). Under paragraph 34, a notice must be displayed at polling stations in each compartment, stating in relation to the constituency election:

"Vote for one candidate only on the constituency ballot paper. Put no other mark on the ballot paper or your vote may not be counted".

A notice must also be displayed, stating:

"Vote once only on the regional ballot paper. Put no other mark on the ballot paper or your vote may not be counted".

Under Part III, paragraph 35 of Schedule 5, each constituency candidate, individual candidate standing for election as a regional member and the election agent of each registered party, can appoint polling agents to attend the polling stations and counting agents to attend the count. The returning officer can limit the number of counting agents. Each constituency candidate must be allowed the same number of counting agents. The number is obtained by dividing the number of clerks employed on the counting by the number of candidates standing as constituency members. The same applies to individual candidates and registered parties. The names and addresses of those appointed as polling and counting agents must be given to the returning officer no later than the second day before polling day.

Under Part III, paragraph 37 of Schedule 5, only certain people, other than electors, can attend a polling station and these are:

❖ Candidates
❖ Election agents
❖ Polling agents
❖ Clerks
❖ Constables on duty
❖ Companions of blind voters
❖ Returning Officers

No more than one polling agent can be admitted at the same time to a polling station on behalf of the same candidate or registered party. Police officers employed during the election to attend particular polling stations can vote at that rather than their own polling station provided they have a certification of employment as specified in the Appendix.

When ballot papers are issued to voters under the procedures set out in paragraph 42 of Part III of Schedule 5, it must be stamped with the official mark, the name and number of the elector as it appears in the register must be called out, the number of the elector must be marked on the counterfoil, a mark placed in the register of electors against the number of the elector to denote that a ballot paper has been received but without showing the particular ballot paper which has been received.

Under paragraph 43 of Part III of Schedule 5, the presiding officer at the polling station can, if a voter is blind or has another physical disability which makes it difficult for them to vote, or who cannot read, in the presence of polling agents, mark the ballot paper in the manner directed by the voter. The name and number of any voters who have voted in this way is then placed on the 'list of votes marked by the presiding officer'. Where a blind voter votes with the assistance of a companion, the companion must have made a written declaration and must not have previously assisted more than one blind person to vote at the election.

A person is qualified to assist a blind voter if he or she is him or herself an elector or is the father, mother, brother, sister, husband, wife, son or daughter of the blind voter and is 18 years of age. The name of electors and their companions who vote in this way must be entered in a list of 'blind voters assisted by their companions'. The declaration is set out in the Appendix to the regulations (in English and Welsh) and is made at the time when the voter applies to vote.

Under paragraph 45 of Part III of Schedule 5 of the regulations, where someone claims to be a particular elector who is not on the absent voters list or where someone claims to be a proxy voters (who does not have a postal vote) and tries to vote after another person of that name and address has already voted, the person concerned is entitled to vote (as they could be the legitimate voter). However, they are given a 'tendered ballot paper' which is a different colour from other ballot papers. It is not put into the ballot box, but is given to the presiding officer and endorsed by him with the name of the voter and his electoral number and is then put into a separate packet. The name and number of the voter is then entered on the register of electors and entered on the 'tendered votes list'.

At the close of polling, the presiding officer must seal the ballot boxes and must then place the following into separate packets:

❖ Unused and spoilt constituency ballot papers

❖ Tendered constituency ballot papers

❖ Unused and spoilt regional ballot papers

❖ Tendered regional ballot papers

❖ Marked copies of the register of electors and list of proxies

❖ Counterfoils of the used constituency ballot papers and the certificates of employment (i.e., police officers on duty at the polling station who have voted there rather than at their own polling station)

❖ Counterfoils of the used regional ballot papers

❖ The tendered votes list, the list of blind voters assisted by companions, the list of votes marked by the presiding officer, a statement of the number of voters whose votes have been marked by the presiding officer under the headings 'physical incapacity' and 'unable to read' and the declarations made by the companions of blind voters

The packets have to be accompanied by a statement by the presiding officer, referred to as the 'ballot paper account' (one for constituency ballot papers and another for regional ballot papers) which shows the number of ballot papers initially given to him or her and an account under different headings of the ballot papers issued, not otherwise accounted for, unused, spoilt and tendered.

The Count

Under paragraph 49 of Part III of Schedule 5, only the following may be present at the count:

❖ The constituency and regional returning officers
❖ The candidates and spouses
❖ The election agents
❖ The counting agents
❖ Others expressly permitted by the constituency returning officer to attend

At the count, the constituency returning officer opens each ballot box in the presence of the counting agents and counts and records separately the number of constituency ballot papers in each box and the number of regional ballot papers. Under paragraph 50 of Part II of Schedule 5 of the regulations, this verification procedure can take place at a different venue from the place where votes are actually counted. Postal ballot papers must be returned in the proper envelope and must reach the constituency returning officer before the close of the poll and must be accompanied by a declaration of identity which has been duly signed and authenticated. Tendered ballot papers are not counted. As ballot papers are being counted they must be kept face upwards to prevent anyone seeing the numbers printed on the back. The constituency returning officer must verify each ballot paper account by comparing it with the number of ballot papers recorded by him and the unused and spoilt ballot papers in his possession and the tendered votes list. He or she must draw up a statement as to the result of the verification, which any election agent may copy.

The following ballot papers would be rejected under paragraph 53 of Part III of Schedule 5 of the regulations:

❖   Those not bearing the official mark
❖   Those on which more than one vote is given
❖   Those on which anything is written or marked which could identify the voter (except the number printed on the back)
❖   Those which are unmarked or void for uncertainty

Some ballot papers are not deemed to be void if the intention of the voter is clear; for example, where the mark on the ballot paper is not in the proper place, where the mark is not a cross, where there is more than one mark. Where a ballot paper is rejected, the constituency returning officer must write 'rejected' on the offending ballot paper and add 'rejection objected to' if an objection is made by a counting agent. A statement is then drawn up showing the number of ballot papers rejected under the following headings:

❖   No official mark
❖   More than one vote
❖   Includes a mark identifying the voter
❖   Unmarked

The constituency returning officer's decision is final, but can be challenged by means of an election petition.

If after the count, two or more candidates in the constituency part of the election have the same number of votes, the constituency returning officer must decide between them by lot (paragraph 55, Part III, Schedule 5). Once the total of votes cast for regional members in any given constituency is known, the constituency returning officer draws up a statement showing the number of votes given for each registered party and each individual candidate standing as a regional list candidate and informs the regional returning officer of the result. The regional returning officer receives the statements form all the constituency returning officers in that region. The following can attend the calculation and allocation of regional seats:

❖   The regional returning officer and his or her clerks
❖   Candidates
❖   Election agents
❖   Constituency returning officers for constituencies in that electoral region
❖   Other specifically permitted by the regional returning officer

After the election, the constituency returning officer must forward to the Assembly the following:

- ❖ The packets of constituency ballot papers

- ❖ The packets of regional ballot papers

- ❖ The ballot paper accounts and statements of rejected ballot papers and statements of the result of the verification of the ballot paper accounts relating to the constituency election

- ❖ The ballot paper accounts and statements of rejected ballot papers and statements of the result of the verification of the ballot paper accounts relating to the regional election

- ❖ The tendered votes list, the lists of blind voters assisted by companions, the lists of votes marked by the presiding officer and the related statements and the declarations made by the companions of blind voters

- ❖ The packets of counterfoils relating to the constituency election

- ❖ The packets of counterfoils relating to the regional election

- ❖ The packets of certificates relating to employment on duty on polling day

- ❖ The packets containing the marked copies of registers and lists of proxies

The Assembly must retain the documents for a year. Documents except ballot papers, counterfoils and certificates of employment are open to public inspection.

Election Addresses

Under Article 66 of Part III of the regulations, each individual candidate or group of party list candidates may send out one free election address to each elector.

Hiring Rooms

Under Article 69, Part III of the regulations candidates are entitled to the free use at reasonable times of school premises.

The Election Agent

Under Part III, Article 32 of the regulations, each constituency candidate and each individual candidate has to name an election agent before the latest time for delivery of notices of withdrawal of candidature. Where parties have submitted regional lists, the candidate whose name appears first on the list declares the name of the agent for that list. Candidates can themselves be election agents. Under the provisions of Article 33, agents may appoint one deputy election agent (sub-agent). Where no name is put forward as agent, the candidate is taken as being the agent (in the case of a regional list this is the candidate whose name appears first on the list). All payments and expenses must be made through and by the election agent during an election campaign and except for items under £20, these all require bills and receipts.

Under Article 41, candidates may pay any personal expenses provided these do not exceed £600 in the case of constituency candidates and £900 in the case of regional candidates. Where a person is both a constituency and regional candidate the amount of personal expenses in both elections must not exceed £900 (the constituency element must not exceed £600). Under Article 42, only candidates, election agents and those authorised by election agents may pay any expenses during an election campaign related to holding public meetings or issuing advertisements, circulars or publications. A return of the expenses which must be authorised by the election agent must be sent to the returning officer within 21 days of the declaration of the election result (the relevant form is set out in Schedule 6). Making a false declaration of election expenses or incurring expenses in contravention of the rules set out above constitutes a corrupt practice. Failure to deliver a return is an illegal practice, but a candidate is not deemed to be liable for an offence committed by his agent if that offence was committed without his consent. The limitations on candidates' expenditure during elections are set out in Articles 46 to 48 of Part III of the regulations. As far as constituency candidates are concerned the limitations are as follows:

❖ For an Assembly constituency which is coterminous with a parliamentary constituency which is a county constituency, £5,229 together with an additional 5.9p for every entry in a register of electors to be used at the election (in the case of a by-election, the amount is £20,920 together with an additional 23.4p for each entry in a register of electors to be used at the election).

❖ For an Assembly constituency which is coterminous with a parliamentary constituency which is a borough constituency, £5,229, together with an additional 4.4p for every entry in a register of electors to be used at the election (in the case of a by-election, the amount is £20,920 with an additional 17.8p for every entry in the register of electors).

The maximum amount for an individual candidate at a regional election (in a general election to the National Assembly) is the total of the amounts that can be spent in individual constituencies (i.e., £5,229 plus 5.9p per elector in a county constituency or £5,229 plus 4.4p per elector in a borough constituency) within that region. In a by-election the relevant figures would be £20,920 plus 23.4p for each elector in a county constituency or £20,920 plus 17.8p for each elector in a borough constituency. The amounts set out above do not cover candidates' personal expenses.

The limits on campaign expenditure for elections to the National Assembly of Wales are set out in Schedule 9, Part III of the Political Parties, Elections and Referendums Act 2000 and are £10,000 for each constituency contested, plus £40,000 for each region. As there are 40 Assembly constituencies each returning one member and five regions each returning four members, the maximum amount of campaign expenditure is £600,000. The relevant period during which the limitations apply is the four-month period ending on the date of the election. These limits replace those contained in Article 47 of the National Assembly for Wales (Representation of the People) Order 1999 (SI 1999/450).

Any claim against a candidate or election agent or registered party in respect of election expenses, which is not submitted within 21 days after the day on which the election result is declared cannot be paid. All election expenses must be paid within 28 days. Contravening these rules is an illegal practice. Where an election agent makes such an illegal payment without the knowledge of the candidate, the candidate's election is not void.

In the case of constituency candidates and individual candidates standing for return as regional members, returns as to election expenses must be submitted to the returning officer, within 35 days as set out in Article 54 of Part III of the regulations. The form in which this should be done is set out in Schedule 6. In the case of registered parties, the return, relating to a regional list, has to be sent in within 70 days after 'the day on which an ordinary election is held' or the day on which the results of a regional election are declared other than at an ordinary election (Article 55). Under Article 56, constituency candidates and individual candidates standing for return as regional members must send a declaration made by their election agent along with their election return (or within seven days of sending the return). Making a false declaration is a corrupt practice. Under Article 57, each party list candidate at a regional election must send in a declaration within seven days of the nominating officer for the party concerned sending in an election expenses return. Where candidates are outside the UK at the time the period is extended to 14 days. If a candidate does not deliver a return or declaration, he or she may not sit or vote in the Assembly and if he or she does the fine is £100 for each day (Article 60). An application can be made to the High Court, an election court or a county court for an exemption on account of illness or the illness of his or her agent (where a return or declaration is not sent in). Returns and declarations are retained by the returning officer for two years in the case of constituency and individual candidates (Article 64) and by the Assembly for two years in the case of returns relating to regional lists. They can be inspected by the public for a fee of £1.50 and 15p per page for each copy.

ELECTION OFFENCES

Bribery and Treating

Under Article 85, Part III of the regulations, bribing (either directly or indirectly) any voter to either vote or refrain from voting by either making or offering a gift of money, or a loan or by procuring or offering to procure a particular office, place or employment, is a corrupt practice. A voter is guilty of bribery if he or she accepts such a gift either before or after an election in order to either vote or refrain from voting. Under Article 86 a person is guilty of a corrupt practice if he or she either before, during or after an election, either directly or indirectly, gives or pays for any 'meat, drink, entertainment' in order to influence someone to vote or refrain from voting. Any elector accepting such an offer is guilty of treating. Under Article 130, Part IV, where a candidate is proved to have been guilty by himself or by any person on his or her behalf, of bribery, treating or undue influence, one vote for each person who voted and is proved to have been bribed, etc., is struck off the total of votes for that candidate or party list.

Undue Influence

Using undue influence to induce of compel someone to vote or refrain from voting is a corrupt practice under Article 87, Part III of the regulations. Undue influence is defined as either directly or indirectly, by himself or by another person on his behalf, using or threatening to use *"force, violence or restraint"* or inflicting or threatening to inflict by himself or by another person, any *"temporal or spiritual injury, damage, harm or loss"* upon someone in order to induce or compel them to vote or refrain from voting or after an election on account of their having voted or not voted. Using abduction, duress or any *"fraudulent device or contrivance"* to impede or prevent someone from freely voting is also undue influence.

233

Personation

Under Part II, Article 27 of the National Assembly for Wales (Representation of the People) Order 1999 (SI 1999, 450) anyone who impersonates another voter or *"aids, abets, counsels or procures"* someone else to impersonate a voter, is guilty of a corrupt practice.

Tampering with Nomination Papers, Ballot Papers, etc

It is an offence under Part II, Article 30 of the regulations to deface or destroy a nomination paper, ballot paper, the official mark on a ballot paper or any declaration of identity or official envelope used for postal voting. It is also an offence to supply a ballot paper to anyone without due authority or to take a ballot paper out of a polling station or to destroy or open a ballot box. Offences under this Article are liable on summary conviction to a fine not exceeding level 5 on the standard scale, to imprisonment for a term not exceeding six months or both. If a returning officer, presiding officer or clerk commits any of the above offences he or she is liable on conviction on indictment to a fine, or to imprisonment for a term not exceeding two years or both or on summary conviction to a fine not exceeding the statutory maximum or to imprisonment for a term not exceeding six months or both.

It is an offence, constituting an illegal practice, under Article 68, Part III of the regulations to issue any documentation which so closely resembles a poll card as to mislead the electors.

Maintaining the Secrecy of the Ballot

Anyone attending a polling station (returning officers, presiding officers, clerks, candidates, election agents and polling agents) must maintain the secrecy of the ballot and must not reveal the name of any elector or proxy, their number on the register of electors, the official mark. They must not attempt to interfere with a voter when voting, obtain information on how he or she voted, tell anyone how someone voted or reveal the number on the back of a ballot paper.

At the count, they must not attempt to ascertain the number on the back of the ballot paper or divulge the mark an elector has made on the ballot paper. Anyone committing any of the above offences is liable on summary conviction to a fine not exceeding level 5 on the standard scale or to imprisonment for a term not exceeding six months.

Other Election Offences

It is an offence under Article 28 of Part II of the regulations to vote more than once in the same Assembly constituency at any Assembly election or to vote in more than one Assembly constituency. It is also an offence to vote in person if entitled to a postal vote or to vote in person knowing that a proxy has already voted on his or her behalf. A proxy voter is guilty of an offence if he votes as proxy for the same elector more than once in the same Assembly constituency or in more than one Assembly constituency. It is also an offence to vote in person as proxy for an elector if entitled to vote by post as proxy or to vote in person as proxy for an elector knowing that the elector in question has already voted in person. These offences constitute illegal practices.

Under Article 67 of Part III of the regulations, it is an offence constituting an illegal practice to broadcast anything from outside the UK with a view to *"influence persons to give or refrain from giving their votes at an Assembly election"*.

Under Article 70, Part III of the regulations, it is an offence constituting an illegal practice to attempt to disrupt an election meeting.

Under Article 72, Part III of the regulations, it is an offence for any police officer to canvass. Any police officer illegally canvassing would be liable on summary conviction to a fine not exceeding level 3 on the standard scale. Paying anyone to canvass is illegal under Article 83, Part III.

Under Article 78, Part III of the regulations it is an offence constituting an illegal practice to publish a false statement about a candidate, unless the person making the statement can demonstrate that he or she had reasonable grounds for making it. Where a candidate's agent other than his or her election agent makes such a statement, the candidate's election would not be considered void unless he or she gave his or her consent. Under Article 79, anyone who induces a candidate to withdraw from an election is guilty of making an illegal payment.

Under Article 81, paying someone to display election material constitutes and illegal practice unless it is part of their ordinary course of business. Under Article 82, all election material must carry the name and address of both the printer and publisher and failure to do so is an illegal practice resulting on summary conviction in a fine not exceeding level 5 on the standard scale.

ELECTION OFFENCES

Under Part IV, Article 93 of the regulations, the following are entitled to present an election petition:

- ❖ A person who voted or had a right to vote as an elector at the election
- ❖ A person claiming to have had a right to be elected at the election
- ❖ A person alleging to have been a candidate at the election
- ❖ A person claiming to have had a right to be returned under Section 9 of the Government of Wales Act 1998 (at a by-election)

A petition must be presented within 21 days after the day on which the name of any member to whose election or return the petition relates has been elected. If the petition alleges a corrupt practice and specifically relates to a payment of money made in pursuance of that corrupt practice, after the election, it can be presented within 28 days after the date of the alleged payment.

Petitions alleging illegal practices must be presented within 21 days after the 10th day after the end of the time allowed for delivering returns relating to election expenses or if later, where the person elected was an individual candidate the day on which the returning officer received the return and declaration relating to election expenses, or where the person elected was a party list candidate the day on which the Assembly received the return and declaration relating to election expenses, or where the return and declarations were received on different days, the last of those days, or where there was an authorised excuse for failing to make the return and declarations, the date of the allowance of the last excuse. Where a petition questions the return on the grounds of an illegal practice and specifically alleges that a payment of money or some other act has been made in pursuance of the alleged illegal practice, then the petition can be presented within 28 days of the alleged payment or other act.

Anyone presenting an election petition must give 'security for all costs' under Article 98 and this can be an amount up to £5,000.

If an election court determines that a regional election was void, the Presiding Officer of the Assembly must set a date for another election in that region within three months.

Where an election court reports that a corrupt practice other than treating or undue influence has been committed with the knowledge and consent of a candidate, he or she is treated as having been reported personally guilty of that corrupt practice. The same applies to illegal practices. Where the election court reports that a candidate was guilty by his agents of treating, undue influence or any illegal practice but that the candidate or his election agent did not sanction it or took all reasonable means to prevent the commission of the offences or the offences were of a 'trivial, unimportant and limited' character and that the election was generally free from corrupt or illegal practices, then the candidate is not treated as being personally responsible for the offences.

The RPA 1983 has been subsequently amended by the PPERA 2000 to ensure that where a candidate or other person is found guilty of a corrupt or illegal practice they may not hold any elective office for five years in the case of a corrupt practice and three in the case of an illegal practice.

Under Article 128, Part IV of the regulations, where corrupt or illegal practices have been so prevalent that they have affected the outcome of the election, the election of the candidate in question is declared void. Under Article 129, if a candidate or his election agent engages as a canvasser or agent someone whom they know or have reasonable grounds to suppose is subject to an incapacity to vote at the election because of having been convicted or reported of any corrupt or illegal practice under the regulations, the RPA 1983, or under the law relating to European parliamentary elections, the Northern Ireland Assembly or the Scottish Parliament, or of having been convicted more than once of an offence under the Public Bodies Corrupt Practices Act 1889, then the candidate or candidates concerned are deemed incapable of being elected. Where party list candidates are concerned the incapacity applies, when an election agent engages such a person, to each candidate on the list and where the election agent does not engage such a person, only to the candidate or candidates who do engage that person.

Under Article 132, Part IV, a person who is guilty of a corrupt practice under the regulations is liable on conviction on indictment in the case of a corrupt practice under Article 27 (impersonation) to imprisonment for a term not exceeding two years, or to a fine, or both and in any other case, to imprisonment for a term not exceeding one year, or to a fine, or to both, or on summary conviction to imprisonment not exceeding 6 months or to a fine not exceeding the statutory minimum or to both.

Under Article 133, Part IV, a person guilty of an illegal practice is on summary conviction be liable to a fine not exceeding level 5 on the standard scale.

Under Article 139, Part IV, a person guilty of an offence of illegal payment, employment or hiring is, on summary conviction, liable to a fine not exceeding level 5 on the standard scale. A candidate or election agent personally guilty of an offence of making an illegal payment, employment or hiring is guilty of an illegal practice.

Under Article 40, proceedings in respect of any offences in the regulations must be commenced within one year after the offence was committed.

Comprehensive results and analysis of the 1999 elections to the National Assembly for Wales can be found at:

http://news.bbc.co.uk/hi/english/static/vote_99/wales_99/html/index.stm

CHAPTER SEVEN – ELECTIONS TO THE NORTHERN IRELAND ASSEMBLY

THE NORTHERN IRELAND ASSEMBLY

Elections to the Northern Ireland Assembly are governed by the Northern Ireland (Elections) Act 1998. There are 108 seats in the Assembly (each UK parliamentary constituency elects six members). The first elections were held on 25 June 1998. The Assembly was suspended on 3 February 2000, but was reinstated on 29 May. On 1 July 2001, First Minister David Trimble resigned, but nominated UUP Minister, Reg Empey as caretaker, triggering a six-week period in which to resolve the impasse that had developed over decommissioning. On 10 August the Assembly was again suspended, being restored on 12 August, setting off another six-week period. On 21 September the Assembly was again suspended. On 18 October the Ulster Unionist Ministers resigned from the Assembly, but after the IRA's announcement on decommissioning on 22 October, David Trimble nominated Ministers to serve in the Assembly. However, David Trimble failed to be re-elected as First Minister by one vote leaving the Secretary of State with the decision as to whether or not to call fresh elections. However, over the weekend of 3rd & 4th November 2001, the Alliance members of the Assembly agreed to re-designate themselves as Unionists, and when a further vote was held, David Trimble was elected as First Minister.

Detailed rules governing the elections were originally set out in the New Northern Ireland Assembly (Elections) Order 1998 (SI 1998, 1287) which was revoked by The Northern Ireland Assembly (Elections) Order 2001 (SI 2001, No. 2599). Elections take place every four years on the first Thursday in May. Northern Ireland is unique in electoral terms in the United Kingdom in that elections are held using the single transferable vote (please see Appendix A for an explanation of STV).

Constituency	Members Elected
Antrim North Total votes – 49,697 Quota – 7,100	Three DUP, one SDLP and two UUP
Antrim South Total votes – 43,391 Quota – 6,285	One Alliance, one DUP, one SDLP, one UKU, two UUP
Antrim East Total votes – 35,610 Quota – 5,088	One Alliance, one DUP, one SDLP, one UKU, two UUP
Belfast East Total votes – 39,593 Quota – 5,657	One Alliance, two DUP, one PUP, two UUP
Belfast North Total votes – 41,125 Quota – 5,876	One DUP, one PUP, one SDLP, one SF, one UU, one UUP
Belfast South Total Votes – 40,724 Quota – 5,818	One DUP, one NI Women, two SDLP, two UUP
Belfast West Total votes – 41,794	Two SDLP, four SF

Constituency	Members Elected
Quota – 5,971	
Down North Total votes – 37,313 Quota – 5,331	One Alliance, one NI Women, one UKU, three UUP
Down South Total votes – 51,353 Quota – 7,337	One DUP, three SDLP, one UUP, one SF
Fermanagh & South Tyrone Total votes – 51,043 Quota – 7,292	One DUP, one SDLP, two SF, two UUP
Foyle Total votes – 48,794 Quota – 6,971	One DUP, three SDLP, two SF
Lagan Valley Total votes – 46,510 Quota – 6,645	One Alliance, one DUP, one SDLP, one UKU, two UUP
Londonderry East Total votes – 39,564 Quota – 5,653	One DUP, two SDLP, one UU, two UUP
Newry & Armagh Total votes – 54,136 Quota – 7,734	One DUP, two SDLP, two SF, one UUP
Strangford Total votes – 42,922 Quota – 6,132	One Alliance, two DUP, one UKU, two UUP
Tyrone West Total votes – Quota – 6,565	One DUP, two SDLP, two SF, one UUP
Ulster Mid Total votes – 49,798 Quota – 7,115	One DUP, one SDLP, three SF, one UUP
Upper Bann Total votes – 50,399 Quota – 7,200	One DUP, one SDLP, one SF, two UUP, one UU

UUP – Ulster Unionist (28 MLAs)
SDLP – Social Democratic and Labour (24 MLAs)
DUP – Democratic Unionist (21 MLAs)
SF – Sinn Fein (18 MLAs)
Alliance – Alliance Party (6 MLAs)
UKU – UK Unionist (1 MLA) (four left to form Northern Ireland Unionist Party, one later joined DUP)
UU – Independents who later formed United Unionist Assembly Party (3 MLAs)
PUP – Progressive Unionist (2 MLAs)
NI Women – Northern Ireland Women's Coalition (2 MLAs)

TIMETABLE FOR ELECTIONS

The timetable for elections to the Assembly is set out in Schedule 1 to the Northern Ireland Assembly (Elections) Order 2001 (SI 2001, No. 2599).

Proceeding	Time
Publication of notice of election	Not later than the 25^h day before the date of the poll.
Delivery of nomination papers	Between 10am and 4pm on the 17th and 16th day before polling day.
Delivery of notices of withdrawals of candidature	Within the time for the delivery of nomination papers at the election.
Making objections to nomination papers	During the hours allowed for delivery of nomination papers on the last day for their delivery and on the 16th day before the date of the poll for the hour following as well: These provisions do not apply to objections made under Rules 15(2). Rule 15(2) relates to candidates disqualified under the provisions of the Representation of the People Act 1981 (candidates serving prison sentences of more than one year) and states that where a candidate is objected to for this reason, that objection must be made between 10am and 4pm on the day after the last day for the delivery of nomination papers.
Publication of statement of persons nominated	At the close of the time for making objections to nomination papers or as soon afterwards as any objections are disposed of.
Polling	Between 7am and 10pm on polling day.

The following days are disregarded in determining the timings above:

- ❖ Saturdays and Sundays
- ❖ Christmas Eve, Christmas Day, Maundy Thursday, Good Friday
- ❖ Bank holidays (as set out in the Banking and Financial Dealings Act 1971 in Northern Ireland)
- ❖ Any day appointed as a day of public thanksgiving or mourning

WHO CAN VOTE?

Those entitled to vote in elections to the Northern Ireland Assembly are those entitled to vote as local government electors in any district electoral partly, or wholly within the constituency concerned, over 18 years of age and registered at an address in the constituency. This includes peers as well as EU nationals and excludes UK residents overseas. Except for the cases stated above, the same disqualifications apply to voting in elections to the Assembly, as apply to parliamentary elections (for example, prisoners and those guilty of corrupt electoral practices cannot vote).

WHO CAN STAND AS A CANDIDATE?

Those eligible to stand for election to the Assembly are those eligible to stand for elections to the House of Commons, with the addition of EU citizens, peers (but not Lords of Appeal in Ordinary) and members of both Houses of the Irish legislature, the Seanad Eireann, the Upper House (Senate of the Republic of Ireland) and the Lower House, the Dail. The effect of the Disqualifications Act 2000 is that members of the Irish legislature may also stand for election to the House of Commons, the Scottish Parliament and Welsh Assembly. Anyone disqualified from membership of the House of Commons under the House of Commons Disqualification Act 1975 or who is otherwise disqualified cannot stand as a candidate. Her Majesty's Lord-Lieutenant of Lieutenant for a county of county borough in Northern Ireland is disqualified for membership of the Assembly for a constituency comprising the whole or part of the county or county borough.

Under the provisions of the Disqualifications Act 2000, Ministers of the Irish Government or chairmen or deputy chairmen of committees of the Irish legislature are disqualified from holding certain offices in the Northern Ireland Assembly, namely those holding ministerial office in Northern Ireland and those members of the Northern Ireland Policing Board drawn from the Northern Ireland Assembly. This means that a Minister of the Government of Ireland may not stand for election, or be elected, as First Minister or deputy First Minister and may not be nominated to hold ministerial office or be appointed as a junior Minister if he becomes a Minister of the Government of Ireland. Any Minister or junior Minister ceases to hold office if he becomes such a Minister.

The Disqualifications Act also amends the 1998 Act so that a Minister in the Government of Ireland or a chairman or deputy chairman of committees of the Irish legislature may not be a chairman or deputy chairman of a statutory committee of the Northern Ireland Assembly or be appointed as a member of the Northern Ireland Assembly Commission set up under Section 40 of the 1998 Act.

Where a candidate who is disqualified under any of the above provisions is returned as a Member of the Assembly his or her election is void and the seat must be vacated.

THE ELECTORAL PROCESS

The rules governing the conduct of elections to the Northern Ireland Assembly are essentially the same as the Election Rules set out in the Representation of the People Act 1983 as subsequently amended the RPA 2000. Schedule 1 of the Northern Ireland Assembly (Elections) Order 2001 sets out those provisions of the 1983 Act, with attendant modifications, that apply to Assembly elections.

The following sections of the RPA 1983 (as amended) apply *unmodified* to elections to the Northern Ireland Assembly:

Section 18(1), (7), (9) (Polling places to be designated for each polling district as established under the Electoral Law Act (Northern Ireland) 1962).

Section 23 (General duties of returning officers).

Section 30 (Taxation of returning officer's account).

Section 50 (Effects of misdescription or persons or places in the register of electors).

Section 54 (Registration expenses of Chief Electoral Officers').

Section 60 (Personation to be a corrupt practice).

Section 65 and 65A (Tampering with nomination papers and ballot papers to be an electoral offence).

Section 66 and 66A (Requirement to maintain secrecy of the ballot).

Sections 67 to 70 (Appointment of election agent, Nomination of sub-agent, Office of election agent and sub-agent, Candidate to be election agent where none named).

Section 71A (Control of donations to candidates - The Political Parties, Elections and Referendums Act 2000 inserts a new Section (Section 71A) into the Representation of the People Act 1983, relating to donations to candidates - The new Section states that if a candidate receives money or other property, whether as a gift or a loan, from anyone other than the candidate or his or her election agent, for the purpose of meeting election expenses, this must be given to the candidate or his or her agent - *see Chapter Nine for more details).*

Section 73 (Payment of election expenses only through election agent).

Section 74 and 74A (Candidates personal expenses).

Sections 76 (Limits on candidates' elections expenses).

Sections 78 to 84 (Time for sending in election expenses, Disputed claims, Returns and declarations of election expenses, Failure to comply with provisions relating to returns and declarations to be an illegal practice).

Section 86 (Allowable excuses for failures as to returns and declarations).

Section 87 (Court's power to require information from election agent or sub-agent).

Section 88 (Publication of election returns and declarations).

Sections 90A to C (The new Section 90A of the RPA 1983 defines 'election expenses' as expenses incurred for the acquisition or use of property or for the provision of services or facilities which are used for the purposes of the candidates' election. - certain expenses are exempt, including: the payment of the candidate's deposit, the publication of an article in a newspaper, magazine (other than an advertisement) or a broadcast, free mailing facilities and services provided by an individual, voluntarily and in his own time - new section 90C of the RPA 1983 states that where property or goods are transferred to the candidate or his election agent free of charge or at a discount of more than 10% of the market value of the property or goods, where the difference between the market value and the value at which the goods are transferred to the candidate is more than £50, the amount must be declared as an election expense).

Section 91 (Right to send free election address).

Section 92 (Broadcasting from outside the UK).

Section 94 (Imitation poll cards to be an electoral offence).

Sections 99, 100 (Officials not to act for candidates, Illegal canvassing by police officers).

Section 106 (False statements about candidates to be an illegal practice).

Section 107 (Corrupt withdrawal from candidature).

Sections 109 to 118 (Paying for exhibition of election notices to be an illegal practice, Details required on election publications, Prohibition of paid canvassers, Providing money for illegal purposes, Bribery and Treating and Undue Influence considered corrupt practices, Rights of creditors, definitions and interpretation).

Sections 119 to 121 (Computation of time, Method of questioning election, Presentation of election petitions).

Section 123 (Constitution of election court).

Section 136 (Security for costs for election petitions).

Section 137 (Petitions at issue – *new section substituted by PPERA 2000*).

Section 140 (Witnesses in election trials).

Section 141 (Duty of witnesses to answer questions).

Section 143 (Expenses of witnesses).

Section 147 (Withdrawal of petition).

Sections 154 to 156 (Costs of petitions, Refusal to pay costs, Provisions relating to costs).

Section 158 (Consequences of election court finding that candidate is guilty of corrupt or illegal practice).

Section 159 (Candidate reported guilty of corrupt or illegal practice).

Sections 161 to 170 (Justices of the Peace reported by election court to be guilty of corrupt practices, Members of legal professions reported by election court, Bribery and treating in licensed premises, Elections to be void and votes to be struck off for general corruption or employing corrupt agent, prosecutions for corrupt and illegal practices).

Section 174 to 176 (Mitigation of findings of election court, Illegal payments, Time limits on prosecutions).

Sections 178 to 180A (Prosecutions of offences outside UK, etc).

Section 181 (Role of the Director of Public Prosecutions).

Section 183 to 186 (Costs, Serving legal notices, Interpretation of Part III, Computation of time in Part III).

Section 200 (Public notices and declarations).

Section 202 (Interpretation).

Section 205 (General application to Northern Ireland).

Schedule 1, Rule 5 (Notice of election) Rule 6A (Nomination papers and names of registered parties), Rules 10 to 17 (delivery of nomination papers, Right to attend nomination, Validity of nomination papers, Withdrawal of candidates, Publication of statement of those nominated, Disqualification by RPA 1981, Adjournment of proceedings in case of riot, Method of election), Rules 19 to 22 (Ballot papers, Official mark, Prohibition of disclosure of vote, Use of school rooms), Rules 23 to 26 (Notice of poll, Postal ballot papers, Provision of polling stations, Appointment of presiding officers and clerks), Rule 28 (Poll cards), Rule 30 (Appointment of polling and counting agents), Rules 31 to 36 (Requirement of maintaining secrecy of ballot, Admission to polling station, Keeping order in polling stations, Sealing of ballot boxes, Questions to be put to voters, Challenge of voters), Rules 39 to 43 (Voting by disabled people, Tendered ballot papers, Spoilt ballot papers, Adjournment of poll in case of riot, Procedure on close of poll), Rule 54 (Sealing up of ballot papers).

Schedule 2A (Schedule 2A was inserted into the RPA 1983 by Schedule 16 of the PPERA 2000 – it contains the details of the measures set out in new Section 71A relating to donations to candidates - the new Section states that if a candidate receives money or other property, whether as a gift or a loan, from anyone other than the candidate or his or her election agent, for the purpose of meeting election expenses, this must be given to the candidate or his or her agent.

Schedule 3 (Returns and declarations of election expenses).

The following sections of the RPA 1983 (as amended) apply *with modifications* to elections to the Northern Ireland Assembly.

Section 29 (but not subsections 1, 2, 6 and 9) and in subsection (5) for "charged on" to "before" is substituted "paid by the Secretary of State on an account being submitted to him, but he may, if he thinks fit, before". The effects of this minor amendment relate to the way in which returning officers' charges are paid.

Section 49 – in subsection (5)(b)(iv) for "a local government" substitute "an". This is a minor amendment to the section which lists the grounds on which a voter must not be prevented from voting.

Section 52(5) – omit from "subsection" to "but"(ensures that in Northern Ireland sections 14(5) and 14A(2) and (3) of the Electoral Law Act (Northern Ireland) 1962 have effect in relation to the Chief Electoral Officer for Northern Ireland in his capacity as registration officer (these sections relate to the appointment of temporary deputies).

Section 61 – in paragraphs (a) and (b) of subsection (1) omit the words "or at parliamentary or local government elections" and "or, as the case may be, at elections of that kind" (minor amendments to the section which sets out other voting offences).

Section 63 – in subsection (3) omit paragraphs (a) and (c), in paragraph (b) omit the words "sheriff clerk" and in paragraph (e) for the words "(a) to (d)" substitute "(b) and (d)" (minor amendments in the section relating to breaches of official duty in parliamentary elections).

Section 75 – omit subsection (4) (minor amendments in section relating to the prohibition of expenses not authorised by an election agent).

Section 77 – in subsection (1), for the words, "a local government" substitute, "an Assembly" (minor amendment to section on expenses limits for candidates at local elections).

Section 87A – omit subsection (1) and in (2) take out "any election" to "above" and insert "an Assembly election" (states that election returns and declarations should be forwarded to Electoral Commission).

Section 89 – in subsections (1) and (2), for the words "two years", in each place where they occur, substitute "12 months" (states that election returns and declarations should be available for inspection for 12 months rather than two years).

Section 93 – omit references to Sianel Pedwar Cymru and insert new subsection (5) *"(5) For the purposes of subsection (1) 'the election period' in relation to an Assembly election means the period beginning with the last day on which notice of election may be published in accordance with the elections rules and ending with the date of the poll".* Defines an election period in relation to Assembly elections, during which broadcasters must adopt a code of practice governing the participation of candidates in local items about the constituency.

Section 97 – substitute new subsection (2) *"(2) this section applies to a political meeting held in any constituency in connection with an Assembly election on any date between the last date on which notice of an election may be published in accordance with the elections rules and the date of the poll".* Section 97 states that a person who disrupts an election meeting is guilty of an illegal practice.

Section 118A – in subsection (2) for "Parliament" substitute "The Assembly" and for "the writ for the election is issued" substitute "the election is held" (minor amendments in Interpretation section).

Section 122 – in subsection (1) for the words from "the return" to the end, substitute "the day on which the relevant result was declared in accordance with rule 50 of the election rules" and in subsection (2) for the words "that return", substitute "that declaration of the result of the election". This amendment means that an election petition must be presented within 21 days after the day on which the result was declared.

The following are all minor modifications to the RPA 1983.

Section 124 – for "the Treasury" substitute "the Secretary of State".

Section 126 – in subsection (1) for "The Shorthand writer of the House of Commons or his deputy" substitute "A shorthand writer" and in subsection (2) for the word "Speaker" substitute "Chief Electoral Officer" and in subsection (3), omit the words "in Scotland" and for the words "section 125" substitute "section 124".

Section 138 – in subsection (3), omit the words from the beginning of the subsection to "local government Act".

Section 139 – in subsection (3) omit the words from "the acceptance" to "notwithstanding", in the third place where it occurs.

Section 144 – in subsections (2), (4) and (6), for the word "Speaker" substitute "Chief Electoral Officer" and omit subsections (5) and (7)

Section 146 – in subsection (2), for the word "Speaker" substitute "Chief Electoral Officer".

Section 157 – substitute new subsection (2) *"(2) Subject to the provisions of this Act and the rules made under it, the principles, practice and rules on which election courts act in dealing with parliamentary election petitions shall be observed, so far as may be, by the High Court and election court in the case of election petitions relating to Assembly elections".*

Section 160 – in subsection (4) after "Kingdom" insert "or local election" and after "Commons" (in each place where it occurs) insert "or the Assembly" and omit subsection 6.

Section 173 – in subsection (1) after "Kingdom" insert "or local election" and after "Commons" (in each place where it occurs) insert "or the Assembly" and in subsection (7) for the words from "House" to "elective office" substitute "Assembly" and for the words "Parliament" to "that office" substitute "the Assembly" and omit subsection 10.

Section 200A – in subsection (3), for the words from "charged" to the end, substitute "paid by the Secretary of State".

These modifications ensure that the Election Rules contained in Schedule 1 to the RPA 1983 apply to elections to the Northern Ireland Assembly.

Schedule 1, Rule 1 – amended timetable for elections (as set out above).

Schedule 1, Rule 2 – in subsection 2 a bank holiday means a day which is a bank holiday under the Banking and Financial Dealings Act 1971 in Northern Ireland.

Schedule 1, Rule 6, in paragraph 3(b) omit the words from "or, where" to the end (Rule 6 relates to descriptions of nominated candidates, and this modification omits the reference to 'The Speaker seeking re-election', which would be irrelevant in elections to the Northern Ireland Assembly).

Schedule 1, Rule 7, in paragraph (5), for the words from "than one nomination" to "delivered" substitute *"nomination papers at the same election than there are vacancies to be filled and, if he does, his signature shall be inoperative on any paper other than the papers first delivered up to the number of vacancies".* (This amendment is necessary to take into account the fact that elections to the Assembly are conducted using STV).

Schedule 1, Rule 8, in paragraph 3(b) for the words "the House of Commons Disqualification" substitute "the Northern Ireland Assembly Disqualification" and for the words "House of Commons" substitute "Assembly". This amends Rule 8 so that those disqualified under the Northern Ireland Assembly Disqualification Act 1975 may not sit in the Assembly.

After Rule 8, a new Section 8A is inserted, which states that when a candidate delivers his or her nomination paper, he or she can also attach the names of no more than six people who may act as substitutes (set out in order of preference); a substitute being a person who, in the event of the candidate being returned at the election but having, subsequently, to vacate the seat, is returned in his or her place. Where a candidate vacated his or her seat but had not selected any substitutes, a by-election would be called in the usual way. Candidates at a by-election cannot nominate substitutes in this way.

Schedule 1, Rule 9 is amended to reduce the deposit from £500 to £150.

Schedule 1, Rule 17, in paragraph (1) for the words "than one person standing nominated" substitute "persons standing nominated than there are members to be elected" and in paragraph (2) for the words "only one person standing nominated, that person" substitute "a number of persons standing nominated which is equal to, or less than, the number of members to be elected, those persons". These modifications are necessary given that elections to the Assembly are held using STV.

Schedule 1, Rule 18, for the words from "result" to the end of the rule, substitute "votes given to each candidate shall be counted and the result of the poll determined in accordance with rules 44A to 44M of these rules". These rules relate to the counting of votes using STV.

Schedule 1, Rule 22, in paragraphs (1) and (2) after "poll" insert "or counting the votes". This allows schools and public rooms to be used for the count as well as for polling.

Schedule 1, Rule 29, in paragraph (5) for the words from "the notice" to the end substitute "the notice set out in the Appendix". The notice in an UK Parliamentary election would state: *"Vote for one candidate only"*, which in the case of elections to the Assembly would be inappropriate as voters may number candidates according to preference. The notice referred to in the Appendix advises voters of this.

Schedule 1, Rule 37, in paragraph (1E)(b) for the words from "the United" to the end substitute "a Member State of the European Community" and omit paragraph 1F and for paragraph (2) substitute *"(2) The voter, on receiving the ballot paper, shall forthwith proceed into one of the compartments in the polling station and there shall – (a) secretly record his vote by placing on the ballot paper "1" opposite the name of the candidate of his first choice and, if he wishes, by placing "2" opposite the name of the candidate of his second choice, "3" opposite the name of the candidate of his third choice and so on in the order of his preference; (b) fold the paper so that his vote is concealed; (c) show to the presiding officer the back of the paper so as to disclose the official mark; and (d) put the folded paper into the ballot box in the presence of the presiding officer".* These amendments are again necessary given the use of the STV method of voting in Assembly elections.

Schedule 1, Rule 38, in paragraph (1) for the words "vote to be marked on a ballot paper" substitute "ballot paper to be marked". This amendment is necessary given the use of the STV method of voting in Assembly elections, where more than one 'vote' is marked on the ballot paper.

Modifications have also been made to Schedule 1, Rule 44 of the RPA 1983, which was amended by the Elections (Northern Ireland) Act 1985. Several new paragraphs are added to Rule 44 to take into account the fact that Assembly elections are conducted using STV. For example; under the provisions of Rule 44C the following ballot papers would be rejected:

- ❖ Those not bearing the official mark

- ❖ Those on which the figure '1' standing alone is not placed so as to indicate a first preference for any candidate

- ❖ Those on which the figure '1' standing alone indicating a first preference is set opposite the name of more than one candidate

- ❖ Those on which anything (other than the printed number on the back) is written or marked by which the voter can be identified

- ❖ Those which are unmarked or void for uncertainty

When the votes are counted, under Rule 44D, the ballot papers are sorted according to the candidates for whom first preferences are given. The number of valid ballot papers is divided by the numbers of members to be elected, plus one. That number, plus one, is the number of votes sufficient to secure the election of a candidate; i.e., the quota. When a candidate's total votes equals or exceeds the quota, he or she is elected. Once a candidate has reached the quota, his or her second preferences are transferred. Where no second preference has been expressed for a candidate, that vote is said to be non-transferrable. That candidate's second preferences are transferred, but at a 'transfer value' which is calculated by dividing the surplus of the candidate from whom the votes are being transferred, by the total number of the ballot papers on which those votes are given. At any point during the count, where no candidate reaches the quota, the candidate with the lowest total of votes is eliminated and their second preferences transferred (for a full description of STV please see Appendix A on electoral systems).

Schedule 1, Rule 50 is amended to include the modifications necessary at the declaration of election results, given that the Assembly elections are conducted using STV.

Schedule 1, Rule 53 is amended so that the number of votes needed to secure a candidate's deposit is one quarter of the quota at any stage of the counting.

The following are all minor modifications to the RPA 1983.

Schedule 1, Rule 55, in paragraph (1), the words "then forward to the Clerk of the Crown" are substituted by "retain" and omit sub-paragraph (i).

Schedule 1, Rule 56, in paragraph (2), for the words "Clerk of the Crown's" substitute "returning officer's", in paragraph (3), omit the words "House of Commons or", in paragraphs (6) and (8), for the words "Clerk of the Crown", in each place where they occur, substitute "returning officer".

Schedule 1, Rule 57, in paragraph (1) (a) for the words "Clerk of the Crown" substitute "returning officer", (b) for the words "forwarded to him in pursuance of these rules by a returning officer" substitute "to which rule 55(1) of these rules applies" and omit the words "House of Commons or", in paragraph (2) for the words from "Clerk of the Crown" to the end substitute "returning officer" and in paragraph (3), for the words "Clerk of the Crown" substitute "returning officer" and for the words "the Treasury" substitute "the Secretary of State".

Schedule 1, Rule 60, in paragraph (1) for the words "as if the writ had been received 28 days" substitute "as if the day appointed for the poll was the first Thursday after the expiry of 30 days", omit sub-paragraph (b) and at the end of the paragraph add the following words "and the period of 30 days shall be calculated in accordance with rule 2 of these rules". These modifications mean that where a candidate dies before the result of the election is declared, a fresh elections takes place on the first Thursday after a 30 day period.

Section 3 of the Elections (Northern Ireland) Act 1985 and section 5 of the Representation of the People Act 1985 are applicd to elections to the Northern Ireland Assembly. Sections 7, 8 and 9 of the latter Act is applied, with modifications, to Assembly elections.

Certain provisions of the Representation of the People (Northern Ireland) Regulations 2001, the Election Petitions Rules 1964 and the Planning (Control of Advertisements) Regulations (Northern Ireland) 1992 are also applied to elections to the Northern Ireland Assembly. The following provisions of the 2001 Order are applied unmodified:

Regulations 5, 6, 7, 8, 9, 10, 11, 12, 47(7)(b), 50, 51, 52, 56, 63 to 79, 81 to 85

The following provisions of the 2001 Order are applied with modifications:

Regulations 3 and 4, 55, 57, 58, 62, 80, 86.

The following sections of the Election Petition Rules 1964 are applied unmodified to elections to the Northern Ireland Assembly: Rule 1, 2, 4, 5, 5A, 6 to 17, 19 to 27, Schedule B. The following sections of the Election Petition Rules 1964 are applied with modifications: Rule 3, Schedule A. Regulations 2 and 4 and Schedules 1 and 2 of The Planning (Control of Advertisements) Regulations (Northern Ireland) 1992 are applied to elections to the Assembly.

For full details of the impact of these regulations on Assembly elections, readers should consult The Northern Ireland Assembly (Elections) Order 2001 (SI 2001, No. 2599).

Under the provisions of Part II of Schedule 9 of the Political Parties, Elections and Referendums Act 2000, the limit on campaign expenses which applies to elections to the Northern Ireland Assembly is £17,000 per constituency. As there are 18 constituencies each returning six members of the Assembly, the maximum amount of campaign expenditure is £306,000. The relevant period during which the limit applies is the four-month period before the election, except in the case of an extraordinary general election, where the period begins on the date when the Secretary of State proposes a date for the election and the day of the election itself.

Comprehensive results and analysis of the 1998 NI Assembly elections can be found on the BBC website at the following address:

http://news.bbc.co.uk/hi/english/events/northern_ireland/assembly_elections/default.stm

CHAPTER EIGHT – ELECTIONS TO THE GREATER LONDON ASSEMBLY

METHODS OF ELECTION

The conduct of elections to the Greater London Assembly (GLA) is governed by the Greater London Authority Act 1999 and subsequent delegated legislation. Elections to the GLA are treated as local government elections by virtue of the application of section 17 of the Act which states that *"Schedule 3 to this Act (which, by amending the Representation of the People Acts, makes provision for and in connection with treating elections under this Act as local government elections for the purposes of those Acts) shall have effect".* Detailed rules governing the conduct of the elections are set out in The Greater London Authority Elections (No. 2) Rules 2000.

The Greater London Authority includes the 32 London Boroughs and the City of London. The Assembly consists of 25 members, 14 of whom are elected as constituency members and 11 of whom are elected as London members (and who do not have a constituency). The Constituency members, London members and the Mayor are all elected at the same time for a four-year period, but by different electoral methods.

❖ **The Mayor** is elected using the Simple Majority System, unless there are more than three candidates, in which case the **Supplementary Vote** is used (as set out in Part I of Schedule 2 to the Act. Under this system voters place a cross beside the name of their first preference and beside the name of their second preference (if they wish to do so). The first preference votes are counted and if one candidate gains over 50 per cent of these votes, he or she is elected. If no candidate receives over 50 per cent of the first preference votes all the candidates, except the two receiving the highest number of votes, are eliminated and their second preferences, where applicable, are allocated to the two remaining candidates. If the person elected as Mayor is also returned as a member of the Assembly, a vacancy is considered to have arisen.

❖ **Constituency members** are elected using the familiar **'First Past the Post'** (FPTP) system. No one may be a Constituency candidate in more than one constituency.

❖ **London members** are elected using the **Additional Member System** (AMS) – with electors casting a vote for a political party.

Elections to the GLA are held on the first Thursday in May in the fourth year after the previous elections, although another day could be substituted by order under Section 37(2) of the RPA 1983.

The Supplementary Vote

The rules governing the use of the supplementary vote electoral system when there are more than three candidates for Mayor are set out in Schedule 2 of the Greater London Authority Act 1999. If one of the candidates receives more than half of all the first preference votes given in the Assembly constituencies that candidate is elected. If none of the candidates receives more than half of all the first preference votes, the two candidates who received the greatest number of first preference votes remain in the contest (if three or more candidates all have an equal number of first preference votes they all remain in the contest) and the other candidates are eliminated. The number of second preference votes for the candidates remaining in the contest by voters who did not give their first preferences to those candidates is determined and then added to the number of first preference votes given to those candidates. The candidate with the greater total number of preference votes is elected. If two or more candidates remaining in the contest each had an equal number of preference votes, the Greater London returning officer would have to decide the election by lot.

London Members

Under the provisions of Part II of Schedule 2 of the Greater London Authority Act 1999, any registered party can submit a list of candidates for election as London-wide members. The list may not contain more than 25 candidates and may not contain the names of any of the following:

* ❖ Anyone who is a candidate for election as a constituency member who is not a candidate of that party

* ❖ Anyone who is included on any other list submitted for the election of London members

* ❖ Anyone who is an individual candidate to be a London member

A person may not be an individual candidate if he or she is:

* ❖ Included on a list submitted by a registered political party for the election of London members

* ❖ A registered party's candidate for Mayor or a registered party's constituency candidate

The number of London-wide votes given for each registered political party list is calculated by adding together the number of London votes given for the party in the Assembly constituencies. This figure is then divided by the aggregate of the number of candidates of the party elected as constituency members, plus one. The number of votes for each individual candidate cast in the constituencies is added together. These figures are referred to as the 'London figure' for that party or individual candidate. Where a party or individual candidate fails to gain more than 5 per cent of the total number of London votes polled by all the registered political parties and all the individual candidates at the election, they are not entitled to any of the London-wide seats. The first of the London-wide seats is allocated to the party or individual candidate with the highest 'London figure'. The second and subsequent seats for London members are allocated to the party or individual candidate with the highest London figure after a recalculation using what is essentially the modified d'hondt formula (for an explanation of the use of this formula please see the example in Appendix A).

Constituency Members

Although the Election Rules governing the election of constituency members, London-wide members, the Mayor and the Ordinary Election Rules are set out in different Schedules in the Greater London Authority Elections (No 2) Rules 2000 (SI 2000, No 427) they have been combined in the sections below and where different rules apply to the elections of different categories of candidates, these have been noted. Schedule 5 of the regulations sets out the various forms to be used in the elections; for example, the nomination papers, official poll card, guidance for voters, etc (as amended by the provisions of the Greater London Authority Elections (No 2) (Amendment) Rules 2000 (SI 2000, No 1040). Schedule 6 sets out the modifications necessary where electronic counting is to be employed. For example, where ballot papers are to be counted electronically, they must not be folded. Schedule 7 contains provisions relating to a combined poll for local London Borough councillors and elections to the GLA and Schedule 8 contains provisions relating to the combination of GLA elections with elections to the European Parliament.

Election Timetable

Proceeding	Time
Publication of notice of election	Not later than the 25th day before the date of the election.
Delivery of nomination papers	Not later than noon on the 19th day before the day of the election.
Publication of statement of persons nominated	Not later than noon on the 17th day before the day of election.
Delivery of notices of withdrawals of candidature	Not later than noon on the 16th day before the day of election.
Notice of Poll	Not later than the 6th day before the day of election.
Polling	Between 8am and 9pm on the day of the election (*between 7am and 9pm at the first set of ordinary elections in 2000 and where poll is combined with local London Borough elections and between 7am and 10pm where combined with parliamentary or European elections*)

In the timetable above, the following days are disregarded:

❖ Saturday or Sunday
❖ Christmas Eve, Christmas Day, Maundy Thursday, Good Friday
❖ Bank holidays (as set out in the Banking and Financial Dealings Act 1971 in England and Wales)
❖ Any day appointed for public thanksgiving or mourning

BY-ELECTIONS

Where a vacancy occurs in a constituency, a by-election takes place within 35 days (excluding Saturdays, Sundays, Christmas Eve, Christmas Day, Maundy Thursday, Good Friday or a bank holiday or a day appointed for public thanksgiving or mourning). If the vacancy occurs within a period of six months preceding ordinary elections to the Assembly, then it is left unfilled until that election. When the seat of a London member is vacant, if he or she was returned as an individual candidate, it remains unfilled until the next election. Where the person vacating the seat was the member of a registered party list then the next person on that list is approached to fill the vacancy.

An Assembly member can resign at any time and an Assembly member who has failed during a six-month period to attend any Assembly meeting, unless that non-attendance has been authorised by the Assembly or results from being a member of the services during war or military emergency, is be deemed to have resigned, thereby creating a vacancy.

WHO MAY STAND AS MAYOR OR AN ASSEMBLY MEMBER?

A candidate may only stand for election as Mayor or as an Assembly Member if he or she is one of the following:

❖ A Commonwealth citizen

❖ A citizen of the Republic of Ireland

❖ A citizen of the European Union

❖ Is at least 21 years of age

❖ Is a local government elector for Greater London, or has during the past year been the owner or tenant of *"land or other premises in Greater London"*, or has worked or lived in Greater London for the past year

The following are disqualified both from being elected as Mayor or as a member of the Assembly:

❖ Members of staff of the GLA.

❖ Those holding any of the offices designated in an order as being offices disqualifying their holders from membership of the GLA (see below for disqualifying offices, set out in the Greater London Authority (Disqualification) Order 2000).

❖ Bankrupts, or those who have made a composition or arrangement with creditors (the disqualification ends, on discharge from bankruptcy or if the order against the person is annulled on the date of the annulment, or where a composition or arrangement with creditors is made the disqualification ends when the debts are paid in full or five years after the date on which the terms of the deed of composition or arrangement are fulfilled).

❖ Those who have within five years before the day of the election, or since their election, been convicted in the UK, the Channel Islands or the Isle of Man of any offence resulting in a sentence of not less than three months without the option of a fine (the date of conviction is the date on which the period allowed for making an appeal or application with respect to the conviction expires, or if where such an appeal or application is made, the date on which it is finally disposed of or abandoned or fails by reason of its non-prosecution).

❖ Those disqualified under Section 85A (Mayoral candidates guilty of failure to make proper returns or declarations of election expenses within the time limit) or Part III of the Representation of the People Act 1983 (those found guilty of corrupt or illegal practices) or Section 17 or 18 of the Audit Commission Act 1998 (unlawful expenditure by members of health service body).

❖ Paid officers of London Borough Councils employed under the direction of any of that Council's committees or sub-committees the membership of which includes the Mayor or one or more persons appointed on the nomination of the Authority acting by the Mayor or a joint committee, the membership of which includes one or more members appointed on the nomination of that council and one or more members appointed on the nomination of the Authority acting by the Mayor.

Disqualifying offices as set out in the Greater London Authority (Disqualification) Order 2000 include those holding any office or appointment which would disqualify the holder from membership of the House of Commons under section 1(1)(a), (c), (c), (d) or (e) of the House of Commons Disqualification Act 1975 (judges, civil servants, members of the armed forces, members of police forces and members of certain foreign legislatures). Parts I and II of the Schedule (Article 2 of the order) include a list of bodies, membership of which precludes a person from being a member of the Greater London Assembly or Mayor. These bodies include the following (this is not an exhaustive list):

❖ The Audit Commission for Local Authorities and the NHS in England and Wales
❖ The Central Arbitration Committee
❖ The Commission for Local Administration in England
❖ The Council of the Advisory, Conciliation and Arbitration Service
❖ The Health and Safety Executive
❖ The Local Government Commission
❖ The London Pension Fund Authority
❖ The Police Complaints Authority

Proceedings for disqualification under Section 92 of the Local Government Act 1972 apply to the GLA as they apply to any other local authority.

If the position of Mayor becomes vacant as a result of his or her resignation or because he or she fails to attend meetings of the Assembly or because he or she is disqualified for any reason, an election is held to find a successor, within 35 days. Where a vacancy occurs within the period of six months preceding an ordinary four-yearly mayoral election, it is left unfilled until the next election.

GREATER LONDON ASSEMBLY ELECTORAL REGIONS

The Local Government Commission recommended the boundaries for the 14 voting areas and these were implemented by secondary legislation under the Greater London Authority Act 1999.

GREATER LONDON ASSEMBLY ELECTORAL REGIONS

ELECTORAL REGION	BOROUGHS
Barnet & Camden	Barnet, Camden
Bexley & Bromley	Bexley, Bromley
Brent & Harrow	Brent, Harrow
Croydon & Sutton	Croydon, Sutton
City & East London	Barking & Dagenham, City of London, Newham, Tower Hamlets
Ealing & Hillingdon	Ealing, Hillingdon
Enfield & Haringey	Enfield, Haringey
Greenwich & Lewisham	Greenwich, Lewisham
Havering & Redbridge	Havering, Redbridge
Lambeth & Southwark	Lambeth, Southwark
Merton & Wandsworth	Merton, Wandsworth
North East London	Hackney, Islington, Waltham Forest
South West	Hounslow, Kingston upon Thames, Richmond upon Thames
West Central London	Hammersmith & Fulham, Kensington & Chelsea, Westminster

Section 35 of the RPA 1983 was amended to enable the Secretary of State to designate by order, the returning officer for the election of Mayor and other Assembly members. The returning officers for the GLA elections were duly set out in the Greater London Authority (Assembly Constituencies and Returning Officers) Order 1999 (SI 1999, No 3380). For example, in the London Boroughs of Croydon and Sutton, which together form one constituency for elections to the Assembly, the returning officer for the GLA elections was the returning officer for the London Borough of Croydon.

Schedule 5 of the RPA 2000 added a new Schedule 3A to the Greater London Authority Act 1999, permitting the free delivery of a booklet of election addresses at the first election of Mayor of London.

The detailed rules governing elections to the GLA are set out in the Greater London Authority Elections (No 2) Rules 2000, made under Section 36 of the RPA 1983, as amended by Schedule 3, paragraph 4 of the Greater London Authority Act 1999.[1] Section 61 of the RPA 1983 was amended by paragraph 10 of Schedule 3, which states that the following also constitute voting offences:

❖ Voting more than once at the same election for Mayor.

❖ Voting more than once at the same election of the London members of the Assembly at an ordinary election.

❖ Voting more than once in the same Assembly constituency at the same election of a Constituency member of the Assembly.

❖ Voting in more than one Assembly constituency at the same ordinary election.

---

[1] Schedule 3 of the Greater London Authority Act 1999 set out the necessary amendments to the RPA 1983

❖ Voting in any Assembly constituency at an ordinary election, or an election for Mayor (when there is a vacancy for that position), where a proxy has already been appointed to vote on the elector's behalf in another Assembly constituency.

A person is also guilty of an offence if he or she votes as a proxy for the same elector:

❖ More than once at the same election of the Mayor of London.

❖ More than once at the same election of the London members of the Assembly at an ordinary election.

❖ More than once in the same Assembly constituency at the same election of a constituency member of the London Assembly.

❖ In more than one Assembly constituency at the same ordinary election.

Paragraph 12 of Schedule 3, amends Section 67 of the RPA 1983 and provides for one person to be named as the agent for all the candidates on a party list of London candidates. One of the candidates can be nominated by the party as the election agent of all the candidates on the list. The same person must be appointed as election agent for all the candidates on the list.

Paragraph 18 of Schedule 3 amends Section 74 of the RPA 1983, which relates to candidates' personal election expenses and provides that a candidate for Mayor is authorised to pay personal expenses, subject to a limit of £5,000. For constituency candidates, the limit is £600 and for London-wide candidates, £900.

Candidates' election expenses are limited by regulations made under Section 76 of the RPA 1983 as amended by paragraph 20 of Schedule 3 of the Greater London Authority Act 1999. This order, the Greater London Authority Elections (Expenses) Order 2000 (SI 2000, No 789) sets out the limits on both the expenses which can be incurred by those other than candidates and their election agents and the limits on the expenses of candidates and agents. For those other than candidates and agents the limits are:

❖ In relation to the election for Mayor, £25,000

❖ In relation to the election of a constituency member, £1,800

❖ In relation to the election of London-wide members, £25,000

For candidate and their agents, the limits are:

❖ For a mayoral candidate, £420,000

❖ For a constituency candidate, £35,000

❖ For an individual candidate standing in the London-wide elections, £330,000

❖ For a party list submitted by a registered party, £330,000

Under Section 81 of the RPA as amended by paragraph 23 of Schedule 3 of the Greater London Authority Act 1999, election returns relating to expenses, on the part of mayoral candidates must be made within 70 days after the declaration of the result of the election. The same time limit applies to individual candidates and party list candidates in the London-wide elections. The existing time limit of 35 days applies to constituency candidates. A candidate for Mayor who fails to make a return of election expenses within the time limit, cannot be elected. An 'application for relief' under Section 86 of the RPA 1983, has to be made within six weeks and disqualification from election does not take effect until that period has expired without such an application being made or, if such an application is made, when it is finally disposed or abandoned. Where a constituency or London-wide candidate fails to make a return of election expenses, a fine of £50 is payable for each day they continue to sit in the Assembly.

Detailed rules governing the GLA elections are contained in the Greater London Authority Elections (No 2) Rules 2000 (SI 2000, No 427) and additionally, the Greater London Authority Election (Early Voting) Order 2000 (SI 2000, No. 826) and the Greater London Authority Elections (No 2) (Amendment) Rules 2000 (SI 2000, No. 1040).

Schedules in the Greater London Authority Elections (No. 2) Rules 2000 (SI 2000, No. 427) contain the following Election Rules:

❖ Schedule 1 – The Constituency Members Election Rules (which have effect at both ordinary elections and by-elections, although in the former case the rules are subject to the Ordinary Election Rules as set out Schedule 4).

❖ Schedule 2 – The London Members Election Rules (which have effect at both ordinary elections and by-elections, although in the former case the rules are subject to the Ordinary Election Rules as set out Schedule 4).

❖ Schedule 3 – The Mayoral Election Rules (which have effect at both ordinary elections and by-elections, although in the former case the rules are subject to the Ordinary Election Rules as set out Schedule 4).

❖ Schedule 4 – The Ordinary Elections Rules.

Nominations

A candidate's nomination paper must state the candidate's full names, home address and if desired, a description. Nomination papers must be attested by one witness whose name and address must be given in full. In the case of London candidates, a registered party's list of candidates must be submitted by the party's nominating officer or someone authorised in writing by him. In the case of both constituency, individual and London candidates and in the case of mayoral candidates, a person is not considered validly nominated unless a consent to nomination is given in writing within one month before the last day for the delivery of nomination papers (this is delivered at the same time as the nomination form). A party list must not contain more than 25 names. The nomination paper of a candidate for Mayor must be signed by 330 electors (10 from each Borough and the City).

Deposits

Each candidate must deliver a deposit of £1,000 along with his or her nomination papers. A candidate loses his or her deposit if he or she polls less than one-twentieth of the total number of votes polled by all candidates. The deposit for individual candidates and list candidates for election as London-wide members, is £5,000. Where an individual candidate or party list does not poll more than one-fortieth of the total number of votes polled by all the candidates and registered parties, they forfeit their deposit. The deposit for mayoral candidates is £10,000, which is forfeit if the candidate does not poll more than one-twentieth of the total number for first preference votes.

Ballot Papers

The ballot papers for the election of constituency members, London-wide members and the Mayor must be different colours. Where votes are to be counted electronically, two or more ballot papers can appear on the same sheet. The same official mark on the ballot paper cannot be used for five years and a different official mark must be used for postal ballot papers. The rules relating to the official mark do not apply where votes are to be counted electronically

Procedure at Polling Stations

Each candidate is entitled to appoint polling agents to attend polling stations on the day of the election. The constituency returning officer can limit the number of polling agents per candidate, provided the number is the same for each candidate. No more than four such agents (or more, if the constituency returning officer so decides) are allowed in the polling station at any one time. Only the following are allowed in the polling station, apart from electors: candidates, election agents, polling agents, clerks, constables on duty and companions of disabled voters. Voting procedure is essentially the same as applied to local elections. After the close of polling, the presiding officer must seal the ballot boxes and then make up into separate packets the following:

- ❖ Unused and spoilt ballot papers

- ❖ Tendered ballot papers

- ❖ Marked copies of the register of electors and the list of proxies

- ❖ Counterfoils of used ballot papers and certificates of employment of those duty on polling day

- ❖ The tendered votes list, the list of disabled voters assisted by companions, the list of votes marked by the presiding officer, a statement of the number of voters whose votes were marked by the presiding officer under the headings, 'physical incapacity' and 'unable to read' and the declarations made by the companions of blind voters

The unused and spoilt ballot papers, tendered ballot papers and counterfoils of used ballot papers in the election for a constituency member must be kept separately from the same items which relate to the election of London-wide members or the Mayor. These items relating to the three sets of elections must be kept separately. The 'ballot paper account' – the statement showing the number of ballot papers issued, the number of unused ballot papers, spoilt ballot papers and tendered ballot papers must accompany the above to the count.

The Count

Electronic counting was used for the first time in the elections to the Greater London Assembly in May 2000. Voters were told not to fold ballot papers, so that they could be scanned at a rate of two a second. However, suspect ballot papers still had to be checked manually and the complexity of the election and the ballot paper meant the count was delayed. The other, unforeseen problem, was the sensitivity of the Data & Research Services (DRS) machines to static electricity, caused by a build-up of dust from the green baize cloths used to cover the counting tables. Early voting was also permitted under the Greater London Authority Election (Early Voting) Order 2000 (SI 2000, No 826), which listed those polling stations where voters could vote prior to 4 May 2000.

Each candidate is entitled to employ the same number of counting agents; this number is determined by dividing the number of clerks employed at the count by the number of candidates. A counting agent appointed by one list candidate is deemed to be appointed by all the candidates on that list. Names of counting agents must be given to the constituency returning officer no later than the fifth day before the poll. Only the following can attend the count:

- ❖ The constituency returning officer and his or her clerks
- ❖ The candidates and their husbands or wives
- ❖ The election agents
- ❖ The counting agents
- ❖ Those permitted by the constituency returning officer to attend

The ballot boxes are opened and the number of ballot papers in each one recorded. The ballot paper accounts from the polling stations are then verified. The postal ballot papers are then counted and finally the ballot papers relating to the constituency members election are put separately from those relating to the London-wide members election and the mayoral election (except where one ballot paper has been used and is to be counted electronically). Ballot papers on which votes are given for more than one candidate (or in the case of London-wide members, more than one individual candidate or party list) or on which anything has been written which could identify the voter (except the number which is printed on the back) or which is unmarked or void for uncertainty are deemed to be void and are not counted. However, when electronic counting is employed and one combined ballot paper used, a ballot paper is not rejected if an elector has not voted in one section of the ballot. For example, an elector could have voted for a constituency member and party list but not have voted in the mayoral election. Ballot papers on which a vote has been marked other than in the correct place or other than by a cross or by more than one mark is not void if the intention of the voter is clear.

When a ballot paper is rejected, this is marked on it and if its rejection is objected to then the words 'rejection objected to' are added. The constituency returning officer must then complete a statement showing the number of ballot papers rejected on the grounds set out above. As in all other elections, candidates and their election agents can demand a recount where the result is close. Where candidates have an equal number of votes, the constituency returning officer has, ultimately, to decide between them by lot. In relation to the mayoral election, where there are more than two candidates, the first preference votes are counted and ballot papers would be rejected for voting for more than one candidate as first preference, marking the ballot paper so as to identify the voter, leaving the ballot paper unmarked or void for uncertainty as to the first preference vote.

After the conclusion of the local count, the constituency returning officer must inform the Greater London returning officer of the number of votes cast for each individual candidate standing for election as a London-wide member and the number of votes cast for each party list. He or she must also inform the Greater London returning officer of the number of first preference votes given for each of the mayoral candidates. The Greater London returning officer then allocates the London-wide seats in the presence of the election agents of the individual and party list candidates and the nominating officers of those parties.

As soon as the Greater London returning officer has received from each constituency returning officer the total number of votes cast for each registered party in that constituency, he or she can then calculate the 'London figure' for each party by adding together these totals and then dividing the result by the aggregate of the number of candidates for each party who were elected as constituency members, plus one. The number of votes for each individual candidate cast in the constituencies is added together. These figures are referred to as the 'London figure' for that party or individual candidate. The first of the London-wide seats is allocated to the party or individual candidate with the highest 'London figure'. The second and subsequent seats for London members are allocated to the party or individual candidate with the highest London figure after a recalculation using what is essentially the modified d'hondt formula (for an explanation of the use of this formula please see the example in Appendix A). The Greater London returning officer must then announces the names of the candidates of the registered parties and the individual candidates who have been elected as London-wide members.

In relation to the mayoral election, where there are more than three candidates, the Greater London returning officer must ascertain the total number of first preference votes given in each of the Assembly constituencies for each candidate. If one of the candidates receives more than half of all the first preference votes given in the Assembly constituencies that candidate is elected. If none of the candidates receives more than half of all the first preference votes, the two candidates who received the greatest number of first preference votes remain in the contest (if three or more candidates all have an equal number of first preference votes they all remain in the contest) and the other candidates are eliminated. The number of second preference votes for the candidates remaining in the contest by voters who did not give their first preferences to those candidates is determined and then added to the number of first preference votes given to those candidates. The candidates with the greater total number of preference votes is elected. If two or more candidates remaining in the contest each had an equal number of preference votes, the Greater London returning officer would have to decide by lots which was to be elected.

After the count the constituency returning officer must forward to the Greater London returning officer the packets of ballot papers, the ballot paper accounts, the statements of rejected ballot papers and the result of the verification of the ballot paper accounts and the packets of counterfoils and certificates concerning employment on duty on polling day.

The marked copies of registers and lists of proxies and the tendered votes lists, lists of blind voters assisted by companions, lists of votes marked by the presiding officer and the related statements and the declarations made by the companions of blind voters are retained by the constituency returning officer. The Greater London returning officer and each constituency returning officer must retain for six months all the above documents forwarded to him or her or retained by him or her and all those apart from ballot papers, counterfoils and certificates relating to employment are open to public inspection.

RESULTS OF THE FIRST MAYORAL ELECTION – 4 MAY 2000

Name	Party	1st Preference	%	2nd Preference	%	Final Total
Ken Livingstone	Independent	667,877	39.0	178,809	12.6	776,427
Steve Norris	Conservative	464,434	27.1	188,041	13.2	564,137
Frank Dobson	Labour	223,884	13.1	228,095	16.0	
Susan Kramer	Liberal Democrat	203,452	11.9	404,815	28.5	
Ram Gidoomal	Christian Peoples Alliance	42,060	2.4	56,489	4.0	
Darren Johnson	Green	38,121	2.2	192,764	13.6	
Michael Newland	British National	33,569	2.0	45,337	3.2	
Damian Hockney	UK Independence	16,234	1.0	43,672	3.1	
Geoffrey Ben-Nathan	Pro-Motorist Small Shop	9,956	0.6	23,021	1.6	
Ashwin Kumar Tanna	Independent	9,015	0.5	41,766	2.9	
Geoffrey Clements	Natural Law	5,470	0.3	18,185	1.3	

No candidate gained more than 50% of the first preference votes and therefore all but the top two candidates, Ken Livingstone and Steve Norris were eliminated and their second preferences redistributed, the result of which was that Ken Livingstone was elected with 58% of the final vote.

RESULTS OF THE ASSEMBLY ELECTIONS

The results of the votes for constituency members was as follows:

Party	Constituency Members	London Members	Total No. London-wide Votes	Total No. Seats
Conservative	8	1	481,053	9
Labour	6	3	502,874	9
Liberal Democrat	-	4	245,555	4
Green	-	3	183,910	3
Christian Peoples Alliance – Ram Gidoomal			55,192	
London Socialist Alliance			27,073	
British National			47,670	
UK Independence			34,054	
Peter Gary Tatchell (Independent)			22,862	
Campaign Against Tube Privatisation			17,401	
Pro-Motorist and Small Shop			13,248	
Socialist Labour Party, Leader Arthur Scargill			13,690	
Natural Law			7,559	
Communist Party of Britain			7,489	
TOTAL	14	11	1,659,630	25

The following table shows how the London-wide seats were allocated. In each round the party's total number of votes is divided by the number of seats which they have won, plus one. The party with the highest total in each round is awarded a seat, which is then added to their total number of seats for the next round.

	Con	Lab	LD (LibDem)	GN (Green)	Others	Party winning top up seat	Comments
London-wide votes	481,053	502,874	245,555	183,910	246,238		
Constituency Seats	8	6	0	0	0		
Round 1 1st divisor Total	8+1 = 9 53,450	6+1 = 7 71,839	0+1 = 1 *245,555*	0+1 = 1 183,910		*LD*	The total votes for each party is divided by the no. of constituency seats it has won, plus one; i.e., the Conservative total of 481,053 votes is divided by 8 + 1 giving 53,450. However, the highest total is achieved by the Liberal Democrats, so they win the first seat in this round.
Round 2 2nd divisor Total	8+1 = 9 53,450	6+1 = 7 71,839	1+1 = 2 122,778	0+1 = 1 **183,910**		*GN*	Only the LD divisor changes, making their total less than the GNs, who take the seat in this round.
Round 3 3rd divisor Total	8+1 = 9 53,450	6+1 = 7 71,839	1+1 = 2 **122,778**	1+1 = 2 91,955		*LD*	Only the GN divisor changes, but this makes their total less than the LDs who win the seat in this round.
Round 4 4th divisor Total	8+1 = 9 53,450	6+1 = 7 71,839	2+1 = 3 81,852	1+1 = 2 **91,955**		*GN*	Only the LD divisor changes, but the GNs have the highest total

	Con	Lab	LD (LibDem)	GN (Green)	Others	Party winning top up seat	Comments
							and therefore win the seat.
Round 5 5th divisor Total	8+1 = 9 53,450	6+1 = 7 71,839	2+1 = 3 **81,852**	2+1 = 3 61,303		*LD*	The GN divisor changes, but the LDs have the highest total and win the seat.
Round 6 6th divisor Total	8+1 = 9 53,450	6+1 = 7 **71,839**	3+1 = 4 61,389	2+1 = 3 61,303		*Lab*	The increase in the LD divisor, results in Labour winning the seat in this round.
Round 7 7th divisor Total	8+1 = 9 53,450	7+1 = 8 **62,859**	3+1 = 4 61,389	2+1 = 3 61,303		*Lab*	Although Lab's divisor increases to 8, they still have the highest total and win the seat in this round.
Round 8 8th divisor Total	8+1 = 9 53,450	8+1 = 9 55,875	3+1 = 4 **61,389**	2+1 = 3 61,303		*LD*	The LDs gain the seat in this round.
Round 9 9th divisor Total	8+1 = 9 53,450	8+1 = 9 55,875	4+1 = 5 49,111	2+1 = 3 **61,303**		*GN*	
Round 10 10th divisor Total	8+1 = 9 53,450	8+1 = 9 **55,875**	4+1 = 5 49,111	3+1 = 4 45,978		*Lab*	
Round 11 11th divisor Total	8+1 = 9 **53,450**	9+1=10 50,287	4+1 = 5 49,111	3+1 = 4 45,978		*Con*	The Conservatives finally win a top-up seat in this final round.

FINAL TOTAL OF TOP-UP SEATS:
LIBERAL DEMOCRAT – 4
GREEN – 3
LABOUR – 1
CONSERVATIVE 1

Comprehensive results and analysis of the 2000 elections to the Greater London Assembly and the result of the mayoral election can be found on the BBC website at: http://news.bbc.co.uk/hi/english/static/uk_politics/vote2000/london/default.stm

CHAPTER NINE – THE REGISTRATION AND FUNDING OF POLITICAL PARTIES AND THE ROLE OF THE ELECTORAL COMMISSION

BACKGROUND TO THE ESTABLISHMENT OF THE ELECTORAL COMMISSION

In its report on the funding of political parties ('The Funding of Political Parties in the United Kingdom', Cm 4057) which was published on 13 October 1998, the Committee on Standards in Public Life recommended the establishment of an Electoral Commission, whose role it would be to ensure compliance with electoral rules and to take over the role of registering political parties, which under the Registration of Political Parties Act 1998, was the responsibility of the Registrar of Companies. The Home Affairs Select Committee also recommended the establishment of an Electoral Commission in its Fourth Report of the 1997/98 Session and the Independent Commission on the Voting System (the 'Jenkins' Committee) suggested that the proposed Electoral Commission take on the functions of the four Boundary Commissions (the Committee on Standards in Public Life disagreed with this recommendation). Provisions to set up the Commission were included in the Political Parties, Elections and Referendums Act 2000.

The Electoral Commission is established under Part I of the Political Parties, Elections and Referendums Act 2000. The Commission has the following functions:

- ❖ Registration of political parties
- ❖ Scrutiny of political parties' income and expenditure
- ❖ Administration of referendums
- ❖ Reporting on elections and referendums
- ❖ Reviewing electoral law
- ❖ Providing guidance in relation to Party Political Broadcasts
- ❖ Promoting and understanding of electoral and political matters
- ❖ Taking on the functions of the former Boundary Commissions and the local Government Commission for England and the Local Government Boundary Commission for Wales (see Chapter Two on parliamentary elections)

The Commission consists of between five and nine members (five have been appointed initially). The Chairman of the Commission is Sam Younger (a former Managing Director of the BBC World Service) and the Chief Executive, Roger Creedon. The Commissioners are Professor Graham Zellick, Pamela Gordon, Glyn Mathias, Karamjit Singh CBE and Sir Neil McIntosh CBE. Details of the Commission's constitution are set out in Schedules 1 and 2 of the Act. The Commission is a body corporate, independent of any government department and which reports to Parliament and whose members are appointed by Her Majesty on the presentation of an Address by the House of Commons. The Commissioners are appointed after consultation with the leaders of the registered political parties, (this only includes parties which have two or more elected MPs). Commissioners serve 10-year terms, can be re-appointed and can only be removed from office on an Address from the House of Commons, which can only be moved if the Speaker's Committee has presented a report to the House stating that it has agreed that a

Commissioner should be removed on the following grounds (as set out in Schedule 1, paragraph 5 of the Act):

- ❖ He or she has failed to discharge the functions of his or her office for a continuous period of at least three months.

- ❖ He or she has failed to comply with the terms of his or her employment.

- ❖ He or she has been convicted of a criminal offence.

- ❖ He or she is an un-discharged bankrupt or his or her estate has been sequestrated in Scotland and he or she has not been discharged.

- ❖ He or she has made an arrangement or composition contract with, or has granted a trust deed, for his creditors.

- ❖ He or she is otherwise unfit to hold the office of Electoral Commissioner or unable to carry out its functions.

Deputy Commissioners may be removed from office by the Commission itself on any of the grounds set out above.

The Commission may also, under Schedule 1, paragraph 7, appoint Assistant Electoral Commissioners.

The aforementioned Speaker's Committee is established under section 2 of the Act. It will oversee the functions of the Commission and will have the power to approve its budget and five year corporate plan, after taking advice from the Treasury and the Comptroller and Auditor General. The Commission's annual estimate and five-year plan will be laid before Parliament as will annual accounts, which will have been certified by the Comptroller and Auditor General before being laid before Parliament. The Commission's annual report will also be laid before Parliament. The Speaker's Committee will also lay its own annual report before the House. The Committee will be chaired by the Speaker of the House of Commons and will have eight other members, consisting of the Home Secretary, the Minister for Local Government, the Chairman of the House of Commons Home Affairs Committee and five Members of the House of Commons appointed by the Speaker. Members are appointed for the duration of a Parliament.

Under section 3(4) of the Act, the following may not be appointed as Electoral Commissioners:

- ❖ Members of registered political parties

- ❖ Officers or employees of registered political parties

- ❖ Holders of certain 'elective' offices as set out in Schedule 7[1]

---

[1] These offices are: MPs, MEPs, MSPs, MLAs, AMs, GLA members, Mayor of London or any elector Mayor and members of local authorities in the UK (excluding parish or community councils)

❖ Anyone who has, at any time in the last 10 years, been an officer of employee of a registered party or held an 'elective' office or who has been named as a donor in the register of donations (as set out under Chapter III or V of Part IV of the Act).

Under Schedule 1, paragraph 3(3) of the Act, an Electoral Commissioner would cease to hold office if he or she accepted a nomination as a candidate at an election.

Section 4 of the Act establishes the 'Parliamentary Parties Panel', whose function it is to submit 'representations or information' to the Commission relating to political parties. Only parties with two or more Members of the House of Commons are qualified to sit on the panel. Section 5 of the Act sets out the general functions of the Commission, which are to report on the conduct of elections and referendums, including general elections to Parliament, the European Parliament, the Scottish Parliament, the National Assembly of Wales and the Northern Ireland Assembly, local elections in England and Wales and Northern Ireland.

Under section 7 of the Act, the Government will be required to consult the Electoral Commission before certain order-making powers are used. The Section lists those regulations where such consultation would be required. These relate to the conduct and administration of elections. Section 8 stipulates that certain powers under existing legislation can only be exercised after a recommendation has been made by the Electoral Commission. These powers relate to giving directions to registration officers under section 52(1) of the Representation of the People Act 1983, making orders relating to expenses in connection with elections to the GLA, the National Assembly of Wales, the Scottish Parliament and the European Parliament.

Section 9 of the Act states that the Electoral Commission may be involved in proposals for pilot electoral schemes as provided for under section 10 of the Representation of the People Act 2000. Several such pilot schemes were conducted during the local elections in May 2000; for example, several local authorities experimented wtih early voting, electronic counting and all-postal ballots. Section 9 of the Act would allow the Commission to sponsor such schemes. The Commission will also take on the functions relating to such pilot schemes as are set out in sections 10 and 11 of the RPA 2000. Section 10 of the Act, gives the Commission the power to give advice and assistance to local authorities and the devolved administrations and international bodies on electoral law and practice. Section 12 of the Act provides for the Commission to give 'policy development grants' to political parties (those with two or more Members in the House of Commons) to assist them with the development of policies 'for the inclusion in any manifesto'. The total amount that can be awarded in any financial year is limited to £2 million. Section 13 of the Act, gives the Commission the role of increasing public awareness of electoral systems, current systems of local and national government and also, more controversially, *"the institutions of the European Union"*.

The Electoral Commission published its first report on the 2001 General Election in July ('Election 2001 – The Official Results', Politico's Publishing / Electoral Commission) with a second report to follow in the spring of 2002. This second report will look in detail at the campaign expenditure returns submitted by the political parties, which must be with the Commission by 7 December 2001.

THE REGISTRATION OF POLITICAL PARTIES

The decision to introduce legislation governing the registration of political parties was made in response to a number of high profile cases in which candidates had stood for election under party labels deliberately designed to confuse the electorate; for example, candidates who had described themselves as 'Literal Democrats' or 'New Labour'. Prior to the provisions of the Registration of Political Parties Act 1998 (now contained in the Political Parties, Elections and Referendums Act 2000) the way in which candidates described themselves on ballot papers was governed by Rule 6(2) of the Election Rules in Schedule 1 of the Representation of the People Act 1983. This Rule said that a candidate's nomination paper must state the candidate's full name and home address and in addition, a description, if desired, of no more than six words. In the European Elections in 1994 Richard Huggett stood as the 'Literal Democrat' in the Devon and East Plymouth constituency. The Liberal Democrats' election petition failed on the grounds that the returning officer could only have ruled the nomination invalid if the particulars of the candidate were not as they should have been by law (Rule 12(2) a, b or c). Rule 12(5) of the 1983 Act also states that a returning officer's decision as to the validity of nominations is final.

Part II of the Political Parties, Elections and Referendums Act 2000 repealed much of the Registration of Political Parties Act 1998 and re-enacted its main provisions with some modifications. Section 38 of the Act amended Rule 6 of the Election Rules contained in the RPA 1983, the effect of which is that a potential candidate must be a member of a registered political party, use the term 'independent' (with no other description) or use his or her name with no accompanying description.[2] At the last General Election, by the deadline to register (17 May – the same day as the publication of notice of an election, not the closing date for nominations) there were 148 parties registered for Great Britain and 31 for Northern Ireland. 118 'independent' candidates had registered and there were 19 candidates with no description. An official list of all nominated candidates and party affiliations is available on the Commission's website. Provisions similar to those contained in section 38 of the PPERA 2000 were applied to Northern Ireland by The Local Elections (Northern Ireland) (Amendment) Order 2001 (SI 2001, No, 417) which amended the Electoral Law Act (Northern Ireland) Act 1962.

Section 23 of the Act replaced the register of political parties maintained by the registrar of companies under the Registration of Political Parties Act 1998 with new registers maintained by the Electoral Commission.

These registers are:

❖ A register of political parties that intend to contest relevant elections in one or more of England, Scotland and Wales – *The Great Britain Register*

❖ A register of parties that intend to contest relevant elections in Northern Ireland – *The Northern Ireland Register*

---

[2] For parish council (England) and community council (Wales) elections, candidates may use up to six words on the ballot paper to describe themselves without the need to register as a party with the Commission. Community Council elections in Scotland fall outside the scope of the PPERA 2000. Minor parties, which only contest parish or community council elections, do not have to register with the Commission.

A party may be registered in both registers, but the two entries constitute two separate registered parties. The aim of the section is to ensure that any organisation whose candidates are standing at a relevant election, must be registered as a political party with the Electoral Commission. Section 24 provides that for every registered party there must be:

- ❖ A person registered as the party's leader (*may also be registered as nominating officer or treasurer or both*)

- ❖ A person registered as the party's nominating officer

- ❖ A person registered as the party's treasurer[3]

The person registered as nominating officer must have responsibility for the arrangements for the following:

- ❖ Submission of lists of candidates

- ❖ Issuing of certificates authorising the description of the registered party on candidates' nomination forms

- ❖ Approval of descriptions and emblems used on nomination forms and ballot papers at elections

The person registered as treasurer must be responsible for complying with the provisions set out in Parts III and IV of the Act relating to party accounts and donations. Unless a party has a registered campaigns officer, the treasurer must ensure the party's compliance with the provisions of Parts V to VII of the Act which relate to campaign expenditure, third party expenditure and referendums. A registered party may have a registered campaigns officer who may also be the party leader or nominating officer or both. The campaigns officer is responsible for compliance with the provisions of Parts V to VII of the Act. Up to 12 deputy campaigns officers may be appointed. The provisions of Sections 72(2) to (10) apply to the campaigns and deputy campaigns officers as they do to the treasurer and deputy treasurer.

Section 26 of the Act sets out arrangements for regulating the financial affairs of registered parties. A party cannot be registered unless it adopts a scheme that is approved by the Commission. The scheme must state whether the party concerned is a single organisation with no division of responsibility for the financial affairs of the party or a central organisation with one or more separate accounting units (for example, constituent or affiliated organisations) responsible for its own financial affairs. This is to ensure that those political parties with a federal structure are covered by the Act.

---

[3] Under Section 74 of the PPERA 2000, the treasurer of a registered party can appoint 12 deputies (essentially one for Scotland, Wales, Northern Ireland and one in each of the nine English regions).

The following are not deemed to be constituent or affiliated organisations in relation to any party:

- ❖ A trade union
- ❖ A friendly society
- ❖ Any other organisation specified in an order made by the Secretary of State on the recommendation of the Electoral Commission

Those organisations which are not considered to be constituent or affiliated organisations in relation to a party are set out in The Registered Parties (Non-constituent and Non-affiliated Organisations) Order 2000 (SI 2000, No. 3183) and include such organisations as the Association of Conservative Peers, the Fabian Society, the Socialist Health Association and the Countryside Forum. Section 26(8)(c) of the PPERA 2000 gives the Secretary of State the power to make an order specifying other organisations which cannot be considered constituent or affiliated organisations. The aforementioned order states that any branch of a students' organisation (funded by a students' union as defined by Part II of the Education Act 1994 (section 20)) cannot be considered a constituent or affiliated organisation.

Section 28 of the Act deals with registration and with some modifications re-enacts the provisions of Sections 2 to 5 and 6(1) to (4) of the Registration of Political Parties Act 1998. A party can apply to be registered with the Commission by complying with the requirements of Part I of Schedule 4 as set out below and by sending in a declaration that the party intends to contest one or more relevant elections in Great Britain and one or more such elections in Northern Ireland, or a declaration that the party intends to contest one or more relevant elections in Great Britain only and is therefore only applying for registration in the Great Britain register. Similarly, a party could apply just to be included in the Northern Ireland register on the same basis. A party could also apply for registration on the basis that it only intended contesting parish or community council elections, in which case it is defined as a 'minor party'.[4] The requirements of Part 1 of Schedule 4 as previously mentioned are:

- ❖ An application for registration must specify the name the party wants to be registered (or a name in Welsh and one in English).

- ❖ Where the name to be registered is not in English the application for registration must include a translation.

- ❖ An application in Northern Ireland must specify the party's name or a name in Irish and also in English.

- ❖ An application must specify the party headquarters' address.

- ❖ An application must include the name and home address of the party leader, the nominating officer and the party treasurer.

---

[4] Certain provisions relating to registration do not apply to minor parties; namely, provisions relating to the registration of a treasurer or campaigns officer, provisions under Section 26 relating to the adoption of a financial scheme and provisions under Section 27 relating to accounting units.

❖ Where the application is to be registered as a party with a campaigns officer, it must also give the name and home address of that person.

An application must be signed by the proposed registered leader or registered nominating officer, by the proposed registered treasurer and where appropriate by the proposed registered campaigns officer.

Only certain types of party name may be registered. Under section 28 of the Act the following would be considered unacceptable.

❖ Names that are either the same as that of a party, which is already registered or would be likely to confuse electors if adopted.

❖ Names consisting of more than six words.

❖ Names that are considered obscene or offensive.

❖ Names including words, which if published would constitute the commission of an offence.

❖ Names that include any script other than Roman script.

❖ Names that include any word or expression prohibited by order by the Secretary of State after consulting the Commission.

The Registration of Political Parties (Prohibited Words and Expressions) Order 2001 (SI 2001 No. 82) which revoked the Registration of Political Parties (Prohibited Words and Expressions) Order 1998 lists those words or expressions which cannot be used as part of the registered name of a political party, except where they form, for example, part of the name of a place or local government area.

Part I of the Schedule to the order lists those words which may only be used in a registered party name where they form part of the name of a place, institution or local government area. They are:

Duke, Duchess, Her Majesty, His Majesty, King, Prince, Princess, Queen, Royal, Royalty

Part II of the Schedule to the order lists those words that may only be used in a registered party name where they are qualified by another word or expression other than the registered name of a party which is already registered in respect of the relevant part of the UK. They are:

Britain, British, England, English, National, Scotland, Scots, Scottish, United Kingdom, Wales, Welsh

Part III of the Schedule lists those words that may not be used unless qualified by another word or expression other than the registered name of a registered party, a word listed in that Part of the Schedule or the word 'party'. They are:

Independent, official and unofficial

Part IV of the Schedule lists those words that may not be used unless qualified by the name of a local government of a geographical area. They are:

Ratepayers, residents and tenants

An application under Section 28 may also include a request for the registration of up to three emblems to be used by the party on ballot papers. Section 29 of the Act states that emblems must not be likely to be confused with another party's emblem and must not be obscene or offensive or of such a character that their publication would be likely to amount to the commission of an offence.

Under the Registration of Political Parties (Fees) Order 2001 (SI 2001/No. 83), which came into force on 16 February 2001 the fee for an application by a party to be registered in the Great Britain or Northern Ireland register, under section 28 and Part I of Schedule 4 of the PPERA 2000, is £150. The fee for altering an entry is £25 (this is also the fee for a party's yearly confirmation of an existing entry).

ELECTION EXPENSES

The campaign expenditure of prospective parliamentary candidates (PPCs) is controlled in a number of ways. Candidates may not spend more than a specified maximum amount in their constituency and no expenditure may be incurred by anyone other than the candidate or his or her agent. Certain expenditure is prohibited altogether; for example, a candidate may not pay someone to canvass on his or her behalf (canvassing may only be carried out by volunteers). No one may be paid to display posters or other election notices unless they are professional advertising agents.

There are two types of expenses: those incurred in connection with the conduct of the election campaign and the candidate's own personal expenses.

The limit on expenses incurred in conducting the election campaign is governed by Section 76[5] of the Representation of the People Act 1983 as amended by the Political Parties, Elections and Referendums Act 2000 Section 132. Under the Representation of the People (Variation of Limits of Candidates' Election Expenses) Orders, the latest being the 2001 Order (SI 2001, No 535) which came into force on 5 March, the following limits apply to parliamentary elections:

❖ for candidates in UK parliamentary general elections in county constituencies, £5,483, with an additional 6.2p for each entry in the electoral register being used at that election;

❖ for candidates in UK parliamentary general election in borough constituencies, £5,483, with an additional 4.6p for every entry in the electoral register to be used at that election.

The PPERA 2000 amends Section 76A of the RPA 1983 under which the above order is made, with a new Section (as set out in Section 133 of the PPERA 2000) which gives the

---

[5] Section 76 of the RPA 1983 is applied to elections to the Northern Ireland Assembly by regulations (see Chapter Seven).

Secretary of State power to vary such sums by order as a result of the effects of inflation and also in order to 'give effect to a recommendation of the Electoral Commission'.

Section 132 of the PPERA 2000 amended the existing limits on by-election expenses as set out in Section 76 of the RPA 1983 (these were: for candidates in UK parliamentary by-elections in county constituencies, £19,863, with an additional 22.2p for each entry in the electoral register to be used at that election; and for candidates in UK parliamentary by-elections in borough constituencies, £19,863, with an additional 16.9p for each entry in the electoral register to be used at that election) and replaced them with one common limit, of £100,000 per candidate, regardless of whether the by-election is to be in a borough or county constituency.

At a local government election (excluding elections to the Greater London Authority and local elections in Scotland and Northern Ireland) the maximum is £242 with an additional 4.7 pence for each entry in the register of electors to be used at that election (Representation of the People (Variation of Limits of Candidates' Expenses) Order 2001 (SI 2001, No 535). In Northern Ireland, the respective limits are £242 and 4.8 pence (Local Elections (Northern Ireland) (Amendment) Order 2001 (SI 2001, No. 417) (which amended the Electoral Law Act (Northern Ireland) 1962).

Article 41 of Schedule 2 to The Scottish Parliament (Elections etc.) Order 1999 (SI 1999, No. 787) limits the election expenses of candidates in elections to the Scottish Parliament. In the case of candidates standing as constituency members or individual candidates standing as regional members and their agents, election expenses are limited to a maximum amount as set out below:

- ❖ For a constituency candidate in a constituency coterminous with a parliamentary constituency which is a county constituency - £5,483, with an additional 6.2p for each entry in the register of electors to be used at that election (in a by-election, the limit is £100,000)

- ❖ For a constituency candidate in a constituency coterminous with a parliamentary constituency which is a burgh constituency - £5,483, with an additional 4.6p for each entry in a register of electors to be used at that election (in a by-election, the limit is £100,000)

- ❖ For a constituency candidate for the constituencies of the Orkney Islands or Shetland Islands - £5,483, together with an additional 6.2p for each entry in the register of electors to be used at that election (in a by-election, the limit is £100,000)

- ❖ For an individual candidate for return as a regional member, the total of the maximum amounts (calculated in accordance with the rules in 1 to 3 above) for a single candidate standing as a constituency member in each constituency within that region

As far the elections to the Greater London Assembly are concerned, election expenses are limited by regulations made under Section 76 of the RPA 1983 as amended by paragraph 20 of Schedule 3 of the Greater London Authority Act 1999. This order, the Greater London Authority Elections (Expenses) Order 2000 (SI 2000, No 789) sets out the limits on both the expenses which can be incurred by those other than candidates and their election agents and the limits on the expenses of candidates and agents. For those other than candidates and agents the limits are:

❖ In relation to the election for Mayor, £25,000

❖ In relation to the election of a constituency member, £1,800

❖ In relation to the election of London-wide members, £25,000

For candidate and their agents, the limits are:

❖ For a mayoral candidate, £420,000

❖ For a constituency candidate, £35,000

❖ For an individual candidate standing in the London-wide elections, £330,000

❖ For a party list submitted by a registered party, £330,000

Under Section 75 of the RPA 1983, election expenses may not be incurred *"with a view to promoting or procuring the election of a candidate"* by anyone other than the candidate, his or her agent or those persons so authorised in writing by the election agent, where those election expenses relate to holding public meetings, issuing advertisements or publications or *"otherwise presenting to the electors the candidate or his views"*. The Section specifically states that this is not intended to restrict newspapers, magazines, broadcasters, etc., from reporting the election. The Section also makes clear that this prohibition on expenses does not relate to expenses up to the level of £5 (see below) provided they have not been *"incurred by an individual and are not incurred in pursuance of a plan suggested by or concerted with others"*.

In the case of Bowman v United Kingdom (February, 1998) the European Court of Human Rights ruled that Section 75 of the Representation of the People Act 1983 was a violation of the right to freedom of expression under Article 10 of the European Convention of Human Rights. As a result, Section 131 of the PPERA 2000 amends Section 75 of the RPA 1983 so that certain expenditure is exempted from the general prohibition on expenses being incurred by anyone other than the candidate or his or her election agent. The current level of such exempted expenditure is £5, but Section 131 raises this level to £500 in respect of a candidate at a parliamentary election, £50 in respect of a candidate at a local government election, together with an additional 0.5p for each entry in the register of local government electors for the electoral area in question. These provisions are extended to Northern Ireland by means of Article 3 of the Local Elections (Northern Ireland) (Amendment) Order 2001 (SI 2001, No. 417) which amends the Electoral Law Act (Northern Ireland) 1962.

Section 131 also replaces the words *"a plan suggested by or concerted with others"* with *"a concerted plan of action"* and adds a new Section (1ZA) to the 1983 Act defining in more detail what is meant by such a plan. The new Section states that a concerted plan of action is one which involves *"that person and one or more other persons"* in incurring expenditure with a view to *"promoting or procuring the election of the same candidate"*.[6]

The candidate's own personal expenses are defined in Section 118 of the Representation of the People Act 1983 and include travelling expenses and accommodation costs. Where incurred by the agent, these expenses, are unlimited; where incurred by the candidate, they are limited by Section 74(1) of the 1983 Act as amended by the Representation of the People Act 1985, to £600. The candidate has to send a written account of his or her expenses to his or her agent within 14 days after the day the election result is declared. When the agent makes his return of expenses, the candidate's personal expenses should be stated separately, as they are not used in determining whether or not a candidate has kept within the maximum permitted election expenditure.

A candidate's expenses begin from the earliest of the following:

- ❖ The time he or she declares him or herself to be a candidate
- ❖ The time the agent is appointed
- ❖ The time he or she is adopted
- ❖ The time he or she is nominated

However, there is no such time set out in statute, so each case has to be decided on its merits. The main principle behind the many judicial rulings handed down over the years is that expenses incurred generally by political parties which promote the party's views, even if circulated in only one particular constituency and with which the PPC may be associated, are not election expenses. However, if the candidate is obviously identified with, for example, political literature promoting his or her candidature, then they are election expenses. Home Office Circular RPA 410 considers whether or not a candidate's use of the internet constitutes an election expense.

Section 134 of the Political Parties, Elections and Referendums Act 2000 inserts a new section (90A) into the RPA 1983 in order to bring the definition of election expenses in the 1983 Act in line with the other provisions of the PPERA 2000 relating to campaign expenditure by political parties, controlled expenditure by third parties and referendum expenses. This means that benefits in kind given to candidates will be regarded as election expenses. The new Section 90A of the RPA 1983 defines 'election expenses' as expenses incurred for the acquisition or use of property or for the provision of services or facilities which are used for the purposes of the candidates' election. Certain expenses are exempt, including: the payment of the candidate's deposit, the publication of an article in a newspaper, magazine (other than an advertisement) or a broadcast, free mailing facilities and services provided by an individual, voluntarily and in his own time. New Section 90C of the RPA 1983 states that where property or goods are transferred to the candidate or his election agent free of charge or at a discount of more than 10% of the market value of the property or goods, where the difference between the market value and the value at which the goods are transferred to the candidate is more than £50, the amount must be declared as an election expense.

---

[6] Section 131(5) of the Political Parties, Elections and Referendums Act 2000 repeals the amendments to the RPA 1983 made by Schedule 3, paragraph 20 of the Greater London Authority Act 1999.

The Political Parties, Elections and Referendums Act 2000 inserts a new Section (Section 71A) into the Representation of the People Act 1983, relating to donations to candidates. The new Section states that if a candidate receives money or other property, whether as a gift or a loan, from anyone other than the candidate or his or her election agent, for the purpose of meeting election expenses, this must be given to the candidate or his or her agent. The details are set out in Schedule 16 of the PPERA 2000 (which inserts a new Schedule 2A into the RPA 1983). The provisions relating to donations are essentially the same as those relating to donations to political parties, which are also set out in the PPERA 2000.

Schedule 16 defines a donation as being:

- ❖ A gift of money or other property.

- ❖ Any sponsorship provided in relation to the party (defined below).

- ❖ Any money spent (otherwise than by the candidate, his election agent or sub-agent) in paying any expenses incurred either directly or indirectly by the candidate.

- ❖ Any money lent to the candidate or his or her, otherwise than on commercial terms.

- ❖ The provision, otherwise than on commercial terms of any property, services or facilities for the use or benefit of the candidate (including the services of any person).

Sponsorship is defined in Section 51 as being:

Any money or other property transferred to the candidate or to any person for the benefit of the candidate in order to help the candidate with meeting any 'defined expenses'.
Defined expenses are taken to mean expenses in connection with any conference, meeting or other event organised by or on behalf of the candidate, the preparation, production or dissemination of any publication by or on behalf of the candidate or any study or research organised by or on behalf of the candidate. The following are not considered as sponsorship: making any payment in respect of any charge for admission to any conference, meeting or other event or the purchase price of, or any other charge for access to any publication, or the making of any payment in respect of the inclusion of an advertisement in any publication where the payment is made at the commercial rate payable.

Schedule 16(5) states that where donations are made to the party for less than their market price, their value is taken to be the difference between the two. Part II of Schedule 16 defines those donors from whom donations are deemed to be permissible and those from whom donations are not acceptable. Donations cannot be accepted from anonymous donors or from those whose identity it is impossible to determine; for example, as a result of 'deception' or 'concealment'. Under the provisions of Section 54(2) foreign donations are not acceptable as the Section states the permissible donors must be any one of the following:

❖ Individuals registered in an electoral register.

❖ Companies registered under the Companies Act 1985 or the Companies (Northern Ireland) Order 1986 and incorporated within the UK or another Member State, which carry on their business in the UK.

❖ Registered parties.

❖ Trade unions entered in the list kept under the Trade Union and Labour Relations (Consolidation) Act 1992 or the Industrial Relations (Northern Ireland) Order 1992.

❖ Building societies within the meaning of the Building Societies Act 1986.

❖ Limited liability partnerships registered under the Limited Liability Partnerships Act 2000, or any corresponding Act in force in Northern Ireland, which carries on its business in the UK.

❖ Friendly societies registered under the Friendly Societies Act 1974 or a society registered under the Industrial and Provident Societies Act 1965 or the Industrial and Provident Societies Act (Northern Ireland) 1969.

❖ Any unincorporated association of two or more persons which does not fall within any of the above but which carries on its business wholly or mainly in the UK and whose main office is in the UK.

Where a 'principal donor' gives a donation to a party along with one or more others, then each individual contribution of more than £50 is treated as a separate donation.

PARTY FUNDING

The question of how to finance political parties was considered in 1976 by the Houghton Committee (Cm 6601) and more recently by the House of Commons Home Affairs Select Committee ('The Funding of Political Parties', 2nd Report, 1993/94 Session, HC 301). However, the composition of the latter at the time of the report (under a Conservative Government) was such that when it came to voting on the contents of the final report, the Committee split along party lines with the Chairman using his casting vote to support recommendations against disclosure of donations, against shareholder approval of company donations and in favour of foreign donations to parties.   The Conservative Government had also prevented the Committee on Standards in Public Life (at that time known as the 'Nolan Committee' after its first Chairman, Lord Nolan) from considering the subject of party financing. It was against this background that the Labour Party pledged in its 1997 General Election manifesto to, *"oblige parties to declare the source of all donations above a minimum figure"*, adding that: *"foreign funding will be banned"*. After the 1997 General Election, the new Labour Government asked the Committee on Standards in Public Life, now chaired by Sir Nigel Wicks (who took over from Sir Patrick Neill QC (Lord Neill of Blaydon) after he resigned in February 2001) to consider questions relating to Party funding.

The Committee on Standards in Public Life published its report, 'The Funding of Political Parties in the United Kingdom' (Cm 4057) on 13 October 1998.   It recommended that donations of more than £5,000 made to a political party nationally and donations of more than £1,000 made to a party locally, should be disclosed. It also recommended an end to foreign donations; an end to anonymous donations of £50 or more (intimidation of anyone as a result of having made such a donation would become a criminal offence); the introduction of tax relief at the basic rate on donations to political parties with at least two MPs, or one MP and 150,000 votes; and, shareholder approval before the making of company donations to political parties. The report was debated in the House of Commons on 9 November 1998. The question of whether or not transparency in donations would actually prevent the improper influence of policy was raised during the debate on the Neill Committee Report, by the then Shadow Home Secretary, Rt Hon Sir Norman Fowler MP (Con, Sutton Coldfield), who made the point (Col. 65) that: *"Transparency does not avoid the dangers of contributions influencing policy"*. Indeed, it is almost impossible to devise a failsafe method of ensuring that contributions, made either openly or anonymously, do not 'influence' their recipients in some way. 'Influence' works on a number of levels and it would not be possible, nor would it be desirable, to seal politicians hermetically in a vacuum, free from anyone or any organisation that might seek to 'influence' them.

On the subject of 'blind trusts', the Committee recommended their abolition and suggested that donations of £1,000 or more to individuals or groups within a party be made through an 'open trust', with disclosure of other donations on the same basis as donations to the party generally. The Committee also proposed a £20 million cap on national General Election expenditure by political parties fielding more than 600 candidates (a lower limit, calculated on a proportional basis, would apply to parties with fewer candidates), a cap on parties' election expenditure for the Scottish Parliament of £1.5m and £600,000 for Wales and £300,000 for Northern Ireland.

Both the Labour Party and the Conservative Party have had to deal with controversies concerning their party finances in recent times. William Hague had just announced that the Conservative Party would no longer accept foreign donations when allegations surfaced relating to a £1m donation from the son of an alleged fugitive drug trafficker in 1994. The son of Ma Sik-chun alleged that the money had been given in return for all charges against his father being dropped. This sort of allegation is almost impossible to prove or refute in the absence of written evidence and demonstrates the difficulties inherent in accepting individual donations of any sort. William Hague announced on 17 December 1997 that the party would disclose the total sum of foreign donations received in the run-up to the 1997 General Elections, but not the individual amounts and sources of donations, on the grounds that past donors to the Party had made donations on the basis of anonymity; it would therefore be wrong to change the rules retrospectively. There has also been controversy in the recent past surrounding the finances of Conservative Party Chairman, Lord Ashcroft, who has donated considerable sums to the party.

The Labour Party has not been exempt from scandal. In November 1997, it was revealed that Bernie Ecclestone, Vice President of the Formula One Association had given a £1m donation to the party. Unfortunately, these revelations surfaced soon after Labour had decided to exempt the sport from a general ban on tobacco advertising. The donation was promptly returned. In his book 'Servants of the People', published just in time for the party conference season in 2000, Andrew Rawnsley alleged that the Chancellor, Gordon Brown had known of the donation when he appeared on the Today programme on 10 November 1997, to deny all knowledge of it. The Prime Minister said he had sought the advice of Lord Neill, Chair of the Committee on Standards in Public Life about returning the donation before journalists began to make enquiries; Andrew Rawnsley claimed the Prime Minister only sought advice after reporters began to break the news. Even if the Chancellor had known the full details of the donation, it seems absurd to suggest that he should have taken the opportunity to 'shop' the Prime Minister live on air, on the Today programme.

All three major parties must now publish the names of donors who give more than £5,000 during any one financial year.

In January 2001, just prior to the provisions on party funding contained in the PPERA 2000 coming into force, it was revealed that the Labour Party had received two anonymous donations of £2 million each (later revealed to be from Lord Hamlyn and Christopher Ondaatje). The Independent, in its leader of 1st January 2001 attributed the worst possible motives to the party's decision to accept a substantial donation prior to the coming into force of new regulations enforcing disclosure of the donor's identity. "The blatant cynicism of this manoeuvre threatens to destroy any credit Mr Blair might have gained by his party's greater openness and its welcome legislation ... it simply cannot fight an election with honour while this issue is unresolved", the newspaper thundered. The Independent suggested that what was required was, not a large number of small donations, but a large number of small ones. This would indeed be nirvana to hard-pressed political parties with declining memberships; sadly, it seems to be an unattainable goal. Individual party membership appears to be on the decline and in the absence of state funding for political parties (opposed in the same Independent editorial) political parties can hardly be blamed for accepting legitimate donations wherever they find them. Piously, the newspaper argued that "The main hope must be that the new regime of disclosure will discourage those rich donors who seek only influence or prestige, forcing the parties to rely on the committed little people on whom democracy ought to depend". Unfortunately, the committed little people seem to be rather thin on the ground and curiously reluctant to become members of any political party. In their absence, it appears that the large donors are here to stay. Any donor advocating a policy, which the Government subsequently adopts, is open to suspicion. Should the Government deliberately adopt a position wholly antagonistic to GM foods in order to prove that it was not influenced by the fact that Lord Sainsbury, a Minister and significant donor, favours genetic modification?

The names of those donating more than £5,000 per annum to Labour can be found in the Annual Accounts of the Labour Party, which forms part of the Party's Annual Report.

The Committee also made recommendations relating to the so-called 'Short Money'. The Short Funds were established by Ted Short, the then Leader of the House of Commons in 1975 (HC, 20 March 1975) to support the activities of the opposition parties in Parliament. Short Money is allocated at a scale of £10,732.69 for each seat won by that Party at the previous General Election, plus £21.44 for every 200 votes cast for that Party. This is uprated yearly in line with inflation – a measure introduced in 1993 (HC Col: 593, 4 November 1993). To qualify, the party concerned must have gained two or more seats at the preceding General Election or gained one seat and 150,000 votes. The motion passed by the House on 4 November 1993 also created a travel fund for opposition parties, to be distributed in the same proportions as the Short Funds.

The Neill Committee recommended an increase in both the Short Money and the 'Cranborne Money Scheme' - a similar fund in the House of Lords. The Cranborne scheme was named after the then Leader of the House, Rt Hon Viscount Cranborne, who proposed its adoption. Their Lordships agreed, by a resolution of the House in November 1996 (HL, 27 November 1996, Col: 267) to make £100,000 available to the main Opposition Party in the House of Lords and £30,000 to the second largest party (to be uprated yearly in line with inflation). Financial assistance to opposition parties in the House of Lords in the year 2000/01 was £312,514.

The Neill Committee recommended that in the House of Commons, the Official Opposition's allocation of Short Money should be fixed and not vary according to the previous General Election result and that a portion of that amount should be earmarked for running the office of the Leader of the Official Opposition. The allocation for the Leader of the Opposition's office was agreed to and has been set at £500,000 per year.

Trade union sponsorship of Labour MPs was discontinued in 1995 in an attempt to break the direct link between unions and MPs – in its place, came 'constituency plan agreements', whereby trade unions gave financial support in return for representation on CLP General Committees.

PARTY ACCOUNTS

Part III of the Political Parties, Elections and Referendums Act 2000 (which is likely to come into effect in January 2002) sets out new provisions relating to party accounts, putting the publication of annual accounts of income and expenditure on a statutory basis. Under Section 41, financial records must be retained for six years and the Electoral Commission can specify what constitutes a financial year for different political parties. Section 42 specifies that the treasurer of a registered party must prepare an annual statement of accounts. Regulations made under the Act will set out different provisions according to the gross income or total expenditure of the party concerned falls into one of the following categories:

- ❖ Up to £5,000
- ❖ Between £5,000 and £250,000
- ❖ Over £250,000

Where gross income or total expenditure is over £250,000, the party's accounts must be audited by a qualified auditor (the Commission can also stipulate a proper audit where income or expenditure is below this level). Section 46 of the Act provides for public inspection of any statement of accounts received by the Electoral Commission. Section 49 of the Act has the effect of ensuring that where a national party has a network of constituency associations and ward-level branches (referred to as 'accounting units'), each one will have to maintain its own accounting records and produce an annual statement of accounts. The requirement to submit an annual statement of accounts to the Electoral Commission will only apply automatically to accounting units with an income or expenditure in excess of £25,000 (this is set out in Schedule 5 of the Act). Campaign expenditure must be calculated inclusive of VAT.

DONATIONS TO POLITICAL PARTIES

Part IV of the Act deals with donations to political parties. Section 50 defines a donation as being:

- ❖ A gift of money or other property.

- ❖ Any sponsorship provided in relation to the party (defined below).

- ❖ Any subscription or other fee paid for affiliation to, or membership of, the party.

- ❖ Any money spent (otherwise than by or on behalf of the party) in paying any expenses incurred either directly or indirectly by the party.

- ❖ Any money lent to the party otherwise than on commercial terms.

- ❖ The provision, otherwise than on commercial terms of any property, services or facilities for the use or benefit of the party (including the services of any person).

Sponsorship is defined in Section 51 as being:

- ❖ Any money or other property transferred to the party, or to any person, for the benefit of the party, in order to help the party meet any 'defined expenses', or to ensure that it does not incur such expenses.

Defined expenses are described in section 51(2) as being:

- ❖ Expenses in connection with any conference, meeting or other event organised by or on behalf of the party.

- ❖ Expenses in connection with the preparation, production or dissemination of any publication by or on behalf of the party or any study or research organised by or on behalf of the party.

The following are not deemed to constitute sponsorship:

- ❖ Making any payment in respect of any charge for admission to any conference, meeting or other event.

- ❖ The purchase price of, or any other charge for access to any publication.

- ❖ The making of any payment in respect of the inclusion of an advertisement in any publication where the payment is made at the commercial rate payable.

The following are not regarded as donations:

- ❖ Policy development grants made by the Electoral Commission.

- ❖ Grants made under Section 170 of the Criminal Justice and Public Order Act 1994 to cover security costs at party conferences.

- ❖ Payments made by the European Parliament to assist MEPs.

- ❖ The transmission by a broadcaster, free of charge, of a party political broadcast or a referendum campaign broadcast.

- ❖ Any other facilities provided in pursuance of any right conferred on candidates, or a party, at an election or a referendum under any enactment.

- ❖ The provision of assistance by a person appointed under section 9 of the Local Government and Housing Act 1989.

- ❖ The provision by an individual of his or her own services which he or she provides voluntarily, free of charge.

- ❖ The interest on a donation that the party cannot accept, but which is returned to the donor.

- ❖ Donations under £200.

- ❖ Donations that are included in a candidate's election expenses return.

- ❖ Payments made to a party to hire a stand at a party conference.

Section 53 states that where donations (other than money) are made to the party for less than their market price, their value is taken to be the difference between the two. Section 54 defines those donors from whom donations are deemed to be permissible and those from whom donations are not acceptable. Donations cannot be accepted from anonymous donors or from those whose identity it is impossible to determine; for example, as a result of 'deception' or 'concealment'. Under the provisions of Section 54(2) foreign donations are not acceptable as the Section states the permissible donors must be any one of the following:

- ❖ Individuals registered in an electoral register.

- ❖ Companies registered under the Companies Act 1985 or the Companies (Northern Ireland) Order 1986 and incorporated within the UK or another Member State, which carry on their business in the UK.

- ❖ Registered parties.

- ❖ Trade unions entered in the list kept under the Trade Union and Labour Relations (Consolidation) Act 1992 or the Industrial Relations (Northern Ireland) Order 1992.

- ❖ Building societies within the meaning of the Building Societies Act 1986.

- ❖ Limited liability partnerships registered under the Limited Liability Partnerships Act 2000, or any corresponding Act in force in Northern Ireland, which carries on its business in the UK.

❖ Friendly societies registered under the Friendly Societies Act 1974 or a society registered under the Industrial and Provident Societies Act 1965 or the Industrial and Provident Societies Act (Northern Ireland) 1969.

❖ Any unincorporated association of two or more persons which does not fall within any of the above but which carries on its business wholly or mainly in the UK and whose main office is there.

Where a 'principal donor' gives a donation to a party along with one or more others, then each individual contribution of more than £200 is treated as a separate donation. Section 55 makes clear that payments out of public funds are not to be treated as donations. This includes such payments as 'Short money' given to assist the opposition parties in the House of Commons and 'Cranborne money', given to assist opposition parties in the House of Lords. Where a party receives a prohibited donation (unless this is anonymous) it must be returned to the donor within 30 days. In the case of anonymous donations, where possible they must be returned to an identifiable financial institution; otherwise they are sent to the Electoral Commission. Where a party does accept a prohibited donation, the Electoral Commission can apply to a court to order the forfeiture of a sum equal to the donation. Section 61 makes it an offence to knowingly assist in the making of a prohibited donation.

Under Section 62 of the Act, party treasurers must prepare quarterly reports of all donations received by the party over the following limits:

❖ Donations of more than £5,000.

❖ Donations which when added to others from the same source in the same calendar year bring the total to £5,000 or more.

❖ Donations of £1,000 or more, from sources which, during that calendar year, have already made donations qualifying for inclusion in a quarterly report.

Constituency and local parties must also report donations, but the relevant figure in their case is £1,000, not £5,000. Political parties will need to maintain records of all donations above £200, in order to comply with all the above requirements.

Under the provisions of Section 63, during a general election campaign, political parties must prepare weekly donation reports, recording donations of £5,000 or more received during the period between the dissolution of Parliament and polling day. Under section 67, the Secretary of State may, after consulting the Electoral Commission and all registered parties, make an order calling for weekly donation reports during European parliamentary elections, elections to the Scottish Parliament, National Assembly of Wales and the Northern Ireland Assembly.

Section 68 relates to multiple small donations of £200 or less, which during the course of a calendar year, total more than £5,000. These must be reported to the Electoral Commission. Section 69 states that donors' home addresses do not have to be published in the register of donations maintained by the Commission. Section 70 provides for special provisions relating to Northern Ireland to be made by order. Schedule 7 covers the control of donations to individual members of registered parties, to associations and office holders (as defined below). It applies the above provisions relating to donations to political parties, to donations made to individuals and associations that are outside the formal party structure; for example, the Tribune Group or the Tory Reform Group. Office holders are any of the following:

- ❖ Members of the House of Commons

- ❖ Members of the European Parliament (if elected in the UK)

- ❖ Members of the Scottish Parliament

- ❖ Members of the National Assembly for Wales

- ❖ Members of the Northern Ireland Assembly

- ❖ Members of a Local Authority (parish or community councils are not included)

- ❖ Members of the Greater London Assembly

- ❖ The Mayor of London

Donations must be reported within 30 days of acceptance.

A membership organisation is defined as one which consists wholly or mainly of members of a registered party. Donations of more than £5,000 in the case of members associations and £1,000 in the case of individuals (a member of a registered party or the holder of a relevant elective office) must be reported under the provisions of Schedule 7, Part III, paragraph 10 (2). Where a donation, when added to previous donations from the same source takes the aggregate amount to more than £5,000 (£1,000 in the case of individuals) that too must be reported. Under Schedule 7, Part IV, paragraph, where small donations (under £200) from the same donor, made over the course of a calendar year, total more than £5,000 (£1,000 in the case of donations to an individual) then they too must be reported. These provisions inevitably mean some overlap between the register of donations maintained by the Electoral Commission and the Register of Members' Interests in the House of Commons.

Chapters I, II and III of Part IV of the PPERA 2000 (and paragraphs 2 to 15 of Schedule 7 to the Act) do not apply to Northern Ireland. Under the provisions of the Political Parties, Elections and Referendums Act 2000 (Disapplication of Part IV for Northern Ireland Parties, etc.) Order 2001 (SI 2001, No. 446) these Chapters, which relate to donations to political parties on the Northern Ireland register, are disapplied in Northern Ireland for four years. This effectively allows parties in Northern Ireland to accept foreign donations as section 54(2)(a) of the PPERA 2000, which states that donees must be registered in an electoral register, is disapplied. The Conservatives opposed the order in the House of Commons on the grounds that it was *"fundamentally wrong that political parties in Northern Ireland are able to obtain funds from abroad when parties based on the mainland are not"* (HC Col: 880, 6 February 2001).

The forms for reporting donations and guidance notes are available on the Electoral Commission website: www.electoralcommission.gov.uk

CAMPAIGN EXPENDITURE

Section 72 of the PPERA 2000 defines the term, 'campaign expenditure' as meaning those expenses incurred by or on behalf of a registered party, which fall within Part I of Schedule 8 and which are spent on the items listed below:

- ❖ Party political broadcasts
- ❖ Advertising
- ❖ Election material sent to electors
- ❖ Manifestos or other policy documents
- ❖ Market research
- ❖ Press conferences
- ❖ Transport costs
- ❖ Rallies and meetings

The following are not considered to fall within any of the categories outline above:

- ❖ Expenses relating to newsletters or similar publications issued by or on behalf of the party and which are designed to give electors in a particular electoral area, information about the opinions or activities of, or other personal information relating to their elected representatives or existing or prospective candidates.

- ❖ Expenses incurred in respect of unsolicited material addressed to party members.

- ❖ Expenses in respect of any property, services or facilities, where those expenses are to be met from public funds.

- ❖ Remuneration or allowances paid to staff.

- ❖ Travelling or accommodation expenses paid by an individual which are not reimbursed.

Limits on spending cover the following elections:

- ❖ Parliamentary general elections
- ❖ European parliamentary elections
- ❖ Scottish parliamentary general elections
- ❖ Elections to the National Assembly of Wales
- ❖ Elections to the Northern Ireland Assembly

There are no limits on local election expenditure, but any expenditure does count against the limits above if incurred during the relevant period (365 days for a general election and four months before the date of the poll in other cases) for one of the above elections. The term 'campaign expenditure' specifically excludes election expenses that fall within the remit of an individual candidate's election expenses return.

Clause 73 brings property, services or facilities provided free of charge (this includes the secondment of an employee to work for a party where he or she is still being paid by his or her employer), or at 10% of market value, within the definition of campaign expenditure. Where an employee is seconded to work for a party during an election campaign, the amount of the donation and the amount the party must declare is the salary paid to that employee by his or her employer (excluding contributions such as National Insurance Contributions). Free transport for a party leader during an election would constitute a 'donation in kind'. Any such items must be declared unless the difference between their real value and the amount paid by the party is less than £200. Campaign expenditure must only be incurred with the authority of the party treasurer or one of his or her deputies.

Limits Applying to Parliamentary Elections

Section 79 and Schedule 9 of the Act set out the limits on campaign expenditure. Part 2 of Schedule 9 states that the limits on expenditure apply where a registered party contests one or more constituencies in England, Scotland or Wales. The limit is £30,000 per constituency multiplied by the number of constituencies contested by the party[7] in the relevant period (365 days) in that part of Great Britain, or the following amounts, if greater (for example, a party might only have candidates standing in three constituencies in England, which would (without the limits below) entitle them to spend only £90,000 – the limit below would allow them to spend up to £810,000):

- ❖ England - £810,000
- ❖ Scotland - £120,000
- ❖ Wales - £60,000

The relevant period is defined as 365 days ending with the date of the election. Where there is more than one election in a year, the relevant period for the second begins the day after the first general election and ends with the date of the second.

	No. Parliamentary Seats	Max. Expenditure (£)
England	529	15,870,000
Scotland	72	2,160,000
Wales	40	1,200,000
Total (GB)	641	19,230,000
Northern Ireland	18	540,000
Total (UK)	659	19,770,000

The Commencement Order which brought Schedule 9 into force on 16 February 2001 (The Political Parties, Elections and Referendums Act 2000 (Commencement No. 1 and Transitional Provisions) Order 2001 (SI 2001, No. 222 (C.11))), provided for transitional provisions specifying a lower limit on campaign expenditure that would (and in the event, did) apply if the General Election was held less than 365 days after 16 February. The limits are set out below:

Period before Election Date	Revised Allowance per Constituency Contested (£)	Limit on Party Contesting all 659 Seats (£ million)
0-3 months	22,500	14,827,500
3-4 months	24,000	15,816,000
4-5 months	25,500	16,804,000
5-6 months	27,000	17,793,000
6-9 months	28,500	18,781,500
9-12 months	30,000	19,770,000

---

[7] This limit also applies in Northern Ireland

As a result, in the 2001 General Election, parties were subject to a constituency allowance of £24,000, with a limit on national spending per party of £15,816 million.

The following revised limits were applied under The Political Parties, Elections and Referendums Act 2000 (Commencement No. 1 and Transitional Provisions) Order 2001 (SI 2001, No. 222 (C.11)) as there were less than 365 days after 16 February before the general election on 7 June:

Period Before Election Date (general election dates between)	Limit on Controlled Expenditure (£)				
	England	Scotland	Wales	Northern Ireland	Total
0-3 months (16 Feb – 15 May)	595,125	81,000	45,000	20,250	741,375
3-4 months (16 May – 15 June)	634,800	86,400	48,000	21,600	790,800
4-5 months (16 June – 15 July)	674,475	91,800	51,000	22,950	840,225
5-6 months (16 July – 15 August)	714,150	97,200	54,000	24,300	889,650
6-9 months (16 August – 15 November)	753,825	102,600	57,000	25,650	939,075
9-12 months (16 November – 15 February)	793,500	108,000	60,000	27,000	988,500

Limits Applying to European Parliamentary Elections

Different limits on campaign expenditure apply to European parliamentary elections. Where a party stands for election in only one electoral region in England, the limit is £45,000 multiplied by the number of MEPs to be returned for that region. Where a party stands for election in two or more electoral regions in England, the limit is £45,000 multiplied by the total number of MEPs to be returned for those regions taken together. Where a party stands for election in Scotland or Wales or one or more candidates stands for election in Northern Ireland, the limit is £45,000 multiplied by the number of MEPs to be returned for that part of the UK.

The relevant period is the four months ending with the date of the election.

Area	Number of Constituencies	Maximum Expenditure
East Midlands	6	£270,000
Eastern	8	£360,000
London	10	£450,000
North East	4	£180,000
North West	10	£450,000
South East	11	£495,000
South West	7	£315,000
West Midlands	8	£360,000
Yorkshire & the Humber	7	£315,000
Total for England	71	£3,195,000
Total for Scotland	8	£360,000
Total for Wales	5	£225,000
Total for GB	84	£3,780,000
Total for Northern Ireland	3	£135,000

Limits Applying to Elections to the Scottish Parliament

There are different limits again applyting to campaign expenditure in Scottish parliamentary elections. There is a limits of £12,000 for each constituency contested plus £80,000 for each region contested (the maximum if all 73 constituencies and all eight regions are contested is therefore, £1,516,000) and the relevant period to which the limitations apply is the four-month period ending on the date of the election.[8] The limits on expenditure replace those set out in Article 42 of the Scottish Parliament (Elections, etc) Order 1999 (SI 1999, 787).

Limits Applying to Elections to the National Assembly of Wales

The limits on campaign expenditure for elections to the National Assembly of Wales are £10,000 for each constituency contested, plus £40,000 for each region. As there are 40 Assembly constituencies each returning one member and five regions each returning four members, the maximum amount of campaign expenditure is £600,000. The relevant period during which the limitations apply is the four month period ending on the date of the election.[9] These limits replace those contained in Article 47 of the National Assembly for Wales (Representation of the People) Order 1999 (SI 1999/450).

Limits Applying to Elections to the Northern Ireland Assembly

The limit on campaign expenditure that applies to elections to the Northern Ireland Assembly is £17,000 per constituency. As there are 18 constituencies each returning six members of the Assembly, the maximum amount of campaign expenditure is £306,000. The relevant period during which the limit applies is the four-month period before the election.[10]

---

[8] The relevant date is four months before polling day except it is five months before what would have been polling day under section 2(2) of the Act if the date of the election is brought forward under section 2(5) of the Act (four months if the day of the election is postponed under 2(5). Where the date of the election is brought forward under any other circumstances the relevant date is the date four months before the date when the poll would have taken place under section 2(2). In the case of an extraordinary general election the relevant period is that beginning with the date when the Presiding Officer proposed a date for the election under section 3(1) of the Act and ending with the date of the election.

[9] The relevant period is four months before the date of the election except that it is five months before the day on which the election would have taken place under section 3(2) of the Government of Wales Act 1998 when the election is brought forward under section 3(3) of the Act or four months when the date of the election is postponed under section 3(2). Where the day of the election is brought forward or postponed in other circumstances, the period is four months before the date when the election would have taken place.

[10] The relevant period is four months before the date of the election except that it is five months before the day on which the election would have taken place if that date is brought forward under section 31(3) of the Northern Ireland Act 1998 or four months where the day is postponed under section 31(3). In other circumstances, the period is four months before the date on which the election would have taken place. In the case of an extraordinary general election the period is the date on which the Secretary of State proposes a date for the election under section 32(1) or (3) of the Act and ending on the date of the election.

Limits Applying to Overlapping Elections

Part III of Schedule 9 deals with the situations where different elections overlap.

European parliamentary elections overlapping with elections to Scottish Parliament or National Assembly for Wales or Northern Ireland Assembly.

This should only happen once every 20 years, with the next occasion being 2019, when the elections to the three devolved legislatures would be on Thursday 2 May, followed by the elections to the European Parliament, five weeks later on Thursday 9 June. The maximum amount of campaign expenditure is essentially the aggregates of the allowable totals in the two campaigns.

Expenditure	Max. amount – European election (£)	Max. amount – Devolved Assembly election (£)	Aggregate limit applying to both (£)
Scotland	360,000	1,516,000	1,876,000
Wales	225,000	600,000	825,000
Northern Ireland	135,000	306,000	441,000

The relevant period in which the aggregated limits apply would be a four-month period starting on the earlier of the two dates on which the respective elections are called; i.e., 3 January 2019 (four months before the date of the ordinary elections to the devolved assemblies).

When a parliamentary general election overlaps with a European parliamentary and/or election(s) to a devolved assembly(ies) aggregated totals below constitute the limits on expenditure. The relevant period will depend on whether the parliamentary election takes place either on the same day or later than the other election(s) or earlier. The Explanatory Notes published alongside the Act give two examples:

❖ Scottish parliamentary election on 5 May 2011 – parliamentary general election on 2 June 2011 – relevant period, 3 June 2010 to 2 June 2011
❖ Parliamentary general election on 31 March 2011 – Scottish parliamentary election – 5 May 2011 – relevant period, 1 April 2010 to 5 May 2011

Expenditure	Max. limit for overlapping parliamentary and European parliamentary election (£)	Max. limit for overlapping parliamentary and Devolved Assembly election (£)	Max. limit for overlapping parliamentary, European and devolved election (£)
England	19,065,000		
Scotland	2,520,000	3,676,000	4,036,000
Wales	1,425,000	1,800,000	2,025,000
Northern Ireland	675,000	846,000	981,000

Where two parliamentary general elections are pending during different parts of the relevant period for a European parliamentary election or an election to a devolved assembly, or a combination of the two, the following are considered the relevant periods.

10 Feb 2009	Four-month period preceding a European parliamentary election starts	
24 Feb 2009	Parliamentary general election takes place	
26 May 2009	Announcement of dissolution of Parliament	First relevant period starts on 26 Feb 2008 and ends on this day
27 May 2009		Second relevant period starts here
9 June 2009	European parliamentary election	
7 Jul 2009	Second parliamentary general election	Second relevant period ends on this day

Other possible combinations are dealt with in Schedule 9.

CONTROL OF THIRD-PARTY EXPENDITURE

Part VI of the PPERA 2000 relates to the control of third-party spending during national election campaigns (this does not include local government campaigns, except where these coincide with a national campaign, when any expenditure incurred would count towards the expenditure limit for the election in question). Section 85 defines 'controlled expenditure' by a third party as expenses incurred by or on behalf of a third party in connection with the production or publication of election material made available to the public.

Election material is defined as being material intended to promote the success of a particular party, or one or more parties, all of which advocate a particular policy, or candidates, all of whom hold a particular opinion. Section 86 applies the same controls as apply to registered parties, to property, services and facilities transferred to a third party free of charge or at a discount of more than 10% of market value, which is to be used by them to promote a particular party, etc., during the campaign. Where the difference between the market value and the amount paid by the third party concerned is less than £200, expenditure controls do not apply. Section 88 of the Act states that in order to be 'recognised', third parties must register with the Electoral Commission.

Third parties are required to register if intending to publish material which promotes one or more of the registered parties or candidates (regardless of whether or not the material refers to a candidate or party by name). This provision was applied for the first time in the 2001 General Election, when organisations ranging form Charter 88 to UNISON registered as third parties. Only those resident in the UK, those registered in an electoral register, registered parties or those who are registered donors under the Act, can send in the required 'notification' to the Commission. Section 94 sets out the limits that apply to controlled expenditure by parties other than recognised third parties. The limits on expenditure during election campaigns are:

- ❖ £10,000 for England
- ❖ £5,000 for Scotland, Wales or Northern Ireland

The limits on controlled expenditure by recognised third parties' during the 'relevant period' relating to parliamentary elections, are set out in Schedule 10 and they are:

- ❖ In England, £793,500
- ❖ In Scotland, £108,000
- ❖ In Wales, £60,000
- ❖ In Northern Ireland, £27,000

The 'relevant period' is the period of 365 days ending with the day of the election.

The limits in relation to European parliamentary elections during the relevant period of four months ending on the day of the election are:

- ❖ In England, £159,000
- ❖ In Scotland, £18,000
- ❖ In Wales, £11,259
- ❖ In Northern Ireland, £6,750

The limit in relation to elections to the Scottish Parliament during the relevant period of four months ending on the day of the election, is £75,800.[11]

The limit in relation to elections to the National Assembly of Wales during the relevant period of four months ending on the day of the election, is £30,000.[12]
The limit in relation to elections to the Northern Ireland Assembly during the relevant period of four months ending on the day of the election, is £15,300.[13]

These figures represent 5% of the total amount a registered party could spend if it contested all the seats in the election in question. Part III of Schedule 10 also sets out the conditions which apply to the limits on controlled expenditure when elections are combined or overlap.

Donations to third parties are covered by the provisions of Section 95 and Schedule 11. Donations to registered third parties are defined as:

- ❖ any gift of money or other property;

- ❖ any sponsorship;

---

[11] The relevant date is four months before polling day except it is five months before what would have been polling day under section 2(2) of the Act if the date of the election is brought forward under section 2(5) of the Act (four months if the day of the election is postponed under 2(5). Where the date of the election is brought forward under any other circumstances the relevant date is the date four months before the date when the poll would have taken place under section 2(2). In the case of an extraordinary general election the relevant period is that beginning with the date when the Presiding Officer proposed a date for the election under section 3(1) of the Act and ending with the date of the election.

[12] The relevant period is four months before the date of the election except that it is five months before the day on which the election would have taken place under section 3(2) of the Government of Wales Act 1998 when the election is brought forward under section 3(3) of the Act or four months when the date of the election is postponed under section 3(2). Where the day of the election is brought forward or postponed in other circumstances, the period is four months before the date when the election would have taken place.

[13] The relevant period is four months before the date of the election except that it is five months before the day on which the election would have taken place if that date is brought forward under section 31(3) of the Northern Ireland Act 1998 or four months where the day is postponed under section 31(3). In other circumstances, the period is four months before the date on which the election would have taken place. In the case of an extraordinary general election the period is the date on which the Secretary of State proposes a date for the election under section 32(1) or (3) of the Act and ending on the date of the election.

- ❖ any money spent in paying any controlled expenditure incurred by or on behalf of the third party;

- ❖ any money lent other than on commercial terms;

- ❖ the provision, other than on commercial terms, of property, services or facilities for the use or benefit of the third party; or,

- ❖ a subscription or other affiliation fee or membership fee.

Sponsorship is defined as money or other property transferred to the recognised third party to assist with meeting 'defined expenses' which are described as expenses in connection with conferences, meetings or other events organised by the third party, the preparation, production, or dissemination of any publication by or on behalf of the third party, or any study or research organised by or on behalf of the third party concerned. Donations under £200 are disregarded. Donations can only be accepted from permissible donors (as set out in Section 54(2) in relation to donors to registered parties) and donations of more than £5,000 must be recorded (this includes amounts which comprise several small donations). Recognised third parties must make a return of any controlled expenditure made during the relevant period to the Electoral Commission. Where that expenditure exceeds £250,000, the return must be examined by a qualified auditor.

POLITICAL DONATIONS BY COMPANIES

Section 139 of the PPERA 2000 inserts Schedule 18 of the PPERA into the Companies Act 1985 as Part XA of that Act. New section 347A of the 1985 Act will control contributions and other donations made by companies to registered parties and other EU political organisations. A donation is defined as anything which constitutes a donation under Sections 50 to 52 of the PPERA 2000. Section 347B sets out a number of exemptions, including EU trade associations and All-Party Parliamentary Groups. Section 347C stipulates that no donation can be made to any registered party or EU political organisation unless authorised by a company general meeting for a four year (or shorter) period.

Special rules apply to subsidiaries under Section 347D and will mean that where a company is not a wholly-owned subsidiary, it will not be able to make a donation or incur any expenditure which has not been approved in a general meeting by both the holding company and the subsidiary. In the case of a wholly owned subsidiary, only a resolution of the holding company is required. Section 347F sets out the remedies available for breach of the prohibitions on company donations. All directors of the company at the time the donation was made will be liable to pay the company the amount of the donation and damages in respect of any loss or damage sustained by the company. Under Section 347H it will be a defence for a director to show that the donation has been repaid, that it was approved in a general meeting, that the notice of the resolution submitted to the meeting made full disclosure of the circumstances under which the donation was made and subsequently repaid to the company. Section 347I provides for shareholders to enforce any of the remedies for a prohibited company donation. However, shareholder action will be limited to 'authorised groups' of shareholders as set out in Section 54(2) of the Companies Act 1985 (those groups entitled to challenge the re-registration of a public company as a private company).

On 26 July 2001, The Boots Company held an Extraordinary General Meeting on the grounds that although it did not, and did not have any intention to make any donations to political parties, the PPERA 2000 could be deemed to cover the provision of additional paid leave to employees elected to local councils and the non company-specific activities of company-paid full time trade union officials. The company allows employees who are local councillors up to 10 days additional paid leave and up to five further days unpaid leave. As the Act required separate authority for company subsidiaries, 17 resolutions were proposed at the EGM.

REFERENDUMS

One of the most contentious issues raised by the Neill Committee was their recommendation that in a referendum campaign, the Government should remain neutral and that there should be equal, core funding, for both sides in the campaign. Donations of £5,000 would need to be disclosed. This would preclude additional Government funding for one side of the campaign. During the debate in the House of Commons, both the Home Secretary and a number of other speakers made the point that it would be almost impossible to ensure Government neutrality during a campaign; Ministers would still be in office and would need advice from civil servants and whilst members of the Government might be on different sides of the debate, there would still be a Government view on the matter in question.

Part VII of the Act sets out the provisions governing referendums in the UK. This only applies to referendums held under Acts of Parliament and not, for example, to referendums held under Section 36 of the Government of Wales Act 1998, which relates to the way in which the National Assembly is governed. The period of the referendum campaign (the period to which expenditure controls would be applied) would be as follows:

❖ In the case of a referendum held in accordance with Schedule 1 to the Northern Ireland Act 1998, the period begins on the date when the draft order under that Schedule is laid before Parliament and ends with the date of the poll.

❖ In the case of a referendum held under the provisions of any other Act, the period is as provided for under that Act.

❖ In the case of a referendum to which Section 101(4) of the Act (a referendum held in pursuance of a provision in a bill or Act) applies, the period is as set out in the order (provided it is no longer than six months) (under Section 101(4) where a Bill is introduced which specifies the wording of the referendum question, or that question is set out in delegated legislation, the Electoral Commission must be consulted on the form the question is to take as soon as possible after the Bill is introduced or before the order is laid before Parliament).

The date of the referendum (if not set out in an Act or delegated legislation) cannot be earlier than 28 days after the end of the period of 14 days referred to in Section 109(3) of the Act, which states that those organisations wishing to campaign in the referendum must apply to the Commission for designation within 28 days beginning with the first day of the referendum period and the Commission must decide on the application within a 14-day-period beginning with the day after the end of the aforementioned 28 day period (the 14 and 28 days can be varied by order).

Section 105 of the Act defines those who can take part in a referendum campaign – the 'permitted participants'. These are:

❖ Registered parties who have made a declaration to the Commission under Section 106 of the Act specifying the referendum to which the declaration relates and the outcome for which the party is campaigning.

❖ Those who have given a notification to the Electoral Commission; namely, any individual resident in the UK or registered in an electoral register, a company registered under the Companies Act 1985 or the Companies (Northern Ireland) Order 1986 and incorporated n the UK or other Member State and which carries on its business in the UK, a trade union, a building society, a limited liability partnership, a friendly society, any unincorporated association of two or more persons (i.e., those set out in Section 54 (2) sub-sections (a), (b) and (d) to (h) of the Act).

Under Section 108 of the Act, certain permitted participants can be designated as organisations to which assistance can be given, as set out in Section 110. Where there are only two possible outcomes to the referendum, the Electoral Commission *may* designate one permitted participant as representing those campaigning for each one of the two outcomes; for example, in a referendum on joining the Euro, where there could be only two possible outcomes to the referendum - 'yes' or 'no' - the Commission could designate one umbrella organisation as being the representative of the 'yes' campaign and another as being the representative body of the 'no' campaign. It could not designate one group as representative of the 'yes' campaign unless it designated another group as representative of the 'no' campaign. If it were unable to designate one group for each side, it would have to forgo designating any group on either side.

Where there are more than two possible outcomes, the Secretary of State *may* after consulting the Commission, specify, by order, the possible outcomes in relation to which permitted participants may be designated. The Commission could, in relation to each of two or more outcomes specified in the order, designate one permitted participant as representing those campaigning for the outcome in question. As outlined above, at least one permitted participant would have to be designated for each outcome, or none at all.

Any group seeking to be designated as an organisation to which assistance may be given under the Act, must apply to the Electoral Commission. Where there is only one application in relation to a particular outcome, the Commission "*shall designate the applicant*" unless they are not satisfied that the applicant adequately represents those campaigning for the outcome in question. Where there is only one application in relation to a particular outcome, the Commission 'shall designate whichever of the applicants appears to them to represent to the greatest extent those campaigning for that outcome' unless they are not satisfied that any of the applicants adequately represents those campaigning for that outcome. Where the Commission does designate umbrella organisations, each is entitled to a grant 'not exceeding £600,000 determined by the Commission' (each designated organisation is entitled to the same amount). Designated organisations have rights (set out in Schedule 12) to the following:

❖ Sending referendum addresses free of charge
❖ The use of rooms free of charge for holding public meetings
❖ Referendum campaign broadcasts

There are limits on the expenditure of permitted participants during referendum campaigns. The expenditure limit on those who are not permitted participants is £10,000. The limits on permitted participants are set out in Schedule 14. Referendum expenses are defined in Part I of Schedule 13, as being:

- ❖ Expenses related to costs of producing referendum campaign broadcasts
- ❖ Advertising
- ❖ Unsolicited material addressed to electors
- ❖ Publications (as set out in Section 125)
- ❖ Market research
- ❖ Provision of services in connection with press conferences
- ❖ Transport
- ❖ Rallies and public meetings

Under Section 112 of the Act, where property, services or facilities are provided for permitted participants either free of charge or at a discount of 10% on market values, then the difference between the real cost and the market value is considered to be referendum expenses and must be declared unless it is less than £200. Under Schedule 14, the limit on referendum expenses for a designated umbrella organisation is £5 million and for a person or organisation falling within section 105(1)(b) (any individual resident in the UK or registered in an electoral register, a company registered under the Companies Act 1985 or the Companies (Northern Ireland) Order 1986 and incorporated in the UK or other Member State and which carries on its business in the UK, a trade union, a building society, a limited liability partnership, a friendly society, any unincorporated association of two or more persons (i.e., those set out in Section 54 (2) sub-sections (a), (b) and (d) to (h) of the Act)), but not designated under section 108, £500,000.

The limit on expenses for registered political parties is as follows, and is based on the percentage of the total number of votes cast for that party at the last election:

Percentage of Vote	Limit on Expenditure (£m)
Less than 5%	0.5
Between 5% and 10%	2
Between 10% and 20%	3
Between 20% and 30%	4
More than 30%	5

These provisions have caused some concern because of their implications for a future referendum on joining the euro. Although two umbrella organisations, one for and one against joining the euro, would have parity in terms of expenditure, the provisions relating to expenditure by registered parties would result in the overall expenditure by the 'yes' campaign being greater than that of the rival 'no' campaign. This is because more parties currently support joining the euro than oppose it.

Where the referendum is not UK-wide, but restricted to a particular area, the above limits are determined by an order made by the Secretary of State. Schedule 15 sets out the controls on donations to permitted participants and these are equivalent to the controls on donations to registered parties. Sections 120 to 124 set out the provisions relating to returns of referendum expenses and Part III of Schedule 15 of the Act states that the return must include a statement detailing the source and amount of donations over £5,000 (including the aggregates of smaller donations).

Section 125 of the Act prohibits the publication of promotional material relating to the referendum by central and local government, or other publicly funded bodies during the 28-day period prior to the date of the referendum. However, this restriction applies to material made available to the public at large, not to specific requests for information from the public. The restrictions do not apply to the Electoral Commission itself, which could produce material designed to encourage people to vote. All publications must include the name and address of the printer, promoter and publisher. As far as referendum campaign broadcasts are concerned, the provisions of Section 127 and Schedule 12(4) apply. Section 127 states that only referendum campaign broadcasts on behalf of designated organisations can be shown by the broadcasters; for example, in a referendum campaign on joining the euro, the 'yes' and 'no' umbrella organisations.

Sections 128 and 129 of the Act related to the conduct of referendums and stipulate that there must be a Chief Counting Officer for the referendum. This will be the Chairman of the Electoral Commission or another person appointed by him or her. The Chief Counting Officer will appoint a counting officer for each relevant area in Great Britain. The relevant areas are the district councils and London boroughs, the City of London, the Isle of Wight or the Isles of Scilly, a local government area in Scotland or a county borough in Wales. In Northern Ireland, the Chief Electoral Officer for Northern Ireland will the Chief Counting Officer for any referendum held only in Northern Ireland. Under Section 129, the Secretary of State can make orders in connection with regulating the conduct of referendums. The intention of this Section is to enable regulations to be made applying provisions similar to those governing ordinary elections in the Representation of the People Act 1983, to referendums; for example, polling hours, voting offences, etc.

APPENDIX A - ELECTORAL REFORM

DIFFERENT ELECTORAL SYSTEMS

Concerns about our current electoral system and calls for its reform are nothing new. However, the First Past the Post System (FPTP) has its supporters as well as detractors and there are strong arguments in favour of its retention. It usually ensures strong majority government, is easy to understand, militates against the undue influence of smaller political parties and avoids the need for coalitions. However, there are equally strong arguments against: it can, and frequently does, result in the election of Members by a minority, rather than a majority, of their constituents; it disenfranchises vast numbers of people in certain parts of the country (for example, Conservative supporters in Scotland); it leads to the under-representation of smaller parties in the House of Commons and it can mean the election of a Government with a larger number of seats but smaller percentage of votes than its main rival (the General Election of 1951 is the best example of this).

The debate about a possible replacement for FPTP has rumbled on for decades. In 1917, a Speaker's Conference on Electoral Reform (Cm 8463) recommended the adoption of a combination of the Single Transferable Vote (STV) and the Alternative Vote (AV). These proposals were rejected by the House of Commons, as were subsequent proposals.

The Labour Party's 1997 General Election manifesto committed the party to holding a referendum on PR, but no timescale was indicated. The Independent Commission on the Voting System was set up in December 1997 under the Chairmanship of the Lord Jenkins of Hillhead and its report (Cm 4090) was published on 29 October 1998[1]. There was no referendum on PR in the 1997 Parliament. This should have surprised no one. It was never really a possibility given Labour's huge majority. Labour's 2001 general election manifesto simply stated that *"The government has introduced major innovations in the electoral systems used in the UK – for the devolved administrations, the European Parliament, and the London Assembly. The Independent Commission on the Voting System made proposals for electoral reform at Westminster. We will review the experience of the new systems and the Jenkins report to assess whether changes might be made to the electoral system for the House of Commons. A referendum remains the right way to agree any change for Westminster"*.

One of the main problems in holding a referendum on PR is just how to word the question on the ballot paper. A referendum on just this issue was held in New Zealand on 19 September 1992. Electors were asked firstly if they wished to alter the current electoral system and secondly, if the answer to the first question was 'yes', which, out of five listed systems they would prefer. A majority supported change and two thirds of those supported a 'mixed member proportional system' similar to AMS. Alternatively, details could be set out first in legislation, with the proviso that provisions relating to PR would not come into effect unless ratified by a majority voting in their favour in a referendum.

Electoral systems can be based on one of the following three principles: Plurality, Majority or Proportionality.

---

[1] 'The Report of the Independent Commission on the Voting System', October 1998, Cm 4090.

Plurality

Our own system of first-past-the-post (FPTP) elections is the best example of plurality; electors vote for one candidate and the candidate with the most votes, wins. The candidate with the most votes is not necessarily the candidate with an overall majority.

Majority

There are three basic majoritarian systems:

- ❖ Second Ballot system
- ❖ Alternative Vote (AV)
- ❖ Supplementary Vote (SV)

These differ from FPTP in that, whilst they are not proportional, they do at least make some attempt to guarantee that MPs are elected by a majority of their electorate.

The Second Ballot

The Second Ballot system is used in France for legislative and presidential elections. In the first ballot, voters select their preferred candidate as they would under FPTP. If any candidate receives an overall majority, he or she is elected. If not, candidates with a minimum of 12.5% of 'registered voters', as opposed to votes cast, proceed to the next round. If more than two candidates go forward there can be no guarantee that the winning candidate will have an overall majority.

The Presidential elections differ in that only the two highest placed candidates can go through to the second ballot. In the French Presidential election in 1995, Lionel Jospin received the most votes in the first ballot, followed by Jacques Chirac and Edouard Balladur. Only Jospin and Chirac went through to the second ballot, where Balladur's votes switched to Chirac, giving him an overall majority.

The Alternative Vote

The Alternative Vote is used for elections to the Australian Lower House. Constituencies elect one candidate, but electors record preferences for the various candidates; e.g.

Twist, Oliver	Labour	1
Nickleby, Nicholas	Conservative	2
Copperfield, David	Liberal Democrat	3

If no candidate gains an absolute majority of the vote, the candidate with the fewest votes is eliminated and his second preferences are allocated to the remaining candidates. This process is continued until a winning candidate is secured. AV was the system recommended by the Jenkins Commission[2] for the constituency section of its AV-Plus electoral system. Under this system, the majority of MPs (80 to 85 per cent) would continue to be elected in constituencies, using AV. The remainder would be elected in small 'top-up' areas from 'open' lists, allowing voters a vote for either a party or a candidate. The number of second votes cast for these list candidates would be counted and divided by the number of constituency MPs elected in the relevant top-up area, plus

---

[2] 'The Report of the Independent Commission on the Voting System', October 1998, Cm 4090.

one (see later for a description of the quotas and divisors which can be used to elected members under a list system).

The Supplementary Vote

This is really a variant of the Alternative Vote and was used in the elections for the Mayor of London.

	Mark X here for your first preference	Mark X here for your second preference
Twist, Oliver – Labour		
Nickleby, Nicholas – Conservative		
Copperfield, David – Liberal Democrat		

The returning officer adds up all the first preferences and if any candidate has gained over 50% of the votes he or she is elected.   If, however, there is no overall majority for any of the candidates, then all except the two with the highest number of second preferences are eliminated. The second preferences on the ballot papers of the eliminated candidates are then added to the totals of the top two candidates (second preferences of eliminated candidates for other eliminated candidates are ignored). Whichever of the two remaining candidates receives the most votes is elected.

Proportionality

Proportional voting systems fall into three main categories:

* ❖ List systems
* ❖ Mixed member systems
* ❖ Single Transferable Vote

Party List Systems - Open or Closed?

There are numerous different list systems, ranging from those that simply allow voters to express a preference for a party, to those that allow full preferential voting; i.e., the voter can list all the candidates in order of preference. Lists are said to be either 'open' or 'closed'. The former allows the electorate to vote for a candidate, the latter allows only a vote for a party. Where a closed list is used the party simply draws up a list of its candidates (in the order it wants them elected) and the elector votes for a party, not for an individual. The number of seats that each party gains in the legislature is proportional to the number of votes received by the party and the most popular candidates from the list are elected.

Preferential or Non-Preferential?

In some party list systems the elector can alter the order of the candidates and in others, the elector has as many votes as there are candidates to be elected and can vote for candidates on different party lists. In Belgium, voters can choose either to vote for the party of their choice or for a candidate. In Luxembourg, voters have as many votes as there are seats to be filled and have three choices as to how they cast them, they can: vote for a party (which gives a vote to each candidate on that party's list); give two preference votes for one candidate (a procedure known as 'cumulation'); or, express preferences for as many candidates as there are seats to be filled on any party's list. In some countries, party lists are unordered and votes for the candidates on the list are the only determinants of who is elected. A vote for a particular party's candidate does not equal a vote for that party, purely a vote for that candidate. Voters can rank candidates preferentially from across the party's lists. Where party lists are ordered, preferential voting may result in reordering of the list, with a candidate lower down the list being elected before a candidate at the top of the party's list. The most proportional list system is one in which the entire electorate forms one large constituency – this system is used in Israel and the Netherlands.

Lists can also be regional or two-tier. There are several varieties of two-list systems. A two-tier system can be used to top-up candidates who may have been elected on a constituency basis, with those elected from a regional list. There are two ways of doing this: 'remainder transfer' or 'adjustment'. In the former, the proportion of additional seats is not fixed in advance (used with largest remainder systems), whereas under the adjustment method, a fixed proportion is set aside (this is usually used with the highest average systems) (largest remainder and highest average systems are explained in the next section). Some lists also allow preferential voting. Before the 1993 reforms, Italy elected its Chamber of Deputies by using the largest remainder Imperiali quota system, with preferential ranking of candidates (this was abolished in 1991), followed by a national top-up. The Senate was elected by using the highest average d'Hondt allocation formula. The system was replaced in 1993 by a system similar in some respects to the 'AV-Plus' system recommended by the Jenkins Commission . Three quarters of both houses are elected in individual constituencies and one quarter is elected from PR lists (the Senate uses the overall vote for the Party to calculate lists seats, whereas the Chamber of Deputies uses a two-vote system, with one vote for constituency candidates and one for a party list).

Quotas and Divisors

Pure list systems employ either a 'quota' or a 'divisor'. Systems which use quotas are called 'largest remainder' systems and those employing divisors are known as 'highest average' systems.

Largest Remainder Systems

Largest remainder systems use one of the three following quotas: Hare (named after Thomas Hare); Droop (after mathematician, H K Droop - also known as the Hagenbach-Bischoff system, after Eduard Hagenbach-Bischoff) or Imperiali. When such quotas are used, in the first round of the election, parties with votes over the quota are allocated seats; for example, using the Hare quota, if the number of total votes was 2000 and the number of seats five, the quota would be 400. Parties with over 400 votes are awarded seats and the remaining seats are awarded to parties in order, with the party with the largest number of votes gaining the first seat, and so on.

The Droop quota divides the total valid votes by the number of seats plus one (where the bracket is equal to the next whole number) i.e., votes divided by seats plus one, plus one (or part thereof). In the above example of 2000 votes with five seats, applying the Droop quota would result in the following: 2000 divided by six, plus one = 334. If there were, for example 54 votes and three seats the quota would be $54 \div 3 + 1 = 13.5$ (plus one or part thereof) = 14.

$$\frac{\text{Votes}}{\text{Seats} + 1}$$

The Imperiali quota divides the total valid votes by the number of seats plus two and the Reinforced Imperiali quota by seats plus three. According to Professor David Butler in his evidence to the Jenkins Commission[4], *"these have no known mathematical justification"*. Using the above example again, the Imperiali quota would result in the following: 2000 divided by 7 = 286. Lower quotas favour larger political parties and vice versa.

Highest Average System

There are three main forms of the highest average system: d'Hondt (named after Victor d'Hondt) pure Sainte-Laguë and modified Sainte-Laguë (named after A. Sainte-Laguë). The d'Hondt system is the most widely used and involves the use of the divisors, 1, 2, 3, etc. The pure Sainte-Laguë system uses the divisors 1, 3, 5, 7, etc, whereas the modified Sainte-Laguë system uses the divisors 1.4, 3, 5, 7, etc. The parties' votes are divided by the divisor to produce an average vote and the party with the highest average vote after each stage of the process wins a seat.

ELECTORAL QUOTAS AND FORMULAS

Largest Remainder	Highest Average
quotas used include:	allocation formulas used include:
Hare (valid votes divided by seats)	d'Hondt (divisors 1, 2, 3, etc)
Droop (valid votes divided by seats plus one), plus one	pure Sainte-Laguë (divisors 1, 3, 5, 7)
Imperiali (valid votes divided by 2)	modified Sainte-Laguë (divisors 1.4, 3, 5, 7)
Reinforced Imperiali (valid votes divided by 3)	

Some examples using the various systems are set out below. These demonstrate the different results that can occur using different quotas and different allocation formulas. The d'Hondt highest average allocation formula is the least proportional and favours larger parties whilst the pure Sainte-Laguë favours smaller parties; the Hare quota favours smaller parties while the Droop and Imperiali quotas favour larger parties.

The following tables are based on examples from David M Farrell's excellent book, 'Electoral Systems: A Comparative Introduction' (see Further Reading).

---

[4] 'The Report of the Independent Commission on the Voting System', October 1998, Cm 4090 - Volume 3, page 24 of evidence – 'Report of group of academics chaired by Professor David Butler, Nuffield College, Oxford University'.

HARE – valid votes divided by no. of seats (2000 votes, five seats)

Party	1st Round	Quota	Seats	2nd Round	Seats	Total Seats
Con	720	400	1	720 - 400 = 320	1	2
Lab	620	400	1	620 - 400 = 220		1
Lib.Dem	300	400		300	1	1
SNP	240	400		240	1	1
Ind	120	400		120		

DROOP – valid votes divided by no. of seats plus one, plus one, or part thereof (2000 votes, five seats)

Party	1st Round	Quota	Seats	2nd Round	Seats	Total Seats
Con	720	334	2	720 - 334 = 386	1	3
Lab	620	334	1	620 - 334 = 286		1
Lib.Dem	300	334		300	1	1
SNP	240	334		240		
Ind	120	334		120		

IMPERIALI – valid votes divided by no. of seats plus two (2000 votes, five seats)

Party	1st Round	Quota	Seats	2nd Round	Seats	Total Seats
Con	720	286	2			2
Lab	620	286	2			2
Lib.Dem	300	286	1			1
SNP	240	286				
Ind	120	286				

d'HONDT – valid votes divided by aggregate of seats plus one (2000 votes, five seats)

Party	divide by 1	divide by 2	Total Seats
Con	720 (1st elected)	360 (3rd elected)	2
Lab	620 (2nd elected)	310 (4th elected)	2
Lib.Dem	300 (5th elected)	150	1
SNP	240	120	
Ind	120	60	

MODIFIED SAINTE-LAGUË– valid votes divided by 1.4, 3, etc. (2000 votes, five seats)

Party	divide by 1.4	divide by 3	Total Seats
Con	720 ÷ 1.4 = 514 (1st elected)	240 (3rd elected)	2
Lab	620 ÷ 1.4 = 443 (2nd elected)	207 (5th elected)	2
Lib.Dem	300 ÷ 1.4 = 214 (4th elected)	100	1
SNP	240 ÷ 1.4 = 171	80	
Ind	120 ÷ 1.4 = 86	40	

PURE SAINTE-LAGUË – valid votes divided by 1, then 3, then 5, etc. (2000 votes, five seats)

Party	divide by 1	divide by 3	divide by 5	Total Seats
Con	720	240	144	2
Lab	620	207	124	1
Lib.Dem	300	100	60	1
SNP	240	80	48	1
Ind	120	40	24	

The Single Transferable Vote

The Single Transferable Vote (STV) is a preferential voting system used in constituencies returning more than one member. It is used in Eire, Malta, Australia (elections to the Senate) and for elections to the Northern Ireland Assembly. It is also used in Northern Ireland for local elections and European Parliamentary elections. Voters mark their ballot paper in order of preference; i.e., '1' against the name of their first choice candidate, '2' against their second preference, '3' against their third choice, etc.

SAMPLE BALLOT PAPER FOR STV ELECTION

Mark Candidates in Order of Preference	
2	Twist, Oliver – Labour
1	Nickleby, Nicholas – Conservative
4	Copperfield, David – Liberal Democrat
3	Rudge, Barnaby – Residents' Association
5	Chuzzlewit, Martin - Independent

The expression of a preference means that if an elector's first choice candidate cannot use the vote (either because he has a surplus of votes and is therefore elected, or because he has too few votes and cannot possibly be elected) his vote can be transferred.

Firstly, a quota has to be calculated. This is the minimum number of votes needed to secure election. The quota is equal to the number of votes divided by the number of seats plus one, and plus one again (the Droop quota).

$$\frac{V}{(S + 1)} + 1$$

In the example set out in the following table, taken from the results of the Sligo-Leitrim Constituency in the Irish General Election of 1969 [5] the calculation of the quota was:

$$\frac{29,974}{4} + 1 = 7,494$$

Any candidate who secured this number of votes was elected. In this example, no candidate reached the quota, therefore the candidate with the least number of votes was eliminated and his votes redistributed. Fallon, Higgins and Mooney were all eventually eliminated and McLoughlin finally reached the quota. His surplus votes were then transferred.

---

[5] This example is taken from 'The People and the Party System', Vernon Bogdanor (Cambridge University Press, 1981)

It is impossible to tell which votes are surplus, so the votes are given a value equal to the ratio of the surplus to the number of transferable votes cast for McLoughlin. McLoughlin's surplus votes (8,011, minus the quota) totalled 517. His transferable votes amounted to 8,011, minus the number of non-transferable votes (205) = 7,806. The surplus, 517 was then divided by the number of transferable votes (517 divided by 7,806) to give $^{33}/_{500}$. Therefore, each continuing candidate received that fraction of every ballot paper showing a next preference for him. Gilhawley received that fraction of every paper showing a next preference for him. He received 1,046 next available preferences out of 8.011 (1,046 x $^{33}/_{500}$ = 69). There were three candidates remaining, Gallagher, MacSharry and Gilhawley. None had reached the quota, but as further transfers would have been pointless (because there were 1,158 votes which were non-transferable; i.e., no further preferences had been marked on the ballot papers and could therefore not be redistributed) MacSharry and Gallagher were elected. If some of those 1,158 votes had been transferred to Gilhawley he could have reached the quota and defeated Gallagher for the third seat.

RESULTS IN THE SLIGO-LEITRIM CONSTITUENCY IN THE IRISH GENERAL ELECTION OF 1969

Candidates by Party	Stage I	Stage II - O'Rourkes votes	Stage III - Gallagher's votes	Stage IV - Fallon's votes	Stage V - Higgins' votes	Stage VI - Mooney's votes	Stage VII - McLoughlin's surplus	Result
Fianna Fail								
Gallagher J	6124	(11) 6135	(70) 6205	(135) 6340	(96) 6436	(645) 7081	(132) 7213	Third
MacSharry R	5616	(18) 5634	(189) 5823	(162) 5985	(424) 6409	(912) 7321	(111) 7432	Second
Mooney J M	2267	(203) 2470	(40) 2510	(11) 2521	(41) 2562	2562 (transferred votes)		Eliminated
	14007	14239	14538	14846	15407	14402	14645	
Fine Gael								
McLoughlin J	6053	(158) 6211	(100) 6311	(527) 6838	(455) 7293	(718) 8011	(517) 7494	First
Gilhawley E	5858	(8) 5866	(111) 5977	(373) 6350	(210) 6560	(48) 6608	(69) 6677	Runner Up
Fallon J	1332	(3) 1335	(44) 1379	1379 (transferred votes)				Lost Deposit
	13243	13412	13667	13188	13853	14619	14171	
Labour								
Higgins T J	1251	(29) 1280	(410) 1690	(122) 1812	1812 (transferred votes)			Lost Deposit
Gallagher J	967	(51) 1018	1018 (transferred votes)	1812				Lost Deposit
O'Rourke P	506	506 (transferred votes)	1690					Lost Deposit
	2724	2298						
Non-transferable votes		25	54 (25+ 54 = 79)	49 (49 + 79 = 128)	586 (128+586 = 714)	239 (239 + 714 = 953)	205 (205 + 953 = 1158)	
Total	29974	29974	29974	29974	29974	29974	29974	

One of the problems with using a quota is the difficulty of deciding which papers to transfer; for example, if a candidate is 100 votes over a quota of 501 – 501 votes will be left in his pile, but 100 will have to be transferred; the question is which 100 votes? This is where an element of chance may creep into STV. For example, the 501 votes left in the pile might all have the Liberal Democrat as their second preference, but the 100 votes which are actually transferred might have the Labour candidate as their second preference. In Australia they deal with this problem by sorting the ballot papers according to the remaining preferences, then apportioning appropriate fractions to them. The Australian Senate elections give voters the opportunity to either vote for a party or to rank candidates in order of preference.

Of all the proportional systems, STV seems to attract the most ardent supporters. Its followers are true believers. Equally, there are those who shudder at its very mention. The traditional arguments against STV are that it inevitably results in coalition government – Ireland is frequently cited. However, coalition government does not always equal unstable government and in fact on average, governments in the Irish Republic have lasted three to four years. Another argument against STV is that it produces what is known as 'alphabetical' or 'donkey' voting; this means is that in some constituencies the list of candidates can be so long that voters have a tendency to rank candidates not in order of preference but in the order of names they recognise on the ballot paper. It has been suggested that the order of names on the ballot paper should be randomised, thereby reducing the tendency towards alphabetical voting. The other main argument against STV, is its non-monotonicity; this is basically the paradox that some first preference votes can actually disadvantage a candidate (see the previously mentioned: 'Comparing Electoral Systems', by David M Farrell).

Mixed Member Systems.

Mixed member systems are known by a variety of different names: for example, Mixed Member Proportional in New Zealand and Additional Member System in Germany.

Under the Additional Member System (AMS) used in Germany, half the Members of the Bundestag are elected by first-past-the-post, whilst the other half are elected from Party lists. The elector has two votes, one for a constituency representative and one for a Party list. The list seats are distributed between the Parties so as to make their total representation in the Bundestag proportional to their respective second votes. Parties need to gain 5 per cent or more the total votes cast, or gain three constituencies in order to be eligible for any seats in the Bundestag. There are no by-elections and all vacancies are filled by co-opting the next candidate on the list. The majority of candidates stand for a constituency and are given a place on their Party's list. The proportion of votes gained by a party in the list section is used to determine the number of additional (if any) constituency Members to which a party is entitled. Under the German system, the number of constituency MPs gained is subtracted from the total votes received by the Party in the list section and any gap is then 'topped-up'. For example; if a party won 30% of the votes in the list section, but only 20% of the seats in the constituency section, it would be entitled to 10% more MPs; these would be allocated from the list section – in the case of the German system, using the Hare allocation formula.

Returning officers must first calculate the results of the constituency elections. If one Party has won fewer constituencies than its overall level of support, as measured by the results of the Party list elections, would indicate, it is compensated by being allocated additional seats from its party list. For example; a Party wins 50 seats out of 500, although its support in the Party list elections indicates that its true level of support is 20% rather than 10%. It would therefore be entitled to 100 seats, so it would retain the 50 constituency seats it had won and be given an additional 50. If one Party exceeds its proportionality quota in the constituency elections, it is allowed to keep those 'extra' MPs and in the case of the Bundestag, this can lead to its temporary enlargement.

Elections to the Scottish Parliament, Welsh Assembly and Greater London Assembly are held using a variant of AMS, with electors voting for both constituency and list members.

In 1979 the Hansard Society's Commission on Electoral Reform recommended a variant of AMS, whereby three quarters of MPs would be elected in single member constituencies, with one quarter being chosen from defeated candidates ('best losers') and allocated to each Party in proportion to its share of the vote in each region. A Party not securing 5% of the vote within the region would not be eligible for seats.

One of the criticisms levelled against AMS is that in the case of the best known example – the system used in Germany – the Free Democrats (FDP) have served in every coalition Government since 1949, except between 1957 and 1960, despite its share of the vote rarely reaching double figures.

Another criticism is the fact that the system leads to the election of two distinct types of MP – a constituency MP and a list MP (usually elected on a regional basis) who does not have the same concerns, or indeed the same responsibilities, as his or her fellow Members.

AMS may also encourage what is known as 'split ticketing' or 'split voting', whereby smaller parties concentrate on the list elections on the basis that they cannot possibly gain any constituency seats, but can gain (if they win enough votes overall) some of the 'top-up' members. AMS can also lead to more pre-election coalitions, as parties standing in the constituency section seek alliances with smaller parties who stand to do reasonably well in the list section.

There are other variants of AMS. In some systems, the two votes from the constituency and lists sections are not subtracted but added together, in others one vote is used twice; firstly to elect the constituency Member and secondly, as a vote for a party in the list section. It is also possible to vary the number of list members; for example, in Italy, the list comprises only 25% of the Members of the Chamber of Deputies and the Senate.

The Independent Commission on the Voting System and AV-Plus

The Jenkins Commission[1], as previously mentioned, recommended replacing our current method of parliamentary elections (FPTP) with a system of 'AV-Plus'. This would be a mixed member system in which between 80% and 85% of MPs would be elected in single Member constituencies using the Alternative Vote, with the remained being elected from 'top-up' areas. In most mixed member systems, the constituency candidates are elected by FPTP, but the Jenkins Commission curiously recommended AV – a system that it rules out as a general replacement for FPTP, elsewhere in its report.

---

[1] 'The Report of the Independent Commission on the Voting System', October 1998, Cm 4090

Under AV-Plus, voters would have two votes: one for a constituency Member and another for a 'top-up' Member, elected from a regional list. There would be 80 top-up areas electing between 15% and 20% of the total number of Members (two in Northern Ireland, five in Wales, eight in Scotland and 65 in England). The top-up areas would be based on existing metropolitan areas and county boundaries. This would mean fewer constituency Members and consequently would entail the readjustment and enlargement of existing constituencies. Parties would not be eligible for top-up seats unless they had contested at least 50% of the constituencies in the top-up area. Votes for an individual party in a particular top-up area would be counted and then divided by the number of constituencies won by that party within the top-up area, plus one. The party with the highest average votes would be allocated a seat.

If a further top-up seat remained then the process would be repeated but the relevant divisor would be 2, not 1 (this is basically an application of the d'Hondt formula). Where vacancies occurred in constituencies, by-elections would continue to be held, but there would be none in the top-up areas, where the next placed candidate would simply be selected.

Lord Alexander of Weedon was the one member of the Commission to dissent from the majority report on this issue. His criticisms of AV are worth noting. He asked in his 'Note of Reservation' (Volume 1, Page 53): *"Why should the second preferences of those voters who favoured the two stronger candidates on the first ballot be totally ignored and only those who support the lower placed and less popular candidates get a second bite of the cherry? Why, too should the second preferences of these votes be given equal weight with the first preferences of supporters of the stronger candidates."*

APPENDIX B - FORMS

Acting returning officers can obtain election stationery from any supplier, provided it conforms to the requirements set out in the various statutes and regulations. For example, the applications to vote by post in the London Borough of Croydon were printed by Shaw & Sons Ltd. Welsh language versions of statutory forms are prescribed in legislation, but the Guidance for Acting Returning Officers in England and Wales 2001 (available on the DTLR website) recommends that although the provision of ethnic minority language versions of forms or notices does not necessarily invalidate an election, *"Acting returning officers should bear in mind, however, that it could be argued that because an election form or notice appeared in one language and not in another, the election was conducted in such a way as to favour a particular candidate or candidates".* It goes on to add that *"There is also the risk of electors being misled by an inaccurate translation. In either case, it is possible that an election might be challenged and subsequently declared invalid by the courts".*

The forms used in local government elections have not been included in this Appendix, due to lack of space, but can be found in the Local Elections (Principal Areas) Rules 1986, as subsequently amended. The forms to be used in elections to the Greater London Assembly can be found in Schedule 5 to The Greater London Authority Elections (No. 2) Rules 2000 (SI 2000, No. 427), The Greater London Authority Elections (No. 2) (Amendment) Rules 2000 (SI 2000, No. 1040) and The Greater London Authority (Elections and Acceptance of Office) Order 2000 (SI 2000, No. 308). Similarly, the forms used in elections to the Scottish Parliament, the Welsh Assembly and the Northern Ireland Assembly have not been included due to lack of space but can be found in the following regulations: The Scottish Parliament (Elections, etc.) Order 1999 (SI 1999, No. 787) and The Scottish Parliament (Elections, etc.) (Amendment) Order 2001 (SI 2001, No. 1399 (S.5)); The National Assembly for Wales (Representation of the People) Order 1999 (SI 1999, No. 450) and The Northern Ireland Assembly (Elections) Order 2001 (SI 2001, No. 2599), the last of which includes the amendments which are necessary to the forms set out in the RPA 1983 and RPA 1985 in order to be effective for elections to the Northern Ireland Assembly. The forms required for European Parliamentary elections can be found in The European Parliamentary Elections Regulations 1999 (SI 1999, No. 1214).

The following is the guidance to voters as set out in the RPA 1983 as subsequently amended.

GUIDANCE FOR VOTERS

1. When you are given a ballot paper make sure it is stamped with the official mark.

2. Go to one of the compartments. Mark a cross (X) in the box on the right hand side of the ballot paper opposite the name of the candidate you are voting for.

3. Fold the ballot paper in two. Show the official mark to the presiding officer, but do not let anyone see your vote. Put the ballot paper in the ballot box and leave the polling station.

4. Vote for one candidate only. Put no other mark on the ballot paper, or your vote may not be counted.

5. If by mistake you spoil a ballot paper, show it to the presiding officer and ask for another one.

Form of declaration to be made by the companion of a voter with disabilities

I, ..., of ...., having been requested to assist ..., (in the case of a voter with disabilities voting as proxy add *voting as proxy for ...)* whose number on the register is .... to record this vote at the election now being held in this constituency, hereby declare that (I am entitled to vote as an elector at the said election) (I am the .... of the said voter and have attained the age of 18 years), and that I have not previously assisted any blind person (except ... of ....) to vote at the said election.

(Signed)...............
.... day of .... 20 ...

I, the undersigned, being the presiding officer for the .... polling station for the .... Constituency, hereby certify that the above declaration, having been first read to the above-named declarant, was signed by the declarant in my presence.

(Signed) ....

.... day of .... 20 ....
Minutes past .... o'clock (am) (pm)

NOTE 1 If the person making the above declaration knowingly and wilfully makes therein a statement false in a material particular, he will be guilty of an offence.

NOTE 2 A voter with disabilities is a voter who has made a declaration under the parliamentary elections rules that he is so incapacitated by his blindness or other incapacity, or by his inability to read, as to be unable to vote without assistance.

The following are the forms required for various electoral purposes as set out in Schedule 3 to the Representation of the People (England & Wales) Regulations 2001 (SI 2001, No. 341)

The Official Poll Card

Front of card

REPRESENTATION OF THE PEOPLE ACTS
OFFICIAL POLL CARD
Constituency
Polling Day
Your polling station will be
Polling hours 7am to 10pm
Number of register
Name
Address

Back of card

PARLIAMENTARY ELECTION

This card is for information only. You can vote without it, but it will save time if you take it to the polling station and show it to the clerk there.

When you go to the polling station, tell the clerk your name and address, as shown on the front of the card. The presiding officer will give you a ballot paper: see that he stamps the official mark on it before he gives it to you.

Go to one of the compartments. Mark a cross (X) in the box on the right hand side of the ballot paper opposite the name of the candidate you are voting for.

Fold the ballot paper in two. Show the official mark to the presiding officer, but do not let anyone see your vote. Put the ballot paper in the ballot box and leave the polling station.

Vote for one candidate only. Put no other mark on the ballot paper, or your vote may not be counted.

If by mistake you spoil a ballot paper, show it to the presiding officer and ask for another one.

If you have appointed a proxy to vote in person for you, you may nevertheless vote at this election if you do so before your proxy has voted on your behalf.

If you have been granted a postal vote, you will not be entitled to vote in person at this election, so please ignore this poll card.

ISSUED BY THE RETURNING OFFICER

The Proxy's Official Poll Card

Front of card

REPRESENTATION OF THE PEOPLE ACTS
PROXY'S OFFICIAL POLL CARD
Proxy's name
Proxy's address
PARLIAMENTARY ELECTION
Constituency
Polling Day
The poll will be open from 7am to 10pm

Back of card

The elector named below whose proxy you are is entitled to vote at the polling station -

To vote as proxy you must go to that polling station. Tell the clerk that you wish to vote as proxy; give the name and qualifying address of the elector, as follows:

Number of register

Name (of elector)

Address

The presiding officer will give you the elector's ballot paper. The method of voting as proxy is the same as for casting your own vote.

It is an offence to vote as proxy for some other person if you know that that person is subject to a legal incapacity to vote, e.g. if that person has been convicted and is detained in a penal institution in pursuance of his sentence. It is also an offence to vote at this election for more than two persons of whom you are not the husband, wife, parent, grandparent, brother, sister, child or grandchild.

The person who appointed you as proxy may himself vote in person at this election if he is able, and wishes, to do so and if he votes before you on his behalf.

ISSUED BY THE RETURNING OFFICER

Return of Expenses Required by Section 75 of the RPA 1983

REPRESENTATION OF THE PEOPLE ACTS
ELECTION IN THE
CONSTITUENCY / LOCAL GOVERNMENT AREA
Date of publication of notice of election
The expenses shown below were authorised in writing in accordance with the provisions of section 75 of the Representation of the People Act 1983 They were authorised by
(name of election agent) for the candidate
(name of candidate) in the above-mentioned election. They were incurred by
(person / association / body of persons). The agent's written authority is attached to this return. Amount of expenses incurred: £
 Signature
Date

Declaration as to Expenses Required by Section 75 of the 1983 Act

REPRESENTATION OF THE PEOPLE ACTS
ELECTION IN THE
CONSTITUENCY / LOCAL GOVERNMENT AREA
Date of publication of notice of election
Name of candidate
Name of election agent
I hereby declare that –
1. I am (the person) or (a director, general manager, secretary or similar officer of the association, organisation or body of persons)* named as incurring expenses in the accompanying return of expenses required by section 75 of the Representation of the People Act 1983.   2. To the best of my knowledge and belief that return is complete and correct.   3. The matter for which the expenses referred to in that return were incurred were as follows
Signature
Office held   (in the case of an association or body of persons)
Date
* enter as appropriate

Proxy Paper

REPRESENTATION OF THE PEOPLE ACTS
Constituency
Polling district
Local government electoral area(s)
European Parliamentary electoral region
Name of proxy
Address
is hereby appointed as proxy for
(Name of elector)
*(who is qualified to be registered for
(Qualifying address)
*(who qualified as an overseas elector in respect of the above constituency) to vote for him / her at
*(the *(parliamentary) *(local government) *(European Parliamentary) election for the above *(constituency) *(electoral area) *(European Parliamentary electoral region) on (date)
*(any *(parliamentary) *(local government) *(European parliamentary) election for the above *(constituency) *(electoral area) *(European parliamentary electoral region))
*(This proxy appointment is not valid until)
*(This proxy appointment remains valid until)
Signature
Electoral Registration Officer
Address
Date
*Delete whichever is inappropriate

YOUR RIGHT TO VOTE AS PROXY

1.	This proxy paper gives you the right to vote as proxy on behalf of the elector whose name is given overleaf. However, you may not vote as proxy at the same election for more than two electors of whom you are not the husband, wife, parent, grandparent, brother, sister, child or grandchild.
2.	Your appointment as proxy may be for a particular election only, or it may be for a definite or indefinite period. If it is for a particular election, you have the right to vote as proxy only at the election specified in the proxy paper. If it is for an indefinite period, you have in general the right to vote as proxy at any parliamentary, European Parliamentary or local government election for which the elector is qualified to vote until the electoral registration officer informs you to the contrary. If it is for a definite period, your right to vote as proxy expires on the date stated on the form.
3.	You may vote as proxy at the polling station allotted to the elector on whose behalf you are appointed. Shortly before polling day you will be sent a proxy poll card telling you where the polling station is. You do not need to take either the poll card or this proxy paper to the polling station but you may find it helpful to do so.
4.	If you cannot vote in person at the polling station, you should consult the electoral registration officer about your right to vote by post.

Certificate of Employment

REPRESENTATION OF THE PEOPLE ACTS
ELECTION IN THE CONSTITUENCY
I certify that (name)
Who is numbered
In the register of electors for the constituency named above cannot reasonably be expected to go in person to the polling station allotted to him or her at the election on *(date of poll)*
by reason of the particular circumstances of his or her employment on that date for a purpose connected with the election – *Delete whichever is*   *(a) a constable inappropriate*   *(b) by me Signature
*Returning officer / police officer (inspector or above).
Date
Note: The person named above is entitled to vote at any polling station of the above constituency on production and surrender of this certificate to the presiding officer.

Declaration of Identity (Parliamentary Election)

REPRESENTATION OF THE PEOPLE ACTS
Ballot Paper No
I hereby declare that I am the person to whom the ballot paper numbered as above was sent. *Voter's signature*
The voter, who is personally known to me, has signed this declaration in my presence.   Witness's signature
Name of witness (WRITE CLEARLY)
Address of witness (WRITE CLEARLY)   SEE INSTRUCTIONS ON THE BACK OF THIS FORM

Back of form

	INSTRUCTIONS TO THE VOTER
1.	You must sign this declaration of identity in the presence of a person known to you. That person should then sign this declaration as a witness, adding his or her name and address. Without this the declaration will be invalid.
2.	Vote for one candidate only. Put no other mark on the ballot paper or your vote may not be counted.
3.	Mark a cross (X) in the box on the right hand side of the ballot paper opposite the name of the candidate you are voting for. Do this secretly. If you cannot without assistance, the person assisting you must not disclose how you have voted..
4.	Put the ballot paper in the small envelope marked "A" and seal it. Then put the envelope marked "A", together with the declaration of identity, in the larger envelope marked "B". Return it without delay. The ballot paper must be received by the returning officer not later than the close of the poll. Alternatively, it may be delivered to a polling station in this constituency on polling day.
5.	If you receive more than one ballot paper, remember that it is illegal to vote more than once (otherwise than as proxy) at the same election.
6.	At this election you cannot vote in person at a polling station, even if you receive an official poll card.
7.	If you inadvertently spoil your ballot paper, you can apply to the returning officer for another one. With your application you must return, in your own envelope, the spoilt ballot paper, the declaration of identity and the envelopes marked "A" and "B". Remember that there is little time available if a fresh postal ballot is to be issued and counted.

Declaration of Identity for Use When Polls are Combined

Front of form

REPRESENTATION OF THE PEOPLE ACTS
DECLARATION OF IDENTITY
Ballot Paper Nos
I hereby declare that I am the person to whom the ballot papers numbered as above were sent.
Voter's signature
The voter, who is personally known to me, has signed this declaration in my presence.
Witness's signature
Name of witness (WRITE CLEARLY)
Address of witness (WRITE CLEARLY)
SEE INSTRUCTIONS ON THE BACK OF THIS FORM

Back of form

INSTRUCTIONS TO THE VOTER

1. You must sign this declaration of identity in the presence of a person known to you. That person should then sign this declaration as a witness, adding his or her name and address. Without this the declaration will be invalid.
2. At the parliamentary election, vote for one candidate only. *(At the election of ...vote for no more than ... candidates). Put no other mark on the ballot paper or your vote may not be counted.
3. Mark a cross (X) in the box on the right hand side of the ballot paper opposite the name(s) of the candidate(s) you are voting for. Do this secretly. If you cannot vote without assistance, the person assisting you must not disclose how you have voted..
4. Put the ballot paper in the small envelope marked "A" and seal it. Then put the envelope marked "A", together with the declaration of identity, in the larger envelope marked "B". Return it without delay. The ballot paper must be received by the returning officer not later than the close of the poll. Alternatively, it may be delivered to a polling station in this constituency on polling day.
5. If you receive more than one ballot paper *relating to the same election,* remember that it is illegal to vote more than once (otherwise than as proxy) at the same election.
6. At these elections you cannot vote in person at a polling station, even if you received an official poll card.
7. If you advertently spoil your ballot paper, you can apply to the returning officer for another one. If you do this you MUST RETURN ALL OF THE POSTAL BALLOT PAPERS YOU HAVE RECEIVED, together with the spoilt ballot paper. In addition, in your application for fresh postal ballot papers you MUST RETURN, in your own envelope, the declaration of identity and the envelopes marked "A" and "B". Remember that there is little time available if a fresh postal ballot paper is to be issued and counted.

*To be completed by the returning officer depending on the election to which regulation 66 applies

318

Declaration of Identity for Use When a Parliamentary Poll is Combined With Another Poll but Postal Ballots are not Combined

Front of form

REPRESENTATION OF THE PEOPLE ACTS
DECLARATION OF IDENTITY
To be returned with the *(insert colour of ballot paper)* coloured ballot paper No
I hereby declare that I am the person to whom the *(insert colour of ballot paper)* coloured ballot paper numbered as above was sent. Voter's signature
The voter, who is personally known to me, has signed this declaration in my presence. Witness's signature
Name of witness (WRITE CLEARLY)
Address of witness (WRITE CLEARLY)
SEE INSTRUCTIONS ON THE BACK OF THIS FORM

Back of Form

	INSTRUCTIONS TO THE VOTER
1.	You must sign this declaration of identity in the presence of a person known to you. *You are required to do this even if you have already signed a similar declaration of identity in respect of another election to be held on the same day.* That person should then sign this declaration as a witness, adding his or her name and address. Without this the declaration will be invalid.
2.	Vote for one candidate only. Put no other mark on the ballot paper or your vote may not be counted.
3.	Mark a cross (X) in the box on the right hand side of the ballot paper opposite the name of the candidate you are voting for. Do this secretly. If you cannot vote without assistance, the person assisting you must not disclose how you have voted.
4.	Different colours are used for the ballot papers for each election. Each ballot paper has its own ballot paper envelope (the smaller envelope marked "A"), the declaration of identity and covering envelope (the larger envelope marked "B"). The covering envelope and declaration of identity for a particular ballot paper are those which refer to the colour of that ballot paper. It is important that you use the correct envelopes and declaration of identity, otherwise your vote may not be counted. You may find it helpful to sort the documents into separate sets, each consisting of a ballot paper, ballot paper envelope, declaration of identity and covering envelope. Then proceed as follows –

	(a) place each ballot paper in the correct smaller envelope and seal it;
	    (b) put that envelope, together with the correct declaration of identity, in the correct covering envelope and seal it;
	    (c) return the covering envelopes without delay. Ballot papers must be received by the returning officer not later than the close of poll. Alternatively, they may be delivered to a polling station in the constituency on polling day.

5.	If you receive more than one ballot paper, remember that it is illegal to vote more than once (otherwise than as proxy) at the *same election.* You are entitled to vote at different elections which are held on the same day.
6.	At this election you cannot vote in person at a polling station, even if you receive an official poll card.
7.	If you inadvertently spoil your ballot paper, you can apply to the returning officer for another one. With your application you must return, in your envelope, the spoilt ballot paper, the declaration of identity and the envelopes marked "A" and "B". Remember that there is little time available if a fresh postal ballot paper is to be issued and counted.

Statement as to Postal Ballot Papers (Form 'K')

REPRESENTATION OF THE PEOPLE ACTS
PARLIAMENTARY ELECTION
Constituency
Date of poll
20

A. *Issue of postal ballot papers*	*Number*
1.	Total number of postal ballot papers issued under regulation 71	
2.	Total number of postal ballot papers issued under regulation 77 (where the first ballot paper was spoilt and returned for cancellation)	
3.	Total number of postal ballot papers issued (1+2)	

B. *Receipt of postal ballot papers*	*Number*
4.	Number of covering envelopes received by the returning officer or at a polling station before the close of poll (excluding any undelivered or returned under regulation 77(1) with spoilt ballot papers)	
5.	Number of covering envelopes received by the returning officer after the close of poll, excluding any returned as undelivered	
6.	Number of postal ballot papers returned spoilt for cancellation	
7.	Number of postal ballot papers returned as spoilt too late for another ballot paper to be issued	
8.	Number of covering envelopes returned as undelivered (up to the date of this statement)	
9.	Number of covering envelopes not received by the returning officer by the date of this statement	
10.	Total Nos. 4 to 9 (This number should be the same as that in 3 above)	

C. *Count of postal ballot papers*	*Number*
11.	Number of covering envelopes received by the returning officer before the close of poll (excluding any undelivered or returned under regulation 77(1) with spoilt ballot papers)	
12.	Number of ballot papers returned by postal voters which were included in the count of ballot papers	
13.	Number of cases in which a covering envelope or its contents were marked "Rejected" (cancellations under regulation 77(5) are not rejections and should be included in items 2 and 6 above)	

Date
Signed
Returning Officer
Address

The following are the forms required for various electoral purposes as set out in Schedule 3 of the Representation of the People (Scotland) Regulations 2001 (SI 2001, No. 497 (S.2)).

Elector's Official Poll Card

Front of Card

REPRESENTATION OF THE PEOPLE ACTS

OFFICIAL POLL CARD

Constituency	Number of register
Polling Day	Name
Your polling station will be	Address
Polling hours 7am to 10pm	

Back of Card

PARLIAMENTARY ELECTION

This card is for information only. You can vote without it, but it will save time if you take it to the polling station and show it to the clerk there.

When you go to the polling station, tell the clerk your name and address, as shown on the front of the card. The presiding officer will give you a ballot paper: see that he stamps the official mark on it before he gives it to you.

Go to one of the compartments. Mark a cross (X) in the box on the right hand side of the ballot paper opposite the name of the candidate you are voting for.

Vote for one candidate only. Put no other mark on the ballot paper, or your vote may not be counted.

Fold the ballot paper in two. Show the official mark to the presiding officer, but do not let anyone see your vote. Put the ballot paper in the ballot box and leave the polling station.

If by mistake you spoil your ballot paper, show it to the presiding officer and ask for another one.

If you have appointed a proxy to vote in person for you, you may nevertheless vote at this election if you do so before your proxy has voted on your behalf.

If you have been granted a postal vote, you will not be entitled to vote in person at this election, so please ignore this poll card.

Proxy's Official Poll Card

Front of Card

REPRESENTATION OF THE PEOPLE ACTS

PROXY'S OFFICIAL POLL CARD

Proxy's name	
Proxy's address	
PARLIAMENTARY ELECTION	
Constituency	
Polling day	
The poll will be open from 7am to 10pm	

Back of Card

The elector named below whose proxy you are is entitled to vote at the polling station -

To vote as proxy you must go to that polling station. Tell the clerk that you wish to vote as proxy; give the name and qualifying address of the elector, as follows:-

Number on register

Name (of elector)

Address

The presiding officer will give you the elector's ballot paper. The method of voting as proxy is the same as for casting you own vote.

It is an offence to vote as proxy for some other person if you know that that person is subject to a legal incapacity to vote, e.g. if that person has been convicted and is detained in a penal institution in pursuance of his or her sentence. It is also an offence to vote at this election for more than two persons of whom you are not the husband, wife, parent, grandparent, brother, sister, child or grandchild.

The person who appointed you as proxy may himself or herself vote in person at this election if he or she is able, and wishes, to do so and if he or she votes before you on his or her behalf.
ISSUED BY THE RETURNING OFFICER

Return of Expenses Required by Section 75 of the 1983 Act

REPRESENTATION OF THE PEOPLE ACTS
ELECTION IN THE
CONSTITUENCY
Date of publication of notice of election
The expenses shown below were authorised in writing in accordance with the provisions of section 75 of the Representation of the People Act 1983. They were authorised
By
(name of election agent)
for the candidate
(name of candidate) in the above mentioned election. They were incurred by
(person / association / body of persons). The agent's written authority is attached to this return. Amount of expenses incurred: £
Signature
Date

Declaration as to Expenses Required by Section 75 of the 1983 Act

REPRESENTATION OF THE PEOPLE ACTS
ELECTION IN THE
CONSTITUENCY
Date of publication of notice of
Name of candidate
Name of agent
I hereby declare that –
I am (the person) or (a director, general manager, secretary of similar officer of the association, organisation or body of persons)* named as incurring expenses in the accompanying return of expenses required by section 75 of the Representation of the People Act 1983.
To the best of my knowledge and belief that return is complete and correct.
The matter for which the expenses referred to in that return were incurred were as follows
Signature
Office held
(In the case of an association or body of persons)
Date
*enter as appropriate

Proxy Paper

REPRESENTATION OF THE PEOPLE ACTS
Constituency
Polling district
Local government electoral area(s)
European Parliamentary electoral region
Name of Proxy
Address
is hereby appointed as proxy for (Name of elector)
*(who is qualified to be registered for (Qualifying address)
*(who qualifies as an overseas elector in respect of the above constituency) to vote for him / her at *(the *(parliamentary) *(local government) *(European Parliamentary) election for the above *(constituency) *(electoral area) *(European Parliamentary electoral region)) *(This proxy appointment remains valid until)
Signature
Electoral Registration Officer Address
Date
*Delete whichever is inappropriate

YOUR RIGHT TO VOTE AS PROXY

1. This proxy paper gives you the right to vote as proxy on behalf of the elector whose name is given overleaf. However, you may not vote as proxy at the same election for more than two electors of whom you are not the husband, wife, parent, grandparent, brother, sister, child or grandchild.

2. Your appointment as proxy may be for a particular election only, or it may be for a particular or indefinite period.

If it is for a particular election, you have the right to vote as proxy only at the election specified in the proxy paper.

If it is for an indefinite period, you have in general the right to vote as proxy at any parliamentary, European Parliamentary or local government election for which the elector is qualified to vote until the electoral registration officer informs you to the contrary.

If it is for a particular period, your right to vote as proxy expires on the date stated on the form.

3. You may vote as proxy at the polling station allotted to the elector on whose behalf you are appointed. Shortly before polling day you will be sent a proxy poll card telling you where the polling station is. You do not need to take either the poll card or this proxy paper to the polling station but you may find it helpful to do so.

4. If you cannot vote in person at the polling station, you should consult the electoral registration officer about your right to vote by post.

Certificate of Employment

REPRESENTATION OF THE PEOPLE ACTS	
ELECTION IN THE	
CONSTITUENCY	
I certify that (name)	
who is numbered	
in the register of electors for the constituency named above cannot reasonably be expected to go in person to the polling station allotted to him or her at the election on *(date of poll)*	
by reason of the particular circumstances of his or her employment on that date for a purpose connected with the election -	

Delete whichever is inappropriate	*(a) as a constable *(b) by me Signature
	*Returning officer / police officer (inspector or above)

Date

Note: The person named above is entitled to vote at any polling station of the above constituency on production and surrender of this certificate to the presiding officer.

Declaration of Identity (parliamentary election)

REPRESENTATION OF THE PEOPLE ACTS
DECLARATION OF IDENTITY
Ballot Paper No
I hereby declare that I am the person to whom the ballot paper numbered above was sent. Voter's signature
The voter, who is personally known to me, has signed this declaration in my presence. Witness's signature
Address of witness
(WRITE CLEARLY)
SEE INSTRUCTIONS ON THE BACK OF THIS FORM

Back of Form

INSTRUCTIONS TO THE VOTER

1.	You must sign this declaration of identity in the presence of a person known to you. That person should then sign this declaration as a witness, adding his or her name and address. Without this the declaration will be invalid.
2.	Vote for one candidate only. Put no other mark on the ballot paper or your vote may not be counted.
3.	Mark a cross (X) in the box on the right hand side of the ballot paper opposite the name of the candidate you are voting for. Do this secretly. If you cannot vote without assistance, the person assisting you must not disclose how you have voted.
4.	Put the ballot paper in the small envelope marked "A" and seal it. Then put the envelope marked "A", together with the declaration of identity, in the larger envelope marked "B". Return it without delay. The ballot paper must be received by the returning officer not later than the close of the poll. Alternatively, it may be delivered to a polling station in the constituency to which the ballot paper relates by the close of the poll on the day of the election.
5.	If you receive more than one ballot paper, remember that it is illegal to vote more than once (otherwise than as proxy) at the same election.
6.	At this election you cannot vote in person at a polling station, even if you receive an official poll card.
7.	If you inadvertently spoil your ballot paper, you can apply to the returning officer for another one. With your application you must return, in your own envelope, the spoilt ballot paper, the declaration of identity and the envelopes marked "A" and "B". Remember that there is little time available if a fresh postal ballot paper is to be issued and counted.

Declaration of Identity for use When Polls are Combined

REPRESENTATION OF THE PEOPLE ACTS
DECLARATION OF IDENTITY
Ballot Paper Nos
I hereby declare that I am the person to whom the ballot paper numbered above was sent. Voter's signature
The voter, who is personally known to me, has signed this declaration in my presence. Witness's signature
Address of witness
(WRITE CLEARLY)
SEE INSTRUCTIONS ON THE BACK OF THIS FORM

Back of Form

	INSTRUCTIONS TO THE VOTER
1.	You must sign this declaration of identity in the presence of a person known to you. That person should then sign this declaration as a witness, adding his or her name and address. Without this the declaration will be invalid.
2.	At the parliamentary election, vote for one candidate only. *(At the election of
	Vote for no more than
	Candidates). Put no other mark on the ballot paper or your vote may not be counted.
3.	Mark a cross (X) in the box on the right hand side of the ballot paper opposite the name(s) of the candidate(s) you are voting for. Do this secretly. If you cannot vote without assistance, the person assisting you must not disclose how you have voted.
4.	Put the ballot paper in the small envelope marked "A" and seal it. Then put the envelope marked "A", together with the declaration of identity, in the larger envelope marked "B". Return it without delay. The ballot paper must be received by the returning officer not later than the close of the poll. Alternatively, it may be delivered to a polling station in the constituency to which the ballot paper relates by the close of the poll on the day of the election.
5.	If you receive more than one ballot paper *relating to the same election*, remember that it is illegal to vote more than once (otherwise than as proxy) at the same election.
6.	At this election you cannot vote in person at a polling station, even if you receive an official poll card.
7.	If you inadvertently spoil your ballot paper, you can apply to the returning officer for another one. If you do this you MUST RETURN ALL OF THE POSTAL BALLOT PAPERS YOU HAVE RECEIVED, together with the spoilt ballot paper. In addition, in your application for fresh postal ballot papers you MUST RETURN, in your own envelope, the declaration of identity and the envelopes marked "A" and "B". Remember that there is little time available if a fresh postal ballot paper is to be issued and counted.

Declaration of Identity (When a Parliamentary Poll is Combined With Another Poll but the Postal Ballots are not Combined)

REPRESENTATION OF THE PEOPLE ACTS
DECLARATION OF IDENTITY
To be inserted with the *(insert colour of ballot paper)* coloured ballot paper No
I hereby declare that I am the person to whom the *(insert colour of ballot paper)* coloured ballot paper numbered above was sent. Voter's signature
 The voter, who is personally known to me, has signed this declaration in my presence. Witness's signature
 Address of witness
 (WRITE CLEARLY)
SEE INSTRUCTIONS ON THE BACK OF THIS FORM

Back of Form

	INSTRUCTIONS TO THE VOTER
1.	You must sign this declaration of identity in the presence of a person known to you. You are required to do this even if you have already signed a similar declaration of identity in respect of another election to be held on the same day. That person should then sign this declaration as a witness, adding his or her name and address. Without this the declaration will be invalid.
2.	Vote for one candidate only. Put no other mark on the ballot paper or your vote may not be counted.
3.	Mark a cross (X) in the box on the right hand side of the ballot paper opposite the name of the candidate you are voting for. Do this secretly. If you cannot vote without assistance, the person assisting you must not disclose how you have voted.

4.	Different colours are used for the ballot papers for each election. Each ballot paper has its own ballot paper envelope (the smaller envelope marked "A"), declaration of identity and covering envelope (the larger enveloped marked "B"). The covering envelope and declaration of identity for a particular ballot paper are those which refer to the colour of that ballot paper. It is important that you use the correct envelopes and declaration of identity, otherwise your vote may not be counted. You may find it helpful to sort the documents into separate sets, each consisting of a ballot paper, ballot paper envelope, declaration of identity and covering envelope. Then proceed as follows -
	
	    (a) place each ballot paper in the correct smaller envelope and seal it;
	    (b) put that envelope, together with the correct declaration of identity, in the correct covering envelope and seal it;
	    (c) return the covering envelopes without delay. Ballot papers must be received by the returning officer not later than the close of the poll. Alternatively, they may be delivered to a polling station in the constituency to which the ballot papers relate by the close of the poll on the day of the election.

5.	If you receive more than one ballot paper, remember that it is illegal to vote more than once (otherwise than as proxy) at the same election. You are entitled to vote at different elections which are held on the same day.
6.	At this election you cannot vote in person at a polling station, even if you receive an official poll card.
7.	If you inadvertently spoil your ballot paper, you can apply to the returning officer for another one. With your application you must return, in your own envelope, the spoilt ballot paper, the declaration of identity and the envelopes marked "A" and "B". Remember that there is little time available if a fresh postal ballot paper is to be issued and counted.

Statement as to Postal Ballot Papers (Form K)

REPRESENTATION OF THE PEOPLE ACTS	
PARLIAMENTARY ELECTION	
Constituency	
Date of poll	
20.. *(year inserted here)*	

A. Issue of postal ballot papers	*Number*
1. Total number of postal ballot papers issued under regulation 71	
2. Total number of postal ballot papers issued under regulation 77 (where the first ballot paper was spoilt and returned for cancellation)	
3. Total number of postal ballot papers issued (1+2)	

B. Receipt of postal ballot papers	*Number*
4. Number of covering envelopes received by the returning officer or at a polling station before the close of poll (including any received in accordance with regulation 79(1) but excluding any undelivered or returned with spoilt ballot papers)	
5. Number of covering envelopes received by the returning officer after the close of poll, excluding any returned as undelivered	
6. Number of postal ballot papers returned spoilt for cancellation in time for another ballot paper to be issued	
7. Number of postal ballot papers returned as spoilt too late for another ballot paper to be issued	
8. Number of covering envelopes returned as undelivered (up to the date of this statement)	
9. Number of covering envelopes not received by the returning officer by the date of this statement	
10. Total Nos. 4 to 9 (This number should be the same as that in 3 above)	

C. Count of postal ballot papers	*Number*
11. Number of covering envelopes received by the returning officer before the close of poll (excluding any undelivered or returned with spoilt ballot papers). This should equal item 4 above and should also equal items 12 plus 13.	
12. Number of ballot papers returned by postal voters which were included in the count of ballot papers	
13. Number of cases in which a covering envelope or its contents were marked "Rejected" (cancellations under regulation 77(5) are not rejections and should be included in items 2 and 6 above)	

Date
Signed
Returning Officer
Address

The following are the forms required for various electoral purposes as set out in Schedule 3 to the Representation of the People (Northern Ireland) Regulations 2001 (SI 2001, No. 400), the Local Elections (Northern Ireland) (Amendment) Order 1987 (SI 1987, No. 168) and the Local Elections (Northern Ireland) Order 1985 (SI 1985, No. 454) as amended.

Official Poll Card

(The form of the poll card is amended under Schedule 3 of the Northern Ireland Assembly (Elections) Order 2001 (SI 2001, No. 2599) in the case of an election to the Northern Ireland Assembly where STV is used and where voters number the candidates in order of preference.)

Front of Card

REPRESENTATION OF THE PEOPLE ACTS

OFFICIAL POLL CARD

Constituency
....

Polling Day
....

Your polling station will be
....

Polling hours
7am to 10pm

Number on register ....

Name ....

Address ....

....

....

....

Back of Card

PARLIAMENTARY ELECTION

This card is for information only. You can vote without it, but it will save time if you take it to the polling station and show it to the clerk there.

When you go to the polling station, tell the clerk your name and address, as shown on the front of the card. The presiding officer will give you a ballot paper: see that he stamps the official mark on it before he gives it to you.

Go to one of the compartments. Mark a cross (X) in the box on the right hand side of the ballot paper opposite the name of the candidate you are voting for.

Fold the ballot paper in two. Show the official mark to the presiding officer, but do not let anyone see your vote. Put the ballot paper in the ballot box and leave the polling station.

Vote for one candidate only. Put no other mark on the ballot paper, or your vote may not be counted.

If by mistake you spoil a ballot paper, show it to the presiding officer and ask for another one.

If you have appointed a proxy to vote in person for you, you may nevertheless vote at this election if you do so before your proxy has voted on your behalf.

If you have granted a postal vote, you will *not* be entitled to vote in person at this election, so please ignore this poll card.

ISSUED BY THE RETURNING OFFICER

Proxy's Official Poll Card

Front of Card

REPRESENTATION OF THE PEOPLE ACTS

PROXY'S OFFICIAL POLL CARD

Proxy's name ....

Proxy's address ....

....

PARLIAMENTARY ELECTION

....Constituency

Polling day ....

The poll will be open from 7am to 10pm

Back of Card

The elector named below whose proxy you are is entitled to vote at the polling station –

....

To vote as proxy you must go to that polling station. Tell the clerk that you wish to vote as proxy; give the name and qualifying address of the elector, as follows: -

Number on register ....

Name (of Elector) ....

Address...

The presiding officer will give you the elector's ballot paper. The method of voting as proxy is the same as for casting your own vote.

It is an offence to vote as proxy for some other person if you know that that person is subject to a legal incapacity to vote, e.g. if that person has been convicted and is detained in a penal institution in pursuance of his sentence. It is also an offence to vote at this election for more than two persons of whom you are not the husband, wife, parent, grandparent, brother, sister, child or grandchild.

The person who appointed you as proxy may himself vote in person at this election if he is able, and wishes, to do so and if he votes before you on his behalf.

ISSUED BY THE RETURNING OFFICER

Return of Expenses Required by Section 75 of the 1983 Act

REPRESENTATION OF THE PEOPLE ACTS

ELECTION IN THE ....……....CONSTITUENCY
Date of publication of notice of election..
The expenses shown below were authorised in writing in accordance with the provisions of section 75
of the Representation of the People Act 1983.
They were authorised
by...…..(name of election agent)
for the candidate ....……..(name of candidate) in the above-mentioned election.
They were incurred by ....…..(person / association / body of persons).
The agent's written authority is attached to this return.
Amount of expenses incurred.   £...........................…..
Signature ....   Date ....

Declaration as to Expenses Required by Section 75 of the 1983 Act

REPRESENTATION OF THE PEOPLE ACTS

ELECTION IN THE ....……....CONSTITUENCY
Date of publication of notice of election..
Name of candidate...
Name of election agent...
I hereby declare that —
1. I am (the person) *or* (a director, general manager, secretary or similar officer of the association,
organisation or body of persons)* named as incurring expenses in the accompanying return of
expenses required by section 75 of the Representation of the People Act 1983.
2. To the best of my knowledge and belief that return is complete and correct.
3. The matter for which the expenses referred to in that return were incurred were as follows
....………....
....………....
....………....
....………....

Signature..……..
Office held...…….
(in the case of an association or body of persons)
Date...………..

* enter as appropriate

Proxy Paper

REPRESENTATION OF THE PEOPLE ACTS

Constituency..

Polling district..

European Parliamentary electoral region................................

Name of Proxy..

Address..

....

....

is hereby appointed as proxy for

(name of elector)..

*(who is qualified to be registered for

(qualifying address)...

*(who qualifies as an overseas elector in respect of the above constituency) to vote for him/her at

*(the *(parliamentary) *(European Parliamentary) election for the above *(constituency) *(European

Parliamentary electoral region))

*(this proxy appointment is not valid until.............................)

Signature..

Electoral Registration Officer

Address..

....

....

Date...

Delete whichever is inappropriate

YOUR RIGHT TO VOTE AS PROXY

1.	This proxy paper gives you the right to vote as proxy on behalf of the elector whose name is given overleaf. However, you may not vote as proxy at the same election for more than two electors of whom you are not the husband, wife, parent, grandparent, brother, sister, child or grandchild.
2.	Your appointment as proxy may be for a particular election only, or it may be for an indefinite period. If it is for a particular election, you have the right to vote as proxy only at the election specified in the proxy paper. If it is for an indefinite period, you have in general the right to vote as proxy at any parliamentary or European Parliamentary election for which the elector is qualified to vote until the electoral registration officer informs you to the contrary.
3.	You may vote as proxy at the polling station allotted to the elector on whose behalf you are appointed. Shortly before polling day you will be sent a proxy poll card telling you where the polling station is. You do not need to take either the poll card or this proxy paper to the polling station but you may find it helpful to do so.
4.	If you cannot vote in person at the polling station, you should consult the electoral registration officer about whether you satisfy the entitlement to vote by post.

Certificate of Employment

REPRESENTATION OF THE PEOPLE ACTS

ELECTION IN THE ....CONSTITUENCY

I certify that (name) .... who is numbered ....in the register of electors for the constituency named above cannot reasonably be expected to go in person to the polling station allotted to him or her at the election on (*date of poll*) .... by reason of the particular circumstances or his or her employment on that date for a purpose connected with the election —

Delete whichever is inappropriate	*(a) as a constable* *(b) by me*
	Signature .... *Returning officer/police officer (chief inspector or above)
Date.............................	

Note: - The person above is entitled to vote at any polling station of the above constituency on production and surrender of this certificate to the presiding officer.

Declaration of Identity

REPRESENTATION OF THE PEOPLE ACTS

Ballot Paper No...............

I hereby declare that I am the person to whom the ballot paper numbered as above was sent.
Voter's signature ....

The voter, who is personally known to me, has signed this declaration in my presence.
Witness's signature ....

	Name of witness .... (WRITE CLEARLY) Address of witness .... (WRITE CLEARLY) ....

SEE INSTRUCTIONS ON THE BACK OF THIS FORM

341

Back of Form

(This is amended under Schedule 3 of the Northern Ireland Assembly (Elections) Order 2001 (SI 2001, No. 2599) in the case of an election to the Northern Ireland Assembly where voters may number the candidates in order of preference)

INSTRUCTIONS TO THE VOTER
1. You must sign this declaration of identity in the presence of a person known to you. That person should then sign this declaration as a witness, adding his or her name and address. Without this the declaration will be invalid.
2. Vote for one candidate only. Put no other mark on the ballot paper or your vote may not be counted.
3. Mark a (X) in the box on the right hand side of the ballot paper opposite the name of the candidate you are voting for. Do this secretly. If you cannot vote without assistance, the person assisting you must not disclose how you have voted.
4. Put the ballot paper in the small envelope marked "A" and seal it. Then put the envelope marked "A", together with the declaration of identity, in the larger envelope marked "B". Return it without delay. The ballot paper must be received by the returning officer not later than the close of the poll.
5. If you received more than one ballot paper, remember that it is illegal to vote more than once (otherwise than as proxy) at the same election.
6. At this election you cannot vote in person at a polling station, even if you receive an official poll card.
7. If you inadvertently spoil your ballot paper, you can apply to the returning officer for another one. With your application you must return, in your own envelope, the spoilt ballot paper, the declaration of identity and the envelopes marked "A" and "B". Remember that there is little time available if a fresh postal ballot is to be issued and counted.

Statement as to Postal Ballot Papers

<table>
<tr><td colspan="2" align="center">REPRESENTATION OF THE PEOPLE ACTS

PARLIAMENTARY ELECTION

Constituency .... Date of poll ...., 20 ....</td></tr>
<tr><td>A. Issue of postal ballot papers</td><td>Number</td></tr>
<tr><td>1. Total number of postal ballot papers issued under regulation 70</td><td></td></tr>
<tr><td>2. Total number of postal ballot papers issued under regulation 76(2) (where the first ballot paper was spoilt and returned for cancellation)</td><td></td></tr>
<tr><td>3. Total number of postal ballot papers issued (1+2)</td><td></td></tr>
<tr><td>B. Receipt of postal ballot papers</td><td>Number</td></tr>
<tr><td>4. Number of covering envelopes received by the returning officer before the close of poll (excluding any undelivered or returned under regulation 76(1) with spoilt ballot papers)</td><td></td></tr>
<tr><td>5. Number of covering envelopes received by the returning officer after the close of poll, excluding any returned as undelivered</td><td></td></tr>
<tr><td>6. Number of postal ballots returned spoilt for cancellation in time for another ballot paper to be issued</td><td></td></tr>
<tr><td>7. Number of postal ballot papers returned as spoilt too late for another ballot paper to be issued</td><td></td></tr>
<tr><td>8. Number of covering envelopes returned as undelivered (up to the date of this statement)</td><td></td></tr>
<tr><td>9. Number of covering envelopes not received by the returning officer by the date of this statement</td><td></td></tr>
<tr><td>10. Total Nos. 4 to 9 (This number should be the same as that in 3. above)</td><td></td></tr>
<tr><td>C. Count of postal ballot papers</td><td>Number</td></tr>
<tr><td>11. Number of covering envelopes received by the returning officer before the close of poll (excluding any undelivered or returned under regulation 76(1) with spoilt ballot papers)</td><td></td></tr>
<tr><td>12. Number of ballot papers returned by postal voters which were included in the count of ballot papers</td><td></td></tr>
<tr><td>13. Number of cases in which a covering envelope or its contents were marked "Rejected" (cancellations under regulation 76(4) are not rejections and should be included in items 2 and 6 above)</td><td></td></tr>
<tr><td>Date...</td><td>Signed.....................
Returning Officer
Address...................</td></tr>
</table>

Form of Proxy Paper for Local Election

District electoral area
Polling district
Name or Proxy
Address
is hereby appointed as proxy for (Name of elector)
who is qualified to be registered for (Qualifying address)
to vote for him/her at
*(the local election for the above district electoral area on (date)) *(any local election for the above district electoral area) *(this proxy appointment is not valid until …..) Signature Chief Electoral Officer Address   *Delete whichever is inappropriate

Your Right to Vote as Proxy
1. This proxy paper gives you the right to vote as proxy on behalf of the elector whose name is given above.
2. Your appointment as proxy may be for a particular election only, or it may be for an indefinite period. If it is for a particular election, you have the right to vote as proxy only at the election specified in the proxy paper. If it is for an indefinite period, you have the right to vote as proxy at any local election until the Chief Electoral Officer informs you to the contrary.
3. When the elector applied for you to be appointed as proxy EITHER he or she was asked to state that he or she had consulted you and that you were capable of being and willing to be appointed as proxy OR you signed a statement stating that you were capable of being and willing to be appointed. You are capable of being appointed as proxy if you are at least 18 years old on polling day, a British or other Commonwealth citizen or a citizen of a Member State of the European Union and not for any reason disqualified from voting. If for some reason you are not capable of being, or willing to be, appointed as proxy, please write to the elector asking him to cancel the appointment.
4. You may vote as proxy at the polling station allotted to the elector on whose behalf you are appointed. However, you may not vote as proxy at the same election for more than two electors of whom you are not the husband, wife, parent, grandparent, brother, sister, child or grandchild. Shortly before polling day you will be sent a proxy poll card telling you where the polling station is. You do not need to take either the poll card or this proxy paper to the polling station but you may find it helpful to do so. Remember that the elector may still vote in person. If he or she applies for a ballot paper at the polling station before you do you will not be able to vote as proxy on his or her behalf.
5. If you cannot vote in person at the polling station the Chief Electoral Officer may be able to allow you to vote as proxy by post. If your appointment is for an indefinite period, you may apply to vote by post throughout the period your appointment is in force if you live in a different ward from the elector's qualifying address. If you are registered for the same ward as the elector, you may apply if you are entitled to vote by post at a particular election if the Chief Electoral Officer is satisfied that you cannot reasonably be expected to vote in person at the elector's polling station. But the Chief Electoral Officer cannot allow an application to vote by post at a particular election if he receives it after midday on the thirteenth working day before the poll.

Ballot Paper for Use in Local Elections in Northern Ireland

Mark order of preference in space below	*
	Emblem included here RUDGE (Barnaby Rudge of 12 Park Lane, Bangor, Co. Down Democratic Unionist Party)
	TWIST (Oliver Twist of 7 Manor Drive, Banbridge, Co. Down Independent)
	COPPERFIELD (David Copperfield of 29 Acacia Avenue, Newry, Co. Down Ulster Unionist Party) Etc., etc.

*Party emblems can now be included on the ballot paper

Directions on how the ballot paper should be printed are included in the Local Elections (Northern Ireland) Order 1985 (SI 1985, No. 454).

Declaration of Identity for Local Elections

ELECTION OF DISTRICT COUNCILLORS

DECLARATION OF VOTER

Ballot Paper No ....

I hereby declare that I am the person to whom the ballot paper numbered above was sent.

Voter's signature ....

CERTIFICATION BY WITNESS

The voter who is personally known to me has signed this declaration in my presence.

Witness's signature .... Date ....

Name of Witness ....
WRITE CLEARLY
Address ....

Back of form

	INSTRUCTIONS TO VOTER
1	You should place the figure 1 opposite the name of the candidate for whom you wish to vote and in addition you may, if you wish, place the figure 2 opposite the name of the candidate of your second choice, the figure 3 opposite name of the candidate of your third choice and so on in the order of your preference. You may indicate by figures as many or as few preferences as you wish.
2	The figure or figures should be placed in the spaces provided at the left-hand side of the paper opposite the name of the candidate for whom you intend it.
3	In no circumstances write anything else on the paper; if you do your vote may be invalid.
4	Immediately after voting you must place the marked ballot paper in the enclosed small envelope on which are printed the words "Ballot paper envelope" and seal it.
5	Then take the sealed ballot paper envelope and the voter's declaration to another elector as a witness and sign the declaration in his presence. He should then certify you signature on the declaration by signing the certification, adding his name and address. Without this, the declaration will be invalid.
6	Enclose the signed and witnessed declaration and the sealed ballot paper envelope in the larger enclosed envelope addressed to the returning officer and despatch it by post without delay. Unless you return the ballot paper at once it may be received by the returning officer too late to be counted.
7	If you received more than one ballot paper it must be remembered that you can vote only once on your own behalf at this election.
8	If you inadvertently spoil your postal ballot paper, you can apply to the returning officer for another one. With your application you must return (in a fresh envelope) the spoilt ballot paper, the declaration of identity and the envelope sent to you with your ballot paper. Remember that there is little time available if a fresh ballot paper is to be issued to you for completion and return before the close of the poll.

Elector's Official Poll Card

Front of Card

....District Council ....District Electoral Area	OFFICIAL POLL CARD Name ....
Polling day .... Polling hours 7am to 10pm Your polling station is At	Number on register .... Address ....
VOTING INSTRUCTIONS Mark your vote secretly by placing in the square provided on the left-hand side of the paper the figure "1" opposite the name of the candidate for whom you wish to vote and, if you wish, the figure "2" opposite the name of the candidate of your second choice and so on in the order of your preference. IMPORTANT – PLEASE READ NOTES ON BACK OF THIS CARD	

Back of Card

THE LAW PREVENTS YOU BEING GIVEN A BALLOT PAPER UNLESS YOU PRODUCE ONE OF THE
FOLLOWING DOCUMENTS:-

(a) a *current* Northern Ireland or Great Britain full driving licence (or a Northern Ireland provisional licence);

(b) a *current* United Kingdom or Republic of Ireland passport

(c) a *current* book for the payment of allowances, benefits or pensions issued by the Dept. of Health and Social Security or the Department of Social Security

(d) a medical card issued by the Northern Ireland Central Services Agency

(e) a current British seaman's card

(f) a card made of plastic issued by the Department of Social Security or the Department of for Social Development with a name and national insurance number embossed on it

(g) in the case ONLY of a woman married within 2 years of polling day, a certified copy or extract of an entry of marriage issued by a Registrar General in the UK

Issued by the Returning Officer

Proxy's Official Poll Card

......................................District Council ....District Electoral Area Polling day .... Polling hours 7am to 10pm Elector's polling station is at	PROXY'S OFFICIAL POLL CARD Proxy's name .... Proxy's address .... Elector's name .... Elector's number on register .... Elector's address ....
INSTRUCTIONS To vote as proxy for the elector named above you must go to the polling station named above. Tell the clerk you wish to vote as proxy and give the name, number and address of elector as given above. The method of voting as proxy is the same as voting as an elector. The person who appointed you as his proxy may vote himself if he votes before you. IMPORTANT: YOU MUST IDENTIFY *YOURSELF* BY ONE OF THE DOCUMENTS SET OUT ON THE BACK OF CARD	

The back of the card is the same as the back of an elector's official poll card set out above.

Form of Certificate of Employment

Local government election

....district electoral area

I certify that (*name*) ....

who is numbered .... in the register of electors used at this district council election in the district electoral area named above is likely to be unable to go in person to the polling station allotted to him by reason of the particular circumstances of his employment on that date

Delete whichever is inappropriate	*(a) as a constable *(b) by me for a purpose connected with the election.
	Signature .... *Police officer (Chief Inspector or above) *Returning officer Date ....
	Note – The person named above is entitled to vote at any polling station in the above district electoral area on production and surrender of this certificate to the presiding officer.

Form of Declaration to be Made by the Companion of a Voter with Disabilities

I, ... of ...., having been requested to assist ... (in the case of a voter with disabilities voting as proxy add voting as proxy for ...) whose number on the register is ..., to record his vote at the election now being held in this district electoral area hereby declare that (I am entitled to vote as an elector at the said election) (I am the * ... of the said voter and have attained the age of 18 years) and that I have not previously assisted any blind person (except ... of ....) to vote at the said election.

state relationship of companion to voter

(Signed) ...,
day of   20..

I, the undersigned, being the presiding officer for the ....polling station for the ....district electoral area, hereby certify that the above declaration, having been first read to the above-named declarant, was signed by the declarant in my presence.

(Signed ...)

day of   20..
minutes past   o'clock (am) (pm)

Note 1: If the person making the above declaration knowingly and wilfully makes therein a statement false in a material particular, he will be guilty of an offence.

Note 2: A voter with disabilities is a voter who has made a declaration under the election rules that he is so incapacitated by his blindness or other incapacity, or by his inability to read, as to be unable to vote without assistance.

FURTHER READING

General Guides

Schofield's Election Law, Rory Mates & Andrew Scallan
(2nd Edition, Shaw & Sons, 1996)

British Politics and European Elections 1999, David Butler & Martin Westlake
(Macmillan Press, 2000)

Elections in Britain: A voter's guide, Dick Leonard & Roger Mortimore
(4th Edition, Palgrave, 2001)

New Britain, New Elections: The Media Guide to the New Political Map of Britain,
edited by Colin Rallings and Michael Thrasher
(Vacher Dod Publishing, 1999)

How to Win an Election, Paul Richards
(Politico's Publishing, 2001)

Election Campaigning: The New Marketing of Politics, Dennis Kavanagh
(Blackwell Publishers, 1997)

Politico's Guide to the General Election, Simon Henig & Lewis Baston
(Politico's Publishing, 2000)

Electoral Change Since 1945, Pippa Norris
(Blackwell Publishers, 1997)

Modern Constitutency Electioneering: Local Campaigning in the 1992 General Election,
David Denver & Gordon Hands
(Frank Cass & Co, 1997)

The Boundary Commissions: Redrawing the UK's Map of Parliamentary Constituencies, D J
Rossiter, R J Johnston and C J Pattie
(Manchester University Press, 1999)

From Votes to Seats: The Operation of the UK Electoral System Since 1945, Ron Johnston,
Charles Pattie, Danny Dorling & David Rossiter
(Manchester University Press, 2001)

Twentieth Century British Political Facts 1900 – 2000, David Butler & Gareth Butler
(8th Edition, Macmillan Press Ltd, 2000)

Election Results (1997 & 2001 General Elections)

Election 2001: The Official Results
(Politico's Publishing, 2001)

Campaign 2001, Nicholas Jones
(Politico's Publishing, 2001)

The British General Election of 1997, David Butler & Dennis Kavanagh
(Macmillan Press, 1997)

Labour's Landslide, Andrew Geddes and Jonathan Tonge (editors)
(Manchester University Press, 1997)

New Labour Triumphs: Britain at the Polls, Anthony King (editor)
(Chatham House Publishers, 1998)

Campaign 1997: How the General Election was Won and Lost, Nicholas Jones
(Indigo, 1997)

Britain Votes 1997, Pippa Norris & Neil T Gavin (Editors)
(Oxford University Press, 1997)

'Democracy in Action: The 2001 UK General Election'
(available from Echo Research, www.echoresearch.com)

Electoral Systems

Electoral Systems: A Comparative Introduction, David M Farrell
(Palgrave, 2001)

Report of the Independent Commission on the Voting System
(Cm 4090, 25 October 1998)

Principles of Electoral Reform, Michael Dummett
(Oxford University Press, 1997)

Electoral Systems and Party Systems: A Study of Twenty-Seven Democracies,
1945-1990, Arend Lijphart
(Oxford University Press,1994)

Why MMP Must Go:The case for ditching the electoral disaster of the century,
Graeme Hunt
(Waddington Press Ltd, 1998)

Making Votes Count: The Case for Electoral Reform, Martin Linton & Mary Southcott
(Profile Books, 1998)

Local Government

Essential Local Government 2000, Ron Fenney
(LGC Information, 2000)

Local Government in Britain, Tony Byrne
(7th Edition, Penguin Books, 2000)

The Parish Councillor's Guide, John Prophet
(17th Edition, Shaw & Sons, 2000)

Local Government in the United Kingdom, David Wilson & Chris Game
(2nd Edition, Macmillan Press, 1998)

Hung authorities, elected mayors and cabinet government, Steve Leach & Chris Game
(YPS, 2000)

Constitution

Constitutional and Administrative Law, A W Bradley and K D Ewing
(12th Edition, Addison Wesley Longman, 1997)

Constitutional and Administrative Law, Hilaire Barnett
(3rd Edition, Cavendish Publishing, 2000)

The Rape of the Constitution, Keith Sutherland (Editor)
(Imprint Academic, 2000)

The British Political Process: An Introduction, Tony Wright (Editor)
(Routledge, 2000)

This Time: Our Constitutional Revolution, Anthony Barnett
(Vintage, 1997)

The Hidden Wiring: Unearthing the British Constitution, Peter Hennessy
(Indigo, 1996)

Constitutional Practice: The Foundations of British Government, Rodney Brazier
(3rd Edition, Oxford University Press, 1999)

United Kingdom Governance, Robert Pyper & Lynton Robins
(Macmillan Press, 2000)

Studies in Constitutional Law, Colin R Munro
(2nd Edition, Butterworths, 1999)

Constitutional Reform: The Labour Government's Constitutional Reform Agenda, Robert
Blackburn & Raymond Plant
(Addison, Wesley, Longman, 1999)

British Government and the Constitution: Text, Cases and Materials, Colin Turpin
(4th Edition, Butterworths, 1999)

The Politics of the British Constitution, Michael Foley
(Manchester University Press, 1999)

Devolved Assemblies and GLA

Dragons Led by Poodles: The Inside Story of a New Labour Stitch-Up, Paul Flynn MP
(Politico's Publishing, 1999)

Redesigning Democracy: The Making of the Welsh Assembly,
Kevin Morgan & Geoff Mungham
(seren, 2000)

Nightmare: The Race to Become London's Mayor, Mark D'Arcy & Rory MacLean
(Politico's Publishing, 2000)

The New Scottish Politics: The First Year of the Scottish Parliament and Beyond,
Gerry Hassan & Chris Warhurst
(TSO, 2000)

Political Parties and Party Funding

The History of British Political Parties, David Boothroyd
(Politico's Publishing, 2001)

British Political Parties Today, Robert Garner and Richard Kelly
(2nd Edition, Manchester University Press, 1998)

'The Funding of Political Parties in the United Kingdom' – Fifth Report of the
Committee on Standards in Public Life
(Cm 4057,13 October 1998)

The Price of Power: The Secret Funding of the Tory Party, Colin Challen
(Vision,1998)

The British Party System, Stephen Ingle
(3rd Edition, Pinter, 2000)

The Modern British Party System, Paul Webb
(Sage Publications, 2000)

Reforming Britain: New Labour, New Constitution?, John Morrison
(Reuters, 2001)

Other

Electoral Law and the Internet: Some Issues Considered, Chris Ballinger & Stephen
Coleman (Hansard Society / The Stationery Office, 2001)

INDEX